ESTONE
D!
BRIDGESTONE
uni-T
Ultimate Tyre Technology
POTENZA
RIDGESTONE
ORS' WORLD CHAMPION 1998

This is a Dempsey Parr Book

Dempsey Parr
13 Whiteladies Road,
Clifton,
Bristol BS8 1PB,
United Kingdom
ISBN 1-84084-388-8
Printed in France

FORMULA 1 YEARBOOK

1998-99

Pictures
Thierry Gromik
Steve Domenjoz
Masakazu Miyata
Jean-Marc Loubat

Conception and texts
Luc Domenjoz

Translated by
Eric Silbermann

Statistics and results
Ruth Domenjoz-Leibold

Drawings and circuit maps
Pierre Ménard

Page layout
Dominique Caussanel

DP
DEMPSEY
PARR

Contents

Foreword

“Here I am, once again in front of a clean sheet of paper, facing the challenge of coming up with an introduction to the «Formula 1 Yearbook.» I can remember how, just one year ago, in these very pages, I told you how much I was hoping that 1998 would help me forget the hardships of 1997. Unfortunately, as you may have noticed, this year did not live up to our high expectations.

I have always managed to bounce back. I can live through difficult times and to overcome the problems, so long as I understand them and can see the light at the end of the tunnel.

And that is exactly the case at Prost Grand Prix, where we quickly realised what were the AP01's faults this season. Unfortunately it was impossible to fix them during the course of the championship, but I am absolutely convinced the new AP02 will allow us to get back on the road to success.

Apart from that, I reckon this year's Formula 1 season was fascinating for race fans and I hope you enjoy reliving its most exciting moments through the pages of this «Formula 1 Yearbook.»

While waiting for next season to start, I suggest you dive into the pages which follow. They will help the time fly by until it is time to start all over again next March.

See you soon,”

Olivier Panis

Hakkinen – Schumacher: total war

PASCAL DRO,
34 years old, married to Florence, one daughter, Martha. Holder of a Science diploma. Finalist in a racing school championship. Took part in three Pau Formula Ford Grands Prix. Switched to the Caterham Cup. Twice entered the Le Mans 24 Hours and three appearances in the Daytona 24 Hours. Started as a road test journalist with Auto Hebdo in 1989, before switching to the Automobile Magazine and then Auto Plus, for whom he covers the Grands Prix.

by Pascal Dro
«Auto Plus»

Ferrari tested 20 different types of tyre at Fiorano and Mugello. They racked up 5000 kilometres in testing between the Luxembourg GP and the final date on the calendar in Japan. They sent four cars and one tub to Japan. Goodyear's main man himself, Perry Bell, was on the pit wall at the test tracks, armed with his temperature gauge. While all this activity went on, a team worked through the night at Maranello to overhaul the cars that Schumacher, Irvine and Badoer had tested during that day. In order to prepare for the possibility of rain in Japan, millions of gallons were sprayed onto the Fiorano track. Scuderia Ferrari's pursuit of at least one championship came pretty close to outright war.
FIAT's honorary chairman, Gianni Agnelli must have written them a blank cheque and even Ross Brawn and Rory Byrne spent their days on the pit wall for all the private tests.

No surrender

The disaster at the Nurburgring was not enough to make Ferrari surrender. Schumacher had promised: «*We have four weeks to work, which is a very long time in Formula 1. We will do all we can to win in Japan. The rest is out of our hands.*» He had set the tone.
For its part, McLaren was also going at it hammer and tongs. It had the advantage in that its car had been the class of the field since Melbourne and that Bridgestone might expect to have an advantage on its home turf at Suzuka, where it tests and also supplies teams in the All Nippon F3000 championship. So Ferrari was looking for progress of a radical nature on both the tyre and chassis front, having chased McLaren since Melbourne when Schumacher was 0.7s slower than Hakkinen in qualifying. It had even come up with a special engine for Japan.
McLaren meanwhile, took a more traditional approach, looking for tyre development and overall reliability. The rest is history. Schumacher dominated qualifying, stalled on the grid and had a tyre explode. Hakkinen took the title, winning eight races.
It was a vintage season, unlike the previous year. In 1997, apart from a couple of strategic errors from Williams, who made a poor tyre choice in the rain at Monaco and Spa, and a few errors from Villeneuve, the Canadian could have wrapped up the title long before Jerez. That and a few comments and lapses of behaviour characterised the series, of which only Villeneuve's final crowning stands out.

70% is down to the tyres

Before the start of the 1998 season, the Ferrari team was bursting with confidence. When the F 300 was unveiled in front of their magnificent new wind tunnel at Maranello, Luca di Montezemolo spoke of a new Ferrari and of victory. The team obviously felt they had got their sums right and that winter testing had started well.
However, news of what the McLarens were doing to their testing stopwatches began to worry the men from Maranello and in Melbourne it was despair for the Prancing Horse. They did not buckle, but got stuck into some serious work. Before Monaco, Schumacher gave Goodyear a verbal pasting: «*70% of the performance we are looking for comes from the tyres.*»
McLaren won Monaco and Hakkinen led Schumacher by 22 points. The American rubber men did not appreciate being snubbed one little bit. They too got down to work and produced a run of three wins in the summer in Canada, France and England, where he took the flag in the pits!
Then he did the impossible, adopting a three pit stop sprint strategy to win Hungary, before Ferrari finally finished first and second on home turf in Monza. It was not enough.
McLaren and Bridgestone fought back. To make matters worse for Schumacher, Lady Luck turned her back on him. Hakkinen suffered an engine failure at Imola, his gearbox went in Canada and the brakes gave up in Monza. The Finn only had one big accident in Spa, where Schumacher also crashed out. In the end, the Finn won 8 to 6.
What the statistics do not show is the sense of fair play which, unusually in recent times, characterised the way the title was played out. For example, when Hakkinen was asked after winning in Luxembourg, why he had been shaking his fist at Irvine, the Finn looked puzzled: «*Oh that!*» he said. «*I was just waving to friends at the side of the track!*» was his lying reply. He burst out laughing, with politics and backbiting the last thing on his mind.

Polished and polite

It is ages since the world championship has been decided in an atmosphere so free of acrimony between the main

players. In the end it is the men and the sport who are the winners.
The drivers have grown up. They have proved that, throughout a 16 race season, after 16 battles and after 6 months of car preparation, 3 months of testing and tens of millions of dollars spent on research and development and parts, it is finally the men who still count for something extra.
It is they who decide if a championship is good or bad and it is they who ensure that a team leaves the world stage in glory as well as crowned with the ultimate prize. Let us leave Jackie Stewart, who knows a thing or two, or even three about winning championships, tell us what is the moral of this tale: «*When you start to do things differently, because the title is up for grabs, then that is when things start to go wrong. Because that is when you are no longer true to yourself.*»
Stalling, whether or not the clutch played up at the start is not something Michael Schumacher is known for, although it is now!
McLaren simply worked at the right pace all year long, while Ferrari got through 20% of its testing in those last few weeks before the final race.
Between Saturday night and Suzuka race morning, Ferrari came up with 16 possible scenarios for the start and how to react to them in terms of strategy. «*But me in front and Michael at the back was not one of them!*» admitted Eddie Irvine. Meanwhile Hakkinen stayed ice cool and passed that feeling on to his team right from the start of practice for the Luxembourg GP to the moment he climbed onto the Suzuka podium. It was a victory for a cool head.
Hakkinen was respected on the track without having to resort to any bullying tactics and none of his opponents were worried he might stab them in the back. He is respected for what he is; a champion who came back from the brink of death. He is a born attacker on the track and above all he is professional as well as a charming guy.
He certainly does not lack for character. His first win was pretty much gifted to him by Jacques Villeneuve at the end of 1997. To that one, he added eight more in 1998 as well as nine pole positions. Keke Rosberg had said it: «*Once he starts winning there will be no stopping him.*» Looking back at the dominance of McLaren in the Prost and Senna era, there is certainly more to come from the Finn. David Coulthard is banking on 1999, but he might not be making many win withdrawals. Of course, Ferrari might be planning to celebrate the twentieth anniversary of Jody Scheckter's title in style. Just two days after the Japanese GP, Michael Schumacher was back in action at Suzuka. 1999 is going to be one tough season.

△
Stop watch war, tyre war, chassis and engine war: The Hakkinen-McLaren versus Schumacher-Ferrari fight, exploited every part of the cars to the limit.

1998 WORLD CHAMPIONSHIP

Drivers :

1.	Mika HAKKINEN	100
2.	Michael SCHUMACHER	86
3.	David COULTHARD	56
4.	Eddie IRVINE	47
5.	Jacques VILLENEUVE	21
6.	Damon HILL	20
7.	Heinz-Harald FRENTZEN	17
	Alexander WURZ	17
9.	Giancarlo FISICHELLA	16
10.	Ralf SCHUMACHER	14
11.	Jean ALESI	9
12.	Rubens BARRICHELLO	4
13.	Mika SALO	3
	Pedro DINIZ	3
15.	Johnny HERBERT	1
	Jan MAGNUSSEN	1
	Jarno TRULLI	1

Constructors :

1.	McLaren / Mercedes	156
2.	Ferrari	133
3.	Williams / Mecachrome	38
4.	Jordan / Mugen Honda	34
5.	Benetton / Playlife	33
6.	Sauber / Petronas	10
7.	Arrows	6
8.	Stewart / Ford	5
9.	Prost / Peugeot	1

Jacques Villeneuve: a leap in the dark

Suzuka marked the last appearance for the Tyrrell team. It was only half an appearance at that, as Riccardo Rosset failed to qualify, leaving Toranosuke Takagi to uphold the honour of this once famous name.
At BAR, there has been little interest in the team they have bought and especially since October, all eyes have been focussed on the «BARrell», the hybrid car driven by Jean-Christophe Boullion, based on a Tyrrell 026 chassis, with a Mecachrome engine and a Reynard rear end.
The day after Suzuka, it was Jacques Villeneuve and Ricardo Zonta who took over. For the Brazilian driver, joining a new team might be the best way to preserve a good image built on his F3000 title in 1997 and the 1998 GT crown, but for Jacques Villeneuve, the outgoing F1 champion, BAR represents a real risk.
Before the Austrian GP, he thought long and hard about the pros and cons of the offer to jump ship. He evidently had offers from the other top teams, but without giving any details about the length of his contract or his salary, he decided to make the move. At the time, the new team already looked pretty well set up. It has a colossal budget in the order of 100 million dollars a year for five years and was busy buying up everything and everyone that was best in F1.
The partnership of Reynard, Villeneuve, the Supertec V10 and some high class personnel poached from other teams looked like a good start.
While it is a genuine risk for the Canadian, there are enough positive points to make it worth taking. The risk fits in with his unconventional attitude to life and as the short term did not look too brilliant if he stayed put at Williams, then why not risk that short term period with BAR?
The thing is, that since last summer, a few spanners seem to have been thrown into the works. Quite how serious they are has yet to be ascertained. Finally, they have been allowed to adopt the name BAR for the team, but FIA has forbidden the team from running its two cars in different liveries and now it seems that Craig Pollock has sold off some of his shares to Barry Greene. So, the team does not move into the winter in the best of health on the political front. Luckily, on the technical side, which is naturally the key to making Villeneuve a winner again, everything appears to be progressing smoothly. However, three key questions remain unanswered. Will the Canadian be a sufficient catalyst to turn to the BAR RP01 into a winner quickly enough? Will all the politics involved weaken the team's effort? And finally, has Villeneuve not simply opted for BAR out of personal interests in the team? Only when these points have been answered will it be possible to guess how successful the team might be in its debut year.

A good start to his third season with Sauber for Johnny Herbert. He scored points in the first grand prix. But it ended in acrimony with claims the team favoured Jean Alesi over him.
▽

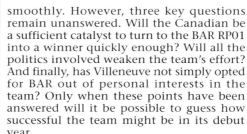

A FEW KEY POINTS

Melbourne. A McLaren one-two. After a mix up over the radio, Mika Hakkinen comes into the pits for no reason, but he re-takes the lead when David Coulthard lets him pass.

Argentina. Starting from pole, David Coulthard is caught by Michael Schumacher, who spears the Scot out of the way, as he heads for victory.

Imola. Victory for David Coulthard and a broken engine for Mika Hakkinen. Central winglets become commonplace, except at McLaren and Arrows. Jordan estimates their cost at around $50,000.

Canada. Three starts, including one behind the safety car because of a major pile- up. Michael Schumacher won, pushing Heinz-Harald Frentzen off the track on his way to the flag.

Great Britain. Hakkinen starts from pole and spins off twice in the rain before giving best to Michael Schumacher, who takes the chequered flag in the pit lane to win.

Austria. In changeable weather conditions, Fisichella sets his first ever pole. Hakkinen wins the race.

Germany. The best a Ferrari can do is fifth place.

Belgium. First one-two finish for Jordan in F1. After an apocalyptic race which saw 13 cars wiped out at the start, Schumacher, in the lead, is about to lap Coulthard but crashes into him and has to retire.

Italy. One-two finish for Ferrari after Hakkinen has brake problems.

Luxembourg. Both Ferraris start from the front row, but they are beaten by a majestic Hakkinen.

Japan. Ferrari dominates qualifying. At the start, Jarno Trulli, then Michael Schumacher stall on the grid and start from the back adding a final twist to the title. Schumacher climbs as high as third but retires with a tyre blow-out.

In the year DC

David Coulthard has a career strategy with the world championship as his goal. He chose to join McLaren and for the moment he is sticking with the team.
As Keke Rosberg said of Mika Hakkinen: *«He conformed to the house style and finally he is a winner.»* So, if there is a house style and not all teams have one, then drivers have to fit in with it.
David Coulthard seems to be moulded in the same style as Ron Dennis demands from his crew, even without having to make any effort. All he has to do now, is to wait and win.
In order not to upset the apple cart, the Scotsman has obeyed team orders and invested his time wisely, in the hope of reaping the benefit in 1999.
Right from Melbourne he made it clear he was prepared to be a team player, although at the time he probably thought he would pick up more than his solitary win at Imola.
In practice, he did what was asked of him, more often than not qualifying right behind Hakkinen and generally, he did all he could to help the team win the championships.
In this, he did better than Irvine at Ferrari as he did actually win a grand prix, taking four points off the German and six off Ferrari, after Hakkinen retired with gearbox problems.
In short, the Scotsman did a good job. However, going from that to winning the title in 1999 is a big step.
He will have to out-qualify Hakkinen more often and hope that bad luck switches camp and joins Hakkinen a bit more often.
He will also have to hope that Schumacher and Ferrari do not turn out to be the dominant team.
He will also have to be as obstinate and determined as the Finn.
Most of all, he will need to find some more speed and have more confidence in the car.
History does not serve his cause as McLaren drivers have often won back to back titles as did Ron Dennis' giant killing team of Alain Prost, champion in 1985 and '86 and Ayrton Senna in 1990 and '91.

△
«But how does Mika find three tenths at this corner?» Faced with the Finn's instinctive speed, the Scotsman had good cause to pull his hair out.

Ferrari world champions in 1999?

If only the season had ended in Monza and that wonderful one -two finish for Schumacher and Irvine. But it was not be and while McLaren boss Ron Dennis could spend the winter hugging trophies, at Ferrari Jean Todt had to settle for looking through his photo album from the Italian Grand Prix.
Since Schumacher joined Ferrari in 1996, he has never been out of the top three in the final classification in the drivers' championship. Since 1993 and the Alesi/Berger duo, the number of points accrued by the Scuderia's lead driver has grown from 18 to 86 points this year. The average number of points taken to win the title in that period is 95.16 points and if Schumacher's points tally continues to grow year by year he should hit the 95 or 96 mark in 1999. It still would not have been enough this season, when Hakkinen ended up with a nice round 100 points. For Schumacher to win next year, he needs the other competitors to improve and start taking points off one another. On the constructor front, Ferrari has been runner up for the past three years and if you accept that Schumacher has always been on top of his game, then the improvement needs to come from Irvine. But if Eddie has not always been able to back up his leader the way they would wish, then Ferrari only has itself to blame as Irvine is the only one of the top ten if not top twelve drivers to be treated as a designated number two driver, rather than a joint number one. If Ferrari gives him more support then they should be capable of increasing their points tally and taking the title next season.
Of course, all this is based on calculations and has little bearing with what might actually happen on the track, but the Scuderia must be in with a chance of winning both championships. Certainly all the ingredients are in place with Jean Todt, Michael Schumacher, Ross Brawn and Rory Byrne all on top of their game. Ferrari will hopefully have learnt their lesson this season and that is that they cannot hope to win unless they are competitive right from the start of the season. In 1998, they had to play catch-up all year long and in the end it was too much for them.

«Ladies, I am sorry, but my heart already belongs to another.» Heinz-Harald Frentzen's sad season did not stop him being popular.
◁▽

The manufacturers go head to head. It was the superiority of the Bridgestone tyres in the early part of the season which allowed Mika Hakkinen to take the title.
▽

Mika Hakkinen – the Finn is finally first in F1

by Eric Silbermann

Almost everyone at Suzuka, with the obvious exception of the Ferrari team, was happy Mika Hakkinen was world champion. There is a feeling that he has paid his dues, has proved his true worth as a very quick and clever driver, whose loyalty to McLaren over so many lean years when he had to do his best with a poor car, should now be rewarded with the ultimate prize. In all those hard times, Mika never once complained in public, he never rubbished his car, his mechanics or even his opponents. It has even been written that Hakkinen deserved the title, because he nearly died in Adelaide, in pursuit of his dream. That of course, is nonsense. Nobody ever asked a young Finnish boy to start karting, to race all around the world and become a grand prix driver. We tend to forget these guys started racing for fun. Mika has always been optimistic. For the past five years, every March, he has told us this was going to be the year he would start winning. The car was great and he was very confident. Listening to this every year, it was like the old story of the little boy who always cried Wolf! It is in his nature to have a positive outlook, something he has had to work on in the past. This year, there was evidently no need for him to psyche himself up and even he admits that in the winter of 97/98 there was a different mood in the McLaren camp. *«I knew when I ran the car for the first time in Paul Ricard, that it felt good and I could drive it the way I liked. I did not have to work on building up some huge motivation inside of me. I did not have to push myself to say it was going to be good. I was able to relax a bit more. Also, I have a lot of experience in F1 and I knew life could only get better.»* Finally and for once, he was right. Hakkinen is living proof that it pays to be loyal. There is no doubt he could have quit McLaren and got another top drive over the past few years and now he is seeing the benefit of staying put.

With the might of Mercedes behind it, the skills of Adrian Newey and determination of Ron Dennis, perhaps Mika might actually stay with the team until it is time for him to retire and look after the kart team of the four children he will probably have by then! *«Ron* (Dennis) *has already said to me that he hopes I finish my F1 career with McLaren and with a lot of success,»* admitted Mika. *«It seems we are heading for that success for a few more years at least. When to stop racing depends on your own physical and psychological strength. How long can you continue? I have been in F1 for eight years and it has been a long road down which time has flown very quickly. I don't mean I am missing something in my life; time with my friends or family for example. However, I believe Formula 1 is a very hard business which takes a lot out of you and one day I will say 'thank you very much' and turn my back on it, but that day is still a long way off.»*

Hakkinen now hopes the next few years might have plenty more winning in them for him. *«The future looks good at the moment,»* he said. *«If you look at the past winners, it seems to go in cycles. The last time McLaren won, they were champions for several years and then Williams did the same, so it would seem that maybe this is the start of another McLaren cycle and that is something to look forward to.»*

Running for the title has changed the way Hakkinen tackled some of the races this season. In the past, still chasing that first ever win, there was almost no risk that was not worth taking in an effort to score maximum points. Now we have seen a more cautious and calculating approach. *«In Argentina, people said to me I could have pushed harder, overtaken Schumacher and won,»* he recalled. *«The car was difficult to drive and I knew if I pushed harder I would go off the track and so I made a conscious decision to maintain my second place. I knew there were other races coming up where I would do better.»* For many onlookers, that brought back memories of two young boys called Schumacher and Hakkinen fighting it out for F3 honours in the prestigious Macau GP. With a race in two parts and having won the first, all young Mika had to do was follow young Michael to the flag to take overall honours, but he was impatient, tried to pass and crashed. He learnt his lesson. *«I don't remember the race at all, it was such a long time ago!»* he lied. The strangest moment of Mika's 1998 season came right at the start in Melbourne, when Coulthard moved over to let his team-mate through. Now, after the Finn has dominated the Scot all year, it seems a perfectly logical move, but at the time nobody could accurately predict who would be the quickest of the pair, although some were pretty convinced it would be Hakkinen. Those extra four Australian points, the difference between coming first and second is exactly the gap Hakkinen had over Schumacher going into the Suzuka race. *«It is all part of the jigsaw puzzle, but it is important to remember the fantastic thing that David did in Melbourne. Next year we will be starting again and David will be fighting even harder. But the reality is that everyone can only go at a certain speed and no faster.»* You see, Mika can make cutting comments when he wants to! The truth is that while others might have been speculating back in March that we would have an interesting year-long duel between the two McLaren drivers, that was never part of Hakkinen's plans. He always felt he was quicker than David. In fact, Mika thinks he is quicker than all of them and he might be right, although Schumacher and his fans would disagree.

Hakkinen himself would only ever want to win in a McLaren, such is his loyalty to Ron Dennis, so what is the boss of McLaren, who we hardly ever see smiling, really like in private and inside his team? *«My relationship with Ron is personal and I do not want to say too much about it,»* said Mika, who has a habit of making simple questions seem like you are asking him for the meaning of life. *«However, I can say, that he thinks everything through very carefully and he always looks to the future. It is as though he can see the future. He never stops to think what happened yesterday-tomorrow and the far off future is the important thing. His family and the company come first. He cares enormously about his staff as he knows that without them McLaren would be nothing. I respect his qualities enormously. When I joined McLaren in 1993 I was still a kid and he took me into the team like part of his family. At that time I was very shy and it was difficult for me to understand what was happening, as Ron Dennis was a big hero of mine. That is a fact. Remember, that I had not long left Finland, where motor racing is very important and everyone talks about the sport all the time and Dennis was a major personality in that sport. For me, as a young guy, the opportunity to work with him was fantastic. He gave me my confidence, even though he was very hard on me and is still very hard on me sometimes. He is very tough, but it is the best way to get the results. He is a very good judge of people's qualities and he knows how to get the most out of them. I have learnt so much from him.»* For his part, Dennis has seen all the time and effort spent on Mika produce a mature race winner now. The human investment has paid off. For a man who has always claimed that both his drivers always have equal status, Dennis has found it difficult to hide the fact that Mika is very much his favourite out of the two, no matter

if they are treated equally in technical terms. «*Even I find it difficult to understand,*» laughed Mika. Perhaps Dennis became a big Mika fan, when his young driver out qualified Ayrton Senna in his first ever GP appearance for McLaren at the Portuguese GP in 1993. «*I don't think so,*» disagreed Hakkinen. «*It might have seemed like something fantastic, what I did that day in Estoril, but I am not sure it was such a good thing for me. The team had given me a fantastic opportunity, but you cannot be the best driver, every day on every track. It just so happened that on that occasion I was quicker than Ayrton, but it did not mean much. After all, he was much quicker than me the next day in the race.*»
Hakkinen has not lacked for deluxe, first class advice, as apart from Ron Dennis he can also count on the support of a certain Keke Rosberg, who used to do a bit of driving in the old days! The 1982 world champion is no soft touch when it comes to keeping his young charger on the straight and narrow path to success. «*F1 is a tough business and if you do not work hard all the time then you will drop out of it,*» said Mika. «*Keke is tough on me to make sure I keep working. He is a blunt talker but there is a logic to everything he says. His position as my manager is not easy. He has a huge responsibility to handle my success and he does not want to fail. If I fail, he fails and so he is as tough on me as he is on himself. He does not really advise me anymore as to how I should do my job, because we both know there is only one way and that is to keep your foot flat down all the time! He did advise me on Sunday just before the Suzuka race. 'Treat it like just another race,' he said. 'Enjoy yourself and go for it. At the finish we can add up the points.' It was good advice! The work he does goes much deeper than what you see on the surface. It all goes on in the background and sometimes even I do not realise what is going on. Everyone at McLaren has helped me over the years and we have been through a lot together. They are very strange people because they understand their work so well and they are so organised. They can be very hard on me and there is not much emotion or pity if a race goes wrong. But if they make a mistake, they admit it immediately, because they know Ron will not sack them from the team. He accepts that everyone makes mistakes and that allows for a good working environment.*»
Unlike some of his fellow F1 drivers, Hakkinen does not use the Royal «*We.*» Schumacher and Villeneuve for example, always talk about «*we did a good lap,*» or «*we managed to go quicker,*» when they really mean «*I.*» Mika does not think he is a king! When Mika says we, he means the team and as we have touched on the subject of his bosses and engineers, I brought up the topic of the two other members of his close-knit group at the track, friend and confidant Didier Coton and wife Erja. «*Oh my God!*» said Mika , laughing loudly. «*Do we have to talk about those people? Didi and I have been on the road together since 1992. He is part of the Rosberg organisation and he is there to look after the day to day business of travelling around the world as you cannot expect a driver to do it all. But after all these years, he is more than that. We have a very strong and important friendship. I know this job can look glamorous but you can get lonely sitting in a hotel room all alone for a week. In these situations it is good to have a friend you can turn to and Didi and I talk a lot. It is almost like therapy for me!*» *At this point I suggested that Mika could have saved a lot of money that he must have spent on engagement and wedding rings and simply married Didier Coton!* «*It is not a bad idea, but there is one big problem with it!*» he replied laughing. «*As for Erja, in the past she did not come to many races, back in 1995 and 1996. I was a bit of a male chauvinist in those days and felt the paddock was not the right place to bring your wife. I thought it would make my mind go weird. But Erja enjoys the atmosphere of the grands prix and it gives her a break from her own work. At the same time it gives us the opportunity to be together. There has to be a certain harmony between you or it will not work. Finally, there is one person who is part of this «family» and part of the organisation. That is Keke's sister Jatta, who runs the Monaco office, but does a lot more besides. She looked after me when I was very green and was only a 19 year old boy, fresh from Finland and racing in Formula Ford. I was in a foreign country, trying to be a professional racing driver. I do not think that Keke's nerves could have put up with dealing with me and my problems and luckily Jatta was there to do it!*»

«*Fish-paste, hat-stand, desk lamp!*» This was the catch phrase of a group of journalists, every time Hakkinen came into the media centre at the race tracks for a press conference. Why? Because Mika was prone to mumble or avoid questions or simply ignore or refuse to answer the question. «*Fish-paste, hat-stand, desk lamp*» seemed to be what he was saying, especially when asked to reply in his native tongue. In fact, he came in for a lot of criticism at the start of the season, for not looking happy on the podium and being lost for words in the press conferences. But gradually that changed as his confidence built up, until his emotions were plain to see when the champagne started to spray. Equally his opinions were plain to understand once he started talking after the races. By the time we got to Monaco, Mika the Mumbler was gone to be replaced by Mika the Master of the press conference. After that emotional win in the Principality, the nearest thing this permanent world traveller has to a home, Mika took command of the press conference and there was something that reminded people of the late Ayrton Senna in the way Mika chose his words carefully to ensure he said exactly what he meant. «*I have learnt to live with the press and that has come with the wins and the success,*» explained Hakkinen. «*Most of the time at the track, I am with the engineers or hiding in the motorhome, but all the pole positions and wins have given me the opportunity to show myself as I really am and what I think. It is important, because people do not know who you really are unless you spend time with them. Having to attend all those press conferences at every race has allowed the media to know me and has also allowed me to get to understand them and what their job is.*» The positive aspect of the conferences at the last few races was the genuine good feeling between the two title adversaries. Over the past few seasons, the Formula 1 world championship has always played out its last few races in a mood of bitterness and anger. Put Schumacher and Villeneuve in the same room in '97 or Schumacher and Hill in '96 and they could hardly bear to look at one another, let alone talk politely to each other. Mika and Michael might not have been best friends but there was respect between them. They could still shake hands and mean it and that was great for Formula 1. So what does Mika think of Schumacher? «*He is one hell of a racer and great driver with a great talent in the car and the way he works with his team. His character is such that some people like him and others don't. Nobody is perfect. Racing with him for the championship, my first thought was that I wish I had been competing against someone who is not so quick, although of course that is not the way it works.*»
«*It has been an up and down season,*» confirmed Mika. «*Sometimes we have left a grand prix in total silence and others we have been laughing our heads off at the good times. What I can say is that winning is everything! It gives you such a great feeling inside that you forget all the stress.*»
By next season, Mika will have learnt to believe he is champion and like all winners of the title he will start the following year in a much stronger frame of mind mentally. We could be in for an even more exciting fight between Hakkinen and Schumacher, the two fastest drivers in the world today.

The actors

This year, there are but 22 players on the stage to fight over the top Grand Prix honours. From the least well known to the superstars, here is the cast of the 1998 world championship.

Marlboro

Williams-Mécachrome

1. Jacques VILLENEUVE

DRIVER PROFILE

- Name : *VILLENEUVE*
- First name : *Jacques*
- Nationality : *Canadian*
- Date of birth : *April 9, 1971*
- Place of birth : *St-Jean-sur-Richelieu, Quebec, CAN*
- Lives in : *Monaco*
- Marital status : *single*
- Kids : -
- Hobbies : *music, computer, movie theatre*
- Favourite music : *rock and pop*
- Favourite meal : *pasta*
- Favourite drink : *milk*
- Height : *171 cm*
- Weight : 66,5 kg

STATISTICS

- Nber of Grand Prix : *49*
- Victories : *11*
- Pole-positions : *13*
- Best laps : *9*
- Accident/off : *8*
- Not qualified : *0*
- Laps in the lead : *634*
- Km in the lead : *2972*
- Points scored : *180*

PRIOR TO F1

1986 : Jim Russel School
1987 : Driving school Spenard-David
1988: Ital. Champ. Alfa
1989-91 : F3 (-, 14th, 6th)
1992 : F3 Japan (2nd)
1993 : F. Atlantic (3rd)
1994 : IndyCar (6th)
1995 : IndyCar (Champion)

F1 CAREER

1996 : *Williams / Renault. 78 points. 2nd of championship.*
1997 : *Williams / Renault. 81 pts.* ***World Champion.***
1998 : *Williams / Renault. 21 pts. 5th of championship*

2. Heinz-Harald FRENTZEN

DRIVER PROFILE

- Name : *FRENTZEN*
- First name : *Heinz-Harald*
- Nationality : *German*
- Date of birth : *May 18, 1967*
- Place of birth : *Mönchengladbach (D)*
- Lives in : *Monaco*
- Marital status : *single*
- Kids : -
- Hobbies : *running, mountain-bike, eating*
- Favourite music : *funk, soul, rap*
- Favourite meal : *fish, paella*
- Favourite drink : *apple juice*
- Height : *178 cm*
- Weight : *64,5 kg*

STATISTICS

- Nber of Grand Prix : *80*
- Victories : *1*
- Pole-positions : *1*
- Best laps : *6*
- Accident/off : *18*
- Not qualified : *0*
- Laps in the lead : *76*
- Km in the lead : *379*
- Points scored : *88*

PRIOR TO F1

1980-84 : *Karting*
1981 : *German Jr Karting Champion*
1885-87 : *F. Ford 2000 of Germany*
1988 : *F. Opel Lotus Champion*
1989 : *F. 3 of Germany*
1990-91 : *F. 3000*
1992-93 : *F. 3000 Japan*

F1 CAREER

1994 : *Sauber / Mercedes. 7 points. 13th of championship.*
1995 : *Sauber / Ford. 15 points. 9th of championship.*
1996 : *Sauber / Ford. 7 points. 12th of championship.*
1997 : *Williams / Renault. 42 pts. 2nd of championship.*
1998 : *Williams / Mécachrome. 17 pts. 7th of championship.*

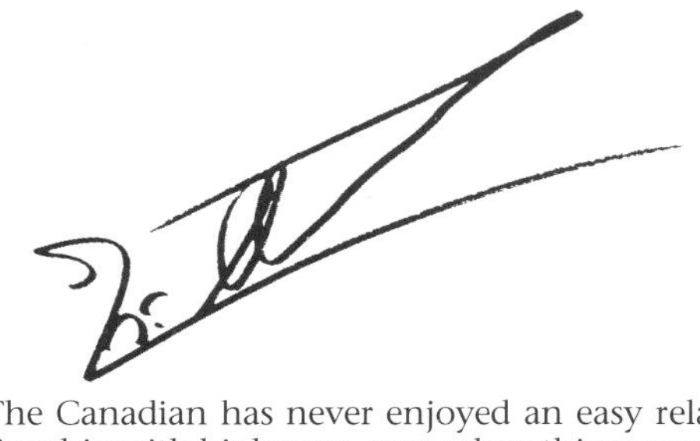

The Canadian has never enjoyed an easy relationship with his bosses, even when things went well and they were winning titles. Imagine what it must be like when things go badly then. It must be hell. Villeneuve has had a very tough year, hoping for a lucky break, gambling on strategy or praying for the misfortune of others to get in the points. He only visited the podium twice, in Germany and Hungary, but the light at the end of his tunnel turned out to be an oncoming train, rather than true improvement with a single point picked up at the final round in Japan. However, he did himself some good, because he proved to be a fighter who never gave up, no matter how bad the car. In many ways this was his best F1 season and now he takes another big risk, joining his former manager, Craig Pollock at BAR.

The German also made the best out of adversity, having a good season on relative terms. Unlike the previous season, this year "HH" regularly beat his more illustrious team-mate, both in qualifying and in the race. Villeneuve found it hard to stomach, especially in the final race in Japan. If his form suffered mid-season, it was because the rumours had already begun that he was being shown the door at the end of the season. Frentzen is something of a sensitive soul, it must be something to do with his mother's Spanish blood and Williams is notorious for regarding its drivers as just another widget that goes in the car somewhere. He managed to show some fighting spirit and in the warmer and more friendly environment he might finally show the promise that once had him billed as being quicker than Michael Schumacher.

Frank Williams did not have much to smile about this season. It was the first time his team had not been scrapping for the title since 1990. ▽

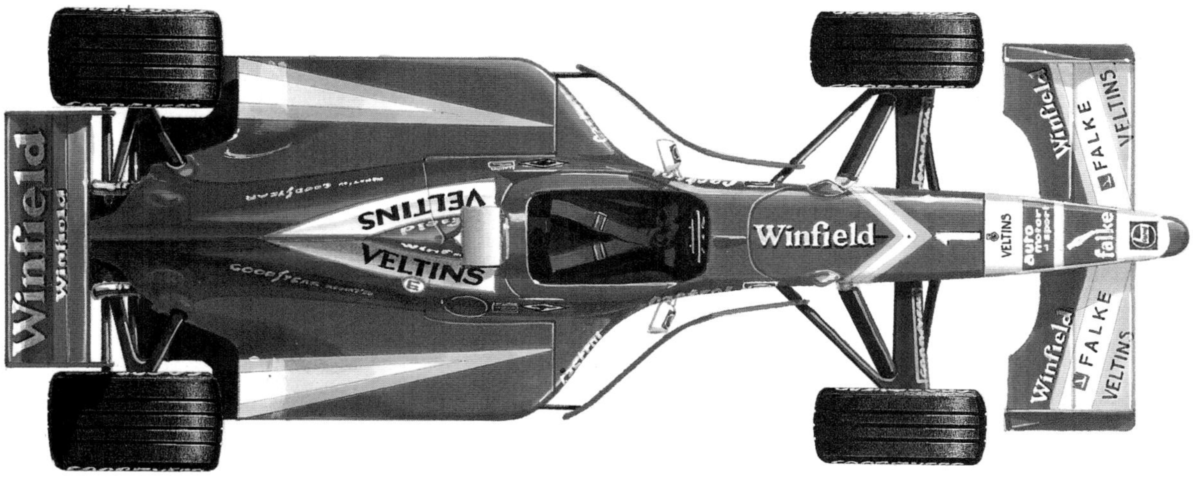

WILLIAMS-MÉCACHROME FW20 –
JACQUES VILLENEUVE
BELGIAN GRAND PRIX

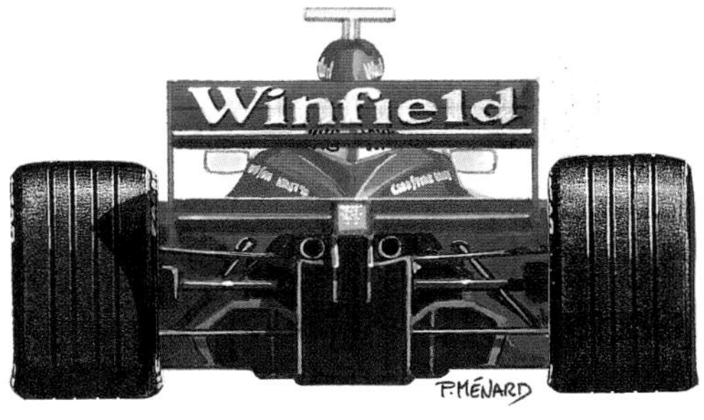

Williams-Mécachrome FW20

SPECIFICATION

- Chassis : *Williams FW20*
- Engine : *Mécachrome V10 GC 37-01*
- Tyres : *Goodyear*
- Wheels : *OZ*
- Fuel / oil : Petrobras/*Castrol*
- Brakes (discs) : *Carbone Industrie*
- Brakes (calipers) : *AP Racing*
- Transmission : *Williams 6 gears*
- Radiators : *Secan (water) / IMI (oil)*
- Plugs : *Champion*
- Electronic mgt : *Magneti Marelli*
- Shock absorbers : *Williams / Penske*
- Suspensions : *Williams, torsion and helicoïdal*
- Dry weight : *600 kg, driver included*
- Wheelbase : *2914 mm*
- Front track : *1460 mm*
- Rear track : *1400 mm*
- Total length : *4392 mm*

TEAM PROFILE

- Address : *Williams Grand Prix Engineering Grove, Wantage Oxfordshire OX12 0DQ, United Kingdom*
- Telephone : *(44) 1235 77 77 00*
- Fax : *(44) 1235 76 47 05*
- Established in : *1969*
- First Grand Prix : *Argentina 1975*
- General director : *Frank Williams*
- Technical director : *Patrick Head*
- Team-manager : *Dickie Stanford*
- Chief mechanic : *Carl Gaden*
- Nber of employees : *220*
- Sponsor : *Windfiel*

STATISTICS

- Number of Grand Prix : *395*
- Number of victories : *103*
- Number of pole-positions : *107*
- Number of best laps during the race : *109*
- Number of drivers' world titles : *7*
- Number of constructors' titles : *9*
- Total number of points scored : *1947.5*

POSITION IN WORLD CHAMPIONSHIP

1975 : *9th – 6 points*	1987 : ***1st – 137 points***
1976 : *not classified*	1988 : *7th – 20 points*
1977 : *not classified*	1989 : *2nd – 77 points*
1978 : *9th – 11 points*	1990 : *4th – 57 points*
1979 : *2nd – 75 points*	1991 : *2nd – 125 points*
1980 : ***1st – 120 points***	1992 : ***1st – 164 points***
1981 : ***1st – 95 points***	1993 : ***1st – 168 points***
1982 : *4th – 58 points*	1994 : ***1st – 118 points***
1983 : *4th – 38 points*	1995 : *2nd – 112 points*
1984 : *6th – 25.5 points*	1996 : ***1st – 175 points***
1985 : *3rd – 71 points*	1997 : ***1st – 123 points***
1986 : ***1st – 141 points***	1998 : *3rd – 38 points*

Williams Technical Director Patrick Head looks towards the future, the year 2000 and the arrival of the BMW engine.
▽

Waiting for BMW

In Formula 1, uncertainty about the future is a daily worry. During the winter, a slight drop in performance from Williams was to be expected, what with Renault quitting the sport and aero-wizard Adrian Newey moving to McLaren. However, the extent of the reigning world champion's fall was spectacular. The FW20 was simply a bad car and although it was improved slightly during the year, it had basic faults which would never be overcome and the team can consider itself lucky to have hung onto third place in the championship. The immediate future does not look much brighter. They will have a completely new driver line up and have to go through another transitional year with the less than competitive Mecachrome engine, while waiting for BMW to come to the rescue in 2000. The saving grace is that, despite their advancing years! Frank Williams and Patrick Head are real racers. The only thing that interests them is winning races. The problem is that this might be something that will have to wait until the arrival of their new German engine partner.

TEST DRIVER 1998

Juan Pablo MONTOYA (COL)
Max WILSON (BRA)

SUCCESSION OF DRIVERS 1998

- Jacques VILLENEUVE : *all Grand Prix*
- Heinz-H. FRENTZEN : *all Grand Prix*

Ferrari

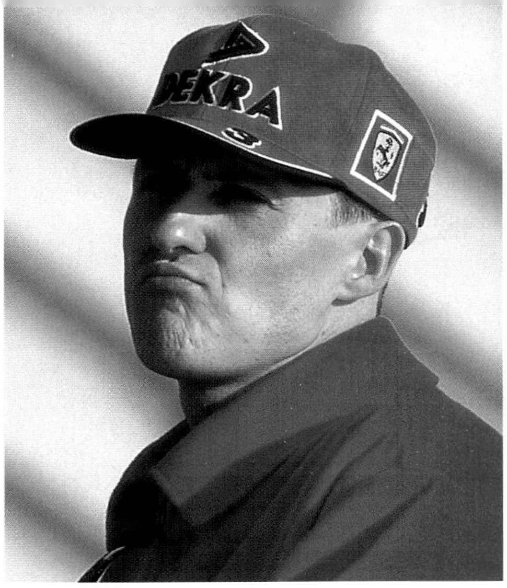

3. Michael SCHUMACHER

DRIVER PROFILE

- Name : *SCHUMACHER*
- First name : *Michael*
- Nationality : *German*
- Date of birth : *January 3, 1969*
- Place of birth : *Hürth-Hermühlheim (GER)*
- Lives in : *Vufflens-le-Château (CH)*
- Marital status : *married to Corinna*
- Kids : *one daughter (Gina Maria)*
- Hobbies : *karting, mountain-bike, biking*
- Favourite music : *Phil Collins, M. Jackson, T. Turner*
- Favourite meal : *Italian cuisine*
- Favourite drink : *apple juice with mineral water*
- Height : *174 cm*
- Weight : *74,5 kg*

STATISTICS

- Nber of Grand Prix : *118*
- Victories : *33*
- Pole-positions : *20*
- Best laps : *33*
- Accident/off : *19*
- Not qualified : *0*
- Laps in the lead : *1837*
- Km in the lead : *8463*
- Points scored : *526*

PRIOR TO F1

1984 : *German junior karting Champion*
1987 : *European karting Champion*
1988 : *German Champion of F. Ford*
1990-91 : *Sportscar championship with Mercedes*

F1 CAREER

1991 : *Jordan / Ford & Benetton. 4 points. 12th du champ.*
1992 : *Benetton / Ford. 53 points. 3rd of championship.*
1993 : *Benetton / Ford. 52 points. 4th of championship.*
1994 : *Benetton / Ford. 92 points.* ***World Champion.***
1995 : *Benetton/Renault. 102 pts.* ***World Champion.***
1996 : *Ferrari. 49 points. 3rd of championship.*
1997 : *Ferrari. 78 points. Excluded from the championship.*
1998 : *Ferrari. 86 points. 2nd of championship.*

4. Eddie IRVINE

DRIVER PROFILE

- Name : *IRVINE*
- First name : *Edmund*
- Nationality : *British*
- Date of birth : *November 10, 1965*
- Place of birth : *Newtownards (IRE)*
- Lives in : *Dublin, Oxford (GB) & Conlig (IRE)*
- Marital status : *single*
- Kids : -
- Hobbies : *golf, swimming, fishing*
- Favourite music : *rock, Van Morrison*
- Favourite meal : *Chinese*
- Favourite drink : -
- Height : *178 cm*
- Weight : *75 kg*

STATISTICS

- Nber of Grand Prix : *81*
- Victories : *0*
- Pole-positions : *0*
- Best laps : *0*
- Accident/off : *25*
- Not qualified : *0*
- Laps in the lead : *24*
- Km in the lead : *129*
- Points scored : *99*

PRIOR TO F1

1983-87 : *F. Ford 1600*
1988 : *F. 3 GB*
1989 : *F. 3000*
1990 : *F. 3000 (3rd)*
1991 : *F. 3000 Japon (7th)*
1992 : *F. 3000 Japon (8th)*
1993 : *F. 3000 Japon (2nd)*

F1 CAREER

1993 : *Jordan / Hart. 0 point.*
1994 : *Jordan / Hart. 6 points. 14th of championship.*
1995 : *Jordan / Peugeot. 10 points. 12th of championship.*
1996 : *Ferrari. 11 points. 10th of championship.*
1997 : *Ferrari. 24 points. 7th of championship.*
1998 : *Ferrari. 47 points. 4th of championship.*

There is no doubt this was his best season. After the opening race in Melbourne, no one would have given him the slightest chance of winning the title. But he pushed his team and especially their tyre supplier to do more. He gave Goodyear a roasting before Monaco and went on to win the next three races! However, up until the summer, it did not seem that his fabled talents at the wheel or race craft would not be enough to turn the tide. He never gave up and Ferrari worked harder than ever, putting in 24 hour days and tested pretty much non-stop at Mugello and their own Fiorano track. In the end it was not quite enough and Schumacher yet again had to suffer the pain of defeat in the last hour of the championship. In 1998, his reputation grew, although it has to be said he was not infallible, making a few driving errors of his own and probably losing the title in the rain in Spa-Francorchamps.

There are some who claim Eddie Irvine has the best job in the world and others who say it is the worst. What is certain is that none of Michael Schumacher's previous team-mates have ever managed to live with the German, either on or off the track, for as long as the laid back Irishman. It is his easy going nature that has led some of the sport's purists to claim he is only in it for the money, but this year's results have proved otherwise. Certainly it has been his best F1 season since he burst on the scene in 1993. He has been a model of consistency, helped by Ferrari's reliability, finishing eleven times in the points, eight times on the podium with two second places to his name. He also qualified on the front row for the first time in his career at the Nurburgring. But next year will undoubtedly be his last with the Scuderia, so he might trying ignoring his radio instructions now and again!

FERRARI F300
MICHAEL SCHUMACHER
FRENCH GRAND PRIX

Ferrari F300

SPECIFICATION

- Chassis : *Ferrari F300*
- Engine : *Ferrari 047 V10*
- Tyres : *Goodyear*
- Fuel / oil : *Shell*
- Brakes (discs) : *Carbone Industrie*
- Brakes (calipers) : *Brembo*
- Transmission : *Ferrari 7 gears*
- Radiators : *not revealed*
- Plugs : *NGK*
- Electronic mgt : *Magneti Marelli*
- Shock absorbers : *not revealed*
- Wheels : *BBS*
- Suspensions : *push rods (ft/bk)*
- Dry weight : *600 kg, including driver*
- Wheelbase : *2953 mm*
- Total length : *4340 mm*
- Total height : *961 mm*
- Front track : *1490 mm*
- Rear track : *1405 mm*

TEAM PROFILE

- Address : *Ferrari SpR, Via Ascari 55, 41053 Maranello (MO), Italy*
- Telephone : *(39) 536 94 91 11*
- Fax : *(39) 536 94 64 88*
- Established in : *1929*
- First Grand Prix : *Monaco 1950*
- General director : *Luca Di Montezemolo*
- Technical director : *Ross Brawn*, *Paolo Martinelli (engines)*
- Concepteur chassis : *Rory Byrne*
- Recherche : *Gustav Brunner*
- Team-manager : *Jean Todt*
- Chief mechanic : *Nigel Stepney*
- Nber of employees : *400*
- Sponsors : *Marlboro, Fiat, Shell, Asprey*

STATISTICS

- Number of Grand Prix : *602*
- Number of victories : *119*
- Number of pole-positions : *124*
- Number of best laps during the race : *131*
- Number of drivers' world titles : *9*
- Number of constructors' titles : *8*
- Total number of points scored : *2215.5*

POSITION IN WORLD CHAMPIONSHIP

1958 : *2nd – 40 points*	1972 : *4th – 33 points*	1986 : *4th – 37 points*
1959 : *2nd – 32 points*	1973 : *6th – 12 points*	1987 : *4th – 53 points*
1960 : *3rd – 24 points*	1974 : *2nd – 65 points*	1988 : *2nd – 65 points*
1961 : ***1st – 40 points***	1975 : ***1st – 72,5 points***	1989 : *3rd – 59 points*
1962 : *5th – 18 points*	1976 : ***1st – 83 points***	1990 : *2nd – 110 points*
1963 : *4th – 26 points*	1977 : ***1st – 95 points***	1991 : *3rd – 55,5 points*
1964 : ***1st – 45 points***	1978 : *2nd – 58 points*	1992 : *4th – 21 points*
1965 : *4th – 26 points*	1979 : ***1st – 113 points***	1993 : *4th – 23 points*
1966 : *2nd – 31 points*	1980 : *10th – 8 points*	1994 : *3rd – 71 points*
1967 : *4th – 20 points*	1981 : *5th – 34 points*	1995 : *3rd – 73 points*
1968 : *4th – 32 points*	1982 : ***1st – 74 points***	1996 : *2nd – 70 points*
1969 : *5th – 7 points*	1983 : ***1st – 89 points***	1997 : *2nd – 102 points*
1970 : *2nd – 55 points*	1984 : *2nd – 57,5 points*	1998 : *2nd – 133 points*
1971 : *4th – 33 points*	1985 : *2nd – 82 points*	

Ferrari gave their all

They made the brave announcement when, with much pomp, they unveiled the new F 300 in front of the new Ferrari 1:1 scale wind tunnel. Neither President Montezemolo nor sporting director Todt had held back. The F 300 was the car that would finally take the team back to the top. It had to win one world title at least. From that standpoint, they very definitely failed. However, the car was incredibly reliable, and performed very consistently. The technical and organisational personnel tackled the challenge without flinching. With such an arsenal of talent, victory cannot be too far away and this Ferrari team will take the title. Second last year as well, Schumacher has been too near the top for too long not to succeed. In 1998, the Scuderia worked better than ever, but no one could predict last winter, just how competitive the McLarens would be.

TEST DRIVER 1998

Luca BADOER (I)

SUCCESSION OF DRIVERS 1998

- Mich. SCHUMACHER : *all Grand Prix*
- Eddie IRVINE : *all Grand Prix*

Jean Todt and Ross Brawn, both directors of the Scuderia; the first sporting, the second technical.
▽

Benetton-Playlife

5. Giancarlo FISICHELLA

DRIVER PROFILE

- Name : *FISICHELLA*
- First name : *Giancarlo*
- Nationality : *Italian*
- Date of birth : *January 14, 1973*
- Place of birth : *Roma (I)*
- Lives in : *Monte Carlo*
- Marital status : *single*
- Kids : -
- Hobbies : *skiing, fishing, football, tennis*
- Favourite music : *disco music, Zucchero*
- Favourite meal : *pasta, pizza, steaks and fish*
- Favourite drink : *orange juice*
- Height : *172 cm*
- Weight : *69,5 kg*

STATISTICS

Nber of Grand Prix :	41
Victories :	0
Pole-positions :	1
Best laps :	0
Accident/off :	10
Not qualified :	0
Laps in the lead :	31
Km in the lead :	154
Points scored :	36

PRIOR TO F1

- 1984-88 : *Karting*
- 1989 : *World Championship Karting (4th)*
- 1991 : *F. Alfa Boxer; karting (EUR) (2nd)*
- 1992-94 : *F 3 (ITA), champion in1994*
- 1995 : *DTM/ITC Alfa Romeo*

F1 CAREER

1996 : *Minardi / Ford. 0 point.*
1996 : *Minardi / Ford. 0 point.*
1997 : *Jordan / Peugeot. 20 points. 8th of championship.*
1998 : *Benetton / Playlife. 16 points. 9th of championship.*

6. Alexander WURZ

DRIVER PROFILE

- Name : *WURZ*
- First name : *Alexander*
- Nationality : *Austrian*
- Date of birth : *February 15, 1974*
- Place of birth : *Waidhofen (AUS)*
- Lives in : *Perchtoldsdorf*
- Marital status : *engaged to Karin*
- Kids : -
- Hobbies : *mountain biking, skiing*
- Favourite music : *Beatles, Pink Floyd, Rolling Stones*
- Favourite meal : *pasta and meat*
- Favourite drink : *apple juice with mineral water*
- Height : *186 cm*
- Weight : *82,4 kg*

STATISTICS

Nber of Grand Prix :	19
Victories :	0
Pole-positions :	0
Best laps :	1
Accident/off :	4
Not qualified :	0
Laps in the lead :	0
Km in the lead :	0
Points scored :	21

PRIOR TO F1

- 1986 : *BMX worldchampion*
- 1989 -90 : *kart (AUS) (2nd) Middle East KW (4th)*
- 1991 : *FFord 1600 (AUS)(1st)*
- 1992 : *FFord 1600 (D)(1st)*
- 1993 : *F3 (AUS) champion*
- 1994 : *F3 (D) (2nd)*
- 1995 : *F3 (D) (6th)*
- 1996 : *Le Mans 24h (1st)*

F1 CAREER

1997 : *Benetton / Renault. 4 points. 14th of championship.*
1998 : *Benetton / Playlife. 16 points. 9th of championship.*

Fisichella had not wanted to leave Jordan at the end of 1997. Now, he is probably not too sure. The young Roman, Italy's best hope of a home grown world champion had an excellent season within the limitations of the equipment available. He was nearly always quicker than his team mate, who had already worked with Benetton as test driver. "Fisico" has made his mark with two second places in Monaco and Canada and proved he can do the one lap flyer as well, by stealing pole in Austria. He was known to be quick, but against expectations, he has shown himself to be cunning on the track and clever on the technical side. The only down side is that he seemed to tail off, scoring only two points in the second half of the season. He has a win to will and so does his team. Now, he just needs a technical package worthy of his talents.

It is important to remind oneself that this was the young Austrian's first full season in Formula 1, because you would never guess it from his calm manner and confidence. Young bloods often qualify well, then throw it all away in the races. The lanky Wurz knew where his priorities lay and was not worried when his team-mate was higher up the grid, preferring to concentrate on the race. The result of this self- discipline that he scored six times out of the first nine races and that is worth its weight in gold to a team owner. While this remarkable record died away in the second half of the season, Wurz took the opportunity to improve his qualifying technique. The future looks bright, given he possesses that rare combination of speed and intelligence.

BENETTON-PLAYLIFE B198
GIANCARLO FISICHELLA
CANADIAN GRAND PRIX

Benetton-Playlife B198

SPECIFICATION

• Chassis :	*Benetton B198*
• Engine :	*Playlife V10F1-01*
• Tyres :	*Bridgestone*
• Wheels :	*BBS*
• Fuel / oil :	*Agip*
• Brakes (discs) :	*Carbone Industrie*
• Brakes (calipers) :	*Brembo*
• Transmission :	*Benetton 6 gears*
• Radiators :	*Benetton*
• Plugs :	*Champion*
• Electronic mgt :	*Magneti Marelli*
• Shock absorbers :	*Bilstein*
• Suspensions :	*push rods (ft/bk)*
• Dry weight :	*520 kg (without driver)*
• Wheelbase :	*3000 mm*
• Front track :	*1800 mm*
• Rear track :	*1805 mm*

TEAM PROFILE

• Address :	*Benetton Formula Ltd.* *Whiteways Technical Centre* *Enstone, Chipping Norton* *Oxon OX7 4EE* *United Kingdom*
• Telephone :	*(44) 1608 67 80 00*
• Fax :	*(44) 1608 67 86 09*
• Established in :	*1970 (under the name Toleman)*
• First Grand Prix :	*Italy 1981*
• General director :	*Flavio Briatore / David Richards*
• Technical director :	*Pat Symonds*
• Team-manager :	*Joan Villadelprat*
• Chief mechanic :	*Mike Ainsley-Cowlishaw*
• Nber of employees :	*175*
• Sponsors :	*Mild Seven, Fed Ex, Korean Air, Akai*

STATISTICS

• Number of Grand Prix :	*267*
• Number of victories :	*26*
• Number of pole-positions :	*16*
• Number of best laps during the race :	*37*
• Number of drivers' world titles :	*2*
• Number of constructors' titles :	*1*
• Total number of points scored :	*830.5*

POSITION IN WORLD CHAMPIONSHIP

1981 : *not classified*	1990 : *3rd – 71 points*
1982 : *not classified*	1991 : *4th – 38,5 points*
1983 : *9th – 10 points*	1992 : *3rd – 91 points*
1984 : *7th – 16 points*	1993 : *3rd – 72 points*
1985 : *not classified*	1994 : *2nd – 103 points*
1986 : *6th – 19 points*	1995 : ***1st – 137 points***
1987 : *5th – 28 points*	1996 : *3rd – 68 points*
1988 : *3rd – 39 points*	1997 : *3rd – 67 points*
1989 : *4th – 39 points*	1998 : *5rd – 33 points*

Comeback backfires

David Richards tenure of the reins at Benetton was brief to say the least. Having been brought in by the Benetton family to replace the extrovert and erratic Flavio Briatore, a great deal was expected of the boss of Prodrive, one of the most successful companies in the world of motor sport. Richards is no F1 expert, nor is he an engineer, so he decided to watch how the team ran itself before planning to step in with some radical plans for 1999. His arrival, when the team was at an all time low, was a great morale booster and there was talk of a return to the glory days of the Schumacher era. There were a few tangible signs of that revival: Fisichella on pole in Austria, his second place in Monaco and until we got to Japan, the team was still in with a chance of winning the Non McLaren/Ferrari title. Not bad for a convalescent period but Richards' radical plans for the future frightened the Benetton family. Richards chose to leave and now Rocco Benetton is in charge, even less knowledgeable about the sport than his charismatic predecessor.

TEST DRIVER 1998

-

SUCCESSION OF DRIVERS 1998

• Giancarlo FISICHELLA : *all Grands Prix*
• Alexander WURZ : *all Grands Prix*

Complicity between Giancarlo Fisichella and Mickey Ainsley-Cowlishaw, Benetton's chief mechanic. "Fisico" did not take long to fit in with his new team.
◁

David Richards did not stop long at Benetton. He joined in September 1997 and left in October 1998, following a disagreement over the choice of engine for 2000.
▽

McLaren-Mercedes

7. David COULTHARD

DRIVER PROFILE

- Name : *COULTHARD*
- First name : *David*
- Nationality : *British*
- Date of birth : *March 27, 1971*
- Place of birth : *Twynholm (Scotland)*
- Lives in : *Monaco*
- Marital status : *single*
- Kids : -
- Hobbies : *motorsport, golf, swimming*
- Favourite music : *Queen, Phil Collins*
- Favourite meal : *pasta*
- Favourite drink : *tea*
- Height : *182 cm*
- Weight : *75 kg*

STATISTICS

- Nber of Grand Prix : 74
- Victories : 4
- Pole-positions : 8
- Best laps : 8
- Accident/off : 11
- Not qualified : 0
- Laps in the lead : 430
- Km in the lead : 2052
- Points scored : 173

PRIOR TO F1

1983-88 : *Karting*
1989 : *Junior F. Ford 1600 Champion*
1990 : *F. Opel Lotus*
1991 : *F. 3 GB (2nd)*
1992 : *F. 3000 (9th)*
1993 : *F. 3000 (3rd)*

F1 CAREER

1994 : *Williams / Renault. 14 points. 8th of champ.*
1995 : *Williams / Renault. 49 points. 3rd of champ.*
1996 : *McLaren / Mercedes. 18 points. 7th of champ.*
1997 : *McLaren / Mercedes. 36 pts. 3rd of champ.*
1998 : *McLaren / Mercedes. 56 pts. 4th of champ.*

8. Mika HÄKKINEN

DRIVER PROFILE

- Name : *HAKKINEN*
- First names : *Mika Pauli*
- Nationality : *Finnish*
- Date of birth : *September 28, 1968*
- Place of birth : *Helsinki (SF)*
- Lives in : *Monte Carlo*
- Marital status : *single*
- Kids : -
- Hobbies : *skiing, swimming, golf, tennis*
- Favourite music : *Michael Jackson, Phil Collins*
- Favourite meal : -
- Favourite drinks : *water, milk*
- Height : *179 cm*
- Weight : *70 kg*

STATISTICS

- Nber of Grand Prix : 112
- Victories : 9
- Pole-positions : 10
- Best laps : 7
- Accident/off : 15
- Not qualified : 2
- Laps in the lead : 641
- Km in the lead : 3022
- Points scored : 218

PRIOR TO F1

1974-86 : *Karting (5 times Champion of Finland)*
1987 : *Champion F. Ford*
1988 : *Opel Lotus Euroseries*
1989 : *F. 3 (GB, 7th)*
1990 : *F. 3 / Champion West Surrey*

F1 CAREER

1991 : *Lotus / Judd. 2 points. 15th of championship.*
1992 : *Lotus / Ford. 11 points. 8th of championship.*
1993 : *McLaren / Ford. 4 points. 15th of championship.*
1994 : *McLaren / Peugeot. 26 points. 4th of champ.*
1995 : *McLaren / Mercedes. 17 points. 7th of champ.*
1996 : *McLaren / Mercedes. 31 points. 5th of champ.*
1998 : *McLaren / Mercedes. 100 points.* ***World Champion.***

In a world of Formula 1 which is currently dominated by the big manufacturers, a driver's talent is not enough to turn him into a winner. If there is one driver who knows that to be true, more than any other, then it is Mika Hakkinen. His first win took eight years, even though he came close on several occasions. His efforts even brought him face to face with death. From the day of his first win at Jerez in 1997, his attitude and his expression changed to that of a world champion. It never changed during the entire course of this season and he pushed everyone - his team- mate, himself, his team, all the way to the title. For him, every moment spent in the McLaren environment is the time to have a discussion with his engineers. With eight wins this season, the championship should have been his long before the final race, but the for the terrible talent of Michael Schumacher at the wheel of a Ferrari.

The man does not lie and he is true to himself. He hangs on to his self-belief. *"I won a grand prix early enough in my career, not to feel under excessive pressure about it."* The complete opposite to Hakkinen. Maybe it was this self-belief that allowed him to obey orders in the Australian Grand Prix and hand victory to the Finn. At the time, he had every intention of settling the score later. But his team mate and Lady Luck decided otherwise. So, he decided to invest in the future and played the supporting role and was the perfect team player. McLaren has often won back to back driver titles, as it did with Senna and Prost and that once the team starts winning, it tends to go on longer than with some other outfits. So, he has a firm belief that 1999 will be his year. There is only one problem with this theory and that is that he has been beaten fair and square by Hakkinen a little too often.

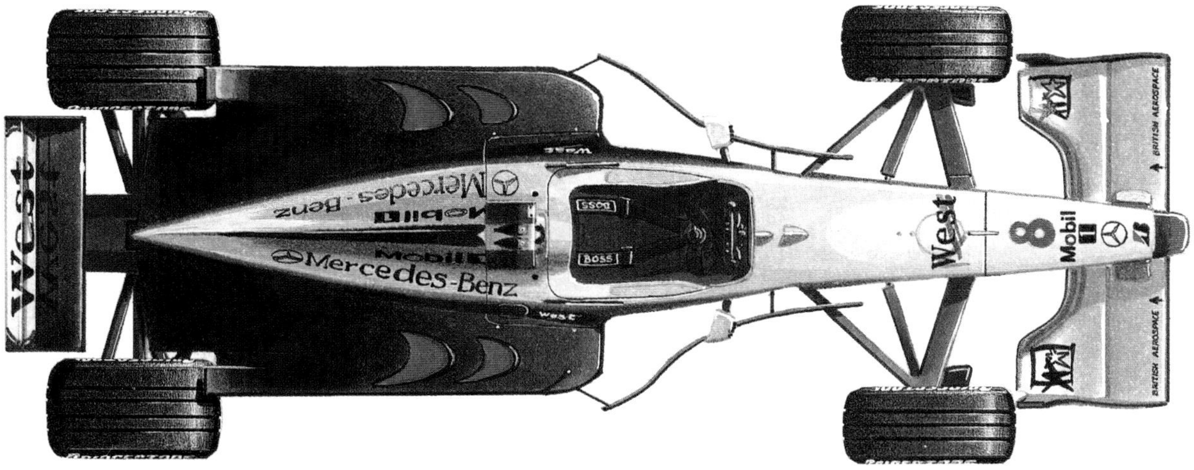

McLAREN-MERCEDES MP4/13
MIKA HÄKKINEN
SPANISH GRAND PRIX

McLaren-Mercedes MP4/13

SPECIFICATION

- Chassis : *McLaren MP 4/13*
- Engine : *Mercedes-Benz V10 FO 110 G*
- Tyres : *Bridgestone*
- Wheels : *Enkei*
- Fuel / oil : *Mobil*
- Brakes (discs) : *Hitco*
- Brakes (calipers) : *AP Racing*
- Transmission : *McLaren 6 gears, semi-autom.*
- Radiators : *McLaren / Calsonic*
- Plugs : *NGK / GS Battery*
- Electronic mgt : *TAG Electronic System*
- Shock absorbers : *Penske*
- Suspensions : *push rods/torsion bar*
- Dry weight : *600 kg, driver included*
- Wheelbase : *4550 mm*
- Front track : *not revealed*
- Rear track : *not revealed*

TEAM PROFILE

- Address : *McLaren International Ltd. Woking Business Park Albert Drive Woking, Surrey GU21 5JY United Kingdom*
- Telephone : *(44) 1483 728 211*
- Fax : *(44) 1483 720 157*
- Established in : *1963*
- First Grand Prix : *Monaco 1966*
- General director : *Ron Dennis*
- Technical director : *Adrian Newey*
- Team-manager : *Jo Ramirez*
- Chief mechanic : *Paul Simpson*
- Nber of employees : *280*
- Sponsors : *Reemtsma, Hugo Boss, Tag-Heuer*

STATISTICS

- Number of Grand Prix : *476*
- Number of victories : *115*
- Number of pole-positions : *92*
- Number of best laps during the race : *80*
- Number of drivers' world titles : *10*
- Number of constructors' titles : *8*
- Total number of points scored : *2205.5*

POSITION IN WORLD CHAMPIONSHIP

1966 : *7th – 3 points*
1967 : *8th – 1 points*
1968 : *2nd – 51 points*
1969 : *4th – 40 points*
1970 : *4th – 35 points*
1971 : *6th – 10 points*
1972 : *3rd – 47 points*
1973 : *3rd – 58 points*
1974 : ***1st – 73 points***
1975 : *3rd – 53 points*
1976 : *2nd – 74 points*
1977 : *3rd – 60 points*
1978 : *7th – 15 points*
1979 : *7th – 15 points*
1980 : *7th – 11 points*
1981 : *6th – 28 points*
1982 : *2nd – 69 points*
1983 : *5th – 34 points*
1984 : ***1st – 143.5 points***
1985 : ***1st – 90 points***
1986 : *2nd – 96 points*
1987 : *2nd – 76 points*
1988 : ***1st – 199 points***
1989 : ***1st – 141 points***
1990 : ***1st – 121 points***
1991 : ***1st – 139 points***
1992 : *2nd – 99 points*
1993 : *2nd – 84 points*
1994 : *4th – 42 points*
1995 : *4th – 30 points*
1996 : *4th – 49 points*
1997 : *4th – 63 points*
1998 : ***1st – 156 points***

"And you want another pay rise? Try asking Frank Williams and see what he says." Ron Dennis in conversation with his technical director, Adrian Newey, reputedly on 3 million dollars a year.
▽

Two McLarens leading the field at the first corner. It was a common sight (here at Monza.)
▽

The new wave

There is so much one can say about the McLaren MP4/13. It was the best F1 car of the year. Its long wheelbase proved hard to copy for the opposition and was a winning novelty. It had an uncanny ability to hold the road and ride the kerbs. Added to all this it an Ilmor-Mercedes V10 which put out well over 800 horsepower, maybe by as much as 20 or 30 horsepower. The team itself was boosted by finding itself back in the winners enclosure, so how come it took it the whole season right up to Suzuka to tie up the title? There were a few strategic errors and some wrong calls on the tyre side; some fine performances from Ferrari and Schumacher - France, Great Britain and Hungary, to name but three.) But above all, McLaren had worrying reliability problems with excessive oil pressure on the engine side and with the brakes, calipers giving trouble at Monza. Up against them was Ferrari which, having been near the top for longer, had wiped out all its reliability problems so that it was always there to pick up the pieces, even if finally it was to no avail.

TEST DRIVERS 1998

- Ricardo ZONTA (BRE)
- Nick HEIDFELD (ALL)

SUCCESSION OF DRIVERS 1998

- Mika HAKKINEN : *all Grands Prix*
- David COULTHARD : *all Grands Prix*

Jordan-Mugen Honda

9. Damon HILL

DRIVER PROFILE

- Name : *HILL*
- First names : *Damon Mark*
- Nationality : *British*
- Date of birth : *September 17, 1960*
- Place of birth : *London (GB)*
- Lives in : *Dublin (IRL)*
- Marital status : *married to Georgie*
- Kids : *3 kids (Oliver, Joshua, Tabatha)*
- Hobbies : *golf, music, motorbike, tennis*
- Favourite music : *Elvis Presley, Otis Redding*
- Favourite meal : *traditional english cuisine*
- Favourite drinks : *milk, wine, beer, champagne*
- Height : *182 cm*
- Weight : *70 kg*

STATISTICS

- Nber of Grand Prix : 100
- Victories : 22
- Pole-positions : 20
- Best laps : 19
- Accident/off : 13
- Not qualified : 6
- Laps in the lead : 1351
- Km in the lead : 6243
- Points scored : 353

PRIOR TO F1

- 1983 : *Motorcycle 500cc*
- 1984 : *F. Ford 1600 (10th)*
- 1985 : *F. Ford 1600 (3rd)*
- 1986 : *F. 3 GB (9th)*
- 1987 : *F. 3 GB (5th)*
- 1988 : *F. 3 GB (3rd)*
- 1989 : *F. 3000 (11th)*
- 1990 : *F. 3000 (13th)*
- 1991 : *F. 3000 (7th)*

F1 CAREER

- 1992 : *Brabham / Judd. 0 point.*
- 1993 : *Williams / Renault. 69 points. 3rd of champ.*
- 1994 : *Williams / Renault. 91 points. 2nd of champ.*
- 1995 : *Williams / Renault. 69 points. 2nd of champ.*
- 1996 : *Williams / Renault. 97 pts.* ***World Champion.***
- 1997 : *Arrows / Yamaha. 7 points. 12th of championship.*
- 1998 : *Jordan/Mugen-Honda. 20 points. 6th of championship.*

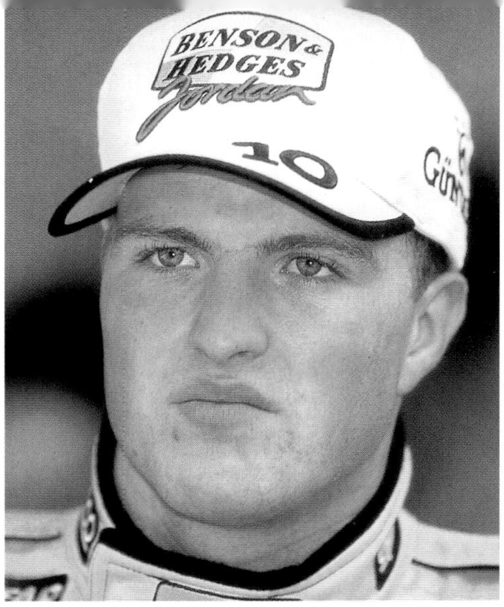

10. Ralf SCHUMACHER

DRIVER PROFILE

- Name : *SCHUMACHER*
- First name : *Ralf*
- Nationality : *German*
- Date of birth : *June 30, 1975*
- Place of birth : *Hürth (D)*
- Lives in : *Monte Carlo*
- Marital status : *single*
- Kids : -
- Hobbies : *karting, tennis*
- Favourite music : *soft rock*
- Favourite meal : *pasta*
- Favourite drink : *apple juice with mineral water*
- Height : *178 cm*
- Weight : *73 kg*

STATISTICS

- Nber of Grand Prix : 33
- Victories : 0
- Pole-positions : 0
- Best laps : 0
- Accident/off : 10
- Not qualified : 0
- Laps in the lead : 0
- Km in the lead : 0
- Points scored : 27

PRIOR TO F1

- 1978-92 : *Karting*
- 1993 : *Jr. Champ. ADAC*
- 1994 : *Champ. F. 3 (D, 3rd)*
- 1995 : *Champ. F. 3 (D, 2nd), winner world final F.3 in Macao*
- 1996 : *F. 3000 Champion (Japan)*

F1 CAREER

- 1997 : *Jordan / Peugeot. 13 points. 11th of championship.*
- 1998 : *Jordan/Mugen-Honda. 14 points. 10th of championship.*

At the launch of the new car, Damon Hill was convinced it would be a winner. However, from the moment it was first wheeled out onto the track, it was obvious he was well wide of the mark. His hopes became doubts and then turned into anger. It seemed that 1998 would be yet another barren year. It takes a lot to get Damon angry. He took ten races to score his first point and that would explain his uncontained joy on the Spa podium. Since then, Eddie Jordan worked on tidying up a few more loose ends, Mugen produced more power. The car was transformed and Damon was a front runner again. Most importantly, he now knows he can win without Williams. Any rumours of retirement can now be scotched.

Ralf Schumacher nearly equalled his brother's feat of winning a grand prix in his second season at Spa. But it was not too be. Although he was closing on Hill at around two second per lap in the Belgian GP, Eddie told him to hold station for the good of the team. He had to be asked three times mind you, before a faint "okay" was heard on the radio. It weighed heavily on his heart but that moment transformed him into a professional racing driver and he used that to grab himself a third place on the Monza podium two weeks later. He is quick, but it seems he might be going into his new adventure with Williams with a more mature frame of mind. It would be a good thing too.

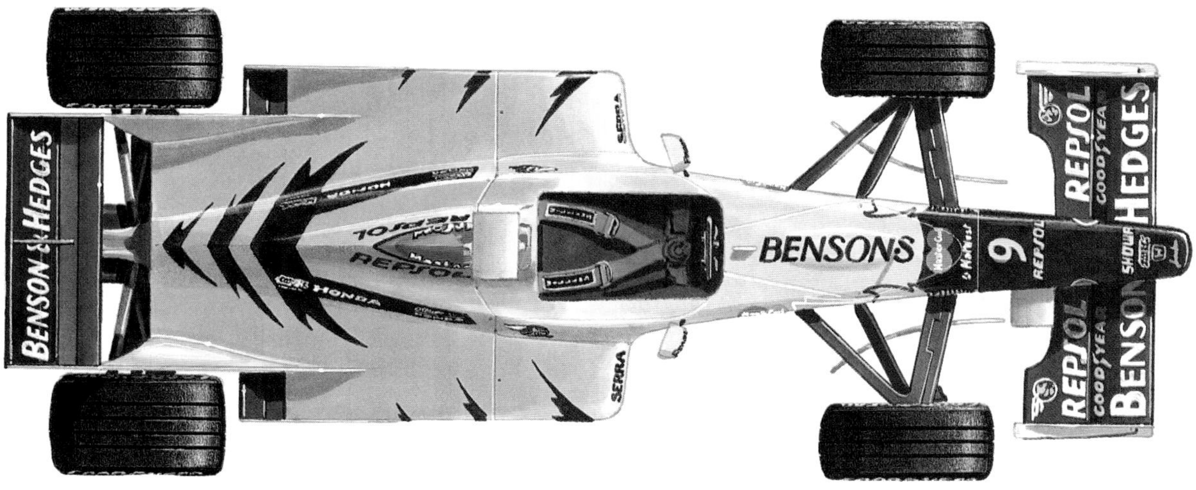

JORDAN-MUGEN HONDA 198
DAMON HILL
BELGIAN GRAND PRIX

Jordan-Mugen Honda 198

SPECIFICATION

• Chassis :	*Jordan 198*
• Engine :	*Mugen-Honda MF 301 HC V10*
• Tyres :	*Goodyear*
• Wheels :	*OZ*
• Fuel / oil :	*Repsol*
• Brakes (discs) :	*Carbone Industrie*
• Brakes (calipers) :	*Brembo*
• Transmission :	*Jordan 6 gears*
• Radiators :	*Secan / Jordan*
• Plugs :	*FIAMM / FIAMM*
• Electronic mgt :	*TAG Electronics*
• Shock absorbers :	*Jordan*
• Suspensions :	*push rods (ft/bk)*
• Dry weight :	*600 kg, driver included*
• Wheelbase :	*2900 mm*
• Front track :	*1500 mm*
• Rear track :	*1418 mm*

TEAM PROFILE

• Address :	*Jordan Grand Prix Ltd. Buckingham Road, Silverstone, Northants NN12 8TJ United Kingdom*
• Telephone :	*(44) 1327 857 153*
• Fax :	*(44) 1327 858 120*
• Established in :	*1981*
• First Grand Prix :	*USA 1991*
• General director :	*Eddie Jordan*
• Technical director :	*Gary Anderson*
• Team-manager :	*Trevor Foster*
• Chief mechanic :	*Tim Edwards*
• Nber of employees :	*140*
• Sponsors :	*Benson & Hedges, Repsol*

STATISTICS

• Number of Grand Prix :	*130*
• Number of victories :	*1*
• Number of pole-positions:	*1*
• Number of best laps during the race :	*2*
• Number of drivers' world titles :	*0*
• Number of constructors' titles :	*0*
• Total number of points scored :	*152*

POSITION IN WORLD CHAMPIONSHIP

1991 : *5th – 13 points*	1995 : *6th – 21 points*
1992 : *11th – 1 point*	1996 : *5th – 22 points*
1993 : *10th – 3 points*	1997 : *5th – 33 points*
1994 : *5th – 28 points*	1998 : *4th – 34 points*

Eddie Jordan in happy mood. After seven years hard labour, the team scored its first grand prix win at Spa.
▽

Back from the grave

One of the highlights of this season was the miraculous transformation of the Jordan team. By the time we got to the season's mid-point at Silverstone, the Irish outfit was literally pointless. The car did not seem to be one of Gary Anderson's best - the technical director flew the coop and joined Stewart by the end of the year - and winter testing was disastrous because of electrical incompatibilities between chassis and engine. For a team which had been poised on the edge of victory, it was a bitter pill to swallow. For once, Eddie Jordan shrugged off his dilettante image and got stuck in and Mike Gascoyne was brought over from Tyrrell as Anderson's replacement, before he had left mind you. Gradually the points started coming and then we had the incredible weekend in Belgium. Winning its first grand prix is always an unforgettable moment for a team, but to do it with a one-two finish is something else. It was the catalyst for other good performances which culminated in Jordan finally breaking into the Top Four of the championship for the first time in its F1 career.

TEST DRIVER 1998

-

SUCCESSION OF DRIVERS 1998

• Ralf SCHUMACHER : *all Grands Prix*
• Damon HILL : *all Grands Prix*

Prost-Peugeot

14. Olivier PANIS

DRIVER PROFILE

- Name : *PANIS*
- First names : *Olivier Denis*
- Nationality : *French*
- Date of birth : *September 2, 1966*
- Place of birth : *Lyon (F)*
- Lives in : *Grenoble (F)*
- Marital status : *married to Anne*
- Kids : *one son (Aurélien) and one girl*
- Hobbies : *bike, karting,*
- Favourite music : *Stevie Wonder*
- Favourite meal : *pasta*
- Favourite drink : *Coca Cola*
- Height : *175 cm*
- Weight : *76,1 kg*

STATISTICS

- Nber of Grand Prix : *75*
- Victories : *1*
- Pole-positions : *0*
- Best laps : *0*
- Accident/off : *13*
- Not qualified : *0*
- Laps in the lead : *16*
- Km in the lead : *53*
- Points scored : *54*

PRIOR TO F1

1981-87 : *Karting*
1988 : *Champion Steering Wheel Elf Paul Ricard*
1989 : *Champion F. Renault of France*
1990 : *F. 3 of France (4th)*
1991 : *F. 3 of France (2nd)*
1992 : *F. 3000*
1993 : *Champion F. 3000*

F1 CAREER

1994 : *Ligier / Renault. 9 points. 11th of championship.*
1995 : *Ligier / Mugen. 16 points. 8th of championship.*
1996 : *Ligier / Mugen. 13 points. 9th of championship.*
1997 : *Prost / Mugen Honda. 16 points. 10th of champ.*
1998 : *Prost / Peugeot. 0 point. not classified*

12. Jarno TRULLI

DRIVER PROFILE

- Name : *TRULLI*
- First name : *Jarno*
- Nationality : *Italian*
- Date of birth : *July 13th, 1966*
- Place of birth : *Pescara (I)*
- Lives in : *Francavilla (I)*
- Marital status : *single*
- Kids : -
- Hobbies : *tennis, karting, swimming*
- Favourite music : *Vasco Rossi, Elton John*
- Favourite meal : *pizza*
- Favourite drink : *Coca Cola*
- Height : *173 cm*
- Weight : *66,2 kg*

STATISTICS

- Nber of Crand Prix : *23*
- Victories : *0*
- Pole-positions : *0*
- Best laps : *0*
- Accident/off : *3*
- Not qualified : *0*
- Laps in the lead : *37*
- Km in the lead : *160*
- Points scored : *4*

PRIOR TO F1

1963-87 : *Karting*
1988-93: *Karting 100 6 times champ.(ITA) 3 times 2nd in world championships*
1994 : *Wordl Champ.125 FC and 100SA karting*
1995 : *Champ. F3 (D), 4th*
1996 : *Champ. F3 (D), 1st*

F1 CAREER

1997 : *Prost / Mugen Honda 3 points 14th of championship.*
1998 : *Prost / Peugeot. 1 point. 15th of championship.*

He had a bellyful. Not since his F1 debut in 1994 has he suffered so much in Formula 1. He hung like a drowning man to his hopes, but fighting for last place in the Monaco and Hungary grands prix is not something he is used to doing. The dreadful AP01 nearly destroyed his legendary strength of character. This was hard to swallow for a man who has won a grand prix and is used to fighting for the podium and for points and unlike team-mate Trulli is no longer an F1 debutant. Panis' reputation suffered slightly this season as maybe some of the motivation died. But going out to find that last tenth of a second, just for twelfth place on the grid is not the easiest thing to get excited about, when one has tasted victory. Just ask Jean Alesi or Damon Hill.

There has never been a shadow of doubt that the Italian is quick. However, what was new this year, was the revelation that he can be opinionated and have a mind of his own. This could explain the growing respect which Alain Prost, a true thinker among drivers in his day, holds for his young charger. Towards the end of the season, Trulli seemed to have the upper hand over Panis in qualifying and seemed to have a bit more luck when it was needed as was the case in Spa. He scored the team's only point of the season. What is not clear, is whether or not he has taken over from Panis as the natural leader of the Prost team. We will have to wait and see, come 22nd December, when the AP02 is due to make its track debut.

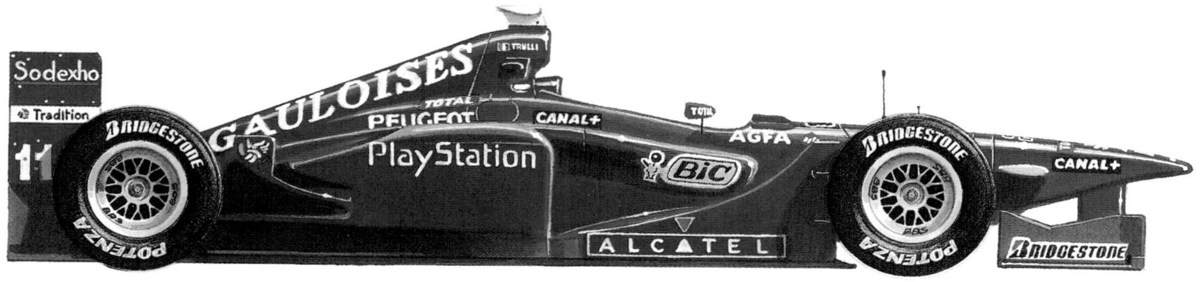

PROST-PEUGEOT AP01
JARNO TRULLI
BELGIAN GRAND PRIX

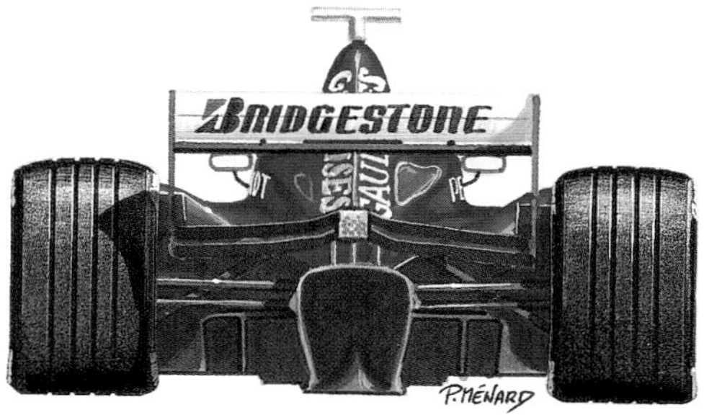

Prost-Peugeot AP01

SPECIFICATION

• Chassis :	*Prost AP01*
• Engine :	*Peugeot V10 A16*
• Tyres :	*Bridgestone*
• Fuel / oil :	*Total*
• Brakes (discs) :	*Carbone Industrie*
• Brakes (calipers) :	*Brembo*
• Transmission :	*Prost-Peugeot 6 gears*
• Plugs :	*NGK / FIAMM*
• Shock absorbers :	*Dynamics*
• Suspensions :	*push rods (ft/bk)*
• Dry weight :	*600 kg, driver included*
• Wheelbase :	*2795 mm*
• Front track :	*1600 mm*
• Rear track :	*1600 mm*
• Total length :	*4135 mm*
• Total height :	*948 mm*

TEAM PROFILE

• Address :	*Prost Grand Prix* *Quartier des Sangliers* *7, Avenue Eugène Freyssinet* *78280 Guyancourt France*
• Telephone :	*(33) 1 39 30 11 00*
• Fax :	*(33) 1 39 30 11 01*
• Established in :	*1997*
• First Grand Prix :	*Australie 1997*
• General director :	*Alain Prost*
• Technical director :	*Loïc Bigois*
• Team-manager :	*Cesare Fiorio*
• Chief mechanic :	*Robert Dassaud*
• Nber of employees :	*155*
• Sponsors :	*Gauloises Blondes, Alcatel, BIC* *Dassault Systèmes, Total,* *Sodexho, Playstation, Canal Plus*

STATISTICS

• Number of Grand Prix :	*33*
• Number of victories :	*0*
• Number of pole-positions :	*0*
• Number of best laps during the race :	*0*
• Number of drivers' world titles :	*0*
• Number of constructors' titles :	*0*
• Total number of points scored :	*22*

POSITION IN WORLD CHAMPIONSHIP

1997 : *6th - 21 points*
1998 : *9th - 1 point*

Alain Prost stays on course. Despite the difficulties encountered by his team this season, the "Professor" is still confident about the long term future.
▽

The devil is in the gearbox

A fragile gearbox shattered this team's dreams at the start of the season. It was strengthened but the extra weight involved did little to improve the already badly balanced car. Furthermore, the suspension was as rigid as a jelly and the chassis itself was not much better. Scoring points under normal conditions could be no more than a dream for Prost. Therefore, right from the start of the second half of the season, they concentrated on the 1999 season. From Hungary onwards, different aerodynamic solutions were tried on both cars and this programme continued over the next few races and in private testing at Barcelona. Four cars were taken to Japan, one of which was a AP01B hybrid, fitted with engine, gearbox and suspension parts scheduled for the 1999 car. It was driven by Jarno Trulli. With double the number of personnel, a move to a new factory now complete and six months work on the new AP02 already under its belt, the team looks to have a brighter future. An added bonus is the imminent arrival of John Barnard which should see Prost attack the 1999 season in much better shape and allow everyone to forget the disaster that was 1998.

TEST DRIVER 1998

• Stéphane SARRAZIN

SUCCESSION OF DRIVERS 1998

• Olivier PANIS :	*all Grands Prix*
• Jarno TRULLI :	*all Grands Prix*

Sauber-Petronas

14. Jean ALESI

DRIVER PROFILE

- Name : *ALESI*
- First name : *Jean*
- Nationality : *French*
- Date of birth : *June 11, 1964*
- Place of birth : *Avignon (F)*
- Lives in : *Nyon (CH)*
- Marital status : *divorced, fiancée Kumiko*
- Kids : *two daughters*
- Hobbies : *skiing, tennis, golf, water skiing*
- Favourite music : -
- Favourite meal : *pasta*
- Favourite drink : *Vichy Menthe*
- Height : *170 cm*
- Weight : *75 kg*

STATISTICS

- Nber of Grand Prix : *151*
- Victories : *1*
- Pole-positions : *2*
- Best laps : *4*
- Accident/off : *23*
- Not qualified : *0*
- Laps in the lead : *239*
- Km in the lead : *1113*
- Points scored : *234*

PRIOR TO F1

1981-82 : *Karting*
1983-84 : *Renault 5 Turbo*
1985 : *F. Renault of France (5th)*
1986 : *F. 3 of France (2nd)*
1987 : *French Champion of F. 3*
1988 : *F. 3000 (10th)*
1989 : *Champion F. 3000*

F1 CAREER

1989 : *Tyrrell / Ford. 8 points. 9th of championship.*
1990 : *Tyrrell / Ford. 13 points. 9th of championship.*
1991 : *Ferrari. 21 points. 7th of championship.*
1992 : *Ferrari. 18 points. 7th of championship.*
1993 : *Ferrari. 16 points. 6th of championship.*
1994 : *Ferrari. 24 points. 5th of championship.*
1995 : *Ferrari. 42 points. 5th of championship.*
1996 : *Benetton / Renault. 47 points. 4th of champ.*
1997 : *Benetton / Renault. 36 points. 4th of champ.*
1998 : *Sauber / Petronas. 9 points. 11th of champ.*

15. Johnny HERBERT

DRIVER PROFILE

- Name : *HERBERT*
- First name : *Johnny*
- Nationality : *British*
- Date of birth : *June 27, 1964*
- Place of birth : *Romford (GB)*
- Lives in : *Monaco*
- Marital status : *married to Rebecca*
- Kids : *two daughters (Amy, Chloe)*
- Hobbies : *golf, squash, fishing*
- Favourite music : *rock, pop*
- Favourite drink : *apple juice*
- Height : *167 cm*
- Weight : *65 kg*

STATISTICS

- Nber of Grand Prix : *129*
- Victories : *2*
- Pole-positions : *0*
- Best laps : *0*
- Accident/off : *17*
- Not qualified : *3*
- Laps in the lead : *27*
- Km in the lead : *149*
- Points scored : *83*

PRIOR TO F1

1984-85 : *F. Ford 1600*
1986 : *F. Ford 2000*
1987 : *GB F. 3 Champion*
1988 : *F. 3000*

F1 CAREER

1989 : *Benetton / Ford & Tyrrell / Ford. 0 point.*
1990 : *Lotus / Lamborghini. 0 point (only 2 GP).*
1991 : *Lotus / Judd. 0 point.*
1992 : *Lotus / Ford. 2 points. 14th of championship.*
1993 : *Lotus / Ford. 11 points. 8th of championship.*
1994 : *Lotus / Honda. 0 point.*
1995 : *Benetton / Renault. 45 points. 4th of champ.*
1996 : *Sauber / Ford. 4 points. 14th of championship.*
1997 : *Sauber / Petronas. 15 points. 10th of champ.*
1998 : *Sauber / Petronas. 1 point. 11th of champ.*

It was nine years ago that Jean Alesi made his stunning debut with Tyrrell. The most experienced driver on the grid has gone through his time with the big teams, Ferrari and Benetton and here he is back in the family atmosphere of Sauber, for what is either the twilight of his career or a re-birth. *"I wanted to prove a driver can do a good job outside the big four teams,"* he explained. It took the man from Avignon a little time to adapt to his new mount, particularly the front end of the car, but once he got his eye in, he did some good work. He put on a display of virtuosity and panache rarely seen at Sauber. The highlights of the year were his demon start at Monaco, where he snaked his way between the barrier and team-mate Herbert to make up five places and also his podium at Spa and his front row grid position in Hungary. For Alesi, Sauber might just turn out to be his winning Tyrrell.

Johnny Herbert was not totally eclipsed by Jean Alesi, but it was a close run thing. He had taken Sauber to the podium in the past, Monaco in 1996 and Hungary a year later. But Alesi had different ideas. "It is him or me," he said at the British Grand Prix. Apart from his ability as a driver, Alesi also brought some Latin temperament to the quiet Swiss team and Johnny was the scapegoat. For 1999, he has found a berth at Stewart. Dominated by Schumacher at Benetton, then by Alesi at Sauber, how will he get on against Barrichello at Stewart?

Peter Sauber and Jean Alesi. It did not take long for the two men to understand one another, despite the language barrier.
▽

SAUBER-PETRONAS C17
JEAN ALESI
BELGIAN GRAND PRIX

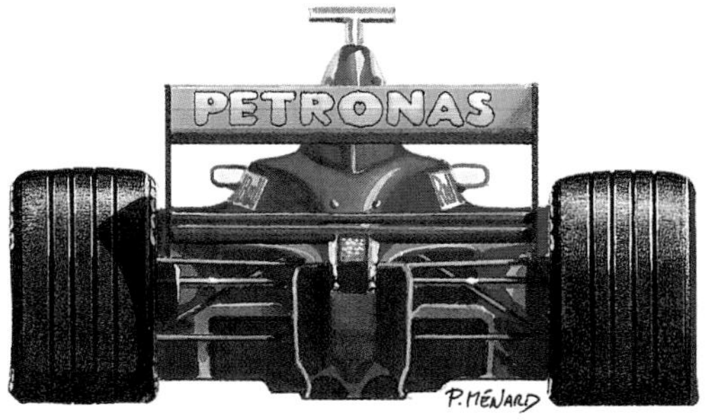

Sauber-Petronas C17

SPECIFICATION

- Chassis : *Sauber C17*
- Engine : *Petronas SP01D*
- Tyres : *Goodyear*
- Fuel / oil : *Petronas*
- Brakes (discs) : *Carbone Industrie*
- Brakes (calipers) : *Brembo*
- Transmission : *Sauber 6 gears longitudinal*
- Radiators : *Behr/Secan*
- Plugs : *NGK*
- Electronic mgt : *Magneti Marelli*
- Shock absorbers : *Sachs*
- Suspensions : *push rods (ft/bk)*
- Dry weight : *600 kg, driver included*
- Wheelbase : *2920 mm*
- Front track : *1470 mm*
- Rear track : *1470 mm*

TEAM PROFILE

- Address : *Red Bull Sauber AG, Wildbachstrasse 9, 8340 Hinwil, Switzerland*
- Telephone : *(41) 1 938 14 00*
- Fax : *(41) 1 938 16 70*
- Established in : *1972*
- First Grand Prix : *South Africa 1993*
- General director : *Peter Sauber*
- Technical director : *Leo Ress*
- Team-manager : *Peter Sauber*
- Chief mechanic : *Beat Zehnder*
- Nber of employees : *90*
- Sponsors : *Red Bull, Petronas, Dassault Systèmes*

STATISTICS

- Number of Grand Prix : *97*
- Number of victories : *0*
- Number of pole-positions : *0*
- Number of best laps during the race : *0*
- Number of drivers' world titles : *0*
- Number of constructors' titles : *0*
- Total number of points scored : *78*

POSITION IN WORLD CHAMPIONSHIP

1993 : *6th – 12 points*	1996 : *7th – 11 points*
1994 : *8th – 12 points*	1997 : *7th – 16 points*
1995 : *7th – 18 points*	1998 : *6th – 10 points*

Classic but tasteful

Sauber has a unique position in the sport. It is not just that it is the only Swiss team, but it comes also from Peter Sauber's equally unique character. Always calm, even in the eye of a storm, he guides his boys like a pater familias, just as he did in his sports car days. He carries the weight of responsibility of the team on his own shoulders and takes an objective view about the work achieved by his staff, be they Swiss, German, English, Italian or French. The team has gone from 7th with 16 points to 6th with 10 points. It was quite a good season, during which Sauber found a driver he liked in Jean Alesi, the Frenchman returning the compliment. In 1999, the team should have a never version of their Petronas-Ferrari engine which could see them move even further up the pecking order.

TEST DRIVER 1998

-

SUCCESSION OF DRIVERS 1998

- Johnny HERBERT : *all Grands Prix*
- Jean ALESI : *all Grands Prix*

Arrows

16. Pedro DINIZ

DRIVER PROFILE

- Name : *DINIZ*
- First names : *Pedro Paulo*
- Nationality : *Brazilian*
- Date of birth : *May 22, 1970*
- Place of birth : *São Paulo*
- Lives in : *Monte Carlo, São Paulo*
- Marital status : *single*
- Kids : -
- Hobbies : *traveling, reading, tennis*
- Favourite music : *soft rock, Sade*
- Favourite meal : *spaghetti alla crudaiola*
- Favourite drink : *mineral water*
- Height : *174 cm*
- Weight : *69 kg*

STATISTICS

- Nber of Grand Prix : *66*
- Victories : *0*
- Pole-positions : *0*
- Best laps : *0*
- Accident/off : *10*
- Not qualified : *0*
- Laps in the lead : *0*
- Km in the lead : *0*
- Points scored : *7*

PRIOR TO F1

1987-88 : *Karting*
1989 : *F. Ford Brazil*
1990 : *F. 3 South America*
1991 : *F. 3 GB*
1992 : *F. 3 GB*
1993-94 : *F. 3000*

F1 CAREER

1995 : *Forti / Ford. 0 point.*
1996 : *Ligier / Mugen. 2 points. 15th of championship.*
1997 : *Arrows / Yamaha. 2 points. 17th of championship.*
1998 : *Arrows. 3 points. 13th of championship.*

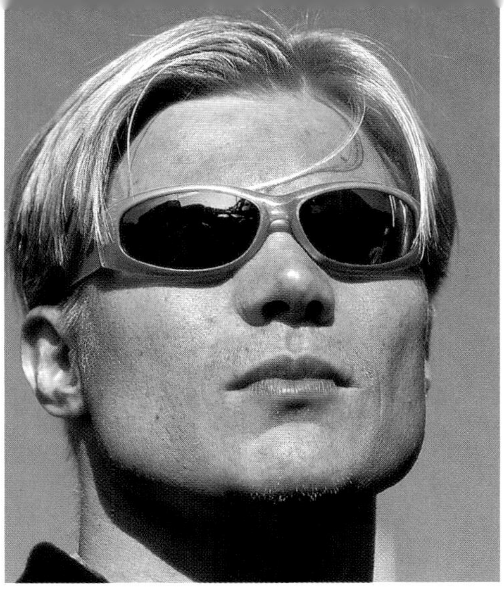

17. Mika SALO

DRIVER PROFILE

- Name : *SALO*
- First names : *Mika Noriko Endo*
- Nationality : *Finnish*
- Date of birth : *November 30, 1966*
- Place of birth : *Helsinki (SF)*
- Lives in : *London*
- Marital status : *single, fiancée Noriko*
- Kids : -
- Hobbies : *ski-doo, squash, mountain-bike*
- Favourite music : *rock*
- Favourite meal : *meat balls, pasta*
- Favourite drink : *milk*
- Height : *175 cm*
- Weight : *66 kg*

STATISTICS

- Nber of Grand Prix : *68*
- Victories : *0*
- Pole-positions : *0*
- Best laps : *0*
- Accident/off : *7*
- Not qualified : *0*
- Laps in the lead : *0*
- Km in the lead : *0*
- Points scored : *15*

PRIOR TO F1

1989 : *British F. 3*
1990 : *F. 3 GB (2nd)*
1991-94 : *F. 3000 Japan*

F1 CAREER

1994 : *Lotus / Mugen. 0 point. (only 2 GP)*
1995 : *Tyrrell / Yamaha. 5 points. 14th of championship.*
1996 : *Tyrrell / Yamaha. 5 points. 13th of championship.*
1997 : *Tyrrell / Ford. 2 points. 17th of championship.*
1998 : *Arrows. 3 points. 13th of championship.*

Diniz has singlehandedly given pay-drivers a good name. Until his arrival in the sport pay-drivers and talent were never mentioned in the same sentence. However, this season he has managed to out-perform his illustrious team-mate on a few occasions and put together some seriously quick drives. From now on, Diniz has to be regarded as a true Formula 1 driver and not just a money box. He is using this fast growing reputation to move up the ranks of the lesser teams and in 1999 he takes a big step up to join Jean Alesi at Sauber. There he will find a chassis which should be as good as his 98 Arrows and a Ferrari engine which has already delivered the goods.

This guy is a mystery. Three years ago he was linked to a Ferrari drive. This year there was talk of BAR or Williams for 1999. He is spoken of as a major talent who can win races and even championships. He is reckoned to be meticulous and stylish and in short, a rare talent in Formula 1. But time is passing by and his brilliant debut with Lotus in 1994 is forgotten now. It is something of a mystery, although Craig Pollock, who wanted him to partner Jacques Villeneuve, reckons the Finn's future is linked to Honda's comeback in 2000. All there is to remember about this year is his fourth place at Monaco. It is not much to go on.

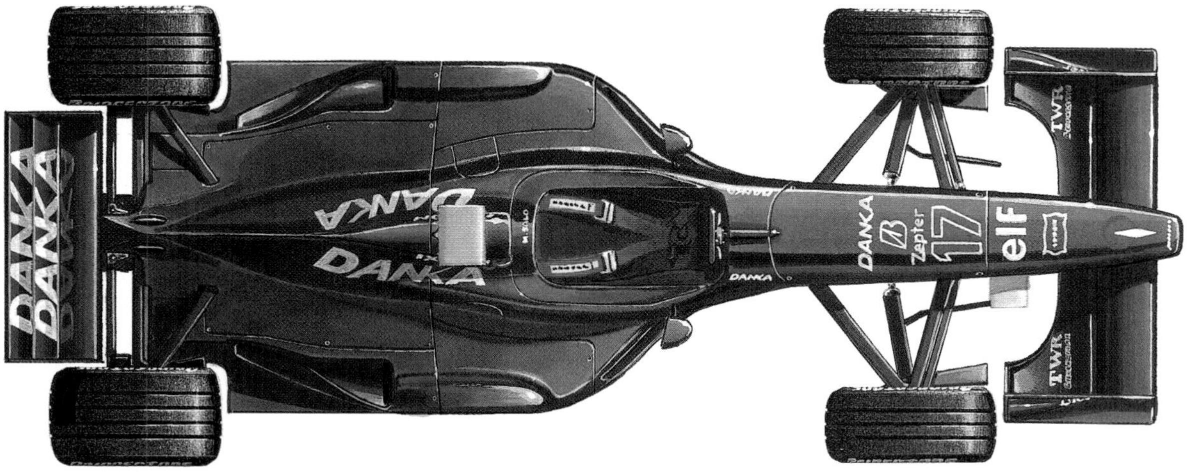

ARROWS A19
MIKA SALO
MONACO GRAND PRIX

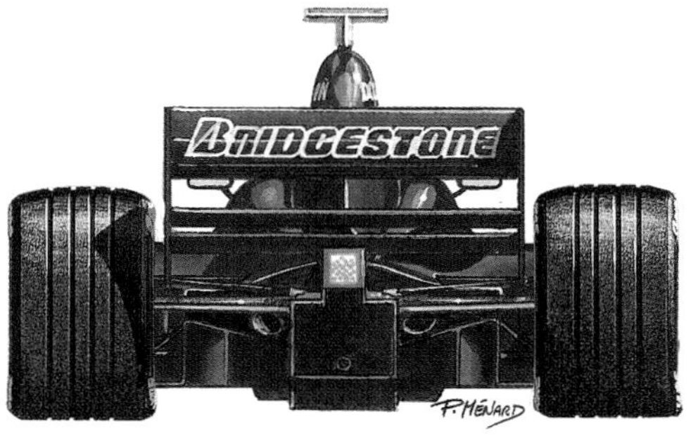

Arrows A19

SPECIFICATION

• Chassis :	*Arrows A19*
• Engine :	*TWR Arrows V10 F1*
• Tyres :	*Bridgestone*
• Wheels :	*BBS*
• Fuel / oil :	*Elf*
• Brakes (discs) :	*Carbone Industrie*
• Brakes (calipers) :	*AP Racing*
• Transmission :	*Arrows 6 gears*
• Radiators :	*Secan*
• Plugs :	*NGK / FIAMM*
• Electronic mgt :	*Zytek*
• Shock absorbers :	*Dynamics*
• Suspensions :	*push rods (ft/bk)*
• Dry weight :	*600 kg, driver included*
• Wheelbase :	*2950 mm*
• Front track :	*1465 mm*
• Rear track :	*1410 mm*
• Total length :	*4410 mm*

TEAM PROFILE

• Address :	*Arrows Grand Prix Int. Ltd.* *Leafield Technical Centre* *Leafield* *NR Witney* *Oxon OX8 5PF* *United Kingdom*
• Telephone :	*(44) 1993 87 10 00*
• Fax :	*(44) 1993 87 14 00*
• Established in :	*1977*
• First Grand Prix :	*Brazil 1978*
• General director :	*Tom Walkinshaw*
• Technical director :	*John Barnard*
• Team-manager :	*John Walton*
• Chief mechanic :	*Lee Jones*
• Nber of employees :	*170*
• Sponsor :	*Danka, Dassault Systèmes* *Bridgestone, Zepter, Parmalat*

STATISTICS

• Number of Grand Prix :	*321*
• Number of victories :	*0*
• Number of pole-positions :	*1*
• Number of best laps during the race :	*0*
• Number of drivers' world titles :	*0*
• Number of constructors' titles :	*0*
• Total number of points scored :	*156*

POSITION IN WORLD CHAMPIONSHIP

1978 : *9th – 11 points*	1989 : *7th – 13 points*
1979 : *9th – 5 points*	1990 : *9th – 2 points*
1980 : *7th – 11 points*	1991 : *not classified*
1981 : *8th – 10 points*	1992 : *7th – 6 points*
1982 : *10th – 5 points*	1993 : *9th – 4 points*
1983 : *10th – 4 points*	1994 : *9th – 9 points*
1984 : *9th – 6 points*	1995 : *8th – 5 points*
1985 : *8th – 14 points*	1996 : *9th – 1 point*
1986 : *10th – 1 points*	1997 : *8th – 9 points*
1987 : *6th – 11 points*	1998 : *7th – 6 points*
1988 : *4th – 23 points*	

Legitimate high hopes dashed

With Mika Salo on board, Pedro Diniz' wallet and John Barnard's talent, Tom Walkinshaw reckoned he had a few aces up his sleeve. The only unknown factor was the engine. Would the Brian Hart V10, now integrated into the TWR group, be good enough? The answer was not long in coming. While it might have been good enough for the Minardi chassis the previous year, it only disappointed Salo and Diniz, who were both so enthusiastic about the Barnard chassis. The result was that on the quick circuits especially, the Arrows duo were left puffing and panting. Where high downforce was required, life was a bit better and both drivers scored points in Monaco. Sadly, mid-season engine development was plagued with unreliability and the budget soon dried up. At Spa, virtually every piece of team machinery was destroyed in the start line prang, which did not help. But for these problems, Arrows had seemed to be on the right road.

TEST DRIVER 1998

Emmanuel COLLARD (FRA)

SUCCESSION OF DRIVERS 1998

• Mika SALO : *all Grands Prix*
• Pedro DINIZ : *all Grands Prix*

◁ *Mika Salo talks to Brian Hart, the team's engine man.*

Team owner Tom Walkinshaw. It was a difficult season for the Scotsman, with his main sponsors leaving at the end of the season. ▽

Stewart-Ford

18. Rubens BARRICHELLO

DRIVER PROFILE

- Name : *BARRICHELLO*
- First names : *Rubens Gonçalves*
- Nationality : *Brazilian*
- Date of birth : *May 3, 1972*
- Place of birth : *São Paulo (BRA)*
- Lives in : *Monaco*
- Marital status : *married to Silvana*
- Kids : -
- Hobbies : *running, jet-ski*
- Favourite music : *pop, rock*
- Favourite dish : *pasta*
- Favourite drink : *Diet Pepsi, Pepsi Max*
- Height : *172 cm*
- Weight : *71 kg*

STATISTICS

- Nber of Grand Prix : *97*
- Victories : *0*
- Pole-positions : *1*
- Best laps : *0*
- Accident/off : *16*
- Not qualified : *0*
- Laps in the lead : *8*
- Km in the lead : *47*
- Points scored : *50*

PRIOR TO F1

1981-88 : *Karting (5 times Brazilian Champion)*
1989 : *F. Ford 1600 (3rd)*
1990 : *Champion Opel Lotus Euroseries*
1991 : *Champion F. 3 (GB)*
1992 : *F. 3000*

F1 CAREER

1993 : *Jordan / Hart. 2 points. 17th of championship.*
1994 : *Jordan / Hart. 19 points. 6th of championship.*
1995 : *Jordan / Peugeot. 11 points. 11th of championship.*
1996 : *Jordan / Peugeot. 14 points. 8th of championship.*
1997 : *Stewart / Ford. 6 points. 13th of championship.*
1998 : *Stewart / Ford. 4 points. 12th of championship.*

19. Jos VERSTAPPEN

DRIVER PROFILE

- Name : *VERSTAPPEN*
- First names : *Johannes Franciscus*
- Nationality : *Dutch*
- Date of birth : *March 4, 1972*
- Place of birth : *Montfort (HOL)*
- Lives in : *Monte-Carlo*
- Marital status : *married to Sophie*
- Kids : *one girl*
- Hobbies : *squash, jogging, mountain-bike*
- Favourite music : *pop, UB40, Phil Collins*
- Favourite meal : *pasta*
- Favourite drink : *Coca-Cola*
- Height : *175 cm*
- Weight : *73 kg*

STATISTICS

- Nber of Grand Prix : *57*
- Victories : *0*
- Pole-positions : *0*
- Best laps : *0*
- Accident/off : *14*
- Not qualified : *0*
- Laps in the lead : *0*
- Km in the lead : *0*
- Points scored : *11*

PRIOR TO F1

1980-91 : karting
1983+84 : HOL Champion
1986 : Benelux Champion
1989 : European Champion
1991 : BEL Champion
1992 : F. Opel Lotus (Benelux Champion)
1993 : Champion F3 D; F. Atlantic

F1 CAREER

1994 : *Benetton / Ford. 10 points. 10th of championship.*
1995 : *Simtek / Ford. Forfeit after 5 races.*
1996 : *Arrows / Hart. 1 point. 16th of championship.*
1997 : *Tyrrell / Ford. 0 point.*
1998 : *Stewart / Ford. 0 point.*

The likeable Brazilian is a paradox in the world of Formula 1. At the start of his career, he was dubbed a genius, the natural successor to Ayrton Senna. By the time he left Jordan, he had used up all his credit with everyone. He was mentally at an all-time low and was thinking of looking towards the States and CART. Luckily he was scooped up by the Stewart team and had his confidence rebuilt. He was quick again and his mind was clear again, a vital ingredient in the tough world of F1. He still had his fans, including Frank Williams, who back in the summer, offered him a drive for 1999. Unable to buy his way out of his Stewart contract, he stayed put. The Stewart SF03 cannot be worse than the SF02 and Williams still has to wait one more year for the BMW V10, so maybe "Rubinho" has made the right decision.

A product of the Mercedes school, Jan Magnussen had driven one grand prix for McLaren and also competed in a few CART races. He had shone in F3 and looked to have a great future, but it was not to be. He basically lost the plot and after scoring one point in Canada, Stewart dumped him in favour of Dutchman Jos Verstappen, who took over as from the French GP. Jos the Boss was not quite a dead loss, but he never really cut it against team-mate Barrichello. As usual, the Flying Dutchman was good at flying off the track. A contretemps at a karting track which saw him arrested and briefly imprisoned for some unscheduled fisticuffs, did little to endear him to the politically correct Stewarts. There is talk of him having a testing role with the new Honda 1 team.

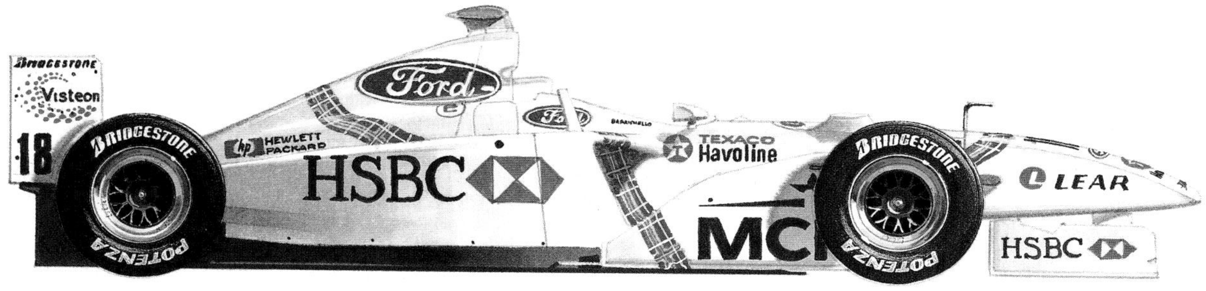

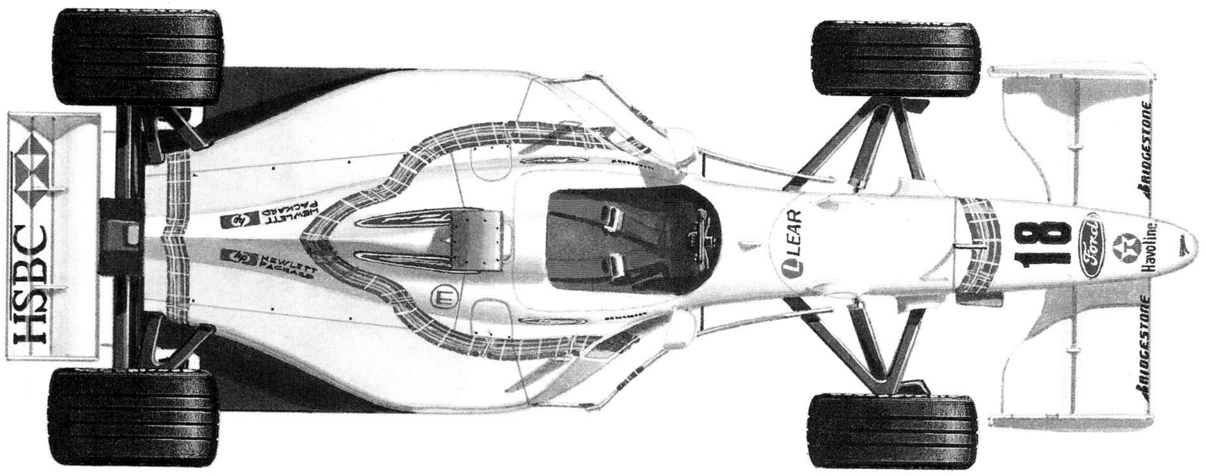

STEWART-FORD SF02
RUBENS BARRICHELLO
SPANISH GRAND PRIX

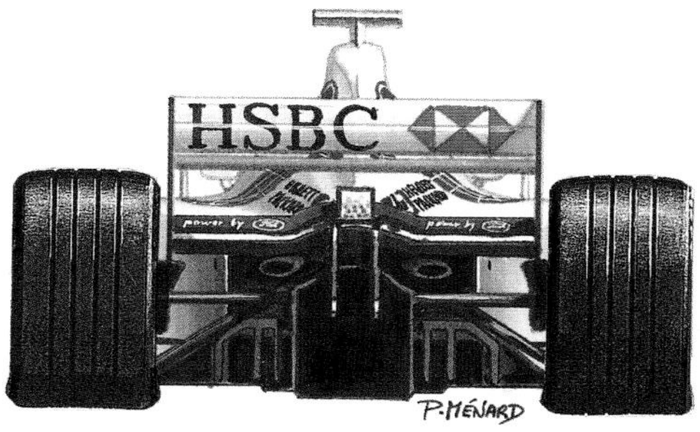

Stewart-Ford SF02

SPECIFICATION

- Chassis : *Stewart Ford SF-2*
- Engine : *Ford Zetec R V10*
- Tyres : *Bridgestone*
- Fuel / oil : *Texaco*
- Brakes (discs) : *Carbone Industrie*
- Etriers : *AP Racing*
- Transmission : *Stewart / XTrac*
- Radiators : *Secan*
- Plugs : *Champion / FIAMM*
- Electronic mgt : *Ford*
- Shock absorbers : *Stewart / Penske*
- Suspensions : *push rods (ft/bk)*
- Dry weight : *600 kg, driver included*
- Wheelbase : *2900 mm*
- Front track : *1470 mm*
- Rear track : *1555 mm*

TEAM PROFILE

- Address : *Stewart Grand Prix, 16 Tanners Drive, Blakelands, Milton Keynes, MK14 5BW, United Kingdom*
- Telephone : *(44) 1908 216122*
- Fax : *(44) 1908 216133*
- Established in : *1996*
- First Grand Prix : *Australia 1997*
- General director : *Paul Stewart*
- Technical director : *Alan Jenkins*
- Team-manager : *David Stubbs*
- Chief mechanic : *Dave Redding*
- Nber of employees : *75*
- Sponsors : *HSBC, Visit Malysia, Havoline, Sanyo, Bridgestone, Ford, Texaco*

STATISTICS

• Number of Grand Prix :	*33*
• Number of victories :	*0*
• Number of pole-positions :	*0*
• Number of best laps during the race :	*0*
• Number of drivers' world titles :	*0*
• Number of constructors' titles :	*0*
• Total number of points scored :	*11*

POSITION IN WORLD CHAMPIONSHIP

1997 : *9th – 6 points* | 1998 : *8th – 5 points*

△
Paul and Jackie Stewart on the long and winding road that is F1.

Even worse than 1997!

The season started badly. The team's first year very nearly saw Rubens Barrichello win at Monaco - he eventually came second, but since then, the Stewarts descended into hell. To start with, rumours as to their financial situation led FIA to ask them for proof they had sufficient funds to race. The SF02 chassis suffered from a chronic lack of grip and Ford grew impatient at the lack of results. Jan Magnussen was sometimes two seconds off his team-mate's pace and finally, after scoring 6 points in 1997, the team could only manage 5 this season. The arrival of Gary Anderson, after ten years at Jordan and one week at Arrows, finally meant that Alan Jenkins could stay at home from the penultimate race onwards, in order to concentrate on the '99 car. Neither Jan Magnussen nor Jos Verstappen worried Rubens Barrichello, who continues to justify his reputation. 1999 will be a key year for the team, which might need a cash injection as its drivers have always complained of a lack of testing. If the car works, then Ford will stay. If not......

TEST DRIVER 1998

-

SUCCESSION OF DRIVERS 1998

- Rubens BARRICHELLO : *all Grands Prix*
- Jan MAGNUSSEN : *AUS-BRE-ARG-S.M-ESP-MON-CAN*
- Jos VERSTAPPEN : *FRA-GB-AUT-HON-BEL-ITA-LUX-JAP*

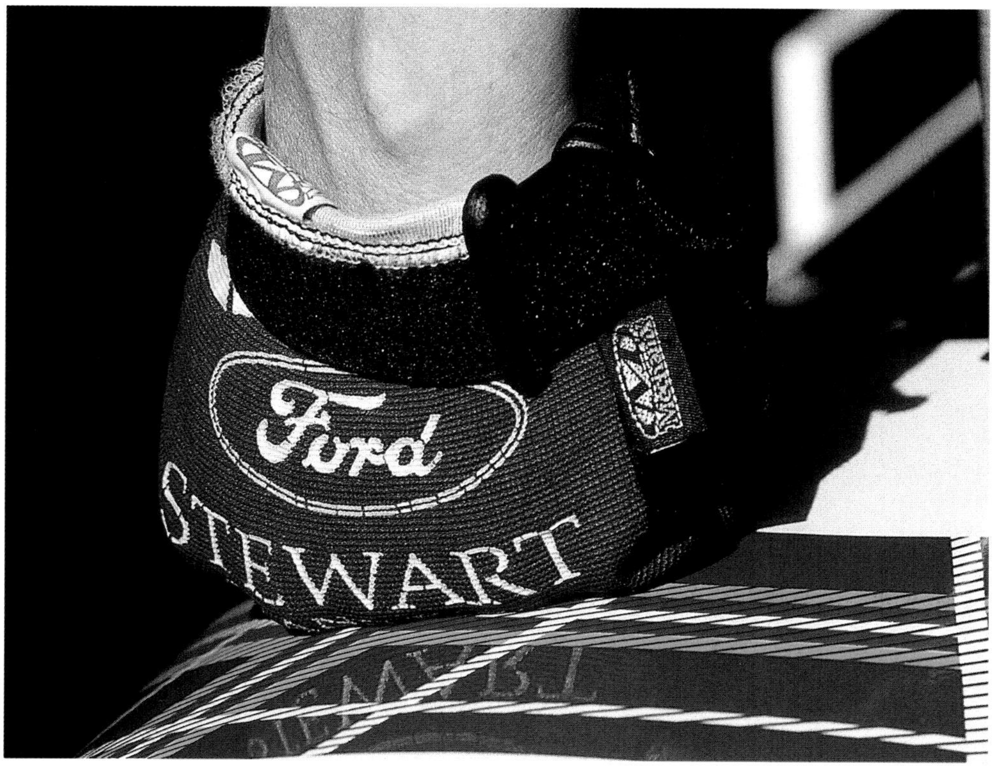

Tyrrell-Ford

20. Ricardo ROSSET

DRIVER PROFILE

- Name : *ROSSET*
- First names : *Ricardo*
- Nationality : *Brazilian*
- Date of birth : *July 27th, 1968*
- Place of birth : *Sao Paulo (BRA)*
- Lives in : *Sao Paulo (BRA), Cambridge (G.B.)*
- Marital status : *single*
- Kids : -
- Hobbies : *music and beach*
- Favorite music : *Phil Collins, Sting*
- Favorite meal : *pasta*
- Favorite drinks : *red wine*
- Height : *174 cm*
- Weight : *69,5 kg*

STATISTICS

- Nber of Grands Prix : *16*
- Victories : *0*
- Pole-positions : *0*
- Best laps : *0*
- Accident/off : *7*
- Not qualified : *5*
- Laps in the lead : *0*
- Km in the lead : *0*
- Points scored : *0*

PRIOR TO F1

1989-90 : *Kart in Brasil*
1991 : *FFord 1600 Brasil (5th)*
1992 : *Euroseries Opel (15th)*
1993 : *British F3 (6th)*
1994 : *British F3 (5th)*
1995 : *European F3000 (2th)*

F1 CAREER

1996 : *Arrows / Hart. 0 point*
1997 : *Lola / Ford. 0 point.*
1998 : *Tyrrell / Ford. 0 point not classified*

21. Toranosuke TAKAGI

DRIVER PROFILE

- Name : *TAKAGI*
- First names : *Toranosuke*
- Nationality : *Japanese*
- Date of birth : *February 12th, 1974*
- Place of birth : *Shizuoka (JAP)*
- Lives in : *Shizuoka (JAP)*
- Marital status : *single*
- Kids : -
- Hobbies : *snowboarding, karting*
- Favorite music : *Pop, Spice Girls*
- Favorite meal : *pasta, indians and chinese meals*
- Favorite drinks : *mineral water*
- Height : *180 cm*
- Weight : *66 kg*

STATISTICS

- Nber of Grands Prix : *16*
- Victories : *0*
- Pole-positions : *0*
- Best Laps : *0*
- Accident/off : *4*
- Not-qualified : *0*
- Laps in the lead : *0*
- Km in the lead : *0*
- Points scored: *0*

PRIOR TO F1

1986-88 : *Karting*
1989 : *Kart A2, Japan (1st)*
1990 : *Kart A2, Japan (1st)*
1992 : *Formula Toyota*
1993 : *All Japan F3 (10th)*
1994 : *All Japan F3 (5th)*
1994 : *Japan F3000 (7th)*
1995 : *Japan F3000 (2th)*
1996 : *Japan F3000 (4th)*

F1 CAREER

1997 : *Tyrrell / Ford. Test driver*
1998 : *Tyrrell / Ford. 0 point.*

F1 is merciless. Sure, Rosset did not enjoy the best of seasons, but to go from there and to declare as Jacques Villeneuve did after the Monaco GP, «that he has no place in F1,» is a bit of a jump. Rosset was still a runner-up in the F3000 championship, he got through a year with Arrows and he out qualified his team mate at Monza and Magny Cours this season. He is also a former F3 racer who was more than the equal of his team-mate Jacques Villeneuve at Macau! While two DNQs are unforgivable, a third, at what was probably his final appearance in an F1 car, is a poor epitaph. For F1 and its short memory, it is unforgivable, even when McLaren is setting the target for the 107% rule. Bet he cannot wait for CART and Brazil!

The lanky Japanese driver is a mystery. Would you believe that neither *«ordinary»* cars nor F1 cars are of any interest to him? All he likes is to attack and nothing else matters. Twenty years ago, he could have been the first Japanese driver to win a grand prix. That is obvious from the speed with which he has adapted to the sport. He lacks neither for talent nor for temperament. But he is lazy. Strangled by his shyness, he still does not speak a single word of English and he is not happy living in Europe. He lacks maturity and any form of professionalism. The only thing that could see him make a comeback is the rumoured arrival of Toyota and return of Honda. In the meantime, even though he eclipsed Riccardo Rosset, he is without a drive for 1999. There is talk of him going to Arrows, which Tom Walkinshaw might be selling into the Yamaha/Toyota family.

TYRRELL-FORD 026 –
TORANOSUKE TAKAGI
AUSTRIAN GRAND PRIX

Tyrrell-Ford 026

SPECIFICATION

• Chassis :	*Tyrrell 026*
• Engine :	*Ford Zetec-R10*
• Tyres :	*Goodyear*
• Fuel / oil :	*Elf*
• Brakes (discs) :	*Hitco carbon*
• Brakes (calipers) :	*AP Racing*
• Transmission :	*Tyrrell 6 speed unit sequential*
• Radiators :	*Secan*
• Plugs :	*NGK*
• Electronique mgt:	*Ford*
• Shock absorbers :	*Koni*
• Suspensions :	*pushrods (front/rear)*
• Dry weight :	*600 kg*
• Wheelbase :	*2900 mm*
• Front track :	*1550 mm*
• Rear track :	*1600 mm*
• Total lenght :	*4350 mm*
• Total height :	*900 mm*

TEAM PROFILE

• Address :	*Tyrrell Racing Organisation Ltd. Long-Reach, Ockham Woking, Surrey GU23 6PE*
• Telephone :	*(44) 1483 284 955*
• Fax :	*(44) 1483 284 892*
• Established in :	*1960*
• First Grand Prix :	*Canada 1970*
• General manager :	*Ken Tyrrell*
• Technical manager :	*Harvey Postlethwaite*
• Sports manager :	*Satoru Nakanjima*
• Team-manager :	*Steve Nielsen*
• Chief mecanic :	*Paul Diggins*
• Nber of employees :	*85*
• Sponsors :	*PIAA*

STATISTICS

• Number of Grands Prix :	*418*
• Number of victories :	*23*
• Number of pole-positions :	*14*
• Number of best laps during the race :	*20*
• Number of drivers' world titles :	*2*
• Number of constructors' world titles :	*1*
• Total number of points scored :	*617*

POSITION IN WORLD CHAMPIONSHIP

1971 : ***1st – 73 points***	1985 : *9th – 7 points*
1972 : *2nd – 51 points*	1986 : *7th – 11 points*
1973 : *2nd – 82 points*	1987 : *6th – 11 points*
1974 : *3rd – 52 points*	1988 : *8th – 5 points*
1975 : *5th – 25 points*	1989 : *5th – 16 points*
1976 : *3th – 71 points*	1990 : *5th – 16 points*
1977 : *5th – 28 points*	1991 : *6th – 12 points*
1978 : *4th – 38 points*	1992 : *6th – 8 points*
1979 : *5th – 28 points*	1993 : *not classified*
1980 : *6th – 12 points*	1994 : *6th – 13 points*
1981 : *8th – 10 points*	1995 : *8th – 5 points*
1982 : *7th – 25 points*	1996 : *8th – 5 points*
1983 : *7th – 12 points*	1997 : *10th – 2 points*
1984 : *not classified*	1998 : *not classified*

Tattered past

13 points, 5 points, 2, points, 2 points and finally zero points this year. The descent into the abyss was a straight line for the Tyrrell team. Watching it struggle along in its final hours with those who stayed faithful to the bitter end, was not a pretty sight. Its final outing in Japan would not provide any last minute consolation either, with Takagi stupidly speared by Tuero at the chicane and Rosset failing to qualify. Thus, 30 years of passion went out with a whimper. Ken Tyrrell had seen it coming and left the sinking ship, which he no longer commanded, even before the first race in Australia. As for the new boss, Craig Pollock was never seen in the colours of a team which was not the one he had created. So, centre stage we had Tora Takagi, Riccardo Rosset and Harvey Postlethwaite. Even the only talent left on the technical side, Mike Gascoyne, upped sticks and headed for Jordan in the middle of the season. As the 1998 budget was not BAR's, hopes were dim, whoever the drivers. Nothing was achieved but who was to blame?

SUCCESSION OF DRIVERS 1998

- Ricardo ROSSET : *all Grands Prix*
- Toranosuke TAKAGI : *all Grands Prix*

Minardi-Ford

22. Shinji NAKANO

DRIVER PROFILE

- Name : *NAKANO*
- First name : *Shinji*
- Nationality : *Japanese*
- Date of birth : *April 1st 1971*
- Place of birth : *Osaka (JAP)*
- Lives in : *Marseille*
- Marital status : *single*
- Kids : -
- Hobbies : *tennis, karting, squash skiing, biking*
- Favorite music : *Tokyo Prin*
- Favorite meal : *pastas, Japanese food*
- Favorite drink : *water*
- Height : *174 cm*
- Weight : *67,5 kg*

STATISTICS

- Nber of Grands Prix : *33*
- Victories : *0*
- Pole-positions : *0*
- Best laps : *0*
- Accident/off : *4*
- Not qualified : *0*
- Laps in the lead : *0*
- Km in the lead : *0*
- Points scored : *2*

PRIOR TO F1

1987 : *Karting (JAP, 2nd)*
1988 : *Champion Super Kart (JAP)*
1989 : *Champ. F3 JAP (7th)*
1990-91 : *F. Opel-Lotus*
1992 : *Champ. F3 and F3000 (JAP)*
1993-94 : *Champ. F3 (JAP)*
1995-96 : *Champ. F3000*

F1 CAREER

1997 : *Ligier / Mugen Honda. 2 points. 19th of champ.*
1998 : *Minardi / Ford. 0 point.*

23. Esteban TUERO

DRIVER PROFILE

- Name : *TUERO*
- First name : *Esteban*
- Nationality : *Argentinian*
- Date of birth : *Avril 22th 1978*
- Place of birth : *Buenos Aires (ARG)*
- Lives in : *Buenos Aires (ARG)*
- Marital status : *single*
- Enfant : -
- Hobbies : *football*
- Favorite music : *Rock & Roll, Eagles*
- Favorite meal : *"Asado" (Argentinian food)*
- Favorite drink : *mineral water*
- Height : *170 cm*
- Weight : *70 kg*

STATISTICS

- Nber of Grands Prix : *16*
- Victories : *0*
- Pole-positions : *0*
- Best laps : *0*
- Accident/off : *6*
- Not qualified : *0*
- Laps in the lead : *0*
- Km in the lead : *0*
- Points scored : *0*

PRIOR TO F1

1985 : *Karting*
1993 : *F. Renault 1400 (ARG)*
1994 : *Formula Honda(1st) and Champ F3 S. Am.*
1995 : *National Trophy FISA F2000 (ITA)*
1996 : *Champ. F 3 (ITA) and Champ. F3000*
1997 : *Formula Nippon(JAP)*

F1 CAREER

1998 : *Minardi / Ford. 0 point.*

Shinji is a calm person. When he has worries, he hunches his shoulders and works even harder. Alain Prost had literally buried him alive last year. Despite that, he had managed an honourable season, twice scoring a point and keeping cool in the storm that followed Panis' accident. He was a regular bloke. Too much of one perhaps. He was certainly less of a loose canon than his irascible team-mate Tuero. When the Argentinean lost his temper, the entire team worried it was going to lose its budget as well. Nakano simply got on with things and regularly out qualified and out raced him. While Tuero was not the gem Minardi had hoped for, Nakano is certainly not the waste of space that Prost claimed he was. He deserves his place, for his turn of speed as much as for his character.

Before the start of the season, the FIA and the other competitors, had demanded that Minardi put Tuero through several thousand kilometres of testing, before granting him his superlicense. He came out of it well, tucking in behind and sometimes pulling ahead of his more experienced team mate. He even had a good start to the season. Then the performance level of his car stagnated and he lost his cool. Getting angry, taking it out on the Minardi scooter, the fans and the numerous sponsors, his growing good image began to fade. Will he be a worthy successor to Carlos Reutemann? One has to doubt it. But he is only 20 years old and maybe there is more to come.

MINARDI-FORD M198 –
SHINJI NAKANO
GERMAN GRAND PRIX

Minardi-Ford M198

SPECIFICATION

- Chassis : *Minardi M198*
- Engine : *Ford Zetec R-V10*
- Tyres : *Bridgestone*
- Fuel / oil : *Agip / Motul*
- Brakes (discs) : *Carbone Industrie*
- Brakes (calipers) : *Brembo*
- Transmission : *Minardi/ XTrac 6 vitesses*
- Radiators : *Minardi*
- Plugs / battery : *Champion / FIAMM*
- Electronique mgt: *Magneti Marelli*
- Shock absorbers : *Dynamics*
- Suspensions : *pushrods/coaxial spring (front/rear)*
- Dry weight : *600 kg, driver included*
- Wheelbase : *2900 mm*
- Front track : *1452 mm*
- Rear track : *1421 mm*

TEAM PROFILE

- Address : *Minardi Team SpA, Via Spallanzani 21 (Z.I.), 48018 Faenza, Italia*
- Telephone : *(39) 546 620 480*
- Fax : *(39) 546 620 998*
- Established in : *1974*
- First Grand Prix : *Brasil 1985*
- Chairman : *Gabriele Rumi*
- General manager: *Gian Carlo Minardi*
- Technical manager : *Gustav Brünner*
- Team-manager : *Frédéric Dhainaut*
- Chief mécanic : *Gabriele Pagliarini*
- Nber of employees : *85*
- Sponsors : *Fondmetal, Avex, Doimo, Roces*

STATISTICS

- Number of Grands Prix : *221*
- Number of victories : *0*
- Number of pole-positions : *0*
- Number of best laps during the race : *0*
- Number of drivers' world titles : *0*
- Number of constructors' world titles : *0*
- Total number of points scored : *27*

POSITION IN WORLD CHAMPIOSHIP

1985 :	*not classified*	1992 :	*11th – 1 point*
1986 :	*not classified*	1993 :	*8th – 7 points*
1987 :	*not classified*	1994 :	*10th – 5 points*
1988 :	*10th – 1 point*	1995 :	*10th – 1 point*
1989 :	*10th – 6 points*	1996 :	*not classified*
1990 :	*not classified*	1997 :	*not classified*
1991 :	*7th – 6 points*	1998 :	*not classified*

Giancarlo Minardi, an ever present passion.

No result awaits at the end of the road, but the efforts is undiminished. Esteban Tuero refuels during a race.

Hope, there is always hope

For Minardi, the 1998 world championship was a whitewash, just as in 1997 and in 1996. It is not easy to make progress in these circumstances as, in order to find sponsors and make some progress, Minardi must score some points. Its existence in the final classification constitutes the sole tangible testament to the huge amount of work accomplished in 1998. The boss Gabriele Rumi decided to do things differently. Since this year, he has invested heavily in his team, establishing closer links with Ford, even though he must still pay for the engines. He employed Frederic Dhainaut and Gustav Brunner, he invested in machinery and plant, but there was still a lack of latest generation engines and serious testing. However, all the other teams progressed even more quickly, which is enough to cause alarm for the little team from Faenza. Despite this, the Minardi cars get better and better. One day they will work well, a big sponsor will come along and pay out the small amounts of money the Italians are asking for.

TEST DRIVER 1998

Laurent REDON (FRA)

SUCCESSION OF DRIVERS 1998

- Shinji NAKANO : *all Grands Prix*
- Esteban TUERO : *all Grands Prix*

The engines

As every year, the engine builders worked flat out to find a few more horsepower here and there; some with more success than others. While Ferrari found at least thirty horsepower in between the first and the last grands prix, Minardi and Tyrrell had to make do with a Ford «customer» engine which hardly evolved at all.
Only changes this season compared to last, the disappearance of the Yamaha engine, which had been both unreliable and slow and the change of name for the Hart unit, which henceforth is known as an Arrows. Of course we also had the arrival of the Playlife engine, but this was simply a different name for the Mecachrome engine.

ARROWS — F1-V10

SPECIFICATIONS

- Output : *700 hp at 15 000 rpm*
- Maximal revs: *16 300 rpm*
- Weight : *120 kilos*
- Capacity : *2996 cc*
- Configuration : *72 degrees V10*
- Material : *aluminium block*
- Valves : *4 per cylinder*

RACE PROFILE

- First Grand Prix : *Australia 1998*
- Team 1998 : *TWR-Arrows*
- Nber of victories 1998 : *0*
- Nber of pole-positions 1998 : *0*

STATISTICS

- Number of Grand Prix : *16*
- Number of constructors' titles : *0*
- Number of pole-positions : *0*
- Number of victories : *0*

FERRARI — 047

SPECIFICATIONS

- Output : *790 hp at 16 500 rpm*
- Maximum revs : *17 300 rpm*
- Weight : *125 kilos*
- Capacity : *2997 cc*
- Configuration : *80 degrees V10*
- Material : *aluminium block*
- Valves : *4 per cylinder*

RACE PROFILE

- First Grand Prix : *Monaco 1950*
- Team 1998 : *Ferrari*
- Nber of victories 1998 : *6*
- Nber of pole-positions 1998 : *2*

STATISTICS

- Number of Grand Prix : *603*
- Number of constructors' titles : *8*
- Number of pole-positions : *123*
- Number of victories : *119*

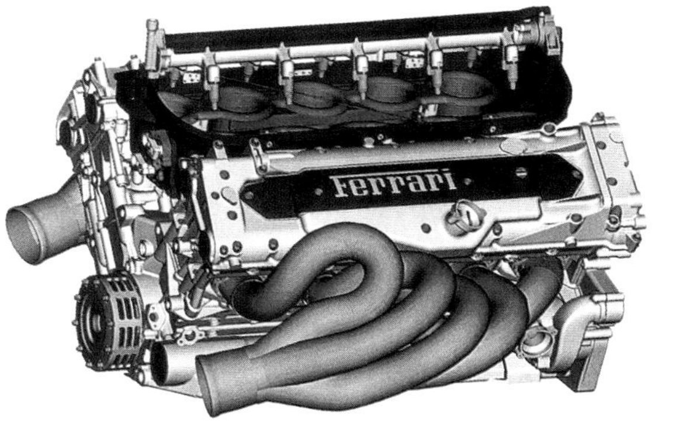

FORD COSWORTH

SPECIFICATIONS

- Output : *705 hp at 14 900 rpm*
- Maximum reves : *15 500 rpm*
- Weight : *125 kilos*
- Capacity : *2998 cc*
- Configuration : *72 degrees V10*
- Material : *aluminium block*
- Valves : *4 per cylinder*

RACE PROFILE

- First Grand Prix : *USA 1963*
- Teams 1998 : *Tyrrell*
  Minardi
- Nber of victories 1998 : *0*
- Nber of pole-positions 1998 : *0*

STATISTICS

- Number of Grand Prix : *467*
- Number of constructors' titles : *12*
- Number of pole-positions : *131*
- Number of victories : *165*

FORD — ZETEC-R V10

SPECIFICATIONS

- Output : *735 hp at 16 000 rpm*
- Maximum revs : *16 800 rpm*
- Weight : *120 kilos*
- Capacity : *2998 cc*
- Configuration : *72 degrees V10*
- Material : *aluminium block*
- Valves : *4 per cylinder*

RACE PROFILE

- First Grand Prix : *Brasil 1994*
- Team 1998 : *Stewart*
- Nber of victories 1998 : *0*
- Nber of pole-positions 1998 : *0*

STATISTICS

- Number of Grand Prix : *82*
- Number of constructors' titles : *0*
- Number of pole-positions : *6*
- Number of victories : *8*

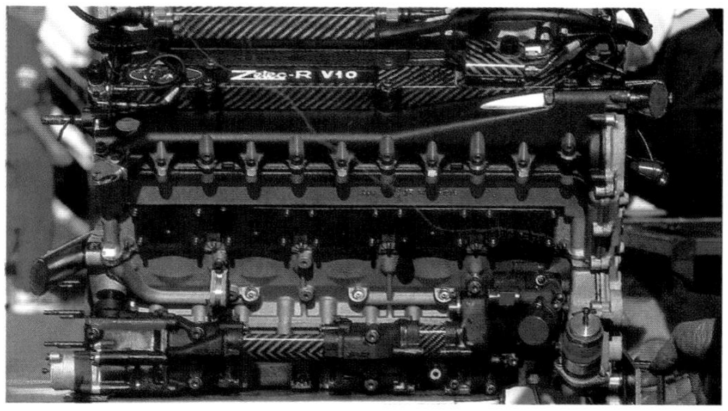

The engines

FO 110G MERCEDES-BENZ

SPECIFICATIONS

- Output : *800 hp at 16 100 rpm*
- Maximum revs : *16 800 rpm*
- Weight : *125 kilos*
- Capacity : *2998 cc*
- Configuration : *72 degrees V10*
- Material : *aluminium block*
- Valves : *4 per cylinder*

RACE PROFILE

- First Grand Prix : *France 1954*
- Team 1998 : *McLaren*
- Nber of victories 1998 : *9*
- Nber of pole-positions 1998 : *12*

STATISTICS

- Number of Grand Prix : *93*
- Number of constructors' titles : *1*
- Number of pole-positions : *25*
- Number of victories : *21*

MF-301HC MUGEN-HONDA

SPECIFICATIONS

- Output : *725 hp at 15 000 rpm*
- Maximum revs : *15 600 rpm*
- Weight : *122 kilos*
- Capacity : *2999 cc*
- Configuration : *72 degrees V10*
- Material : *aluminium block*
- Valves : *4 per cylinder*

RACE PROFILE

- First Grand Prix : *South Africa 1992*
- Team 1998 : *Jordan*
- Nber of victories 1998 : *1*
- Nber of pole-positions 1998 : *0*

STATISTICS

- Number of Grand Prix : *114*
- Number of constructors' titles : *0*
- Number of pole-positions : *0*
- Number of victories : *2*

SPE-01D PETRONAS

SPECIFICATIONS

- Output : *770 hp at 14 800 rpm*
- Maximum revs : *15 600 rpm*
- Weight : *120 kilos*
- Capacity : *2998 cc*
- Configuration : *75 degrees V10*
- Material : *aluminium block*
- Valves : *4 per cylinder*

RACE PROFILE

- First Grand Prix : *Australia 1997*
- Team 1998 : *Sauber*
- Nber of victories 1998 : *0*
- Nber of pole-positions 1998 : *0*

STATISTICS

- Number of Grand Prix : *33*
- Number of constructors' titles : *0*
- Number of pole-positions : *0*
- Number of victories : *0*

A16 PEUGEOT

SPECIFICATIONS

- Output : *765 hp at 15 200 rpm*
- Maximum revs : *16 100 rpm*
- Weight : *125 kilos*
- Capacity : *2998 cc*
- Configuration : *72 degrees V10*
- Material : *light alloy*
- Valves : *4 per cylinder*

RACE PROFILE

- First Grand Prix : *Brasil 1994*
- Team 1998 : *Prost Grand Prix*
- Nber of victories 1997 : *0*
- Nber of pole-positions 1997 : *0*

STATISTICS

- Number of Grand Prix : *82*
- Number of constructors' titles : *0*
- Number of pole-positions : *0*
- Number of victories : *0*

GC 37.01 MÉCACHROME

SPECIFICATIONS

- Output : *775 hp at 15 600 rpm*
- Maximum revs : *16 500 rpm*
- Weight : *121 kilos*
- Capacity : *2999 cc*
- Configuration : *71 degrees V10*
- Material : *aluminium block*
- Valves : *4 per cylinder*

RACE PROFILE

- First Grand Prix : *Australia 1998*
- Teams 1998 : *Williams*
  Benetton
- Nber of victories 1998 : *0*
- Nber of pole-positions 1998 : *1*

STATISTICS

- Number of Grand Prix : *16*
- Number of constructors' titles : *0*
- Number of pole-positions : *1*
- Number of victories : *0*

GAULOISES
PlayStation

Spotlights

In order to provide a better understanding of the different facets of this Formula One season, five international experts have submitted it to their scrutiny. Here we have the results of their analyses, before moving on, as is the "Formula 1 Yearbook" tradition, to look at the more technical aspect of the discipline.

1998 : a British point of view

Ron Dennis: a winning philosophy

by Nigel Roebuck
«Autosport»

As he left for Japan, Mika Hakkinen took with him a four-point lead in the World Championship, and the knowledge that second place at Suzuka - even if Michael Schumacher were to win - would be enough to give him the title. He did not, though, entertain the idea of racing for other than the win.

«It makes absolute sense, doesn't it?» said Keke Rosberg, Mika's manager, and himself a former McLaren driver. *«You can't really plan to finish second - it's as easy to aim for a victory. So what he needs to do is get pole position, then win the race. That«s the best way to stop Schumacher from getting 10 points...»*

Whatever the outcome of the World Championship, though, no one could seriously claim that Hakkinen had driven a brilliant Grand Prix season, nor that the McLaren-Mercedes MP4/13 had been other than the best car of the year - not the most reliable, perhaps, but emphatically the fastest.

It is amazing, in light of the team«s performances in 1998, to remember that for three whole seasons, 1994-96, McLaren failed to win a single race. After all those years of glory, with Niki Lauda, Alain Prost and Ayrton Senna, from 1982 to 1993, the team rather lost its way.

> *«I could give lots of reasons why we were out of the picture for some time...»*

It didn't help, of course, that the design team, after five years of working with Honda, had to adapt, in successive seasons, to motors from Ford (1993), Peugeot (1994) and finally Mercedes (1995 to date). But there was more than that behind McLaren's fall from grace. For one thing, there was no longer a Prost or Senna on board, no longer a driver with the ability and experience to win with an average car - and for some years, McLarens were just that, average. Hakkinen clearly had the talent to get the job done, but he was still a man in the infancy of his Formula 1 career.

At the beginning of 1995, Ron Dennis even hired Nigel Mansell, something he had previously said he would never do. True, it was at the behest of the sponsor of the time, Marlboro, who wanted a «star» name aboard, and predictably it was a disaster - Mansell left the team after only two undistinguished races - but more to the point was the fact that his very signing had been untypical of McLaren, untypical of Dennis.

People began to speak of Ron and his team in the past tense, but one who never did was Frank Williams. *«Yes, I know they're having a bad time at the moment,»* he said in 1995, *«and we at Williams know all about that, too, because we've had periods like that. But some guys you just know are going to come back - and Ron is one of them.»*

Dennis himself was only too aware that, for everyone at McLaren, losing was a new experience, and not a pleasant one.

«I don't think that people at McLaren were very unhappy back then,» he said, *«but, equally, I don't think they were very happy, either...»*

«They're very very loyal, and if something from outside threatens the company, they have a strong defence mechanism that stimulates them, bringing them together to a point where they are supportive. And then you feel it's all worth it.»

«I could give lots of reasons why we were out of the picture for some time, and those reasons will sound like excuses. As you try to move forward - as a company - inevitably you look back on things and find yourself not particularly happy with the way they were executed. That might be something you have done, or it might be something done by a manager. In those situations there is a double frustration, because inevitably one«s ego says, «If I'd done that, I might have done it better.» *So it's quite painful, because over time I removed myself into a position where I could take a more strategic role in the company.»*

«Some people may think I didn't do it fast enough, that I wasn't strong enough, in terms of the functioning of the group. Other people felt that I wasn't taking decisions that I should have been taking.»

«As hard as I tried to be what people want me to be, the reality is that you only have so much time in the day. When you try to apportion that time, you find yourself asking, «Have I moved forward on all fronts, or have I done purely a damage limitation exercise? What is the quality of the work I have done? Have I just dealt with a pile of paperwork - none of which has made the cars go faster?»»

«I can find long periods where I haven't achieved anything because of the constant avalanche of administrative stuff that comes on to my desk. Some people can be absolutely ruthless about handling these sorts of things. They can make an imperfect decision, and can live with the consequences, whereas I always want to make the best decision on every issue. So then I have to ask myself whether I have got my time management under control, whether I have balanced my strategic role within the group against my day-to-day role within the individual companies.»

«It is so frustrating, because the formula by which you win Grands Prix is constantly changing. What you really need is the ability to second-guess what is going to happen - not at the next race, sometimes not even next year, but in the longer term. That was where I needed to apply my time.»

«I always knew what McLaren could achieve; I knew the formula by which the company needed to be run in the future, the direction that was right. Satisfaction comes in different forms for me. Most of the people in the race programme really felt the failure, becau-

NIGEL ROEBUCK,
51 years old, decided to quit his industrial job and enter journalism at the age of 24. In 1971, he starts writing for the American magazine «Car & Drivers», before joining the British weekly motorracing magazine «Autosport» in 1976. He is covering Formula One since 1977, while working for the «Sunday Times», for «Auto week» and the Japanese magazine «Racing On».

se we were losing. My job was to effect change in such a way that we came back as quickly as possible to a position of winning again.»
«That was not about getting involved in the optimisation of the car's fuel system, or whatever. I know I have the ability to grasp most areas of a grand prix car - if I totally immerse myself in it. But the company wasn«t going to get out of me what it should if I allowed myself to slip back into that sort of hands-on approach.»
«Believe me, I understood those who said that life at McLaren was not as they wanted it to be. But I always felt that they would understand in the end, and I hoped that not too many would choose to leave. As as a company, I think McLaren is very loyal; we try desperately at that. In principle I will do anything for anybody here as long as there is a fairness and balance to it.»
«A great many folk would testify to that», Alain Prost among them. *«I was there a long time,»* he said, *«and I know that, from the outside, McLaren looks very cold. From the inside, though, it's completely different - easily the most supportive team I ever drove for, a family, if you like. OK, I didn't enjoy my last season there, and Ron knows my feelings about that, but we«ve remained good friends, and even now I still think of it as «my» team...»*

«After the 1995 European Grand Prix at the Nurburgring there was a meeting to discuss the overall strategy and results within the Mercedes-Benz motorsport programme»

It was in Melbourne, in 1997, that the victory drought finally ended, with David Coulthard winning, and Hakkinen finishing third.
Later Coulthard also won at Monza, and Hakkinen - after coming close so many times - took his first Grand Prix victory at Jerez.
Essentially, though, the season had been fought out between Williams-Renault and Ferrari. Often the McLarens were a serious factor, but they were not a threat for the World Championship.
That was to change emphatically in 1998 - not least because Dennis was able to persuade Adrian Newey to leave Williams. No one in the modern era is a match for Newey when it comes to designing a Grand Prix car.
The car, though, is only one half of the equation, and Dennis is fulsome in his praise for Mercedes-Benz. *«After the 1995 European Grand Prix at the Nurburgring - which was less than spectacular for us - there was a meeting between myself, Roger Penske and others, to discuss the overall strategy and results within the Mercedes-Benz motorsport programme. We each discussed the negatives of our programmes - not the positives - and there was also an overall discussion designed to share with each other the problems that each of the teams encountered.»*
«That year Roger had the embarrassment of his team's poor performance at Indianapolis to deal with, and I had the embarrassment of poor performances in the Grands Prix, so nobody was sitting there with a smug grin on his face. But the overwhelming point of the meeting was the desire by Helmut Werner and Jurgen Hubbert to convey to us the absolute support that Mercedes had for its motorsport strategy.»
«They radiated commitment, and any questions they had were designed to understand how they could contribute more to achieving on-circuit success. When I left that meeting I felt that I was not partnered by simply fair-weather friends, and that meant a lot to me.»
Everything has come together in 1998. The Newey-designed MP4/13 made a sensational debut in Australia, Hakkinen and Coulthard quite literally playing with the opposition in both qualifying and race.
The only negative aspect was the criticism faced by the team for suggesting, after a pit stop mix-up with Hakkinen, that Coulthard should move over, and allow him to win. This David duly did, but there were suggestions - primarily from those with no understanding of Grand Prix racing - that the result had been *«fixed.»*
Fifteen races into the year, with only Suzuka to come, Hakkinen had won seven, and Coulthard one, but indisputably both should have had more - particularly David, who lost apparent certainties in Montreal and Monza.
A number of mechanical failures are to be expected in the course of a season, but some of those which have cost McLaren points in 1998 have not been of a kind one anticipates from this team: in Canada, for example, Coulthard's throttle linkage stretched, preventing him from getting more than half-power, and in Budapest Hakkinen's front roll-bar came adrift.
After the unexpected Ferrari 1-2 at Monza (where David Coulthard had engine failure while leading, and Hakkinen ran out of brakes), many were quick to suggest that McLaren were on the run, that psychologically the momentum of the season was now with Schumacher and Ferrari. Thus, the Luxemburg Grand Prix was a stern test of Dennis and his boys.

No excuses from Ron Dennis

Initially, it did not look as though they had responded well, for the Ferraris took the front row, and Hakkinen and Coulthard - unable to get their cars handling properly - were only third and fifth. Typically, there were no excuses from Ron: *«We simply didn't get the best out of our cars today. Simple as that...»*
There is huge resilience at McLaren, though. By the time of the race morning warm-up set-up changes to his car had made Mika a happy man again, and in the race he drove quite beautifully, resisting the temptation to panic in the early laps as he ran behind Eddie Irvine, with Schumacher racing away in the lead. Having passed the second Ferrari, Hakkinen took over the lead for four laps when Schumacher made his first stop, and ran them at such an extraordinary pace that he was able, after his own stop, to squeeze out of the pits ahead.
Thereafter, Mika was untouchable, and the elation on Dennis«s face, as he hugged his driver afterwards, spoke volumes. *«This,»* Ron said, *«is probably the most important victory in the history of McLaren.»* Schumacher, meantime, looked simply shocked.
Twenty-four hours earlier, the race had looked his for the taking.
Japan, though, was still five weeks ahead, allowing an unusual amount of time for testing and planning.
Neither Dennis nor Hakkinen was taking anything for granted: *«We all know how it is with Michael,»* said Ron.
«Whenever we have a problem, he's there, ready to pounce.»
Whatever, the feeling in the paddock all year long had been that the World Championship was McLaren's to lose. Dennis's team, after a long period in the wings, were back to centre-stage at last. As Ron always knew it would be.

△
Ron Dennis reached his goal this season, taking the McLaren team to the top of the pile once again.

△◁
(above)
First grand prix and first success for the McLaren team. At the time, Ron Dennis expressed a desire to see his team win all 16 races of the season.

Ferrari 1998: springboard to success

1998 : punto di vista Italiano

by Christiano Chiavegato
«La Stampa»

This past season has been the one that has finally seen Ferrari come to maturity, in terms of course of the latest generation to carry the sacred flame. This is the generation led by Jean Todt since 1993, who faced the difficult task of reorganising the Scuderia. The work began soon after the arrival of Luca di Montezemolo, who had taken on the role of president and figurehead of the company, having already had one successful stint when he had been the team's sporting director in the mid-Seventies. The results have now started coming and, as promised before the start of the season, the Maranello firm has fought from start to finish for the world championship, even if the campaign has had its ups and downs. The start of the season brought mixed fortunes, in part disappointing, before a period of continuous improvement, which can only be put down to a staggering amount of work undertaken by all the Ferrari staff from the top to the bottom, who never stinted their efforts. To put some figures to this workload, consider this inventory of work undertaken from January to November: 36 thousand kilometres of testing carried out with great consistency while the F 300 car also underwent a continuous development programme of all its component parts - chassis, mechanics, aerodynamics, electronics and engine.

The F 300 was the 44th single seater built by Ferrari to compete in the F1 world championship, the third to be fitted with a V10 engine. In fact the car's number indicates the capacity of one of its cylinders. The car was completely new compared with last year's, because of the drastic changes to the regulations aimed at reducing the car's cornering speeds which involved a reduction in the car's width and aerodynamic downforce as well as making the chassis more resistant to impact. Every part was redesigned, including the engine, where the V was opened up to 80 degrees and the centre of gravity was lowered thanks to a smaller diameter clutch which allowed the crankshaft to be lowered. The engine, code named 047, was lighter and able to rev higher. The use of new materials meant the V10 could operate at higher running temperatures, which in turn meant the car could get by with smaller radiators, which improved the overall aerodynamic efficiency of the car. The engine already underwent a modification in time for the opening round in Australia, where in qualifying, Michael Schumacher was able to use a version with a new high-tech ignition system. The German used the same spec engine in the Argentinian race and Eddie Irvine also had it in Brazil. A further step forward was made allowing different specification engines to be used for Spa

and Monza, and although the team would not confirm it, probably also for the final race in Japan. Overall, modifications made over the year produced horsepower increases that totalled around thirty horsepower. The gearbox was also a new sequential, seven speed and longitudinal unit. It is compact and light and linked to a viscous limited slip differential. The front suspension was also completely redesigned. The only area which did not change much was the structure of the team itself. Ross Brawn is the technical director with Rory Byrne at his side as chief designer. Stefano Domenicali was confirmed as team manager, Paolo Martinelli headed up the engine side, while Ignazio Lunetta an Luca Baldisseri took care of the cars of Michael Schumacher and Eddie Irvine respectively. The team staged a major coup with the announcement that Schumacher had signed to stay with the team until 2002, while the agreement with the Irish driver was extended for 1999. In the role of test driver, along came Luca Badoer.

Although Ferrari was one of the first to unveil its 1998 creation- the new car was being tried at Fiorano in «natural» black before Christmas and the official presentation at Maranello on 7th January- things did not go smoothly from the start. *«When we were designing the car, we wanted it to have near perfect balance and very fine lines,»* explained Ross Brawn, the Englishman who runs the technical side of the Italian team. *«But we had also wanted a car that would be very reliable and we soon realised that the high level exhaust system we had adopted ran the risk of causing overheating to the rear end of the car, especially the rear wing. For this reason we had to come up with some compromise solutions. That compromise affected the car's overall performance to the tune of around three to four tenths of a second per lap. This immediately put us in a difficult situation when compared with our nearest competitors.»*

However, the major problem for Ferrari at the opening race of the season was the tyre choice. It became apparent right from the winter testing work that the rival Bridgestone tyres had gone through a major evolution and were very competitive and were going to set the pace in Melbourne. The Italian team immediately put Goodyear under a lot of pressure and the American company called all hands on deck. By the time of the race in Argentina, the F 300 was able to use wider front tyres with a different construction, which immediately produced the goods. It was to be a never ending development programme, throughout the season which eventually saw Ferrari in a position to challenge for overall honours, in qualifying as well as the race. Qualifying had been a problem at the start of the season, but there was a major step forward in this area around the time of the French GP at Magny Cours.

One of Ferrari's major strengths was its ability to read a race and find the right strategy. The result was that occasionally the team won races that had appeared unwinnable on Saturday night. There is no denying that a handful of wins came from an aggressive and imaginative race strategy, although there were times, qualifying at the Nurburgring was one example, when Ferrari was a match for the McLarens, who generally dominated qualifying. *«Sometimes, the plans you make on Saturday evening or Sunday morning*

CHRISTIANO CHIAVEGATO,
57 years old, was introduced very young in journalism. He started at «La Stampa» in 1959, while still attending various sporting events for «La Gazzetta dello Sport» for fifteen years. He has covered about ten Olympic Games, summer and winter, before concentring on motorsport at the end of the sixties. Since 1976, he has not missed a single GP and has written many books on Ferrari, and a biography of Niki Lauda.

have to be changed during the race,» explained Jean Todt. *«There are too many factors to take into account. In Michael Schumacher we have what is certainly the most reliable and precise racer in Formula 1. But even he cannot defend himself if he does not have sufficient means at his disposal. In any case, Ferrari has dedicated a lot of time and effort to the whole question of race strategy. When we are testing, either in private sessions or during official practice, some people might ask themselves why we try out certain things.*

Overall, we must have produced about a dozen different front wings, to meet the demands of the various circuits and then modified the rear wings accordingly

The answer is simple: we must not leave anything to chance as every tiny detail has a value as part of the whole. We have produced certain programmes which we use to apply all the parameters of data at our disposal, from the configuration of the car, to tyre wear, to fuel consumption, to the type of track we are about to tackle. Even elements such as the entrance and exit to the pit lane are taken into consideration. To these factors, have to be added all the uncertain variables that can affect us: overtaking moves and the weather which can change from one moment to the next. From this veritable mass of data we try and find the right compromise as well as working on an emergency strategy which can allow for a quick change to the programme. Because, no matter how well prepared one is, the need to improvise can always crop up. The whole thing is poised on a knife edge. We also rely on the great level of professionalism of our engineers and our mechanics. They have to be cool headed to stand the situation. It's part of the game, but it seems to me that we achieved that overall, with a regulation that demands at least one pit stop per race, Ferrari is capable of turning the situation to its advantage.»
Returning to the technical development of the F300, it has to be said that Ferrari has made progress in every area and that it did not stop for a single moment during the championship, from moving forward on this front. *«Once we had got over the basic problems with the car,»* continued Todt, *«we managed to concentrate on a programme of improvements based on its emerging potential from the massive amounts of data we had gathered from the large number of test sessions we carried out. In the course of the year we were able to reduce the weight of the F 300 by various means and that allowed us to improve the weight distribution. We worked constantly on the electronics, on the development of the car as a whole and on the suspension. The bodywork underwent various modifications and therefore so did the aerodynamics. Remember the side wings, which undoubtedly gave us an advantage, but were unfortunately used only at Imola as FIA banned them shortly afterwards. Overall, we must have produced about a dozen different front wings, to meet the demands of the various circuits and then modified the rear wings accordingly. All of this was made possible by the commissioning of our new wind tunnel to full use. Designed by the famous architect, Renzo Piano it is right next to the factory. Operational from 1997, one of the most modern and advanced in the world, it nevertheless needed some fine tuning work and data collation, which meant we have not yet been able to get the most out of it. Therefore we cannot really say that the F300 was born out of this new technological centre which is at our disposal. But we intend reaping the benefits of this important investment made by Ferrari for next year.»*
«Another major step forward came when we transformed the car into a long wheelbase chassis, which made its debut in the unfortunate Belgian Grand Prix before proving victorious at Monza. It was a very complex operation which took a lot of time and both human and financial resources. Although the car apparently was much the same as the standard length chassis, as the increase in length came from a spacer between the engine and gearbox, in truth the engineers had to redesign several parts both on the mechanical and aerodynamic side. Although we obtained some success with it, the long wheelbase did not convince everyone, which is why we had to return to work with the standard car as we prepare to tackle the final and decisive race of the season. That way we can keep our options open right to the very last minute,giving us a choice for Suzuka. We have certainly left nothing to chance in our efforts to give Schumacher everything he needs to fight for the title and a win in the concluding race in Japan. Our overall result this season has been satisfactory, as we have won more races than in 1997. Above all, it is a year, which we at Ferrari consider as a year of establishing itself and its 450 staff. It has been a springboard for a long period of continuity and a permanent place at the very highest level in Formula 1.»

△
The Ferrari team's nerve centre during a grand prix is on the pit wall: a glass of water, a calculator and a strategy plan. Note that it is impossible to see the track! From left to right; Ignazio Lunetta, Ross Brawn and Jean Todt.

Victory at Monza was the high point of the 1998 season for Scuderia Ferrari.
▽

Villeneuve's awfully big adventure

by Philippe Cantin
«La Presse»

Back in July, at the British Grand Prix, a cold hard rain was falling on Silverstone circuit. In the press office, while waiting for practice to start, the French journalists were busy singing the praises of Aime Jacquet, the national soccer coach. Despite a captivating battle for the drivers' world championship, the round ball dominated all conversation that weekend. It was hard to believe, but the home side was actually going to play in the final of the World Cup!

The success of its footballers was in sharp contrast to the disarray of another French team, namely Prost Grand Prix. Despite a hike in its budget, a larger workforce and a move to a new state-of-the-art factory in a Parisian suburb, Alain Prost and his boys were tripping over their own feet this season. Life was so bad, that technical director Bernard Dudot decided to confront the situation with a press release. *«A team can quite easily get to the third or fourth row of the grid,»* he explained. *«But making it onto the front row demands a phenomenal amount of work. It is very difficult to break into the inner circle of the top three or four teams. It is possible that those of us at Prost have not made this clear enough to the outside world. That has resulted in the creation of false hopes which have now turned to disappointment.»*

> *«If BAR potters around in the middle of the grid and does not bring that breath of fresh air promised by Craig Pollock, then Villeneuve will not escape some degree of blame, whether his hair is red, mauve or black!»*

Reading these words of wisdom, from the pen of a man rich in deep experience of Formula 1, it made me think of the BAR (British American Racing) team, which will make its Formula 1 racing debut in the Australian Grand Prix next March. Since the 2nd December 1997, the day when millions of dollars from a tobacco multinational bought Craig Pollock his entre into the inner circle of Formula 1 team owners, the man has been blowing his own trumpet to attract the attention of his peers. Right from the first press conference, Jacques Villeneuve's former manager set the tone. *«We will bring a breath of fresh air. The arrival of BAR will mark an important moment for motor sport. We want to stand out through our open spirit and a desire to be close to our public. Our team will not be hidden away as the plaything of a rich owner and our supporters will have a sense of belonging.»*

This marked love of the self-congratulatory, twinned with the pleasure of goading the opposition at the same time, rapidly became the new outfit's calling card. An example: In the week prior to the British Grand Prix, BAR invited the international press to a marketing operation of little interest, the capping off ceremony of its Brackley factory, 15 minutes drive from Silverstone. A photo was distributed showing Pollock with a spanner in his hand. This was not without irony, as unlike Frank Williams or Ron Dennis, the BAR owner has never laid spanner to car for a living. Six slides were also included in the press kit, of which three of them were of Pollock. Without any shame or even humility, the team has adopted as its motto: *«BAR, a tradition of excellence.»* Coming from a group which is still wet behind the years and so far achieved nothing, it smacked of a solid dose of conceit.

In Quebec, the birth of the BAR team generated a lot of interest. It was hardly surprising, as although Jacques Villeneuve enjoyed playing the game of suspense, it was obvious he would turn up as the new team's number one driver. At Silverstone, the Canadian driver gave the best indication yet that this move was on the cards. *«Yes, I might accept an offer from a new team. As long as it offers a winning combination. In these circumstances why not?»* To no one's surprise, a few days later, Craig Pollock confirmed the move. In accepting this proposition, Villeneuve listened chiefly to his heart. And that is no bad thing. The young man certainly has the right to work in a pleasant environment with friends he trusts. Pollock, his skiing instructor back in the days when he was at an up-market private school in Switzerland, falls into that category. Their complicity is clear to see. The two men will work in harmony, which was not always the case for Villeneuve when dealing with Frank Williams and Patrick Head. Despite taking the 1997 drivers and constructors' championships, the trio never really hit it off as the following anecdote goes to show.

Last March, on arrival in Melbourne for the first grand prix of the 1998 calendar, Villeneuve was more than a little surprised to read in a local paper, a rather cutting appraisal of his abilities from Patrick Head. Emphasising the fact the Canadian found it difficult to communicate with his engineers, the Williams technical director went on: «Jacques can tell us what he prefers, but he cannot really tell us why. He will have to get people to think his way rather than operating on dictates.» In the same interview, Head went on to express his admiration for Michael Schumacher. And this just five months after the German driver's unforgivable move on the Canadian in the European Grand Prix at Jerez. Hardly a lesson in diplomacy! As for Villeneuve's discourse with his engineers, it is certainly not as bad as Head made out. Otherwise,

PHILIPPE CANTIN,
39 years old, studied law before turning to journalism in 1984. He has covered the Olympics Games, the Tour de France and many other top-levels sporting events in the United States and Europe. He has also been a political correspondent. In addition to Formula One, he his particulary interested in economics and sport in general.

Jock Clear, his race engineer since 1996, would not have chosen to follow him to BAR.
The 1998 season was tough for Villeneuve, as the Williams team was incapable of getting its cars to perform in line with the new regulations. Unfortunately, the 1999 season is hardly likely to be much better for the former world champion. BAR may well have invested 400 million US dollars in the hope of getting the team to the top in record time, but the team has yet to gel. It will take them time to start channelling all their energies in the same direction. Unlike McLaren, Williams or Ferrari, BAR does not yet possess what Bernard Dudot refers to as *«technical memory;»* a tool which only comes with time. In short, BAR will find it difficult to reach the desired level, which its directors have promised us. They would do well to take heed of Michael Schumacher's words on the subject. *«The BAR team will have to go through school. It will be a difficult time and it is a different gamble to the one I took on joining Ferrari. We have developed an established team, whereas BAR is starting from nothing.»* David Coulthard had this to add: *«This type of operation is always a gamble. The examples of the last ten years proves that the big teams stay in front and the small ones still cannot break through.»*
Jacques Villeneuve is an excellent driver, but is he the ideal candidate to develop a car? Will he have the necessary patience, when his team goes through the inevitable black periods? The answer is unclear but what is clear is that this will be the biggest challenge the 27 year old has faced in his career. He reckons the Supertec Renault engine and the Adrian Reynard developed chassis represents a winning combination. Joining forces with his mates, Villeneuve will have the chance to find the limits of his talent. If he takes a BAR car to victory, much of the credit will be his and his detractors will perhaps stop minimising his achievement in winning the 1997 world championship, claiming that any driver could have won in that year's Williams. On the other hand, if BAR potters around in the middle of the grid and does not bring that breath of fresh air promised by Craig Pollock, then Villeneuve will not escape some degree of blame, whether his hair is red, mauve or black!
The creation of the BAR team and its employment of Jacques Villeneuve were not the only high points of the Formula 1 season in Montreal. The thorny subject of the future of the Canadian Grand Prix also solicited controversy. At the heart of the matter, just as in several European countries, is an anti-tobacco legislation forbidding cigarette manufacturers from putting their branding on racing cars. The federal government had promised an amendment in order to keep the race in Montreal. This finally happened in June, five months later than planned. The race has been given a five year stay of execution. Normand Legault, the president of the Canadian Grand Prix was relieved to hear the news as there had been a real danger of Bernie Ecclestone switching the North American leg of the F1 world championship to the United States. *«Five years is not a long time,»* commented Mr. Legault. *«But in the world of tobacco, it is also an eternity. Anything can happen between now and then. The FIA is itself studying the possibility of banning tobacco advertising. If they take a different decision then we will have to look at the situation again in 2003. But this reprieve gives us space to breathe and we will no longer be fire fighting the problem.»*

The facilities at the Ile Notre Dame circuit are in need of urgent modernisation. The paddock is tiny and the teams do not know where to put their tyres. The media centre also needs urgent attention. The promoters also want to increase the available seating as the event is an undoubted success. On 7th June last, over 100,000 spectators saw Michael Schumacher take victory at the end of an action packed race. On Friday, for free practice, over 60,000 people filled the grandstands. *«Ten years ago, we did not have that sort of crowd on race day,»* commented Normand Legault. In short, the Villeneuve effect is still seducing the public. Unfortunately, Quebec's favourite son had a difficult race in front of his fans. He tried a risky overtaking move on lap 23, while there was still everything to play for, showing surprising impetuosity. Usually such a clear thinker, on this occasion he chose recklessness. Of course, if he had pulled off the move, then he would have been seen as a hero.
The Canadian Grand Prix marked a turning point in the calendar. Up until the Montreal date, the McLarens of Mika Hakkinen and David Coulthard had devastated the opposition. In order to upset their impetus and keep his chances of pulling off a third world championship, Schumacher had to lay all his cards on the table here. His sense of spectacle transformed a rather dull event into a race full of unexpected twists and turns. For that we thank him.
Victory for his nemesis certainly hit Villeneuve hard. Relations have remained strained since their coming together in the European Grand Prix in October 1997. An attempt at reconciliation took place in Australia before the first race of the season, but it was not a resounding success. Schumacher came up to Villeneuve in a hotel and invited him to share a cup of coffee. After some little reticence, the Canadian accepted, but Schumacher did not apologise for the Jerez incident. Over the next few months, Villeneuve often criticised his German rival's behaviour. *«On the track, you must have mutual respect,»* he reminded everyone. *«It is right to take a risk but putting one's rivals in danger is not. This attitude goes beyond what is acceptable. Drivers must obey a simple rule: do not do to others what you would not want them to do to you. But I suppose if you believe nothing bad can happen to you, if you think you are a superior being, then I suppose everything is permitted.»*
At the wheel of his Williams, Villeneuve was incapable of taking on Schumacher on equal terms in 1998. Deep down, he feels that BAR will help him realise his ambitions in 1999. *«As long as there is a Fangio with five world titles to his name, a Prost with 51 wins and a Senna with 65 poles, then there is still a lot to accomplish,»* he says. *«It does not matter what level you are at, there is always a new challenge to conquer.»* Despite his worthy good intentions, he is facing a colossal challenge.

△
Craig Pollock, the main man with the new British American Racing team.

1998 aus deutscher Sicht

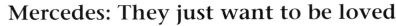

Mercedes: They just want to be loved

by Anno Hecker
«Frankfurter Allgemeine Zeitung»

They have almost everything: money, influence, elegance and success. But that is not enough. Mercedes wants more, Mercedes wants it all. Mercedes wants to be loved.
It would be the final step on the road to perfection, which has seen the German company take several years to reach its place in the sun in Formula 1.
The Germans have poured in millions of deutschmarks since 1993 before reaching their goal. Now it is time to take the final step. As a winner, Mercedes still has to win the affection of all and develop a human image which would protect them from hatred when they fail and make the image shine when they triumph.

Mercedes does not feel loved

But Mercedes comes up against a barrier in what ought to be the open world of Formula 1. «*Mercedes has always been respected, but we have never been adored or even just liked,*» admitted Norbert Haug, their motor sport director back in the spring, before adding: «*I think this is beginning to change.*» A phrase which implies both a need and an under-estimation of the situation at the same time.
Firstly, Mercedes evidently does not feel loved and secondly the engine supplier is keen to start a love affair with the general public. The entire group is in on the act. It was a market study and good sense which pushed Daimler-Benz to look at modifying its general image by using Formula 1. The company's products must come across as serious and of good quality, but also young, sporty and dynamic, while being loved at the same time.

«They buy everything and they have no humanity.»

That is why Mercedes wants, above all, to make a good impression with those responsible for conveying the image to the public. When the three pointed star entertains the press, nothing is too much trouble. Sea food salad between the motorway and the Hockenheim track, medallions of pork on the lawn at Silverstone, it always has to be the best at Mercedes.
That is how the entire team presents itself, as polite but with an iron determination to win. Team members do not need to express their secret ambition because it is etched on their foreheads. Their own way of looking at things after the switch from Sauber to McLaren, at the end of 1994, was strange to say the least. The guys from Stuttgart had failed in their first mission which carried the motto: veni, vidi, vici. But instead of accepting their fate in public, boss Haug clung to nebulous calculations based on tenths gained here and there on split times, thousandths made up in the final section, while the result was at best a sixth place. This collage of bits of seconds only hid some of the problem and demonstrated a certain cowardice when it came to facing facts and admitting to defeat and weaknesses. Losing was not allowed.

All that is in the past. Mercedes and its partners are winners at last. McLaren and its sponsor Reemtsma (West) the cigarette company, brought in by Mercedes, go well together. At least that is the impression in the paddock.
The «partners» try to out-do one another with their two storey motorhomes and large awnings. West's mobile palace which made its debut at Spa this year, has a glass fronted verandah with a revolutionary system which sucks up the ash of the expensive Cuban cigars offered to its guests.
Everything is designed to show off their «*we have it all here*» attitude. But not everyone in Formula 1 wants to dance to this tune. While at first, it might have been seen as a mix of good business sense and

a sporting spirit, it now seems far less convincing. Wherever you look you see the Mercedes symbol. The Formula 1 car parks are dominated by the cars from Unterturkheim, from the Safety Car, to the marshals cars to chauffeur driven VIP cars, they all have the same badge on the bonnet.
Even Bernie Ecclestone, who usually favours Audi, had no choice. An S Class is at his disposal over the grand prix weekends. And one energetic secretary in the Stuttgart factory has ensured that its noble product is available at knock-down prices to all the grand prix drivers, team owners and their families. Formula 1 drives a Mercedes. But it is not necessarily delighted about it. Such a heavy presence becomes a bit too much for the F1 folk, normally the last to turn down a free gift. The German magazine «Stern» printed the first signs of disapproval. «*They buy everything and they have no humanity.*» They also lack a certain sense of tact. 30 years after the invasion of the Warsaw Pact states in Prague, which put an end to the political springtime, the West McLaren Mercedes troops have invaded the race circuits, turning them into go kart tracks for publicity purposes.
At the end of the day it is just a business and the public seems well aware of this. If sporting success was the only aim, the number of Mercedes and Schumacher fans in 1998 should have been about equal. But a quick glance at the grandstands at Hockenheim, Nurburgring, Spa or Monaco, reveals that on any of the 16 tracks around the world, the red Schumacher caps far outnumber the silver ones which glorify Mercedes.
Machinery cannot win against Man. It might be perfect, but it is still cold. It might react to a problem with a turn of a screw, but it can never show emotion. Who, apart from engineers and obsessed fans, can identify with a ten cylinder engine? A powerful engine can incite surprise or amazement, but it will never provoke passion.
This is not the only reason German race fans find it difficult to take Mercedes to their hearts. There is nothing for them to grab hold of and with McLaren they present themselves as a complete entity. Their doctrine is one of control and perfection combined with an air of diplomacy. «*With us the star is the team,*» is one of Haug's favourite sayings.
This sounds sound: no exaggerated admiration for a driver and his moods. But a close look shows that the roles at McLaren and Mercedes are simply devised in a different fashion to those at Ferrari, so a «*team strategy*» often hides the vanity of its directors. When one driver is not particularly dominant and is not the centre of

ANNO HECKER, 34 years old, worked first as a physical education instructor before turning to journalism in 1986. After working as a political correspondent for a Bonn news agency, he joined «Frankfurter Allgemeine Zeitung» in 1991 to cover motor sports. He specialised in stories combining politics and sport.

attention for the media, someone else must take responsibility for the success. Surely not Haug or Dennis? «*We do not like it when certain team members are singled out,*» says the Mercedes press officer, when asked for an interview with a Mercedes team member. In fact, interviews have to be read and approved, whether it is with technical director Adrian Newey or with engine designer Mario Ilien or with a mechanic or truck driver.

«Hakkinen would never be as popular in Germany as Michael Schumacher, even if he went on to win several more titles. Hakkinen give the impression of being a nice guy and nothing more. Schumacher grabs the attention.»

Mercedes realised that the drivers were not so important alongside the car and engine. That is why the factory decided to mount an advertising campaign in Germany, with Finland's Mika Hakkinen, proving as an aside, which driver was Mercedes' favourite.
In fact Hakkinen saw his popularity increase with some humorous television commercials. Apparently, he is particularly popular with women and manages to convey some of that fresh Formula 1 driver image to Mercedes diesel cars. Although this has not actually been proven.Nevertheless, the factory must have learnt one thing.
Despite his success, Hakkinen would never be as popular in Germany as Michael Schumacher, even if he went on to win several more titles.
Hakkinen give the impression of being a nice guy and nothing more. Schumacher grabs the attention of those who line the race tracks, of the millions who sit at home and watch on television, giving up 100% support to exclusion of all others.
It is for this reason and not just his skill behind the wheel, which led Mercedes to try and lure Schumacher to McLaren last spring. The fact a deal was not done had nothing to do with money. «*I would not have been worse off at McLaren-Mercedes,*» admitted Schumacher. The parties could not reach an agreement because Ron Dennis would not allow the German driver the slightest influence over the way the team was run or its choice of personnel. «*At Ferrari I have been granted the freedom I need to control my own future,*» concluded Schumacher.
Mercedes might have become more popular with the arrival of Schumacher, but only superficially. Because, while Schumacher's fans currently have some respect for Ferrari, the day their hero switches teams, so too their allegiance will change to another team.
At the end of the day, Schumacher could have posed a threat to Mercedes. His wins are normally credited to his own talent, while his defeats are put down to mechanical failures.
In any case there are no guarantees that Schumacher would have managed to banish the prejudices the marques has been up against for several years.
The impression most Germans have of Mercedes owners is that they are rich, arrogant and always put themselves first and not just in terms of traffic on the road.
Michael Schumacher is a millionaire known for his aggressive driving style. Is that what Mercedes needs?
As part of the Daimler-Benz group, Mercedes is too strong, too perfect and too rich to engender pity. On the contrary, after the disaster with the A class, it was easy to see what sort of reputation the company had in its own country. There was a feeling of malicious joy running through Germany!
That situation can neatly be transposed to Formula 1. Mercedes guarantees reliability, quality and finally success. That is why the marque is respected, but not really loved by the fans. Even the 1998 titles will not have changed that.

(left page)
Jurgen Hubbert, President of the Daimler-Benz board of directors, is here to check that his cash is being well spent at the race track. Seen here with David Coulthard.
◁

The imposing figure of Norbert Haug, a former journalist and now motor sport director of the three pointed star marque, has seen his efforts rewarded this year.
▽

1998 wo hurikaeru

Honda should give up its plans

by Kunio Shibata
«GPX Press», Tokyo

For the past five years, enthusiasm for Formula 1 has waned in Japan. But 1998 saw a young hopeful make his debut, then Bridgestone started winning and finally the giant Honda decided to return. Despite this, there is still not much enthusiasm. Why the cold shoulder? Maybe it is because Honda would do better to shelve their plans. Here's why.

Tora! Tora! Tora!....and then what?

Just twelve months ago in these pages, I strongly criticised the behaviour of young Japanese driver, Toranosuke Takagi. At the time, he was discovering Europe for the very first time, taking part in the Porsche Supercup.
He had come to familiarise himself with motorsport on the old continent, as he was due to make his Formula 1 debut the following season. But Tora did not react like all the other driver apprentices when faced with new surroundings. He was not at all interested in what went on around him, either on the track or in the pits. At the time, I predicted he would not be very quick in F1, given that he never even made it to the podium in the Porsche.
Well, I was wrong! Tora is quick enough. Right from winter testing he was consistently putting in quick lap times. Trained in karts, he had always preferred a nimble car. «The Porsche is too heavy. Even an F3000 car does not handle the way it should. With an F1 car, I finally feel comfortable again, like I was in karts,» he said. In his very first qualifying session in Melbourne, he was 13th. The car was good from the start, but because of constant mechanical problems, he had only managed to do a few laps in private testing prior to the first event. Despite that, his Tyrrell was quicker than the Prosts or Stewarts, even though these cars had works engines. What is more, he did not feel at a disadvantage being at a track he had never seen before. It was a pleasant surprise for me.
His exploits continued. At every track, he was quick right from the start, which definitely set him apart from his Japanese predecessors like Aguri Suzuki or Ukyo Katayama. Sadly the banning of the centrally mounted winglets literally clipped his wings.
Furthermore, just prior to the first grand prix of the season, Ken Tyrrell decided to sell up and many of the staff left, starting with technical director Mike Gascoyne, who was the key to the car's development. Then, the test team was swallowed up by the newly formed British American Racing and mid-season test sessions became something a rarity. The pace of development of the car slowed down and Tora's sparkle was tarnished.
By the end of the season, he had not scored a single point. This result, mediocre at best, cannot simply be attributed to the deterioration of a team which was on its way out. Tora's behaviour is also at fault, as it showed no signs of improvement.

«Toranosuke Takagi makes no effort whatsoever to communicate with anyone, even with Japanese»

Tora is a naturally quick driver and he is certainly talented enough to be the best of all the Japanese drivers. But watching him closely since the start of the season, I am really worried he is simply wasting the opportunity. There are two reasons for this. First, his knowledge of English is still very poor. Tora, he can get by with his engineer. However, the man in question says he often finds it difficult to communicate, especially over the radio. I have spoken on several occasions about the importance of his learning English to his boss, Satoru Nakajima, but his reply was always the same: *«It's not worth it.»* Probably because, when he was an F1 driver, he could not speak a word. But one has to remember that, at the time, he was a Honda protege. All necessary communication with the team was done through Honda. Tora's situation is completely different and sadly, neither he nor his master seem to understand this.
Furthermore, at least as far as I can see, he makes no effort whatsoever to communicate with anyone. He does not like to talk about his hopes or his feelings and that applies even in Japanese. I sometimes wonder if this guy wants to be in Formula 1 at all. Because, right from his days in F3, it was always Nakajima who told him what to do. Tora only had to keep his mind on racing, while everything else from contract negotiations to hotel and restaurant reservations were made by Nakajima's organisation staff and these people are with him at all times, even in the team motorhome. It is not easy for a journalist to get to him through this wall of people. If the journalist does get through. Tora does not have much to say. One day, a French colleague was stunned and angry after an interview (if one can call it that) with him. «I intended doing a two page story for my magazine. But all he said was *«yes,» «no,»* or *«I don't know. I will only write a couple of lines!»* Despite this, Tora was still courted by several team owners at the end of the season. He has sponsors, most notably, Japan Tobacco and through Nakajima he has close links with Honda.
One of those team owners was Peter Sauber. Impressed with Tora's driving, he decided to have a meeting back in August. But it was the same as with the journalists. Apparently, during a forty minute meeting, Tora was as dumb as a mute. «I knew the Japanese were a different race to us, but this one is an extra-terrestrial!» was Peter Sauber's dry comment to one of his engineers. Tora used to say and he still believes that, a driver only needs to express himself on the track. But even Michael Schumacher makes an effort to put his point across to the press. For the moment therefore, Tora's future is uncertain.

Bridgestone: can they maintain their motivation?

Bridgestone had a sensational debut season in Formula 1 in 1997. While only supplying second division teams, Bridgestone made its mark right from the opening races, with Olivier Panis' third place in

KUNIO SHIBATA, 42 years old, he left Japan, giving up his job in journalism in 1982 to move to Paris and study Political Science. He became a freelance producer for Japanese television and having always been interested in motor racing, he began covering the Grands Prix for a press agency in 1987 when Satoru Nakajima arrived on the scene. He has written for the specialist Japanese magazine «Grand Prix Xpress» since 1991.

Brazil and Ruben Barrichello's second at Monaco. It was these outstanding results that attracted Benetton and McLaren to the Bridgestone camp.
As you have seen, McLaren dominated the 1998 season, or at least the first two thirds of it. It is very difficult to assess what part the tyres played in this success, but it is clear that Bridgestone concentrated on the English team, building tyres on demand, sometimes to the detriment of their other teams. This year, the new rules forced the tyre companies to produce grooved tyres, which for Bridgestone, meant having to forget just about everything it had learnt the previous season. But the Japanese engineers did rather well, because there was at least one driver on the podium wearing a Bridgestone cap at the end of each race. Already the previous year, the Japanese company's rain tyres had a good reputation for incredible levels of grip. And this year, Bridgestone managed to wipe out the understeering tendency, by coming up with wider front tyres. These larger tyres had a negative effect on the very sensitive aerodynamics of these cars and it caused a few discussions, especially at McLaren, but eventually, it proved to be the correct solution.
At the start of the season, Bridgestone was totally dominant. But as time went by, the old Goodyear lion rose from its slumbers and mounted an effective counter- attack. The Bridgestone tyres sometimes only suited Mika Hakkinen's driving style and other drivers complained of a lack of responsiveness, too much understeer and of an over cautious approach, which favoured reliability rather than performance. In short, Bridgestone found it hard to maintain its early season advantage.
At the end of the day, the American-Japanese tyre brought many things: knowledge, engineering motivations and global publicity among others. Bridgestone had succeeded in winning an awesome challenge against the Americans.

The return of Honda: What are they trying to do?

Honda will be back in Formula 1 in 2000, this time as a complete team, with the company building both chassis and engine. In the modern F1 era, only Ferrari has succeeded in doing this by spending a fortune and throwing manpower at the project. It is a real challenge, even for a major player like Honda with a 1997 turnover of thirty billion dollars and 69 victories from 151 grands prix between 1983 and 1992.

As for Postlethwaite himself, he is one of the big names in F1. But his great days as an engineer in F1 are long gone.

At the time of writing, there are no details of this project. But according to sources, Honda has already set up a team to work exclusively on F1. There is talk of the Italian manufacturer Dallara, acting as technical partner, while Harvey Postlethwaite is billed as Technical Director and Satoru Nakajima as Managing Director. For the moment, all this is simply rumour. And I would like it to remain so for ever and for several reasons. Firstly, if Honda has really decided to come in with a 100% effort, I would prefer it not to be a pseudo «*complete team.*» Of course, it is better for them to rely on people who already have experience in this field, but let us not forget what Honda did 35 years ago. When Mr. Honda decided to enter F1, he at first thought of simply supplying engines. Lotus' Colin Chapman had suggested the idea and then at the last moment, Lotus broke the contract. Most of those behind the Honda project were in favour of dropping it, but the project leader, Nakamura («Naka-san») sent Chapman a telegram: «*We are going it alone, without you and with determination.*» This simple motorcycle manufacturer, who had never built a car, came into F1 as a complete team. It was the start of the Honda adventure. If that «Honda Spirit» is still alive today, a spirit which excludes all attempts at concession or imitation, then it is time to try and cross the desert alone.
Secondly, if Honda had decided on seeking outside help, maybe it should have done its research first. Dallara is already reckoned to have build the Honda chassis. Is it a simple research exercise or the sign of a partnership between the two companies? Dallara has never shone in F1. Could it be Postlethwaite who has pushed Honda in this direction? Dallara is actually one of his «*Italian connections,*» dating back to his time at Ferrari. As for Postlethwaite himself, he is one of the big names in F1. But his great days as an engineer in F1 are long gone. Technical Director at Tyrrell for several years, he is no longer at the cutting edge of success, in the way he was during the Eighties, neither from a technical nor a strategic point of view.
What of Nakajima himself? What a joke. What can one expect of a man who speaks no English and has no links with the current Formula 1 scene? In short, since Honda pulled out of Formula 1 at the end of 1982, it seems the company has not kept tabs on this world in a continuous and systematic fashion. If they had, their choices might have been more judicious. Tora-Bridgestone-Honda. Each one of them has the potential to regenerate Japanese interest in F1. But for the time being, not one of them seems capable of doing it. Could we one day see Tora win a grand prix at the wheel of a Honda fitted with Bridgestone tyres? Only time will tell.

◁
Bridgestone tyres played a major part in Mika Hakkinen's world title. It was a big success for the Japanese company.

◁◁
(left page)
Toranosuke Takagi, or the extra-terrestrial as Peter Sauber described him, was pretty impressive this season. At least, that was the case on the track, because off it, «Tora» lacked the social graces.

With two titles in its back pocket, Bridgestone has won its challenge

Although the Japanese company is only in its second season of Formula 1, it won both the drivers' and constructors' titles. For Bridgestone, the challenge it accepted has been a total success.

Champagne, then beer when the champagne ran out. The atmosphere was euphoric in the Bridgestone camp at Suzuka and with good cause. The Japanese company had just taken its ninth win of the season, but more importantly they had won both world titles. After barely two years competing in F1, the result was all the more exceptional in that the company had thus beaten Goodyear with its 34 years experience in Formula 1 and its 368 wins.
This achievement delighted Bridgestone MD, Yoichiro Kaizaki, who had made the trip to Suzuka. «*We are doubly satisfied to see both titles decided in our favour, here on our home turf in Japan,*» he declared. «*This is a very important event in the history of our company. I want to express my extreme gratitude to all the members of the West McLaren Mercedes team and especially to the drivers, Mika Hakkinen and David Coulthard.*»
For Hiroshi Yasukawa, Bridgestone's motorsport boss, all their goals had been achieved. «*When we decided to tackle Formula 1, our first goal was to gather knowledge and to increase sales on a world scale. But after our first season In F1, we realised we had the potential to be very competitive. We all knew this would involve joining forces with a top team, who was also looking for a world title.*»
Hiroshi Yasukawa also underlined all the hard work wich had been necessary to get to this glorious day. «*Today's result represents a reward for all the sacrifices made by our staff, especially the lack of sleep! Their determination and will to win were the two main contributing factors in this success.*»
In fact, while we had to wait until the final round of the season to know who would be champion, Bridgestone's success was built up throughout the year. Because, after the Japanese company's first F1 win in Melbourne, it was obvious they had a superior product to Goodyear. The American company did work very hard to close the gap, but it was too late by then.
The advantage McLaren had in the early part of the season through their tyres had already decided the championship, as Michael Schumacher himself admitted after the final race.
For Hirohide Hamashima, Bridgestone's technical director, this result rewarded a colossal amount of work. «*Our Formula 1 development programme kicked off in 1989, without official approval, I have to say! Now we are finally reaping the success from these seeds. Our first results came in 1996, when we first tested our products on a real F1 car, an Arrows. I must say, we have always respected what Goodyear has done. Without them, Formula 1 might have come to an end. And now we are very much aware of the task which faces us next season. We will make the maximum effort to allow Formula 1 to continue as the top level of motor racing.*»

The importance of Formula 1

When Bridgestone arrived in Formula 1, its stated aim was to increase brand awareness for the company and thus to increase sales around the world. It wanted to reach the target of a 20% market share of global tyre sales. «*We want to be the clear leader in tyre sales around the world and to increase our actual share from 19% to 20%,*» declared Yoichiro Kaizaki. A television audience of around 5.4 billion people around the world watch Formula 1, especially in Europe and South America, but also in Japan, North America and Australia. According to Bridgestone, participation in F1 constitutes an excellent method of improving the marque's visibility.
And it is working: In 1997 Bridgestone commissioned a market research survey to see how well known its name was among the general public. In Germany, Great Britain, France, Italy and Spain, the five biggest European markets, brand awareness had increased by 12% from 1996 to 1997. As a comparison, it had only increased by 0.8% between 1992 and 1996.
At the same time, sales of Bridgestone tyres in the replacement market for road cars increased by 20% from 1996 to 1997.
According to Bridgestone management, both these spectacular results can be put down to F1. «*Our successful participation in Formula 1 has been particularly effective in improving brand awareness in Europe,*» confirmed Kaizaki.
So, despite the huge amounts invested in F1, the investment has proved to be worthwhile for the Japanese company.

Bridgestone's technical director, Hirohide Hamashima. One of the key men in the company's 1998 success. ▽

Making tyres: a mixture of technology and family secrets

While the design of an F1 tyre may be very simple, with three grooves at the front and four at the rear to comply with the 1998 regulations, Bridgestone still uses two very powerful Cray T90 computers to calculate how the compounds will react. The surface temperature can be visualised in colour on the screen and the tyre's profile can be modified to study the new shape as temperature controls tyre wear.
A test bench is also used to put the tyres through a punishing routine on a sandpaper rolling road where speeds can exceed 300 km/h. Tyres wear out in a matter of seconds, which allows engineers to study how the rubber which is torn off is forced back on the tyre thus deforming the profile. This test bed can also measure the tyre's lateral traction, in other words its ability to hold the road in a corner.
Depending on downforce generated by the wings on a car, the track temperature and the make up of the asphalt, an F1 tyre can withstand lateral forces of between 200 kilos and 1.6 tonnes, or over six tonnes for the four tyres on a car. This explains why drivers complain about G-forces. Of course, nothing is left to chance. Along with testing on a rolling road and the track, tyres are also examined in the laboratory with an electronic microscope which can magnify the rubber up to one million times. This allows the actual molecules to be studied. It can also be a way of studying a rival company's compounds from samples scraped off the track surface after a test session. With such complex machinery and legendary Japanese working practices, this year, Bridgestone produced tyres which helped the McLaren team win nine race and both world championships.

◁ *The Kodaira-shi factory on the outskirts of Tokyo is one of many Bridgestone production facilities. The company employs around 96,200 staff.*

The story of a little stone bridge

The Bridgestone company was founded on 1st March 1931 by one man, Shojiro Ishibashi, in a little town on the island of Kyushu, in the south of Japan. «Ishibashi» means bridge of stone and so the man decided to call his company «Bridgestone.»
From a family concern, Bridgestone has grown today where it is the biggest tyre company in the world in terms of its turnover - 18 billion dollars, way ahead of Michelin and Goodyear, who are second and third respectively in the world. These three companies dominate the world tyre market, leaving only a few crumbs for the other brands.
Today, Bridgestone has 41 factories in 21 countries. At Kodaira-shi alone, which operates around the clock, seven days a week, 33,460 tyres are produced every day- 28,000 for road cars, 5400 truck tyres and 60 aircraft tyres. These figures do not include a few Formula 1 tyres, which do not feature in the commercial figures as they are suppled free of charge to the teams.
Ten years ago, Bridgestone bought Firestone, which had been the second largest American company after Goodyear.
The Firestone brand was retained to sell the cheaper range of tyres, while Bridgestone is the name given to the top of the range products. They are original equipment on several models from Porsche, Ferrari and BMW. The little bridge of stone has become a viaduct.

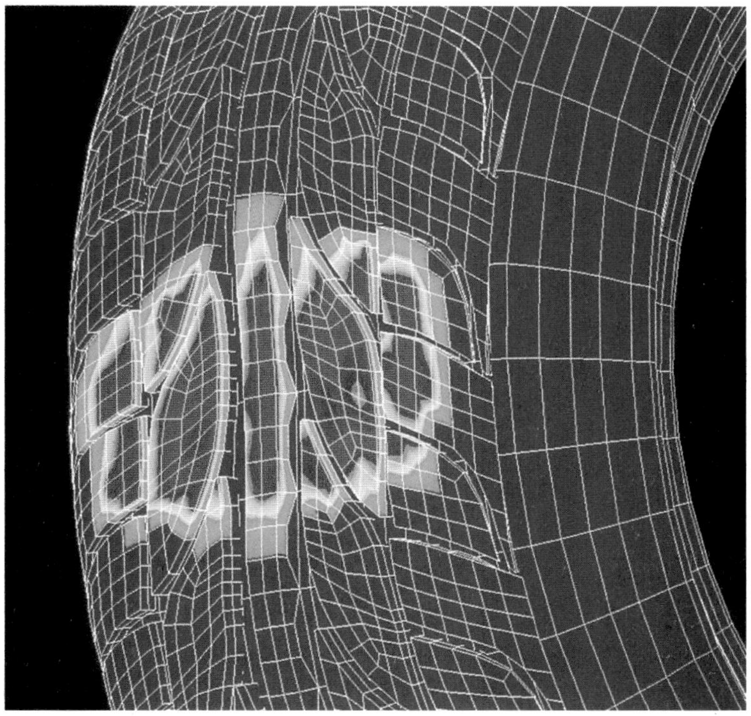

△ *Simulation of the spread of temperatures across a road tyre.*

Making the tyres: a complex process

Inside the huge building where the tyres are actually made, the visitor is surprised by an overpowering smell and by the haphazard layout of the factory with machinery littered everywhere.
For anyone who knows nothing about it, a tyre seems rather a simple thing. If you cut through one, you discover a «U» shaped carcass covered in rubber. But in fact the number of stages leading to this product is astounding. Here it is made as simple as possible.
While road car tyres are made from natural rubber, Formula 1 tyres are made from synthetic rubber, which does not last as long but provides greater grip. Apart from this fundamental difference, the two tyres are made in pretty much the same way.
First of all the rubber, synthetic or natural, is mixed mainly with sulphur and carbon dust, which is what gives tyres their black colour. It is in this mix that the future hardness of the tyre is decided and this is where experience and a bit of black magic comes into play.
Then the tyre is shaped. The paste is first squeezed into a long strip of rubber less than a millimetre thick.
Two of these strips are used to sandwich steel cables before it is all cut at an angle to the steel. The tyre carcass is now complete and it is the angle of the cut that leads to the type of tyre being called «radial.»
This is then covered with a thicker strip of pure rubber. This is then all fitted in a mould which inflates from inside to give the tyre its shape, which is a spectacular operation.
From then on, all that is left is the vulcanising process, which involves heating it to 170 degrees for about ten minutes in a mould which contains the outside design of the «tread.» In the case of a Formula 1 tyre, the circumferential grooves.
After a final inspection, the tyre is ready for track or street.

Adrian Newey went from Williams to McLaren. So did success.

Adrian Newey joined McLaren as technical director on 1st August 1997 and since then the silver arrows have been remarkably effective, while Williams has struggled. This situation cannot be a simple coincidence. Interview with one of the paddock's top boffins.

A nice unassuming sort of person, Adrian Newey is not one of the poseurs in the paddock and photographers wanting to capture him on film often have a long wait.

Adrian Newey is the man Ron Dennis has been looking for since the departure of John Barnard, over ten years ago, Recently, the technical director's seat at McLaren has been all too empty, his duties being divided between Neil Oatley, a former Williams engineer and the former Ferrari aerodynamicist Henri Durand. But this time Ron Dennis got the man for the job.

At the age of 39, Newey is regarded as an aerodynamics genius. Having made his F1 debut with March, he moved to Williams in the autumn of 1990. He was behind the cars which won the world championship five times; 1992, 1993, 1994, 1996 and 1997. In November 1996, the Englishman decided to leave the Frank Williams and Patrick Head team. «*It would have been easy for me to stay at Williams,*» said Newey. «*It would have been the most comfortable solution. I had been at Williams for a long time and I really liked my work there. I had a lot of friends there and I had a good time. But I also had the impression I had gone as far as I could and I felt I had to do something to progress in my career. I had to take up a new challenge and my position at Williams was static. I was also frustrated and that is why I left.*»

His departure was not a sweet affair. While Newey quit Williams in November 1996, he was not able to start work for McLaren until 1st August 1997, or at least officially. «*The first three months were horrible,*» recalled Newey. «*There were interminable legal discussions and a sort of open war with Williams. It was a bit stupid, but these things happen. I cannot say too much about it. Let's say the team saw things one way and I saw them another when it came to my contract.*»

This enforced nine months without work at least gave Newey the opportunity to enjoy a break, to spend time with his family, to go skiing and to tinker with his old pre-war Jaguar, with which he entered a few rallies. «*The free time was the good thing about this period. I really did not think about work, even though I did think about Formula 1 and the way it was heading.*»

On arriving at McLaren, Newey could have expected some problems with Neil Oatley and Henri Durand, especially as the rumours abounded that the new technical director's salary was in the region of three million dollars per year, or a lot more than the combined salary of the two other men.

In fact everything went off smoothly, Adrian Newey not being much of a dictator. He led the team by example, letting everyone get on with their jobs. From this point of view, the structure of the McLaren team is much better than at Williams. «*I think the two teams are pretty similar, apart from the management. As far as the mechanics, the workshops are concerned there is not much to choose between them. However, the structure of the two teams is different. I would say that McLaren is definitely much better organised with a better structure, especially at the very top.*»

Today, with the success of the MP4/13, Adrian Newey is considered responsible for the team enjoying its best season for ten years. Quiet to the point of shyness, he does not particularly like reading the pages of praise in the motoring press. «*I consider myself to be someone who likes his work and likes the challenges which go with it. I don't think I am a genius. I work hard but the pressure comes mainly from within. It is the fear of failure which motivates me most, rather than what people think of me.*»

Newey has been interested in aerodynamics since he was a kid. «*It was my father who got me interested in motor racing,*» *he continued.* «*He was also an engineer and had all sorts of cars to tinker with. He had a workshop and did some races and that is what got me interested. It is what I wanted to do, when it was time to go to university. I reckoned aeronautical engineering might be more relevant to racing cars than automotive engineering itself. I think I was right and I was lucky to get my first job in racing once I had a degree.*»

Adrian Newey reckons a technical director's best asset is an open mind. «*A good designer has to be inventive and must always bring new ideas. He must always question his work and challenge preconceived ideas. He must also be prepared to work hard. The worst thing about this job is how hard the work is and how long one must spend in the office. I have done this job for so long that I am used to it, but it is still tiring. I like working as part of a team.*»

A team that had already done a lot on the new MP4/13 when Newey joined McLaren last August. «*Henri Durand had done a lot of aero research. When I started we sat down and looked at all the results obtained so far. I had to add my experience to theirs. There is no big secret about this car. It is just an excellent package where everything fits.*»

Bridgestone: the good choice

Naturally, Bridgestone tyres had a lot to do with the success of the MP4/13. It was at the end of the year that the team left Goodyear to join the Japanese company, a decision that Newey was very keen on. «*Personally, I was in favour of this move. In any case, switching to grooved tyres meant a lot of work for us, so switching to Bridgestone did not add that much to our efforts. We had to make some changes to the suspension, which meant the car was a bit late coming out. The decision to switch was made by Ron Dennis and managing director Martin Whitmarsh and myself. I pushed them because I reckoned we would have a much closer relationship with the tyre manufacturer. We could develop our car along with the tyres and Bridgestone could make their tyres suit our car. We have a good working relationship with them. Their main advantage is their working method. They have excellent engineers who really listen to what we tell them.*»

Evidently, tyres were very important this year and it seems much easier to gain two seconds through the tyres than with a chassis or engine modification. This could be frustrating for chassis engineers. «*Not really,*» said Newey. «*In fact, with the very big changes to the technical regulations we had to face this year, the tyre companies are still on a learning curve and that is why progress is very rapid.*»

Ron Dennis is certainly a big fan of Newey's. «*When you run an F1 team, you are always searching for people who can improve your results. Adrian simply brought an additional element to our mix, just as if Mobil had come up with a new lubricant which reduced friction still further in the engine. He brought his own style, which involves sharing all his information so that everyone can contribute. He does not think he knows it all and works with others. He is open and he is still learning; learning every day.*»

New materials come to the aid of braking

The thousands of tifosi who invaded the track at the end of the Italian Grand Prix, owe a French company a great debt of gratitude. There is little doubt that Ferrari's one - two finish that day owed much to the new brake discs Carbone Industrie supplied to the team that day.
Because, this year, the situation as far as brakes is concerned, was critical. The technical regulation demanded that disc thickness be limited to 28 millimetres, as opposed to dimensions as high as 34 millimetres seen the previous year, at least on hard braking tracks like Melbourne, Montreal and Monza.
For the Carbone Industrie engineers, this ruling presented them with a new challenge, something the company was used to. On the eve of the 1998 season, Carbone Industrie could boast of having won all the world championships since 1984 and an average of nine wins from ten races in the same period. Indeed, it won its 200th grand prix when Michael Schumacher was first across the line in Argentina.
This year, as in 1997, the Villeurbanne based company yet again supplied all the Formula 1 teams, with the exception of Tyrrell and McLaren. The engineers immediately realised that with the increase in competitiveness of this last team, Carbone Industrie risked not taking its fifteenth consecutive world championship this year. Combined with the change in the rules, this possibility galvanised the French company into evolving its braking materials - in fact it is practically a new material - in time for the Italian Grand Prix. *«The 28 millimetre limit forced us to look for new solutions and take a big step forward,»* explained Philippe Rerat, Carbone Industrie's chief engineer.
It took some time before it was possible to test these applications in the field and that caused a few worries. *«At Montreal we were rather anxious. In fact the three appearances of the safety car were a godsend,»* continued Rerat.
At Monza, Michael Schumacher's win was clearly down to the brakes, on a day when McLaren was suffering with theirs - Mika Hakkinen having practically used up all his braking material when he came in for his pit stop, before limping home to finish. The two Ferrari drivers were able to attack hard, without giving a second thought to their brakes from start to finish of the race. The Scuderia bosses could be sure of this as wear rate sensors were fitted to the disc brakes of the F 300 - sensors which the McLarens did not have. *«Last winter we pushed the teams we work with to fit these sensors,»* continued Philippe Rerat. *«It is part of our race philosophy: not only to supply the very best equipment, but also to supply the best technical back-up at the tracks, which is an added value. Thanks to these sensors, we were able to tell the Williams team at Monza, that Heinz-Harald Frentzen had to slow his pace down or he would not finish the race.»*
Essentially, the new material which was produced by Carbone Industrie, does not really come from a revolutionary process, but simply from a new fabrication method. Philippe Rerat was not prepared to reveal any more on the subject. *«We have been looking for a long time and this is the first time we have come up with a far reaching solution.»*
The results from the test bed having been confirmed in private testing, Carbone Industrie was confident enough to introduce the new product at Monza.

△ *Michael Schumacher, his wheels locked. In Argentina, the German's win was Carbone Industrie's 200th Formula 1 victory from 229 starts.*

In Monza, Michael Schumacher's win owed a great deal to the new material introduced that day by Carbone Industrie, solely for the Ferraris, as the company did not have enough parts to supply its other teams. *«This new material meant the cars could start heavier and therefore only need to stop once to take on fuel,»* revealed Rerat. *«It is a new friction material which represents real progress on the wear front. Thanks to that, we are perfectly prepared for 1999, because then we will be able to supply it to all our teams.»*
The new product was discovered by accident during research carried out at Villeurbanne. *«The science of frictions is not a precise study and therefore our development programme for new products is pretty much empirical. Our researchers try and think of new concepts, new manufacturing procedures and then they try them out. Thanks to collecting all this data from the test bench and validating it on the track, we are beginning to have a better understanding of the subject.»*
But even if the company has the situation under control on the wear front now, development will not stop there. Carbone Industrie has now provided Scuderia Ferrari with clutch housings, which were successfully used for the first time at the Argentinian Grand Prix. *«We have been working on clutches since the Eighties,»* recalled Philippe Rerat. *«But since then, speed of revolution has increased and the parts were breaking. But in this case also, since we have used a new material, there are no more problems.»*
Endlessly developing and fine tuning its products and its manufacturing methods, Carbone Industrie seems well armed to set off to conquer more F1 world titles.

And now on the roads

◁ *After its successes on the race track, the French company Carbone Industrie is now looking at being equally successful on the roads. Here, a close up on the discs of an RUF CTR2.*

Carbone Industrie had been cultivating this project for a long time, notably with Venturi.
Now, the idea has become reality and it is possible to get road cars fitted with Carbone Industrie brake discs - in this case, the Porsche 911 modified by German tuning company RUF. *«To arrive at this agreement, we had to develop a carbon brake caliper as well as solve numerous other technical problems,»* related Philippe Rerat. In fact, to ensure compatibility of calipers, discs and pads, Carbone Industrie had to make all these individual components to create CIBS -Carbone Industrie Braking System.
The development of the calipers first of all caused something of a rift between Carbone Industrie and AP and Brembo, a problem which has since been solved. *«We wanted to move forward in this area. That is part of our company strategy,»* concluded Rerat. On sale for the first time at the Mondial de L'Automobile, it should be a big sales success.

The making of a Peugeot engine

The men from Vélizy

by Dominique Caussanel
«Drapeau à Damier»

Like all perfect structures which evolve in Formula 1, Peugeot Sport, based at Velizy, around ten kilometres from the Prost Grand Prix factory, has a development department which beavers away in secrecy and solitude away from the hubbub of the grands prix themselves, working on the Peugeot V10 of the future.

Over 110 engineers and mechanics thus concentrate all their expertise on the engines that Olivier Panis and Jarno Trulli will use in 1999 and 2000, to uphold the honour of France's only Formula 1 team. Their job keeps them away from the tracks, but it is their engines which sit behind the drivers.

Dominique Cavazzi has the height and appearance of a basket ball player and captain, planning his team's next move. Like all high flying engineers, he is a cross between student and pupil. The professor invokes his theories while the student always wants to know more. To work on a Formula 1 engine is to be permanently at the cutting edge of the limits of research. For this man, charged with the development of the engine, there are two main aims; power and reliability.

Whatever modifications are carried out to the engines, the latest version has to be more powerful and at least as reliable as its previous incarnation. Cavazzi is responsible for Peugeot's F1 research department, the test beds, the quality control areas and the assembly. Once this sequence has validated a new evolution of the engine block it is passed on to Guy Audoux and the team. As it makes this move, the V10 becomes a star and the slightest hitch in its progress is carried out under the harsh spotlight of the media.

Storage room at Vélizy.

Unlike Cavazzi's team, Audoux and his men do their work out in the open and whether in testing or at a race, at circuits all over the world.

Dominique Cavazzi loves engine technology and he explained to us what decisions are involved in the creation and development of an F1 engine. «*We hold regular meetings with the specialist engineers and the project chiefs to discuss the best choices and solutions for the development of an engine. My role is like that of the conductor in an orchestra who must assist the best soloists in producing the best sound in the symphony. During these meetings, Formula 1 boss at Peugeot Sport, Jean-Pierre Boudy decides on the direction we should go in with our research. Given how long it takes to produce an engine, we have to work out a time scale long in advance and of course that is done in conjunction with Prost Grand Prix. Peugeot's involvement in Formula 1 followed on from its participation in endurance racing and the 905. We were forced to modify our original plan as the two disciplines meant different requirements from the engine. Since that time, we have moved on and made several changes, some of them because of changes to the regulations, for example the change from 3.5 to 3 litres. With the A14 engine, we entered into a phase of weight reduction and also pursued plans to make the unit more compact; a phase which continues today with the A16 and A18. The A20 will involve us in making another step forward in terms of the search for more power, weight and size reduction. It is a natural tendency, common to all motor manufacturers, who even adopt these principles for their road cars. The Prost Grand Prix engineers want this type of work done as it is easier to integrate such an engine with their chassis and allows for more efficient aerodynamics. The engine is one of the main sources of power on a Formula 1 car, but it is also the one the engineers would like to be as neat and unnoticeable as possible. It is not enough to have a good engine to win. It must integrate perfectly with the chassis so that the car can use its performance in the optimal situation. That is why there are almost as many staff working at Velizy, exclusively on the engine, as there are in the Prost team. Today, because of all the means at our disposal, we know it is almost impossible to come up with something really new in the field of engine technology and the rules laid down by the sport's organisers limit and prevent us from building the ultimate engine. Most commonly, in our research with F1 engines, we try to find new materials and the evolution of those we already use, or the adaption of technologies already in use elsewhere to the area of Formula 1. A Formula 1 engine is built to survive for a few hundred kilometres, during which time it must survive some very heavy loads. We are always evolving near the limits of what is known, working with computers capable of ever more complicated calculations. Naturally, we call on our experience, but also we take these computers to new and higher levels. Each time we start to look at an engine evolution, we put our simulation process to work to help the specialist engineers in collaboration with the research labs in order to define a choice. These studies allow us to reduce mass and friction and especially to ensure that parts will not break later. Over the years, the experience we have acquired is blended with the data from our simulation tools, thus providing a panoply of scientific solutions which will improve our future developments. We are not a pure research and development department in the sense that we have*

General view of Peugeot Sport's offices.

a target of supplying F1 engine. This means that while looking far into the future, we must also remain realistic. We also have to solve problems which occur during a grand prix which means we have to react very, very quickly to solve them. Our work is a mixture of empiricism and pragmatism in the field of science. We produce between two and three development engines per month and around 80 engines to be used in a season. Our development engines only ever get as far as the test bed, before being stripped down and examined. That way we can move on by looking at what the weak points were.»

Dominique Cavazzi's team lives a step or two ahead of the grands prix and the outline of the engine for the year 2000 is already on the computer screens and it is in an office run by Patrick Le Mens that non-existent V10s gradually take shape in the bowels of the computers. *«In this department, everything is defined around the work of specialist engineers. These are the people whose creations are then taken up by Jean-Pierre Boudy and Dominique Cavazzi and check the ideas are coherent. The designers here are at their disposal to give form to their concepts and the calculation department is there to validate their ideas before moving onto the costly prototype stage.*

We are there to try various simulations on all the possible design of parts before moving onto the test bed stage. In order to ensure the engine will mate perfectly with the chassis, we have the same equipment as Prost Grand Prix, so that we can see our engine fit into the chassis. This means that we can resolve any fitting problems before we try and physically mate the two units.

All this work is done in far less time and with far less money than in the days before all this simulation equipment was available. Now, three different routes can be tried out overnight, when in the past, the need to build prototypes meant this same process could take around ten months.

Our role is therefore to make available all our know-how through all the tools available to us within the PSA group, in order to achieve the best possible results. Our philosophy is that the engine should be an «accessory» which should thanks to its dimensions and weight, be easily forgotten when it comes to designing the chassis around it. When we go to a grand prix, we do not so much see our engine race as the whole Prost-Peugeot car, because our engine is only built for a team to fit into a chassis.»

Thus every part of the engine goes through a simulation test programme before being finally made for real. Of the 3240 parts which make up a Formula 1 engine, some are only used once, no matter what condition they are in. But the majority have a longer life than that. Therefore each part is examined by the metrology department under the control of Christian Noiret.

In the quality control department, the technicians follow the path of the engine parts and note their life span on computer. In a very well isolated laboratory, where all the most sophisticated measuring instruments are kept, each part is checked one at a time on a regular basis. After being used, each engine is completely stripped down and the puzzle is carefully kept in a box. These checking procedures make it possible to control reliability and to work out which parts on an engine can be re- used. Not included in this process are the parts which, automatically, are only used just the once.

Those which will be used again are checked geometrically as well as having their

Numerical simulation of the engine's air intake.

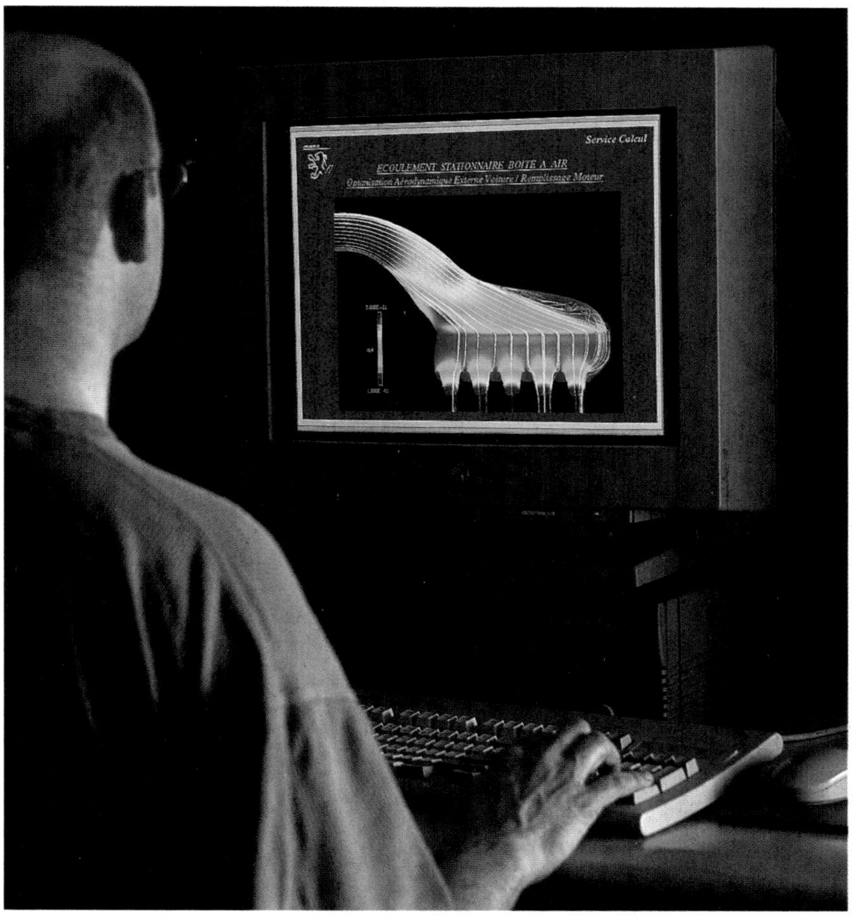

Technical meeting at Vélizy.

age noted. Christian Noiret explains to us what his department does to the V10 engine on a daily basis.

«Here we never see a complete engine! They come to us in bits, cleaned and filed in order. With around one hundred engines in circulation during the course of the year, engine building and dismantling takes place about twice as often as that over the same period. In our department, we check about one engine per day... To completely dismantle an engine takes about two days. In order to rebuilt it, the build shop, run by Frederic Coisnon has to count on five days. To check everything, it takes three people half a day. The first controller goes through the classic range of measurement, while the second concentrates on checking for cracks on the cast pieces. A development technician completes the trio and checks the entire the dismantling procedure.»

Each of these reports is attached to the dossier of each part along with its drawing. The parts are then stored by computer. *«All the data acquired is integrated in a data basis which allows us to trace the reliability of all the parts. On some key engine parts, like heads, camshafts, rings and so on, we can log their progress down to the last kilometre.»*

The engine/gearbox test bench. A web of connections to the various computers.

It is the sort of work that requires discipline more usually found in a colony of ants, a trait found in other areas of Peugeot Sport. Before an engine is assembled, each part is measured to check it conforms to its drawing. Given the ever growing complexity of some of these parts, the measuring equipment has to be ever more sophisticated.

«We have a numeric imagery test bed, which lets us photograph each defective part,» continued Christian Noiret. *«The numerical document is kept with the part's technical dossier. The most sophisticated measuring device is a three dimensional one which has a measuring head which actually scans the part in one continuous movement while another piece of equipment is used solely for volumetric measurements using lasers.»*

Although not strictly parts, the different joints used in the engine also have to be tested and checked. For these elements, a non-contact measuring device is used to measure the joints «at rest.» Noiret has a whole host of other very complex machines at his disposal, although some still rely on the good old eyesight of a man operating the equipment. *«The principle is simple. Each metal part which is susceptible to cracking is plunged in a bath containing a fluorescent liquid. Through capillary action, this liquid enters any cracks. The part is then washed. While it is drying, the surface tension means the liquid emerges slowly from the crack, instantly showing the fault in the part.»*

Noiret's department is also responsible for finding out the cause of any engine failures, rather like the work of a coroner's office, although Christian Noiret prefers the measuring side of his work to this performance of engine autopsy.

In another building, Lionel Greck runs all the department's test beds. The roles of the different test beds are many. Some check ignition, others test all the various pumps, oil, water and so on, while some control the flow of air through the engine. Every single V10 takes its first steps on a test bed. At Peugeot Sport, Lionel Greck has some traditional test beds, others are for frictional work while others still are for dynamic testing. It is these last two that are used to test the V10, fitted to the gearbox in race simulation conditions.

The test beds are in constant use, checking the engines before the grands prix. Other benches are used for future development. Performance testing or validating work, Lionel Greck, like all the men of Velizy, loves it all and talks about «his» engines.

«We are charged with measuring every single aspect of the V10 in dynamic conditions. Our aim is to reproduce situations, while at the same time thinking about new mea-

suring possibilities. When an engine is on the test bed, we have to «listen» to it with as many sensors as we can use, without the number getting to the point where they interfere with the actual measurements. Jean-Pierre Boudy and Dominique Cavazzi suggest different programmes to us and we bring our experience in materials analysis to bear. At the same time, we also compare the performance levels of different engines. Furthermore, we have to be on our toes and keep an eye on current testing to anticipate any possible engine failures, in order to come up with better analyses. This way, we can call on our own research and development department to keep improving our test equipment. I was in at the birth of Peugeot's first Formula 1 V10 engine, the A3 and today, when looking at the progress made with our new A18, we take encouragement from the fact we can still improve a great deal.»

Far removed from the race tracks, Lionel Greck can bring an almost clairvoyant expertise to the situation.

«It is true that the engine alone does not determine the performance of the team. However, if targets are not met, it is usually the engine builder who is asked to come up with something better. This is because the chassis designers go about their work taking the engine very much into consideration. Each team has its own engine manufacturer, who can no longer settle for being a simple supplier of horsepower. The idea of a technical partnership is a real one. Apart from engine testing, our work at the end of this season is more involved with the entire engine/transmission assembly of the future AP02 rather than just the engine. It is the only way for us to move forward with our engines and the cars that use them.» On the test bed, computers and electronics are part of everyday life. Research is not simply restricted to the mechanical side of the engine, but also takes in all the electrical aspects, which are getting ever more important in the development of a Formula 1 engine these days. All the effort that goes into producing the wonderful mechanical components of a Peugeot V10, would be as nothing without the constant development of the electrical and computer side of the business. Guy Micard is the man responsible for this side of Peugeot-Sport's activities.

His department configures the electronic systems which allow the drivers to get the most out of the engines. For several years now, the F1 driver has had paddles fitted on the back of the steering wheel and other devices, which replaces the traditional gear lever and other vital functions. The department is divided into four sectors, each with a specific task to do: on board electronics, hydraulics and automation and computer developments.

Peugeot Sport works closely with TAG Electronic Systems as far as the computerisation side is concerned.

Getting rid of bugs is a big part of the work and is on-going throughout the process. *«It is a question of security and reliability. For example, it might well have been a bug which caused Michael Schumacher's start line problem in Japan,»* explained Guy Micard.

Another job of this department is to adapt the engine characteristics to the driving style of a particular driver. *«Contrary to popular belief, a driver does not have to get used to the electronics of an engine.*

It is in fact the other way around. We have to configure our engines to suit the driver's style as he must have final control. Jarno Trulli does not use the throttle in the same way as Olivier Panis and so he uses a different set up on the fly by wire system which supplies the air fuel mixture in relation to the angle of the throttle pedal. The electronics are just there to help the driver stay concentrated on his actual driving and car control. Only this way can the drivers get the most out of the engines with which we provide them.»

Just like the mechanical parts, the electronic side also has to undergo a rigorous trial by test bed, as Guy Micard explained. *«There are both race and development versions of these computers. Often in race conditions, the electronics are disturbed by their surroundings and all the electronic messages that are everywhere to be found at a race track. While mechanical parts might have a life which can be measured in kilometres, the electronics can suffer deterioration after certain periods of time.*

△
Assembling the Peugeot V10.

All the connectors, sensors and so forth are computer controlled and we aim to put as much data as possible in the on-board control units in order to give the drivers as much help as possible in controlling the engine, gearbox and clutch. Of course, the more complex the computers, the harder they are to check. This is very important in terms of the rules laid down by FIA, which is fighting to ensure the legality of the sport.»

Jean-Pierre Boudy, the boss of Peugeot-Sport's F1 department knows there is still a vast area to be investigated in terms of future technologies.

«The future evolution of the engines lies in better centring of the masses and making the whole engine/gearbox unit more compact, but at the same time we will have to work on increasing power output. That could mean a loss of reliability and it is this area where we can make the biggest gains in the future. Basically, there will be nothing revolutionary and it is in these different areas that we must concentrate our research.

Of course, our main aim at the moment is to improve our results and once everything is well established and that we have gained in reliability, then we will be able to step up our evolution programmes. If all goes well in this area in 1999, we can foresee three evolutions of our A18 V10 instead of two for the A16 which we had this year. Our ultimate aim is to get the A20 up and running as soon as possible.»

Tri-dimensional check of an engine size.
◁◁

Real worlds of virtual design

by Dominique Caussanel
«Drapeau à Damier»

Formula 1 has for long conveyed the image of people working in seclusion, cloistered in their universe, isolated from the rest of the world by an often emperical and small scale technic, made up of tricks and a lot of know-how.
But one notices today that this circle is attempting to use the most forefront design technics to meet the requirements of safety and performance imposed by a more and more *«merciless»* regulation and competition.
Alain Prost is part of those who know that in Formula 1, nothing must be left to chance and that the tools which must help engineers to design the best one-seater are an integral part of the success of a in the forefront team.
This is why, as from the creation of the Prost Grand Prix team, its new boss has seeked the support of partners of international fame, capable of offering him the most homed products to succeed in his challenges. As from the creation of Prost Grand Prix, on February 14th, 1997, Alain Prost has clearly defined what his vision of a technological partnership was: *«I wish to have along my side firms which have an international vocation and a global vision capable of providing my team with the best technologies, but also the largest competences, all of that in a spirit of full cooperation. With Dassault Systemes and IBM, I knew that I would have two of the biggest names in the world of industrial computing to help me design entirely my racing cars with the CATIA software.»*
CATIA is a a very powerful sofware, running more than 113 tools which can design and develop parts or group of parts, assemble them, make them evolve and then test them by computer before they have to be manufactured and tested physically. It was not so long ago that the design of a new car would imperatively have to follow a set process which would often be spread over a period of three or four years, with no guarantee of avoiding teething problems. With the CATIA software, engineers can do the same job in a matter of months and what is more, this time, total success is guaranteed.
The CATIA 3D Digital Mock-up allows for an exchange of information between the original research and development departments and the production workshops, so they can pass information between them simultaneously. Together, they can create and test the quality and compatibility of whole assembles and thousands of components. Essentially, the strenght of the CATIA system is to put those responsibile for one single element of a project in permanent contact with those overseeing the entire programme. Each part designed with CATIA can be integrated virtually into its environment to check that it fits properly, rather like a piece of jigsaw puzzle. CATIA means there is no longer the need to actually build a model until the final stage of its conception. CATIA therefore abolishes the most time consuming steps in the creation of a model and allows each step of the creation process of a product to be fully modified or to evolve it in a new direction or get it to suit the market requirements.

Realistic rendering of Prost-Peugeot AP01 car. CATIA - Prost Grand Prix document.

3D wireframe design of the Peugeot AP-01 car. CATIA - Prost Grand Prix document.

CATIA and Formula 1

Today, one of the objectives of the partnership between Dassault Systemes and Prost Grand Prix is to produce the first ever virtual model of an F1 car. Therefore, in the design offices of Prost Grand Prix at Guyancourt in the Paris suburb, Prost project leader and chassis designer, Loïc Bigois is assisted by around twenty engineers, who elaborate at CATIA stations the Formula 1 car of tomorrow. For these men who work with CATIA in the present, the CAD/CAM tool and computer simulation are part of those tools necessary for the development of their projects. They spend their days with computers which are already reaching out to the future. Taking advantage of the latest versions and developments of CATIA first they are considered as privileged development partners, to validate the technologies to be integrated into the CATIA software.
The objective of signing an agreement with Prost Grand Prix was to bring CATIA up to speed in the world of Formula 1 and to enable other teams to take advantage of future CATIA developments. Therefore, Prost Grand Prix is regarded as a development team, just as McLaren is regarded as Bridgestone's top team for the approvement of the new tyres.
Bernard Dudot, Prost Grand Prix Technical Manager has, as from his arrival, given a new dimension to this partnership: *«With the building of our ultra-modern new factory of Guyancourt, we want to accept the challenge of the Digital Enterprise. This will is renforced by the determination of our partners and our common vision of making the CATIA Digital Mock-up the center of our firm information system. this will allows us to manage and control the access to all quantitative and qualitative data related to the about 3000 parts which today make up a Formula 1. This includes the geometrical data such as 3D models, the scale drawings and assembles, as well as the lists of parts and data supporting processes such as projects management, manufacturing, maintenance and operating. Our processes shall then be optimized and we shall be able to design more quickly and earlier in the season our future cars».*

Realistic rendering of the Prost-Peugeot AP01 gear-box. CATIA - Prost Grand Prix document.

With Prost Grand Prix, Dassault Systemes's aim is to adapt the virtual modelling to the manufacturing process of a F1. Other technical aspects are on the agenda, but they must remain confidential for the time being. As much, for example with Mercedes, who is a major car manufacturer using CATIA, the customer gives information about his working and research methods and asks the Dassault Systemes development engineers to help him optimise his system.

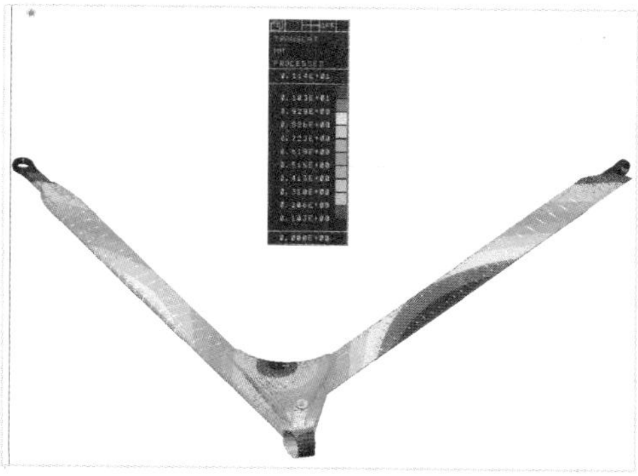

F1 is a new world for CATIA, especially in terms of time cycle. The production cycles related to the world of competition at highest level have nothing to do with those of the traditional car manufacturers. If CATIA can adapt to the F1 rythm, then it will become even more efficient for its customers of the road car business who are taking a close interest in this new partnership type at the level of F1.
Further to its managers' will, Prost Grand Prix wants to be a small business before being a team. The aim of this firm is to manufacture a car which must be the best. At Prost, management is installing almost industrial working methods which must match the realities of F1 and the sporting challenge it represents. This mentality is completely different to that of the F1 teams in the Eighties and early Nineties when the F1 manufacturer was essentially an assembler of added various components to which he brought his experience know- how in order to make a difference.
At Prost Grand Prix, the CATIA data of Digital Mock-up are precious for management and planning of the manufacturing, sub-construction, the purchases and other aspects relying on the qualitative and quantitative information they contain. Today Prost is a car industry in «*miniature*». The time elapsed between each evolution of a part of the car must must be as short as possible. Once the season is underway, this deciding time factor is the gap between two grands prix, hence the interest in virtual modelling. Today, with this system, one can avoid the long and costly creation of a prototype model each time its part is redesigned. The digital programme allows to validate its evolution directly at the design level, on the computer. This entire digitization programme already exists with CATIA at BMW. The fundamental difference between these two users which Prost Grand Prix and BMW comes from the industrial challenge related to the time scales specific to F1. The Prost Grand Prix engineers quickly understood the advantages of using Digital Mock-up. At the start of the '98 season, mechanics spent more than half a day trying unsuccessfully to get two parts to fit together. No one had realized that this task was impossible and that the only solution was to modify one of the parts to get a perfect fit. With this virtual modelling, the designer would have immediately spotted in 3 D, at the drawing stage, the smallest defect and thus saving valuable time and the gain in efficiency would have been immediate. Such examples are commonplace in the design departments of all major manufacturers or within the workshops of F1 teams. To convince oneself, one has to look at the problems Ferrari encountered at the start of the season with its exhaust system. The same pattern on an assembly line of production cars was punished by a two to three weeks delay wich has been written off the deficit colum of the project books. Other teams are already interested in this concept of virtual modelling. Prost Grand Prix is well aware of that, but, thanks to its partnership with Dassault Systemes, it knows that it is one step ahead of his competitors.

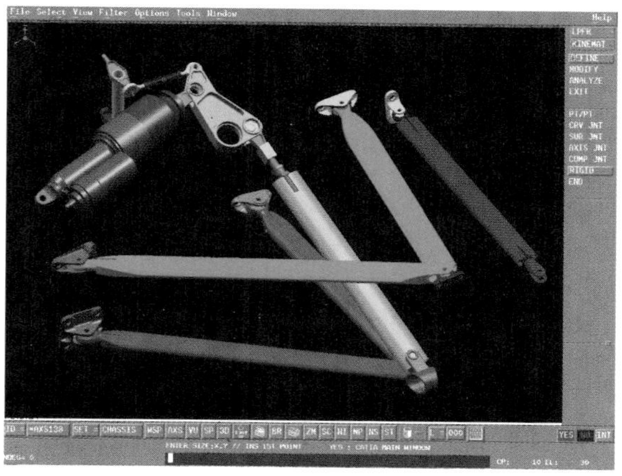

◁

CATIA screen capture showing the front suspension of Prost-Peugeot AP01, all the distinc elements are shown in different colors.
CATIA - Prost Grand Prix document.

◁◁

CATIA screen capture - Infrastructure Analysis Tool - showing the computing of resistance on the front suspension wishbone of the Prost-Peugeot AP01. Hot colors mean the most stressed areas.
CATIA - Prost Grand Prix document.

When Osamu Goto joined the team with the special responsibility of looking after the Ferrari engines, Petronas gave the green light to go ahead with the production of Sauber's own engine, the Petronas Formula 1 V10 and a four cylinder Petronas destined for the Malaysian motor industry.
On the engine manufacturing side, it has been seen, CATIA has been used at Peugeot Sport, but also at Renault Sport for more than seven years and is actually working on the development of F1 engines which are currently on the grid under the various names of Mecachrome, Mugen-Honda, Playlife and Supertec for 1999.
But F1 is not the only favourite field of CATIA. Another queen category, the sports prototypes producing cars even faster that the Formula 1, require a technology in all points similar to the Prost Grand Prix or Ferrari one-seaters. An independant manufacturer, Courage Competition based in Le Mans, has now used its partnership with

Realistic rendering of Courage C51 Le Mans prototype car.
CATIA - Courage Compétition document.
◁

CATIA and Motorsport

In the field of motor sport today, CATIA is used at Prost Grand Prix, but also Ferrari, Sauber, TWR-Arrows, Renault Sport, Peugeot Sport, Costworth, Honda and Yamaha. At each of these manufacturers, the programmes are very different, especially at Sauber and Costworth where the installation of new technologies is closely linked to the engine side. (The English engine manufacturer commercialises its own working methods under two identities, Racing and Engineering). As far as Sauber is concerned, CATIA is involved at two levels, the chassis for the team side and the engines.

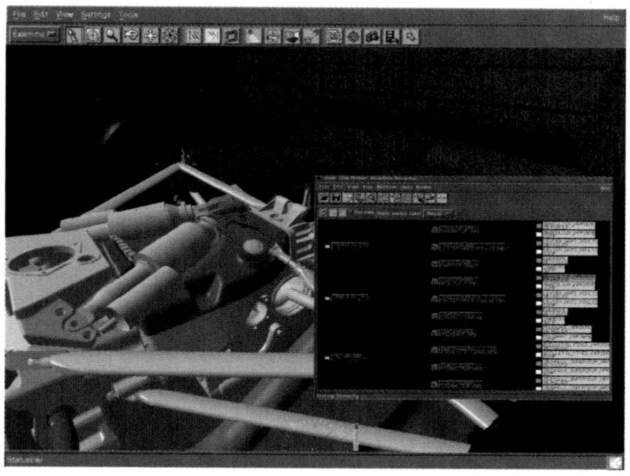

CATIA screen capture of 3D navigation in the Prost-Peugeot AP01 digital mock-up. The window indicates the logical links between parts and assemblies, where are located the pushroad elements higlighted in orange color.
CATIA - Prost Grand Prix document .
◁

CATIA et la Formule 1

The F1 world has known CATIA for a long time and today the references make CATIA the leader in this field: 30% of the chassis manufacturers and 60% of the engine manufacturers.

Chassis : Ferrari, Sauber, Prost, Arrows

Engines : Ferrari, Peugeot, Renault - Mécachrome, Mugen-Honda, Yamaha.

Without taking into account the equipment fitters such as Brembo, Carbone Industrie, Bosch, Goodyear, Bridgestone, etc.. and in matching up the uses of CATIA between chassis and engines, one notices that almost 70% of the F1 cars run with CATIA on board!

And the future could even announce a reinforcement of this presence of CATIA in F1! To be continued...

Realistic rendering of Chrysler Viper. CATIA - CHRYSLER CORPORATION DOCUMENT.

CATIA for five years to manufacture its cars which run at the 24 Hours of Le Mans. It is, in fact, historically speaking, the first partnership developed by Dassault Systemes with a motor race team. Today, thanks to in

HIGH TECHNOLOGY

«A Formula 1 takes more after a plane than after a car» says Loic Bigois, in charge of development at Prost Grand Prix.

In this industry, jobs and technologies are among the most in the forefront of progress. A Formula 1 is made up for 80% of its volume of composite materials and for 50% of its weight in metal parts or casting (Aluminium Magnesium, Beryllium).

the forefront technology he uses and in which the four CATIA stations he owns are totally part, Yves Courage can give a new dimension to his team, thanks to the agreement signed with the Japanese manufacturer Nissan which is taking a great interest in the methods set up at Courage with CATIA. Another star of the 24 Hours of Le Mans and last winner up to date is Porsche with its impressive GTI, also designed in less than six months for the first one, with CATIA within the German research departments of Stuttgart; and, while we are talking about GT, why not talk of one of the monsters that make more than one Le Mans spectator dream, the Dodge Viper, in fact a pure Chrysler origin, straight out from the Americans wild imagination.

Real nose and fwings of the Prost-Peugeot AP01 car, 100% carbon composite made.

Indeed, Chrysler appears as avant-garde in the world of the car industry. It is the first, thanks to its optimum use of the CATIA softwares, to have reduced the design costs by 10% and is in a position to gain as much on its production costs with the installation, not only of the virtual modelling, but also of the virtual factory. The Detroit firm has, indeed, managed to totally integrate its processes of production of the virtual modelling. Today it uses the computing tools of the Dassault Systemes (CATIA, CCPLANT, CATWEB, ENOVIA and Deneb) to design even the factory which will be used to produce its cars, its assembly lines, the tools, the programming of the welding robots, etc..

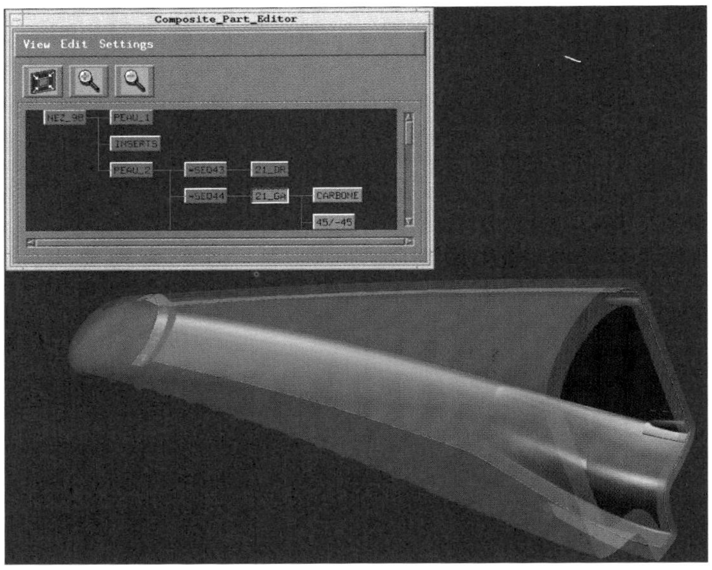

CATIA screen capture- Generative Composite Covering Tool - for the design of the Prost-Peugeot AP01 nose CATIA - PROST GRAND PRIX DOCUMENT.

Competition, catalyst of the motor industry

Two worlds having nothing in common at first, but which use the same tools to always go further in performance. A F1 constitutes a real technological laboratory for all the car industry in the chassis field as well as in engines and equipments. The technics and materials used are probably those which will be used on all production cars in the years to come, anti-skidding system, sequential gearboxes, active suspensions, new materials (alloys, composites). One understands better why the perfect knowledge of these new technics allows CATIA to adapt in order to offer the manufacturers the tools and forefront process to implement them To reach its aims of total digitization of the F1 it manufactures, Prost Grand Prix must have in a close future at disposal around thirty CATIA stations. At PSA, CATIA has been present with Peugeot, before being used at Peugeot Sport.

With numerous manufacturers, CATIA has been chosen for its capacities of entire integration of the various functionalities of its range, which allow the realization

DASSAULT SYSTEMES, IBM AND CATIA

Dassault Systemes is world leader on the markets of XAO softwares and technical data management systems of the new generation (PDM II).

CATIA-CADAM Solutions and *Deneb,* digital factory enterprise, address the process-oriented CAD/CAM/CAE market. Thanks to a unique strategic partnership, the ***CATIA-CADAM Solutions*** are marketed and supported worldwide by IBM. This partnership is now extended to the new generation data magement systems (PDMII)

SolidWorks, subsidiary of Dassault Systemes, addresses the design-centric market. The firm develops and markets mechanical design softwares on Windows and has a dedicated distribution channel.

In the network computing environment, the ***CATWEB*** product line which leans on the Java-based technology, offers a graphic window on the native product data.

On the market of the Product development management (PDM II), ***ENOVIA Corp.***, subsidiary of Dassault Systemes, offers two lines of products, ***ENOVIAVPM*** and ***ENOVIAPM***, which provide a new multi-CAD collaborative and inovative environment for the virtual product and process modeling and management across the extended enterprise.

www.dsweb.com www.deneb.com
www.catia.ibm.com www.solidworks.com
www.enovia.com

Formula 1 coordination : jean-marc_galea@ds-fr.com

of a project from its design to its manufacturing and its maintenance in operation. In fact, these manufacturers have chosen to continue developing their ties with CATIA and have asked the engineers of Dassault Systemes for a new rythm of development of CATIA. From a software version each two years CATIA today brings out three versions per year, while products which had attempted to establish themselves on this fast expanding CADCAM market, have disappeared totally or in part. The results, for CATIA and its customers have exceeded all expectations. A design operation on a Peugeot gearbox which would take 200 hours of calculation at the beginning of the '90 now requires less than 10 hours.

A study carried out over the past eighteen months, shows that CATIA has become a standard in the world of car industry.

CATIA originated in the aeronautical industry and the first company to use the virtual modelling was Dassault

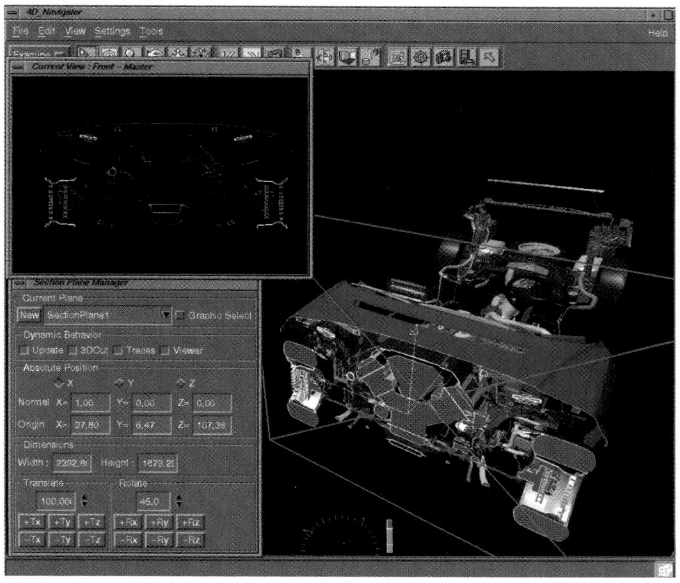

Aviation with the Falcon 2000. About ten years ago, Boeing and Dassault Aviation were leaders in the field of Digital Mock-up, until the Canadian firm Bombardier caught up and passed them, going ever further in the digitilization of its projects.

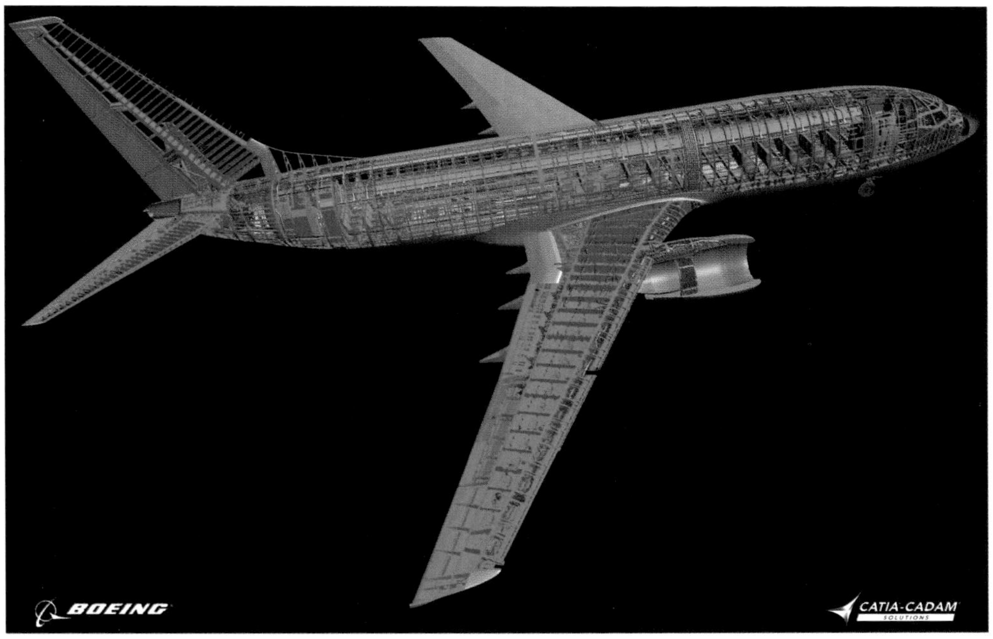

This was the spur which promoted Boeing and Dassault Aviation to redouble their efforts and they came out with a new work concept which integrates three fundamental stages in the establishment of digital systems:

- the Digital Mock-up of the product associating product and process
- the digital manfucaturing integrating directed production technics
- the improvement in dividing and exchanging data between the various teams of the manufacturer and his partners

These three steps of digital design constitute the basis of the precepts of the Digital Enterprise which Dassault Systemes offers today to manufacturers to reach their optimum production.
In this way Boeing has created and assembled 700.000 parts which make up the new 777 in a 100% virtual manner. This new way of working is that which today all car manufacturers wish setting up.
In the Digital Enterprise advocated by Dassault Systemes through the CATIA SOLUTIONS, the life cycle of a product may be consulted at any moment.
The engineer-designer permanently follows the evolution of his product and makes it live in its virtual environment by simulations which exceed reality. He can even go and explore places unaccessible to the human eye.
The power of CATIA allows to enter inside a set of parts and to validate on the screen its functionalities by all the concerned corporations, from the designer to the manufacturer, what is more if they are not at the same place. Indeed digitization of all data allows to exchange information throughout the world thanks to the Internet.
The CATWEB product line from Dassault Systemes offers the possibility for a person far from the factory, to check the good running of a project, or the kinematics of a landing gear.

Dassault Systemes and the Technological Partnership

Dassault Systemes exploits this partnership in many ways :

- External : Prost Grand Prix opens its doors wide to Dassault Systemes. Not only does the CATIA Solutions logo appear in all the team environment: carbodies, teams trucks, pits, overalls of drivers and mechanics. But Prost Grand Prix also allows Dassault Systemes to associate its customers, Business Partners, consultants and journalists to this adventure inviting them to visit the Guyancourt factory and to take part in the private trial sessions, or even, apotheosis, to a Grand Prix. Therefore Dassault Systemes has been present in 7 Grand Prix this year. Immersed in the heart of the sports event, the guests then apprehend perfectly the technological stakes allowing to reach those extraordinary performances. On each Grand Prix, a demonstration of CATIA advanced Digital Mock-up solutions illustrates in concrete terms the tools used to design and manufacture this race one-seater.
- Internal : This partnership is also a source of motivation and pride for the Dassault Systemes developers. Indeed, the latters have the possibility of illustrating in an extremely concrete and exciting way the mathematical algorithms they develop. Our aid enginneers and assigned to Prost Grand Prix may also acquire a know-how and unique competences concerning methodologies, processes and stakes of this industry, to have all the CATIA products benefit from it.

The mechanical engineer will be directly able from his Laptop PC, to return from the race pits the information gathered during a trial session, concerning the part to modify for the next Grand Prix, in that way saving an always precious time for his team.
Prost Grand Prix new design methods and processes already show their worth, with the promising trials of the APO1-B car, a laboratory car which was at Suzuka for the last Grand Prix of 1998. The next Prost-Peugeot APO2 without doubt will benefit from this technological revolution which the CATIA virtual modelling is.
Lets bet that we will have the opportunity to hear about it as from the start of the Formula 1 season of 1999, which looks exciting for Prost Grand Prix and Dassault Systemes.
F1, high tech software, two industries which require excellence,reactivity, creativity and the same goldsmith know-how.

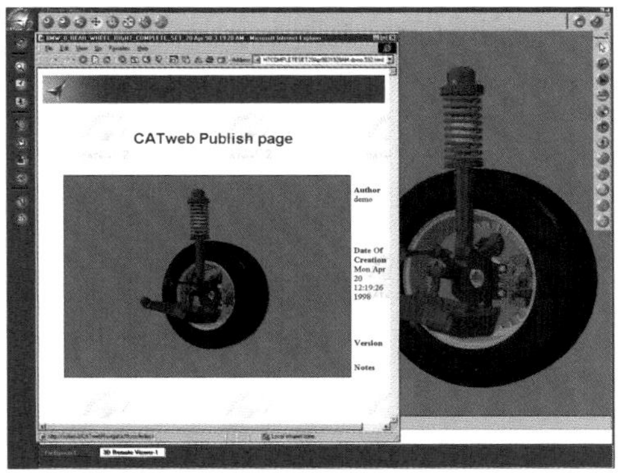

◁ *CATIA screen capture of 4D Navigator Tool in the digital mock-up of BMW car with 3D sectioning. The plan materialized by the red frame shows the place of the cutting section. The contours of this section appears in real-time in a window, as the engineer moves the plane with the computer mouse.*
CATIA - BMW DOCUMENT .

◁ *Full digital mock-up of the Boeing 737.*
CATIA - BOEING COMMERCIAL AIRPLANE DOCUMENT .

Navigation through internet inside the CATIA digital mock-up with CATWEB
DOCUMENT CATIA -
◁◁

Dassault Systemes guests in front of the Prost Grand Prix pits during the Luxemburg Grand Prix at Nürburgring '98.
◁

Jim Clark, March, 24th 1936 – April 7th 1968

Portrait of a remarkable champion

by Jacques Vassal
«Auto Passion»

On 7th April 1968 motor racing lost one of its greatest masters, along with its last illusions of innocence and invulnerability. Not only was Jim Clark a great driver, skilful and imbued with sang-froid and thought by all to be almost invincible, he was also a great champion and a great man.

On that morning, it was raining and cold on the Hockenheim circuit in Germany. That Sunday, Jim Clark should have been at Brands Hatch for the BOAC 500 where he was to give the Alan Mann Ford Cosworth F3L prototype its maiden outing. But Mann had not confirmed their agreement in writing and Clark, scrupulous to the last decided to drop the project.
He was still tied to Team Lotus of course, so he flew his plane to Germany where he joined his old friend and team mate Graham Hill for the F2 race.
They were driving Lotus 48s with 1600cc Ford Cosworth engines and the cars were painted in the same red, white and gold Gold Leaf colours of their new sponsor as the 49 in Formula 1. In practice, Clark had fuel supply problems and qualified in seventh spot, behind the Matra MS 7s of Jean-Pierre Beltoise and eventual winner Henri Pescarolo.
On lap five of the first leg he was running eighth when, at the long corner in the forest, he started to swerve at over 250 km/h. Maybe it was a puncture or maybe because of a loss of power, the Lotus 48 of the double world champion was out of control. According to an eye witness on this part of the track where spectators were not permitted to stand, Clark seemed to have caught the slide for a moment but the car went the other way and even the best driver of his age could do nothing about it.
The fragile car left the track, hit a tree and broke up. The poor man died of fractures and internal injuries before he could be taken to hospital.
The death of Clark was a cruel blow felt by all the other drivers who had lost in him a friend and a role model and who had learnt that even the best in the world are not shielded from the risk of death. It was also a blow for the public, who shared his colleagues respect and affection mixed with admiration.
This brilliant young sportsman was not only a very good racing driver, he was also a champion who was the epitome of loyalty and honesty, both on and off the track.

Sheep and Latin

Jim Clark was a man of the Scottish countryside and was the son of a cattle and sheep farmer. James Clark his father owned a 400 hectare farm at Kilmany in Fife, between the Tay and Forth estuaries to the north and south respectively. The future world champion was born there on 4th March 1936, the last child and only boy in a family of four girls. Jim was only six when the family moved house. On one of his many trips to the cattle markets, his father found a farm in Edington Mains near Duns in Berwickshire. The farmer had already been thinking in the Borders, just a few kilometres north east of England. In May 1942 he bought the 300 hectares of grazing, 200 of crop and 80 of forest. The farmhouse would be home for a long time and for Jim until 1966.
Jim and his sister Betty, who was three and half years older went to primary school at Chirnside, the next village to Edington Mains and he went there on foot or by bicycle. Jim and his sisters were keen on sport; tennis in the summer, skating in winter and board games like Monopoly. As the only son, he also learnt how to look after the stock and sometimes went to market with his father, thus discovering a world where a man's word was his bond. After three years in Clifton Hall boarding school near Edinburgh, Jim went to Loretto in 1949, a private school with strict discipline, where uniforms were compulsory

JACQUES VASSAL, is a writer and a translator and also a confirmed Ferrari fan. He has been with the french history magazine "Auto-Passion" since 1989 for who he writes features, portraits and interviews of racing drivers. For this story, he made the trip to Scotland to meet those who had been close to Jim Clark.

◁
Clark was in the lead at the start of the 1964 Monaco Grand Prix, but a little knock resulted in a broken rear anti-roll bar on his Lotus-Climax, costing him the win in this race which strangely eluded him. He finished fourth, having adapted his driving style to suit the wounded car.

and each morning started with a cold bath. He was there four years.
His school friends remember a secretive boy, taciturn and independent who seemed to have few close friends. As a student, he made the grade, but no more, in all subjects, even though he later admitted to asking himself: «*What possible use could Latin be for a farmer.*» He was already talking about his passion for cars and as soon as he was old enough he spent the holidays driving around Edington Mains.
Once he boasted of having already driven at 90 mph, but his school chums refused to believe him.

Young farmer at the wheel

Jim displayed a precocious talent at the wheel. At nine, he was driving the humble paternal Austin Seven, at ten the farm tractors and at twelve, the heavy Alvis Speed Twenty. The young Clark, who was a small lad, had to first declutch, select first gear and let the clutch out without seeing over the dashboard, before jumping onto the bench seat and driving off using the hand throttle, which was a fortuitous fitting on the Alvis. One day, as he was reversing out of the garage, this throttle lever got caught in the young man's sleeve and the inevitable brick wall was waiting. The Alvis being a tough car and the wall being even tougher, Jim had no need to admit to this incident until several years later.
At the age of 16, Jim had to leave Loretto and his studies.
One after the other, his grandfather and uncle died and almost overnight, James Clark found himself with three farms to run. He roped his son in to help and put him in charge at Edington Mains. Jim was less than pleased to leave school but got on well in his new role. According to his sister Betty, he also liked getting re-acquainted with the tractor and his car. His passion for things mechanical continued to grow, as he subscribed to various magazines and joined the Ednam Young Farmers, who organised car gymkhanas. He met Ian Scott-Watson, another farmer's son, six years older than him who rallied an MG. Curiously, Jim Clark attended his first motor race, not in Scotland but in England, where a cousin took him to Brands Hatch. Back home, he came across the three C Type Jaguars of Ecurie Ecosse, whizzing down the Kelso road. He saw them race not long after in October 1952, a few miles from his home on the Charterhall circuit, a wartime airfield. That day, Giuseppe Farina, the 1950 world champion was driving in Formula 1 in a Thinwall Special. Also taking part were the Belgian Johnny Claes in a Talbot-Lago and Prince Bira at the wheel of an OSCA.
Ian Stewart, at the wheel of an Ecurie Ecosse C-type Jaguar won the sports car race. But more than the drivers, it was the cars and their engines which fascinated the young farmer.
In 1954, James Clark bought a Rover, leaving Jim the Sunbeam-Talbot MkIII. It only had 12,000 miles on the clock. It was his first ever car and he used it to take part in his first gymkhanas.

The Border Reivers driver

With friends from the Ednam Young Farmers club, renamed for the event, «Ecurie Agricole,» the young Clark took part in the Scottish International Rally in May 1955 as co-driver to his cousin Billy Potts. On a link section he took the wheel of the Austin Healey 100 and proceeded to stun its owner with his skill when he stuck to the back of another Healey which had just passed them. For the first time in his life, Jim had gone over the magical 100 mph. However, as Scott-Watson was keen to relate: «*as a navigator he was hopeless. He would read the map with it lying across the back seat, while he knelt on his seat reading the directions in the opposite direction!*»
Scott-Watson was in fact the first to spot Jim Clark's potential as a driver, who was starting to learn the skills of car control, sliding his Sunbeam around autocross tracks. Ian owned a little DKW Sonderklass with a two stroke engine which he entered in the Crimond race, near Aberdeen on Saturday 16th June 1956. Naturally, he took Clark with him «as a mechanic.» Actually, he had put Jim's name down as the driver. In practice, he was three seconds quicker than the car's owner.
Jim was persuaded to enter a handicap race for «prototype cars» and he finished last. All the same, Ian had such faith in him, that he packed in driving himself to devote his energies and his money to moving Jim's career along.
Clark had to overcome two obstacles: the objections of his parents, who felt racing was a waste of time and money, not counting the danger and then the-

Jim Clark and Colin Chapman enjoyed a perfect relationship. To such an extent that Clark refused all offers from other teams keen to steal him away from Team Lotus, while Chapman built several of his cars, most notably the Lotus 49, specifically to fit his shape!
▽

Jim Clark scored his fourth consecutive Belgian Grand Prix win at Spa Francorchamps in 1965. Here he shares the podium with a promising young compatriot, Jackie Stewart, who was making his Formula One debut in this event, finishing second in a B.R.M.

re was his own inhibition. Yes, Jim Clark lacked self confidence, something which lasted a long time. One of Scott-Watson's first jobs was to persuade his charge as to his own abilities.
Another task was to find some competitive machinery. To this end, Scott-Watson, along with old friend Jock McBain, himself an amateur driver and garage proprietor, relaunched the Border Reivers team, a banner under which they had both competed. This time the only driver would be Jim Clark. In 1957, Ian sold the DKW and bought a Porsche 1600 Super which Jim used to take his first major win.

From the farm to the circuits

In 1958, Jim Clark's status as a professional racing driver took off. He won the «Rest and be thankful» hillclimb in a Triumph TR2. This time, Scott-Watson with help from McBain, pulled off a coup in buying a «customer» Jaguar D-type which had raced the 1957 season in the hands of Henry Taylor (1st at Snetterton, 3rd at Spa) and put Jim in it.
He won 12 of the 20 races entered. When he had his first run in the car at Charterhall he was impressed with the power it put out, but he did more than just cope with the power and on his first outing in the Jaguar, he set a new lap record at an average speed of over 100 mph at Full Sutton in Yorkshire. The farm truck having broken down, Jim drove the Jag all the way to York, a distance of almost 300 km in a snowstorm.
Scott-Watson took the plunge and entered Jim in a GT race in the Porsche and in the Sports Car race in the Jaguar at Spa-Francorchamps in May. It was his first trip abroad and the 14 km track impressed him with its outline and its traps. He finished second in the 2 litre class in the GT race.
In the other race, he was up against stiff opposition: Masten Gregory and Archie Scott-Brown in Lister-Jaguars, Olivier Gendebien in a Ferrari Testa Rossa and Paul Frere in an Aston Martin DBR1. Jim made a cautious start and was lapped by Gregory. Clark considered packing it as he found the pace astounding. On the third lap, Scott-Brown went off in a heavy downpour just before the La Source hairpin where Richard Seaman died in 1939. The Lister caught fire and its unfortunate driver died a few hours later in hospital from his burns. Clark detested Spa, even though he would go on to win four consecutive grands prix there, including one in the pouring rain.
In the autumn of 1958, Scott-Watson organised a meeting to get Clark to try a Formula 2 Lotus 12 at Brands Hatch in front of constructor Colin Chapman and his drivers, Cliff Allison, Innes Ireland and Graham Hill.
Clark amazed everyone with his easy style and his lap times. Hill climbed into the 12 and although he beat his best time, he lost a wheel and crashed. Clark vowed never to get in a Lotus single seater again. He tried a GT Elite coupe and loved it. Scott-Watson bought an Elite and entered Clark in the Boxing Day meeting. Jim almost beat Chapman himself at the wheel of another Elite.
The constructor-engineer vowed to have Clark drive for Team Lotus one day.

The early grands prix

1958 Scottish champion, thanks to his wins in the Jaguar, his career moved ever upward the following year.
Until now, he had regarded racing as a great pastime. He always felt he could return to farming, which is what he did during the week anyway.
The problems was the increasing number of days he had to be away and the greater distances he had to travel to get to the races. Eventually he had to dig out the accounts to prove to his family that even if his racing was not making a profit, he was at least doing well enough to cover his expenses.
Even when fame and fortune came his way, he would maintain this careful nononsense attitude and his close links with his family. In the autumn of 1965, having just won the Indy 500, he visited his father, who had just been operated for a stomach ulcer and he was on the point of stopping racing to pick up the family business, but contracts already signed for 1966 meant he could not.
1959 saw Jim Clark share his time between the big Lister-Jaguar which replaced the D-type and the Border Reivers Lotus Elite. In this, he and John Whitmore entered his first ever Le Mans 24 Hours. He was tenth overall at an average speed of 144.212 km/h. Not bad for a little 1216cc car. Jim was Scottish champion yet again with 23 wins, when on Boxing Day he had his first ever single seater race at Brands Hatch.
The Gemini Formula Junior he had been lent was not a match for the new Lotus 18. Luckily his 1960 season was looking good. True to his word, Chapman gave him a Formula Junior contract in one of these Lotus 18s.
He would put together an impressive string of wins and became British and European champion.
On 5th June, Chapman entered him for his very first F1 grand prix in the Netherlands at Zandvoort, followed by the Portuguese GP on 14th August at Oporto, where Jim scored his first world championship points, finishing third in a Lotus-Climax.
Chapman was absolutely strapped for cash and needed this result to continue, which made him all the more grateful towards Clark, who would go on to often cajole a tired and broken car to the finish line.

An exceptional champion

At the wheel of an Aston Martin DBR1, recently acquired by Border Reivers, Clark finished third in the 1960 Le Mans 24

The Edington Mains farm, near Duns, Scotland. Here, Clark spent a good part of his younger years. It was still home in the final months of 1966, when tax reasons saw him take on an adress in Bermuda and an apartment in Paris.

Hours along with Roy Salvadori. Jim continued to race in sports cars and GT with Aston Martin, then with the Lotus 23 as well as tin top racing in a Ford Lotus Cortina and even in the big Galaxies. In each case he demonstrated an incredible adaptability, to a new car, a new track or a new discipline.
These different skills were exceptional but they were also part of an F1 driver's lot in those days. His irresistible rise to the top was delayed only by Wolfgang von Trips' fatal accident at Monza, which also accounted for the death of several spectators. It was claimed that Clark had involuntarily caused the accident by failing to notice the German's Ferrari outbraking him and causing him to crash. The inquiry dragged on for years.
Clark and Chapman were bothered by the Italian authorities after winning at Monza in 1962 but the conclusions were uncertain. Whatever, it was the only time in his career that Clark's driving and sporting correctness was ever called into question and he was badly affected by it. As he was in 1960 at Spa, where he had to cope with the death of Chris Bristow in the race and of Alan Stacey in practice as well as Moss' injuries, these last two both driving for Lotus.
However, Clark never lost faith in his boss Colin Chapman, even though the founding father of Lotus was often accused of building cars that were too light and flimsy. Clark knew what he owed Chapman and lived in awe of him to a certain extent. At the end of the '61 season, his elder team-mate Innes Ireland, who had just given Team Lotus its first ever grand prix victory in the United States, was suddenly kicked out by Chapman. Jim Clark was the number one driver.
On 17th June 1962, with the Lotus 25 monocoque mated to a Climax engine, he won the Belgian GP at Spa, his first success in the world championship.
24 other wins, each put together with brio and intelligence, would follow until the South African race in January 1968 at the wheel of the Lotus 49 Ford, which Chapman had built especially for him - the width of the monocoque was built to fit the width of Clark's backside.
Other wins escaped him, simply though bad luck, as at Monza for the 1967 Italian GP, one of the most important races of his career. While Clark won two Drivers' titles in 1963 and '65, he should have added two more (1962 and 64) but for mechanical failures, which were not his fault. He should also have won the Indy 500 at his first attempt in 1963, but for the organisers fiddling the results to the benefit of Parnelli Jones.
Yes, Jim Clark truly was an exceptional champion, but more than that he was a remarkable and humble man.

Jacques Vassal

English translation :
Éric Silbermann
Pictures :
Bernard Cahier, DPPI Agency, Graham Gauld
Bibliography:
«*Jim Clark, the legend lives on,*» by Graham Gauld (Patrick Stephens Publ. London 1989;)
«*Jim Clark, tribute to a champion,*» by Eric Dymock, Foulis/Haynes Publ., London 1997.)

The 1968 South African Grand Prix at Kyalami on 1st January: Clatk flies to what would be, sadly, his final Grand Prix win at the wheel of the Cosworth powered Lotus 49. It was with this car that he won the 1967 Dutch Grand Prix at Zandvoort, the first win for this car. He went on to do it again at Silverstone, Watkins Glen and Mexico. Reliability problems with the Cosworth DFV robbed him of other wins.

Lotus 18
Coventry-Climax FPF MK2,
A.C.F. Grand Prix
1960

Lotus 21
Coventry-Climax FPF,
Dutch Grand Prix
1961

Lotus 25
Coventry-Climax MK3,
Italian Grand Prix
1963

Lotus 33
Coventry-Climax MK4,
Dutch Grand Prix
1965

Lotus 43
B.R.M. H16,
United-States Grand Prix
1966

Lotus 49
Ford-Cosworth DFV,
Dutch Grand Prix
1967

1968 - 1969 MATRA, TYRRELL AND STEWART A TALE OF MIXED FORTUNES

From the MS9 to the MS80, via the MS 10, the Matra-Ford made its mark on the 1968 and 1969 F1 world championships. Thirty years ago, thanks to Ken Tyrrell with Jackie Stewart at the wheel, the Anglo-French project was under way and the French chassis (if not the engine) was to triumph. When will Prost start winning?

A Surrey timber merchant, Robert Kenneth «Ken» Tyrrell had dabbled in motor racing as a driver from 1952 to 1958. First in Formula 3 (500cc) then Formula 2 (1500cc.) Realising his limitations as a driver and having a taste and talent for management, he hung up his helmet and started his own race team. First with Cooper Formula Juniors and then the new 1000cc F3 cars, he became a tough competitor and a discoverer of new talent. In 1964, his latest find, a young Scotsman called Jackie Stewart became European Formula 3 champion with a Cooper-BMC. The momentum moved up to Formula 2, 1000cc then 1600cc. In December 1965, when Stewart was in Formula 1 with BRM, that a cooperation agreement was signed between the French company, Matra-Sports, a racing division of Engins Matra and the famous British team manager, after some promising tests at Goodwood, with a Matra MS5 chassis fitted with a 1000cc F2 BRM engine. Another English team, belonging to John Coombs would sign a similar agreement and in 1966, it lined up Matra-BRMs in Formula 2. Jackie Stewart and the Belgian Jacky Ickx, another Tyrrell protÈgÈe, drove the Tyrrell Matras, sometimes with BRM engines, sometimes with Ford Cosworth powers. In 1967, Formula 2 switched to 1600cc and Tyrrell's Matra MS7-Cosworth, still with Stewart and Ickx at the wheel were regularly sizing themselves up against the works machinery of Beltoise, Servoz-Gavin and Pescarolo.

A promising Formula 1 debut

But «Uncle Ken» wanted to move up into Formula 1. It was at the Dutch Grand Prix weekend at Zandvoort he learnt that the Ford Cosworth V8 DFV, which was supplied solely to Team Lotus for the new Type 49 driven by Jim Clark and Graham Hill would be available to a few other teams at the end of 1967. Tyrrell made sure that he, like McLaren, would be on the list. As for the chassis, Jackie Stewart had declared himself delighted with the Matra MS7, particularly in terms of its precision and traction. The two men saw Matra, who were also working on their own V12 engine, as the constructor most likely to help them achieve their goals. The Matra engineers, led by Bernard Boyer set to work..

▷ Victory champagne for Ken Tyrrell - they still drank it in those days - at the end of the 1971 British Grand Prix, along with Goodyear's Leo Mehl (on left) and Jackie Stewart. It was an association which would bring the driver and his manager turned constructor, the championships at the end of the year.

Kyalami, 1st January 1968. Jackie Stewart debuts the Matra MS9, a Formula 2 MS7 adapted to accept the Cosworth DFV at the South African Grand Prix. For a long time it was the meat in the sandwich between the two Lotus 49s of Jim Clark, who went on to win and Graham Hill, who went on to be World Champion. ▽

They began by adapting an MS7 chassis to the 3 litre Ford V8.

They used the principle of the engine as stressed member, bolted to the cockpit bulkhead, the idea invented by Colin Chapman for the Lotus 49. The Matra engineers added a sub-frame to hang the gearbox and suspension from, so that the engine could be removed without touching these parts. The front suspension used inboard torsion bars like the company's F2 and F3 cars.

The MS9, the first example of the first ever Matra F1 car was sent to Kyalami for practice for the South African Grand Prix. Jackie Stewart showed its potential by qualifying third, right behind the Lotus of Clark and Hill. Tyrrell and his driver therefore decided to enter this «laboratory» car in the race. Stewart led for the first lap and then ended up as the meat in the Lotus sandwich in second place, before being let down by a broken valve.

During this time, back at Velizy, work on the first two real chassis was underway, the MS10 for Ken Tyrrell's Matra International team, to be mated to the Cosworth V8 and the MS11 for the works cars, to be fitted with the brand new Matra V12 developed by a team of engineers led by Georges Martin.

Stewart was naturally the designated driver for the MS10 in grands prix, while Jean-Pierre Beltoise would debut the MS11. French oil company Elf would stump up the funds and technical support.

A season of purgatory

Things did not quite go as planned. The Scotsman did debut the MS10 (chassis 1) but it was not in a grand prix. It was at the «Race of Champions,» a non-championship race entered by all the official teams and held at Brands Hatch on 17th March. Stewart came sixth. The next outing was on 12th May at Barcelona for the Spanish GP. In the meantime, Ken Tyrrell's number one driver had fractured his right scaphoid when he crashed in an F2 race at Jarama. As the MS11 was not yet ready, it was Jean-Pierre Beltoise who stood in for Stewart at the wheel of the brand new 02.

The former French motorcycle champion, who both knew and liked the Montjuich track had a great race. After leading for four laps, he unfortunately had to pit with an oil leak.

Nevertheless, he finished fifth in the grand prix and took the lap record.

On 26th May for the Monaco GP, Stewart was still not fit enough to race, but Beltoise finally gave the MS11 and its V12 engine its first outing. So, this time it was Johnny Servoz-Gavin who replaced the Scot at the wheel of 01. The brilliant young F2 and sports car driver for Matra, was making his first appearance in F1. Well coached by Ken Tyrrell and by Jackie Stewart himself, he caused a sensation by snatching pole position. Tearing off into the lead, Johnny hit a chicane on lap 3, which was later found to be caused by a broken suspension and he had to retire. Fifteen days later, Jackie Stewart was finally back in harness for the Belgian Grand Prix at Spa-Francorchamps.

With the 01 he finished fourth. But it was on 23rd June at Zandvoort that all the hard work of Ken Tyrrell and Matra and its two star drivers was going to pay off.

In driving rain, Stewart led the race from start to finish and to add to the party, Beltoise brought the MS11 home in second place, despite a spin. On 4th August, Stewart took 02 to a fantastic victory in the German Grand Prix on a rain soaked and foggy Nurburgring, beating second placed Graham Hill by a staggering four minutes. After the race, Jackie admitted he had been helped, as at Zandvoort, by some excellent new Dunlop rain tyres.
In Italy, Stewart retired (engine) and Servoz-Gavin came second in 02. In the States, Stewart won his third grand prix win of 1968, but in Mexico, problems saw him struggle home seventh. Hill and Lotus were world champions in the drivers and constructors categories.

The MS80 and the 1969 title
In the winter, work was already well underway at Matra on the replacement for the MS10, the MS80. It was still from Bernard Boyer's team and had a wider mid section to the tub in order to accommodate the fuel cells in the sides. The front suspension had out board springs which worked between the side of the chassis and the lower wishbones. More wind tunnel work had been undertaken and the wings underwent several evolutions during the season. The gearbox was still a Hewland DG 300 with 5 speeds and the Cosworth engine put out about 430 bhp at 9500 rpm. Given the difficulties they had run into with their own V12, this was to be used only for sports car racing where it would do very well. In Formula 1 they stuck with the Ford Cosworth engine.
Matra International, still run by Ken Tyrrell, would line up two cars in 1969 for Stewart and Beltoise.
The 1st March in South Africa marked the last appearance for the MS10 and 02 duly won in Stewart's hands and also claimed the lap record. Beltoise was sixth in 01. The MS80-01 had only taken part in practice. But on 16th March, Stewart used it to win the Race of Champions.
It was a good omen for the Spanish GP, where Stewart and 01 were invincible. The race was marred by several breakages of the thin support arms on the rear wings of many cars, including Graham Hill's Lotus 49B. Beltoise had a good race, finishing third in 02. At Monaco, by which time high level wings had been banned, Graham Hill won and both Matras retired. Stewart was to get his revenge winning the Dutch Grand Prix with ease, setting a new lap record on the way.
The French GP was held at Charade on 6th July. Stewart put together another of his majestic performances on this twisty track and Beltoise, cheered along by his home crowd on a track he particularly liked, stole second place away from Ickx' Brabham on the very last lap.
The Scot won again at the British GP while Beltoise was tasked with practising in the heavy four wheel drive MS84, which he, Servoz-Gavin and others really hated. In Germany, Stewart and Beltoise came second and sixth and at Monza, Stewart won an incredible Italian grand prix, with Jean-Pierre Beltoise third. Despite retiring in Canada and the States (engine) and a modest fourth place in Mexico, Jackie Stewart was the 1969 world champion with 63 points to Ickx' 37.
Matra won the Constructors' trophy with 66 points to Brabham's 49.

Charade, 6th July 1969: this French Grand Prix would be another glory day for winner Jackie Stewart and also for Matra and Ken Tyrrell's team. Jean-Pierre Beltoise, was in second car and knowing this circuit like the back of his hand from his days as a motorcycle racer, managed to take second place off Jacky Ickx (Brabham-Ford) aat the end of a very tough duel.

Different fortunes
The seasons from 1970 onwards would be marked by varied fortunes for the principle players in this adventure. Matra continued to operate under the Simca banner - the company itself owned by Chrysler and the cars were called Matra-Simcas.
From then on they could not use Ford engines. Stewart and Tyrrell, who had never believed in the potential of the French V12, went their own way.
To start with they went to March while engineer Derek Gardner worked on the design of the Tyrrell 001, a car which had something of the Matra MS80 about it. Stewart would take the title again in 1971 and '73 at the wheel of Tyrrells. Beltoise stayed with Matra with the V12 and the went to BRM with another V12 in 1972. Elf continued as sponsor and technical partner with Tyrrell.
The V12 would continue in sports cars and reappeared later in Formula 1 with Ligier and Shadow. As for Ken Tyrrell, he would sell his team to British American Racing at the start of 1998, while Jackie Stewart was embarking on his second year as a team owner.
As usual in F1 the wheels are not the only things that keep rolling along.

Jacques Vassal

Pictures : Bernard Cahier, DPPI Agency, Dominique Pascal archives.

Matra MS 9 Ford-Cosworth Jackie Stewart, South-African Grand Prix 1968

Matra MS 10 Ford-Cosworth Jackie Stewart, German Grand Prix 1968

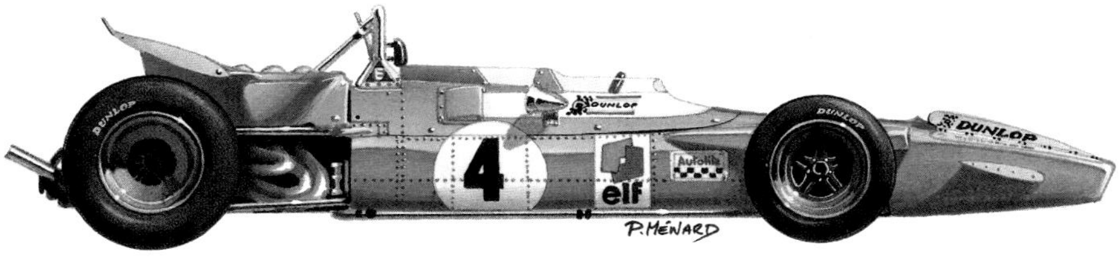

Matra MS 80 Ford-Cosworth Jackie Stewart, Dutch Grand Prix 1969

Atmosphere

Atmosphere. It is the reason why millions of spectators the world over choose to give up the comfort of their seat on the sofa and the television, in order to tackle crowds, heat, cold and rain. It is all worth it, just to see these speed machines in the flesh, to smell the oil and to hear the howl of the V10 engine.
The atmosphere in F1 is unique and here it is distilled into its essence.

Girls and chassis

In Formula 1, everything is a question of aerodynamics and a well proportioned chassis. This rule applies not only to the cars on the track, but also to life in the paddock.

GÜNTHER
sparco
HEWLETT PACKARD
REPSOL
HONDA

BENETTON

ENZO e DINO FERRARI

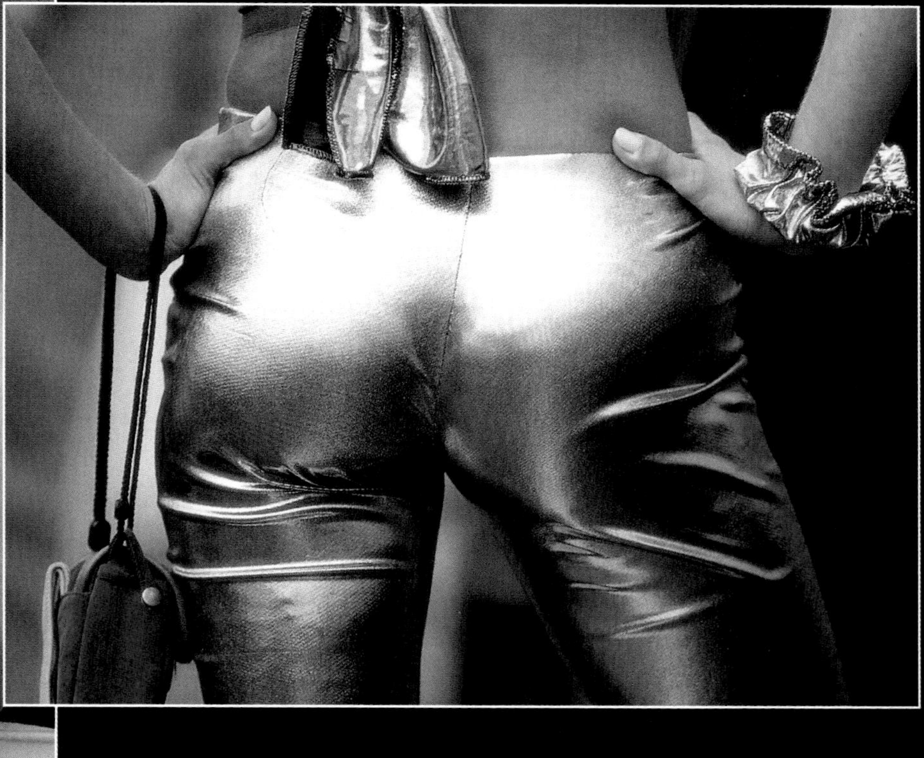

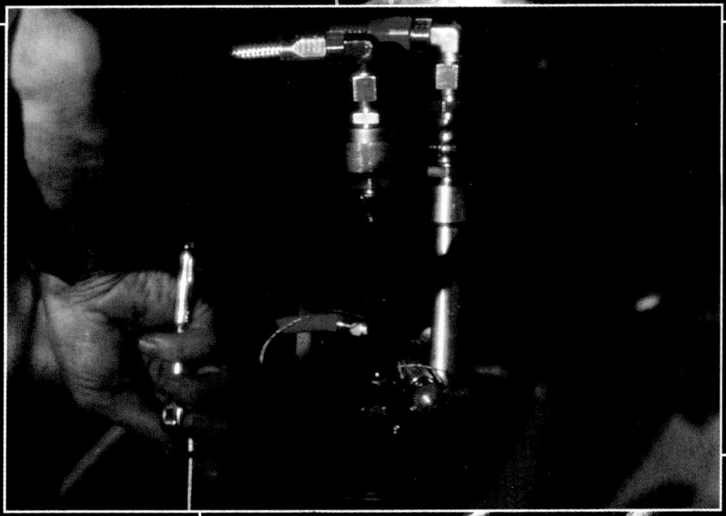

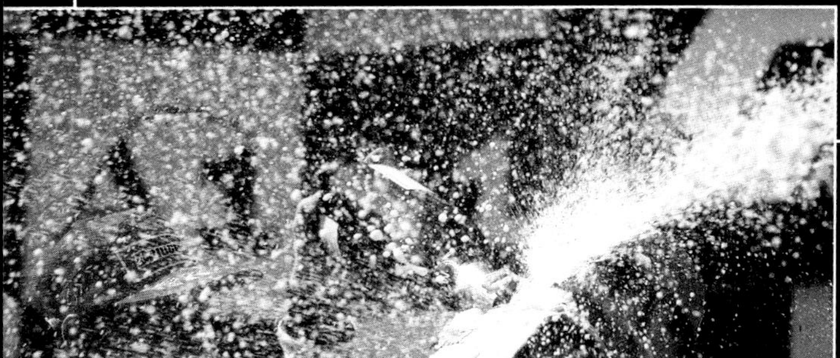

Night & Day

For a photographer, light is the source of all his work, so why not play with it now and again.

Nuts & Bolts

Formula 1 is a spectacle a business and sometimes it is just a sport. But above all it revels in beautiful machinery.

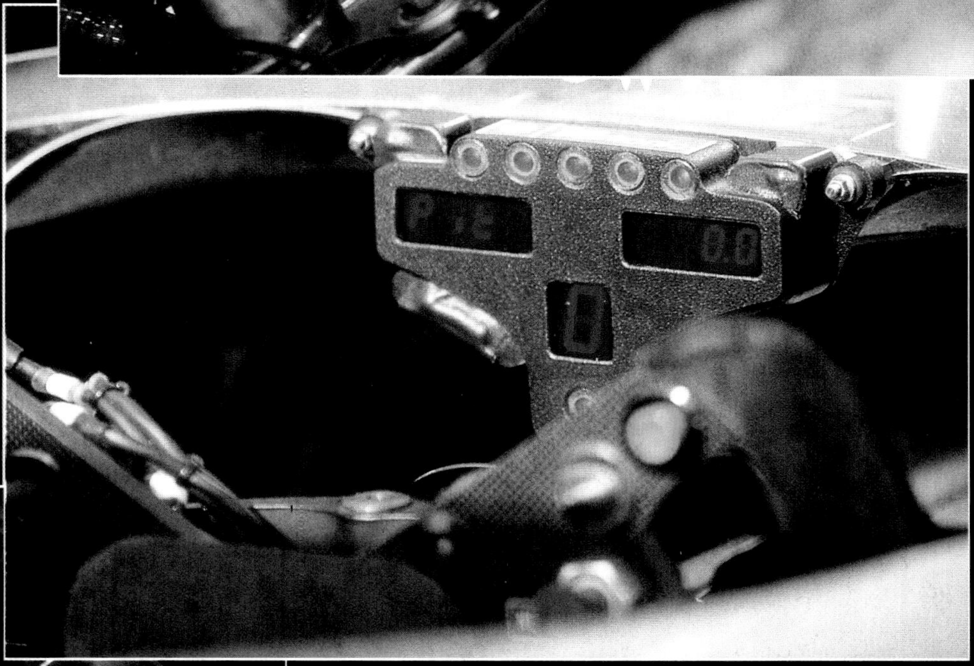

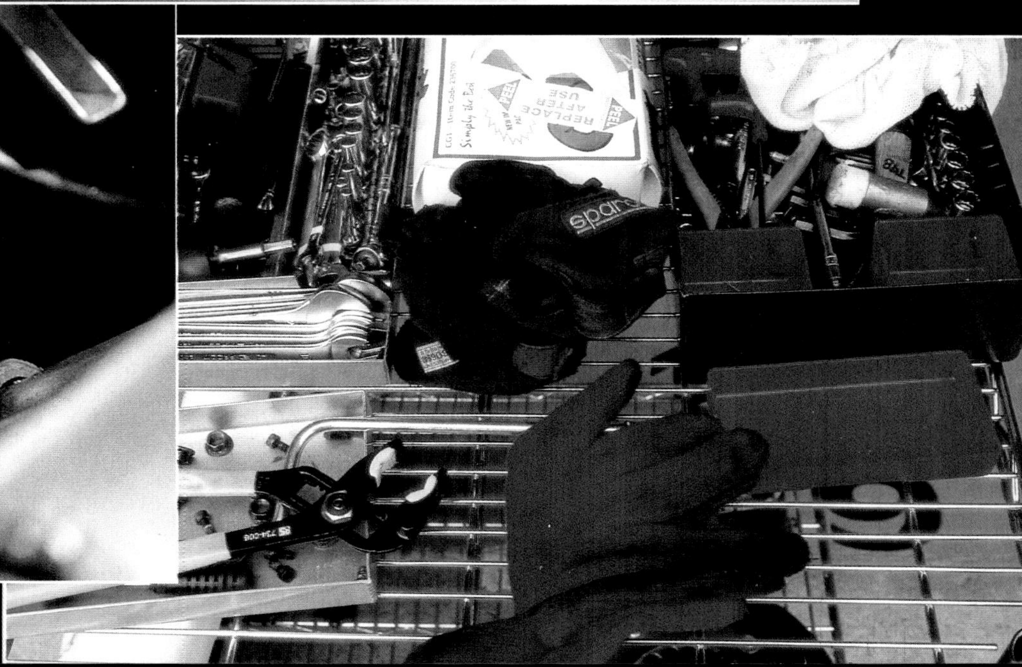

PETRONAS
SAUBER
Red Bull
PlayStation
FONDMETAL
MAGNETI MARELLI
Ford
DOIMO
MORSE
GOOD YEAR
PIAA
LYCRA
DANKA
P. DINIZ
HSBC
HEWLETT PACKARD

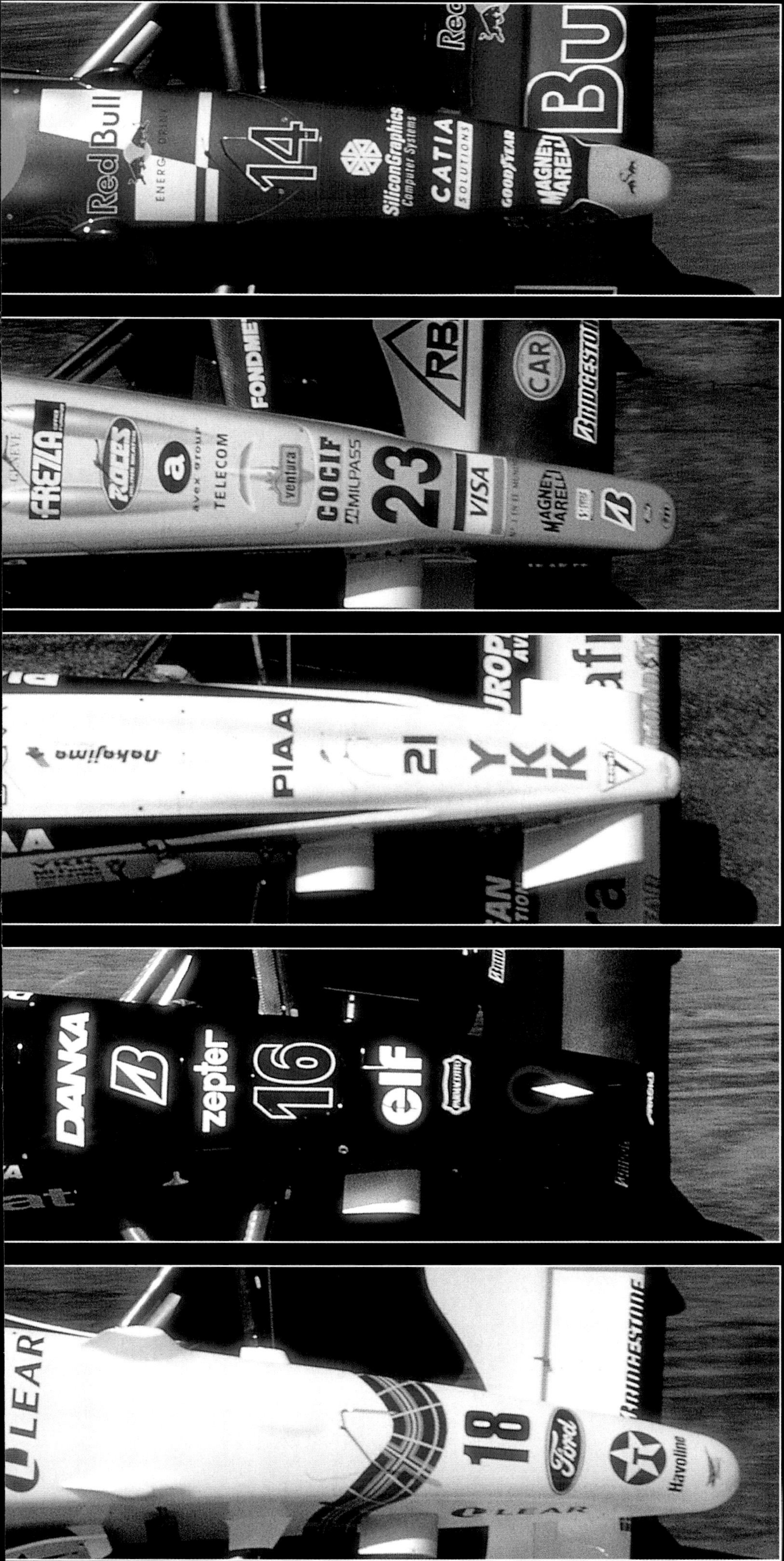

Views from the hot seat

Comfortable is not the word that first springs to mind when looking at a Formula 1 cockpit. Narrow, with belts done right up tight, almost touching the ground, the drivers do not ask for more. In fact, all they care about is the speed.

ATMOSPHERE

Bet on Red

Going up in the world. With the arrival of Michael Schumacher at the Scuderia, followed by that of technical director Ross Brawn, the Italian team has gained in efficiency what it has lost in Latin temperament. The Reds are no doubt on the road to success long into the future.

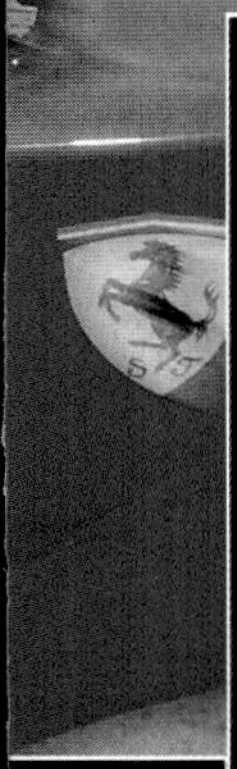

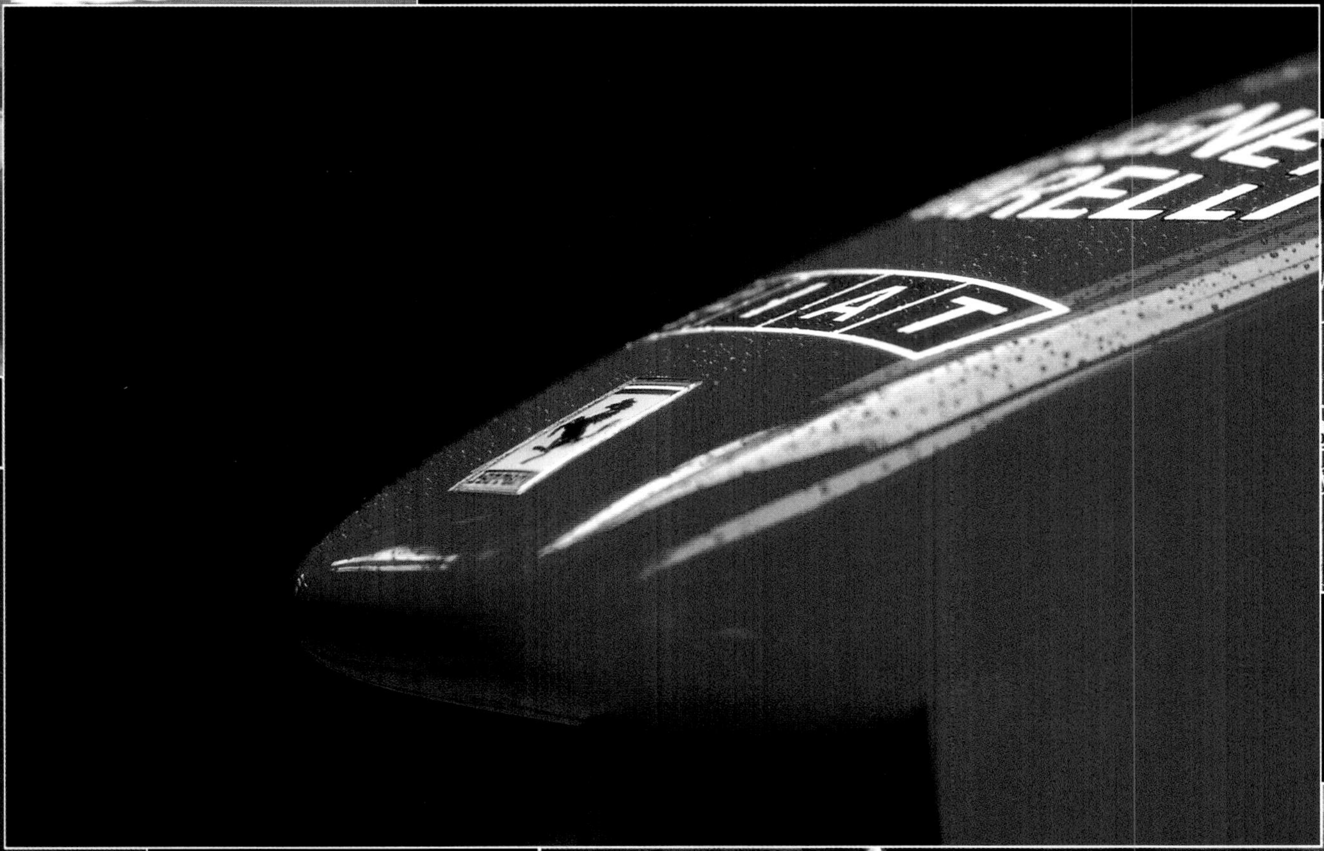

A barren season

The Prost Grand Prix team did not shine this season. Partly because of a gearbox which was too heavy and partly because of a less than perfect weight distribution, the AP01 never kept its promises. Behind the scenes, the team was still undergoing construction and it was soon time to look to 1999.

PlayStation
AGFA
PEUGEOT
TOTAL
CANAL+
BIC
PANIS

GAULOISES
PEUGEOT
CANAL+
AGFA
PlayStation
BIC
Sodexho
LVS

GAULOISES
12
TOTAL
ALCATEL

Sodexho
Tradition
PEUGEOT
PlayStation
AGFA
CANAL+
BIC
ALCATEL
BRIDGESTONE

BRIDGESTONE
Sodexho
Tradition
11

The 16 Grand Prix

If travel broadens the mind, then what can one say about a season of Formula 1? In the space of just eight months, the 16 Grand Prix making up the championship put the F1 folk through a whistlestop tour of tens thousands of kilometres. Most of the time, the demands of the job and the frenetic pace of F1, mean that there is no chance to admire the view.
But now, it is time for action. Start your engine!

A chivalrous gesture

One in the bag for Mika Hakkinen. In Melbourne, the McLaren team crushed the opposition, both in practice and the race, giving everyone a first glimpse of what lay ahead for Formula 1 this season.
While the Finn might have won, it was only down to the honourable behaviour of team-mate David Coulthard. After a misunderstanding, Mika Hakkinen wasted time in the pit lane, letting the Scotsman into the lead. A gentleman to the tip of his fingers, he slowed down to let the Finn be first past the chequered flag.

QANTAS AUSTRALIAN GRAND PRIX MELBOURNE

And a pole for Mika Hakkinen!

The new regulations do not seem to have slowed the pace in Melbourne.

Even quicker than in '97!

«Wait and see Jan, we will get on like a house on fire this season.» Jackie Stewart shares a joke with Jan Magnussen on the grid. Their divorce would be finalised just three months later.

Incredible but true: although the regulations have reduced the width of the cars by 10%, or 20 centimetres, thus greatly reducing aerodynamic downforce and also introducing grooved tyres, the 1998 F1 cars are quicker than last year. On Saturday, the qualifying session effectively brushed away FIA's hopes of reducing the speed of the cars in order to improve their safety. According to computer simulations, the '98 regulations should have slowed lap times by between four and seven seconds. They were wrong. On Saturday, the McLarens lapped 1.7 seconds quicker than their 1997 times and they got within tenths of last year's pole, set then by Jacques Villeneuve in a Williams.

It was a big shock. *«Yes, I have to admit I am surprised,»* admitted Mika Hakkinen. *«It is even very impressive, because it shows that if we still had slick tyres, we would be quicker still. I have to say the team has done a huge amount of work this year and the car's road holding is definitely better than last year.»* Indeed the McLaren drivers had nothing to complain about when it came to the handling of their cars as the two silver arrows claimed the front row for their own on Saturday, separated by just 43 thousandths of a second. *«I think it is the drivers who have improved most at McLaren,»* joked Hakkinen.

«But to be serious, we do have new tyres, but they are not the sole reason for our success. It is the whole package, but I have to admit I am surprised at the size of our advantage.»

For his part, David Coulthard, was not bothered about missing out on pole. *«It took me a long time this morning to get through my programme. In Formula One, you can never make up for lost time and I never really got to grips with my understeer problem. By the end of the session, when the car was better, the track was too hot to improve my time. It has to be said, our car appeared very late, which means we have not done as much testing as we would have liked. For example, we are not sure how it will cope with 50 laps of a race.»*

14 centimetres too many

At Benetton there was disappointment that Fisichella was only seventh and Wurz eleventh on the grid. «This morning the chassis was well balanced, but this afternoon as it got hotter, the car started to oversteer unexpectedly,» explained Giancarlo. While Alexander Wurz spun and had to qualify with the spare car, set up for Fisichella and on which the settings had to be changed in a matter of minutes. Bear in mind, the two Benetton boys are not exactly built the same way, the Italian being 172 cm tall while the Austrian towers over him at 186 cm.

Break of day at Ayers Rock or «Uluru» to give its new official name. For the F1 village, this first trip of the year is also one of the favourites as the atmosphere is much more laid back than in Europe. Also because the countryside is magnificent, as long as you get a few miles away from Melbourne.

Michael Schumacher is third and already blaming Goodyear

△
Michael Schumacher driving his mobile office. The German claimed he was not surprised to have qualified third.

Third on the starting grid, Michael Schumacher was also quicker than in last year's qualifying. «*If you think about it, it makes sense,*» was his analysis. «*Last year our car had a lot of problems at the start of the season, while the new F 300 works a lot better. Also, it was cooler today than last year which automatically makes the track quicker. However, I still think we will be around two to three seconds slower on the more conventional circuits.*»
He was to prove right, of course.
The German was not too far behind the McLarens, giving away only seven tenths of a second. «*We realised during testing at Barcelona, that the McLarens would be very competitive this season. But we also know our Goodyear tyres are not quite as good as the Bridgestones at the moment. It is vital that we make progress in this area if we are to win grands prix. I expected to qualify third here, it is normal.*»
Unluckily for him, Michael Schumacher had been blocked on a quick lap by Damon Hill, who was coming out of the pits. The Englishman did a bit of blatant zig-zagging which worried the German. «*I don't want to talk about it, but we will have to sort it out,*» he concluded.

A bad start

Behind both McLarens-Mercedes and Michael Schumacher's Ferrari, Williams were the big losers in Saturday's qualifying.
It was the first time in three years that the reigning world champions did not have a car in the first three on the grid.
«*Of course I am a bit disappointed,*» confessed Jacques Villeneuve.
«*We had hoped the McLarens would not be as quick as they seemed to be in Barcelona, but we were right to be worried. If they do not have any problems, I don't know how we can beat them.*»
He therefore lined up alongside Michael Schumacher, his sworn enemy from the previous year. «*It doesn't bother me at all. I am not interested in Michael, it is McLaren we have to beat.*»
Heinz-Harald Frentzen was sixth in the other Williams, further disappointed to have been beaten by his team-mate, rather than just because he was a long way off pole position.

«70 kilos and it's all muscle ladies!» Esteban Tuero, only 19 and already discovering the joys of Formula 1 at his very first grand prix.
◁

STARTING GRID

		Mika HAKKINEN 1'30''010
David COULTHARD 1'30''053	-1-	
		M. SCHUMACHER 1'30''767
Jacques VILLENEUVE 1'30''919	-2-	
		Johnny HERBERT 1'31''384
Heinz-H. FRENTZEN 1'31''397	-3-	
		G. FISICHELLA 1'31''733
Eddie IRVINE 1'31''767	-4-	
		R. SCHUMACHER 1'32''392
Damon HILL 1'32''399	-5-	
		Alexander WURZ 1'32''726
Jean ALESI 1'33''240	-6-	
		Toranosuke TAKAGI 1'33''291
R. BARRICHELLO 1'33''383	-7-	
		Jarno TRULLI 1'33''739
Mika SALO 1'33''927	-8-	
		Esteban TUERO 1'34''646
Jan MAGNUSSEN 1'34''906	-9-	
		Ricardo ROSSET 1'35''119
Pedro DINIZ 1'35''140	-10-	
		Olivier PANIS 1'35''215
Shinji NAKANO 1'35''301	-11-	

△ Mission accomplished! Just like a parade, the two McLaren-Mercedes crossed the finish line less than one second apart.

One lap ahead of the second division

Giant tears streamed down Mika Hakkinen's face as the Finnish National Anthem was played. Understandably, as this was only the second win of his career and the second in a row after the 1997 European Grand Prix and emotion was therefore permitted. *«I am sorry about the tears,»* he mumbled moments later. *«But I could not stop myself. I am not used to winning yet, but I hope that will change.»*
It was Mika Hakkinen who was first across the finish line, but it had not exactly been a piece of cake for the Finn. On lap 36, when he had been leading since the start, he drove through the pit lane without stopping. It was a strange move which let David Coulthard into the lead. *«I had just come up behind Eddie Irvine, when I heard some noises over the radio,»* recounted Hakkinen. *«I thought I had to come in and refuel. As I was level with the pit lane entry I dived in without having time to check with the radio. And when I drove past my pit there was no one there!»*
The Finn was back on the track without having stopped, but stopping for real this time, four laps later, he was now 13 seconds down on Coulthard. He had no chance of getting back in the lead, except that David decided to hand him back his position (see right) respecting the plan drawn up by Ron Dennis.
«As we had not been able to test the reliability of our car, I asked my drivers not to fight for the lead after the first corner. I asked them to race for the team and not for themselves. However, after the Brazilian Grand Prix they can do what they like,» said the boss as if justifying the incident
A great chassis aided by a clever braking system, (see page 94,) Bridgestone tyres superior to the Goodyear product and a reliable engine: the McLaren-Mercedes had put on an impressive display. It had all looked so easy that it brought back memories of 1988, when the team won 15 grands prix from 16 starts.

Keep it under your helmet

It was an act of true bravura; one of those chivalrous gestures we thought had been erased from the Formula 1 vocabulary. On lap 44, the McLaren pit informed David Coulthard by radio that Mika Hakkinen had lost the lead because of a misunderstanding. Over the next few laps the Scotsman thought long and hard about what to do, before telling his pit he was going to let Mika through.
It was an admirable gesture of fair play, when you consider the desire to win that motivates all F1 drivers. *«It was a very difficult decision to take,»* conceded David Coulthard after the race. *«But I was alone out in front without any pressure which allowed me think about it calmly and to reach the decision that this race was Mika's by right.»*
The Scotsman confirmed that the two drivers had made a non-aggression pact for these first two grands prix. *«When I accepted that we would not fight after the first corner, I thought I would be the one who would make the best start,»* he joked. *«But I was caught out. We were held for a long time on the grid under the red lights and my engine began to smoke. I was watching it at the precise moment the lights went out.»*
The Finn did not know how to accept his team-mate's gesture. «What David did was exceptional,» stressed Hakkinen. *«I have not seen anything so correct since I have been in Formula 1. Not many drivers would have done what he did.»*
Hakkinen was then asked if he would have done the same thing for Coulthard in a similar situation. *«Er, yes, yes, of course, of course,»* he exclaimed after a moment's hesitation amid an outburst of laughter in the press room. *«And will you hand over your bonus to David?» «Er, yes of course. But, er, what bonus? Do you get a bonus if you win?»* he asked his team-mate. The atmosphere was certainly relaxed between the two heroes of the hour.

Fixed wins

In Melbourne, Mika Hakkinen won his second pre-arranged victory - at Jerez in 1997, Jacques Villeneuve had let him pass. *«I know that seen from the outside, it looks as though both my victories were not genuine,»* he admitted. *«But from my point of view, I feel quite comfortable with it, because it is very hard to drive an F1 car. These two wins were not handed me on a plate. I had to work for them.»*

Fourth place for Eddie Irvine, the only Ferrari driver to get to the finish. ▽

Jacques predicts an open championship

Everything moves fast in Formula 1. It was only Friday of practice for the first race of 1998 and already Jacques Villeneuve was being questioned about 1999.
The Canadian could do nothing to get away from the subject. Last December, at the launch of the British American Racing team, scheduled to make its debut next year, Craig Pollock, the team boss and Villeneuve's manager confirmed that he would like to have his driver in his team. Frank Williams immediately asked Villeneuve to give an answer for 1999 by July.
This little matter did not seem to bother the party concerned. *«The rumours about a move to the BAR team are nothing more than speculation,»* he stated. *«I have a contract with Williams for 1998 and that is the main thing at the moment. It might seem stupid not to plan for the future but I do not want to take my briefcase and start talking to other teams. I have not got the time and anyway I might stay with Williams.»*
With a world championship in his pocket and a winter of resting and skiing behind him, Jacques Villeneuve declares that his batteries are fully charged. *«I think it will be even closer than last season,»* he continued. *«It seems there are more cars capable of winning races and the championship will be very open. It will be very, very tough, even though last year was also harder than I would have liked. Winning was a relief. I would have found it hard to get back in the groove if all that hard work had ended in failure.»*

△
«I am very pleased with you my son.» Ron Dennis congratulates David Coulthard.

Room for improvement

Four seconds. That was the staggering difference in best lap times between Mika Hakkinen and Jacques Villeneuve in the Australian GP.
In Melbourne, only Heinz-Harald Frentzen saved some honour for Williams by climbing onto the podium in third place. Jacques Villeneuve however, could do no better than fifth, chased home all the way by Johnny Herbert's Sauber. *«It is really tough finishing such a long way back from the winners. It is actually unacceptable,»* said the reigning world champion. *«We really took one hell of a pasting today. My set-up was not right and the car had no downforce at all and on top of that I had overheating problems which meant I had to back off. I am not at all happy with the work we have done this winter. Okay, we made a mistake. It can happen. Now we must improve at all levels.»*
According to Villeneuve, this work would not take effect immediately. *«In Brazil and Argentina we will have to make do as best we can. But after that, I hope we will be competitive again for the San Marino Grand Prix».* Heinz-Harald Frentzen had decided to slow down to save his brakes - last year they had broken two laps from the end. *«I certainly did not want the same thing to happen again and anyway, the McLarens were out of reach,»* explained the German, who was a bit more optimistic than Villeneuve about the immediate future. *«I think the McLarens were on another planet today, but I am sure we will react before the next race. The Williams engineers are very good at finding our weak points and reacting quickly. Actually I have never come across such an efficient team.»*

Schumacher optimistic

Michael Schumacher did not get very far in Melbourne, as he had to park his Ferrari on the grass after just six laps. *«I am not really sure what happened,»* he said after the race. *«The temperature started to rise and the engine let go suddenly. It is a real shame as we have not had a single problem with it all winter.»*
Overall, he was not too unhappy with his weekend. *«I think the gap between us and the McLarens is not as big as it looks. I could just about follow their pace in the early part of the race and I was only going to stop once, while they were on a two stop strategy. I am reasonably confident for the rest of the season.»*

Jacques Villeneuve spent the whole race under pressure from the pack and all for a modest fifth place. What a difference a winter can make.
▽

IN THE POINTS

1.	Mika HAKKINEN	West McLaren Mercedes	1 h 31'45"996
2.	David COULTHARD	West McLaren Mercedes	at 0"702
3.	Heinz-H. FRENTZEN	Winfield Williams	at 1 lap
4.	Eddie IRVINE	Scuderia Ferrari Marlboro	at 1 lap
5.	Jacques VILLENEUVE	Winfield Williams	at 1 lap
6.	Johnny HERBERT	Red Bull Sauber Petronas	at 1 lap

Fastest lap : Mika HAKKINEN, lap 39, 1'31"649, avg. 208.303 km/h

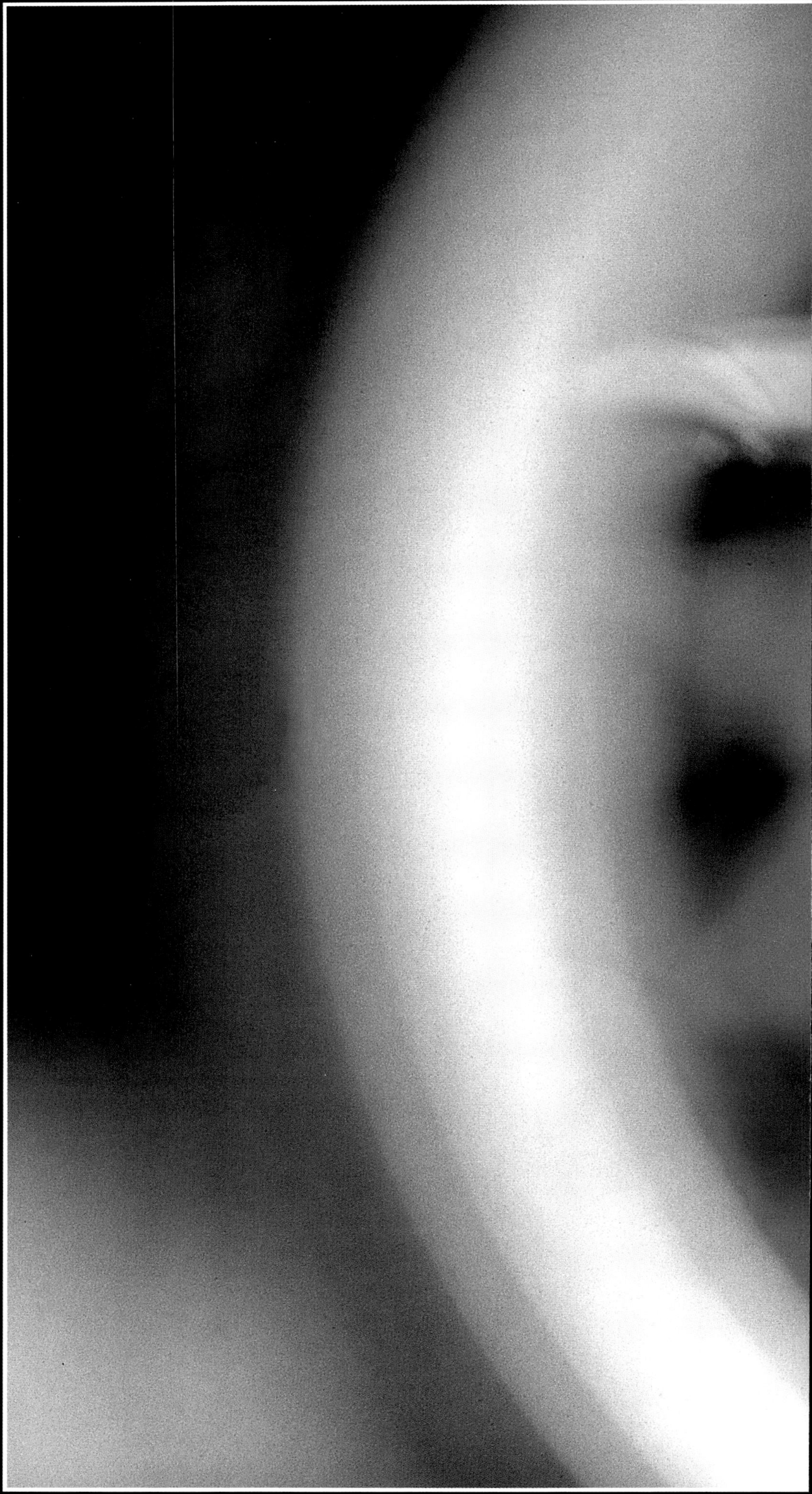

Close up on Mika Salo. For 1998, «the other Finn» moved from Tyrrell to Arrows, but it did not produce the desired results. In Melbourne he retired on lap 24 with gearbox problems. It was the first of a long series of retirements.

«But I've wiped my feet.» Jarno Trulli prepares to climb aboard his brand new Prost- Peugeot AP01. The Italian retired 19 laps from the finish, let down by his gearbox. Olivier Panis finished last.

The secret is all in the brakes

In Melbourne, it was fashionable for many of the technical directors to claim that McLaren's victory was down to its steering brake system. Triggered by a button on the steering wheel it can act on one rear brake at a time, thus limiting wheel spin on the exit of corners. There was apparently nothing illegal about it.
Faced with this situation, Ron Dennis did not mince his words on Sunday night. *«We have used the steering brake system since the middle of last season. At the time, everyone laughed at us. Now that it is working, they are complaining. They basically look a bit stupid for not having copied it earlier.»* The race ended over one hour ago and the McLaren boss is in fine form, pouring scorn on anyone who claims the system is illegal.
«We entered into a lengthy correspondence with the FIA Technical Delegate, Charlie Whiting, who assured us that this diagonal braking system was authorised,» he continued. *«I don't care about those who say it is not, as I have proof of the contrary. The attitude of my competitors is childish. They want the system banned because they do not have it. It is ridiculous.»*
Some teams were complaining about the cost of developing such a system and again, Dennis brushed aside these comments. *«The equipment used in this system cost less than 100,000 dollars. It's peanuts. The others should not pretend they cannot afford it but they should admit they do not have the brains to develop it.»*
The McLaren drivers were tight lipped when it came to discussing how the system worked. *«This sort of system, does not explain a gap of four seconds per lap,»* was Patrick Head's contribution to the argument. The Williams technical director added: *«It can gain you one second per lap at the most. Mind you, stopping wheelspin, prevents the tyres going off too quickly and that is where you have to look to find the McLaren's advantage.»*
A self confident Ron Dennis maintained that the Melbourne race had been but a dress rehearsal. *«I don't think this circuit suited us very well,»* he gloated. *«I expect our advantage to be even bigger in Brazil.»* But nothing is certain, as other teams, including Williams, were already preparing similar systems for Brazil.

Ferrari spies on McLaren and admits it.

It was the first race for the new grooved tyres and also the first win for Bridgestone. It was party time in the Japanese camp come Sunday night.

On the Saturday of practice, McLaren-Mercedes team boss Ron Dennis was torn between two conflicting emotions. On the one hand, happiness: his two cars were both on the front row of the grid, something which had not happened since 1991.
On the other hand, blind rage: *«Nothing surprises me about F1 anymore,»* he began ominously. *«Each team has a different style. But some have no style at all. On Thursday, we had to throw a photographer out of our garage, who was taking pictures of our car and who eventually admitted he was the brother-in-law of an aerodynamicist who works for another team. During private testing at Barcelona, we already had to deal with this same aerodynamicist. It is unforgivable.»*
Indeed, one month earlier, the Austrian Wilhelm Toet, then an engineer at Ferrari, had been caught taking pictures of the new McLaren MP4/13. He had turned up in Barcelona wearing normal clothes, while the Scuderia were back in Italy testing. Recognised by some of the McLaren mechanics, he had his camera confiscated and was kicked out of the garage.
In Melbourne, Wilhelm Toet was at it again, but this time he had roped in his brother- in-law. *«We are considering legal action,»* continued Ron Dennis in a real lather against Ferrari, although he never actually mentioned the other team by name. *«We will in any case ask FIA to protect our intellectual property against such acts. There exists a sort of code of good behaviour in F1, but certain teams appear willing to ignore it. I hope that my statement will at least have caused their people some embarrassment.»*
Quite the contrary at Ferrari where no one seemed bothered by Ron Dennis' outburst. *«All the teams spy on us,»* claimed the Scuderia's sporting director Jean Todt. *«The one time we do it and people are making a song and dance about it. This is no doubt part of the difference between Ferrari and the other teams.»*
For his part, Ferrari's press officer, Claudio Berro preferred to make a joke of it: *«The McLaren is a very beautiful car. It's normal for people to want to photograph it, don't you think?»*

The first for Bridgestone

Mika Hakkinen's win also belonged to Bridgestone. Exactly one year after its Formula 1 debut, the Japanese company thus had its first success, putting to an end a Goodyear monopoly which went back to the Canada 1991, the last win for Pirelli tyres.
On Sunday night, everyone in the Bridgestone camp was very happy with the weekend's work, as well as with their association with McLaren. *«A new team, a new regulation and a fantastic result!»* exclaimed Hiroshi Yasukawa at the finish. *«I would like to say a special thank you to all our staff who gave up their Christmas and New Year holiday. Everyone has worked very hard for this result.»*
This win was indeed the result of a level of work which is hard to comprehend. *«We never stop developing new products,»* said one of the company bosses. *«Last week in private testing with McLaren, we tried ten different types of different compound. It is impossible to say when the new tyres arrive as there are so many of them.»* During the winter, the McLaren team completed around 8000 kilometres on its Bridgestone tyres. That is equivalent to 26 grands prix. It seemed to have paid off.

Building a commercial centre around an old factory is certainly an Australian type of idea. Melbourne boasts an impressive shopping area which houses hundreds of shops under the one roof.

PRACTICE TIMES

No	Driver	Car/Engine/Chassis	Practice Friday	Practice Saturday	Qualifying	Warm-up
1.	Jacques Villeneuve	Williams/Mecachrome/FW20/3 (G)	1'35"023	1'31"178	1'30"919	1'35"401
2.	Heinz-Harald Frentzen	Williams/Mecachrome/FW20/2 (G)	1'36"741	1'31"624	1'31"397	1'35"497
3.	Michael Schumacher	Ferrari/F300/184 (G)	1'33"826	1'31"432	1'30"767	1'34"346
4.	Eddie Irvine	Ferrari/F300/183 (G)	1'37"891	1'32"465	1'31"767	1'35"192
5.	Giancarlo Fisichella	Benetton/Playlife/198/5 (B)	1'38"860	1'31"581	1'31"733	1'35"215
6.	Alexander Wurz	Benetton/Playlife/198/4 (B)	1'35"270	1'33"588	1'32"726	1'36"257
7.	David Coulthard	McLaren/Mercedes/MP4-13/3 (B)	1'35"409	1'30"456	1'30"053	1'34"257
8.	Mika Hakkinen	McLaren/Mercedes/MP4-13/4 (B)	1'34"432	1'31"436	1'30"010	1'34"126
9.	Damon Hill	Jordan/Honda/198/3 (G)	1'37"102	1'32"518	1'32"399	1'35"033
10.	Ralf Schumacher	Jordan/Honda/198/4 (G)	1'35"708	1'32"667	1'32"392	1'35"030
11.	Olivier Panis	Prost/Peugeot/AP01/4 (B)	1'37"102	1'35"913	1'35"215	1'37"215
12.	Jarno Trulli	Prost/Peugeot/AP01/3 (B)	1'36"231	1'34"837	1'33"739	1'36"246
14.	Jean Alesi	Sauber/Petronas/C17/3 (G)	1'36"095	1'32"514	1'33"240	1'36"081
15.	Johnny Herbert	Sauber/Petronas/C17/1 (G)	1'35"876	1'31"870	1'31"384	1'35"081
16.	Pedro Diniz	Arrows/A19/2 (B)	1'37"928	1'36"351	1'35"140	1'36"868
17.	Mika Salo	Arrows/A19/3 (B)	1'36"897	1'35"539	1'33"927	1'35"411
18.	Rubens Barrichello	Stewart/Ford/SF2/1 (B)	1'37"023	1'33"965	1'33"383	1'36"690
19.	Jan Magnussen	Stewart/Ford/SF2/3 (B)	1'37"605	1'34"543	1'34"906	1'36"160
20.	Ricardo Rosset	Tyrrell/Ford/026/2 (G)	1'37"144	1'35"010	1'35"119	1'38"487
21.	Toranosuke Takagi	Tyrrell/Ford/026/1 (G)	1'38"817	1'34"600	1'33"291	1'37"482
22.	Shinji Nakano	Minardi/Ford/M198/1 (B)	1'39"044	1'35"069	1'35"301	1'37"772
23.	Esteban Tuero	Minardi/Ford/M198/3 (B)	2'16"609	1'35"850	1'34"646	1'36"021

LAP CHART

position:	1	2	3	4	5	6	7	8	9	10	11	12	13	14	15	16	17	18	19	20	21	22
start:	8	7	3	1	15	2	5	4	10	9	6	14	21	18	12	17	23	19	20	16	11	22
1	8	7	3	1	5	15	2	4	9	6	12	14	17	10	19	21	23	20	11	22	16	
2	8	7	3	1	5	15	2	4	9	6	12	17	14	23	20	11	22	16				
3	8	7	3	1	5	15	2	4	9	6	12	17	14	23	20	11	22					
4	8	7	3	1	5	15	2	4	9	6	12	17	14	23	20	11	22					
5	8	7	3	1	5	15	2	4	9	6	12	17	14	23	20	11	22					
6	8	7	1	5	15	2	4	9	6	12	17	14	23	20	11	22						
7	8	7	1	5	15	2	4	9	6	12	17	14	23	20	11	22						
8	8	7	1	5	15	2	4	9	6	12	17	14	23	20	11	22						
9	8	7	1	5	15	2	4	9	6	12	17	14	23	20	11							
10	8	7	1	5	15	2	4	9	6	12	17	14	23	20	11							
11	8	7	1	5	15	2	4	9	6	12	17	14	23	11	20							
12	8	7	1	5	15	2	4	9	6	12	17	14	11	20	23							
13	8	7	1	5	15	2	4	9	6	12	17	14	11	20	23							
14	8	7	1	5	15	2	4	9	6	12	17	14	11	20	23							
15	8	7	1	5	15	2	4	9	6	12	17	14	11	20	23							
16	8	7	1	5	15	2	4	9	6	12	17	14	11	20	23							
17	8	7	1	5	15	2	4	9	6	12	17	14	11	20	23							
18	8	7	1	5	15	2	4	9	6	12	17	14	11	20	23							
19	8	7	1	5	15	2	4	6	12	14	17	9	11	20	23							
20	8	7	1	5	15	2	4	12	14	6	17	9	11	20	23							
21	8	7	1	5	15	2	4	12	14	6	17	9	11	20	23							
22	8	7	1	15	2	4	12	14	5	6	17	9	11	23	20							
23	8	7	1	15	2	4	12	14	5	6	17	9	11	20								
24	7	8	1	15	2	4	12	14	5	6	9	11	20									
25	8	7	1	15	2	4	12	14	5	6	9	11	20									
26	8	7	1	15	2	4	12	14	5	6	9	11										
27	8	7	1	2	4	14	5	15	6	9	11											
28	8	7	2	4	14	5	1	15	6	9	11											
29	8	7	2	4	5	1	15	6	9	14	11											
30	8	7	2	4	5	1	15	6	9	14	11											
31	8	7	2	4	5	1	15	6	9	14	11											
32	8	7	2	4	5	1	15	6	9	14	11											
33	8	7	2	5	4	1	6	15	9	14	11											
34	8	7	2	5	4	1	6	15	9	14	11											
35	8	7	2	5	4	1	6	15	9	14	11											
36	7	8	2	5	4	1	15	9	14	6	11											
37	7	8	2	5	4	1	15	9	14	6	11											
38	7	8	2	5	4	1	15	9	14	6	11											
39	7	8	5	2	4	1	15	14	6	9	11											
40	7	8	5	2	4	1	15	14	6	9	11											
41	7	8	2	4	5	1	15	14	6	9	11											
42	7	8	2	4	1	15	5	6	9	11												
43	7	8	2	4	1	15	5	6	9	11												
44	7	8	2	4	1	15	6	9	11													
45	7	8	2	4	1	15	6	9	11													
46	7	8	2	4	1	15	6	9	11													
47	7	8	2	4	1	15	6	9	11													
48	7	8	2	4	1	15	6	9	11													
49	7	8	2	4	1	15	6	9	11													
50	7	8	2	4	1	15	6	9	11													
51	7	8	2	4	1	15	6	9	11													
52	7	8	2	4	1	15	6	9	11													
53	7	8	2	4	1	15	6	9	11													
54	7	8	2	4	1	15	6	9	11													
55	7	8	2	4	1	15	6	9	11													
56	8	7	2	4	1	15	6	9	11													
57	8	7	2	4	1	15	6	9	11													
58	8	7																				

Best result for a Bridgestone shod runner:

Mika Hakkinen, McLaren-Mercedes, 1st

CHAMPIONSHIPS

(after one round)

Drivers :

1. Mika HAKKINEN 10
2. David COULTHARD 6
3. Heinz-Harald FRENTZEN 4
4. Eddie IRVINE 3
5. Jacques VILLENEUVE 2
6. Johnny HERBERT 1

Constructors :

1. McLaren / Mercedes 16
2. Williams / Mecachrome 6
3. Ferrari 3
4. Sauber / Petronas 1

CLASSIFICATION & RETIREMENTS

Pos	Driver	Team	Time
1.	Hakkinen	McLaren Mercedes	in 1h31'45"996
2.	Coulthard	McLaren Mercedes	at 0"702
3.	Frentzen	Williams Mecachrome	at 1 lap
4.	Irvine	Ferrari	at 1 lap
5.	Villeneuve	Williams Mecachrome	at 1 lap
6.	Herbert	Sauber Petronas	at 1 lap
7.	Wurz	Benetton Playlife	at 1 lap
8.	Hill	Jordan Mugen Honda	at 1 lap
9.	Panis	Prost Peugeot	at 1 lap

Lap	Driver	Team	Reason
1	Barrichello	Stewart Ford	gearbox
2	Takagi	Tyrrell Ford	spin
2	Magnussen	Stewart Ford	accident
2	R. Schum.	Jordan Mugen Honda	accident
3	Diniz	Arrows	gearbox
6	M. Schum.	Ferrari	engine
9	Nakano	Minardi Ford	transmission
23	Tuero	Minardi Ford	engine
24	Salo	Arrows	electronics
26	Rosset	Tyrrell Ford	gearbox
27	Trulli	Prost Peugeot	gearbox
42	Alesi	Sauber Petronas	engine
44	Fisichella	Benetton Playlife	rear wing

FASTEST LAPS

	Driver	Time	Lap
1.	Hakkinen	1'31"649	39
2.	Coulthard	1'32"356	23
3.	Frentzen	1'33"554	32
4.	Irvine	1'33"790	32
5.	Hill	1'34"196	56
6.	Fisichella	1'34"319	40
7.	Panis	1'34"319	55
8.	Wurz	1'34"738	55
9.	Alesi	1'34"878	27
10.	Trulli	1'34"885	24
11.	Herbert	1'35"624	23
12.	Villeneuve	1'35"661	53
13.	M. Schum.	1'35"774	2
14.	Salo	1'36"032	17
15.	Tuero	1'36"475	20
16.	Rosset	1'38"116	20
17.	Nakano	1'39"676	2
18.	Diniz	1'39"916	2

FIRST ROUND

QANTAS AUSTRALIAN GRAND PRIX, MELBOURNE

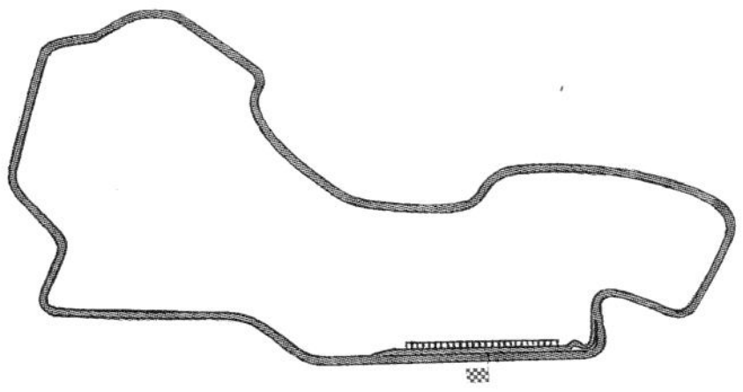

Date : March 9, 1998
Length : 5302 meters
Distance : 58 laps, 307.574 km
Weather : sunny, 30 degrees

RACE SUMMARY

- The two McLarens make the best start, while Michael Schumacher tries in vain to pass David Coulthard.
- The Ferrari driver just about manages to hang on to the infernal McLaren pace, but he is forced to retire on lap 6.
- That hands third place to Jacques Villeneuve, chased by Giancarlo Fisichella.
- Drama on the 36th lap when Mika Hakkinen comes into the pits unexpectedly. He drives straight out again but loses first place.
- In the lead, David Coulthard slows and lets the Finn overtake him. It is the first McLaren one-two finish of the season. It will not be the last.

WEEK-END GOSSIP

- **No smoke without fire**

A sudden volte face from FIA President Max Mosley. In October 1997, he had launched a virulent attack on the European union which was threatening to ban all tobacco advertising on its territory from 2006. *«Formula 1 cannot do without a budget of around 300 million dollars a year,»* he had thundered. *«If it comes to that we will only keep three races in Europe and we will move the championship to the Far East.»*
By Melbourne he had changed his tune. *«Studies we have carried out show that tobacco advertising does not encourage young people to start smoking, but simply makes existing smokers change brands. This seems perfectly logical to me. If I don't like whisky, no amount of advertising will make me drink it. The European union now claims that there are links between the advertising and people taking up smoking. If our own research confirms this, then we will review our position as the FIA does not want to contribute to damaging the health of young people.»*
By taking a self-regulatory stance, F1 would gain public approbrium for its brave move. It would also avoid having to move to Asia, which would not be popular in Europe.

- **Crash test headache**

There were worried faces in the Prost team on the Wednesday before the race. The AP01 was the only chassis not to have yet passed the compulsory crash test and the team's engineers who had stayed back at base were now trying once again in England on the Thursday. It passed, but if it had not, the team would have had to get the approval of all the other competitors in order to line up for the start of the Australian Grand Prix.

- **Casino for the bookies**

Australians like a flutter. The Melbourne casinos are always busy and people bet on anything, including the grand prix and the odds for all the drivers gave a clear indication of who was favourite for the race. Jacques Villeneuve was 2 to 1, Michael Schumacher 3 to 1, David Coulthard 7 to 2 and Mika Hakkinen 9 to 2. At the other end of the scale, those putting a dollar on Toranosuke Takagi or Esteban Tuero stood to win 250 dollars in the event of a win.
This situation caused problems after the strange ending to the Australian Grand Prix, as those who had backed Coulthard felt they had been cheated, as the Scotsman was the moral victor of the event. The bookmakers refused to hand back the stake money.

«All these people, just for me?» The traditional start-of-season photo call, Jacques Villeneuve ▽ *can judge at first hand what the world championship has done for his popularity.*

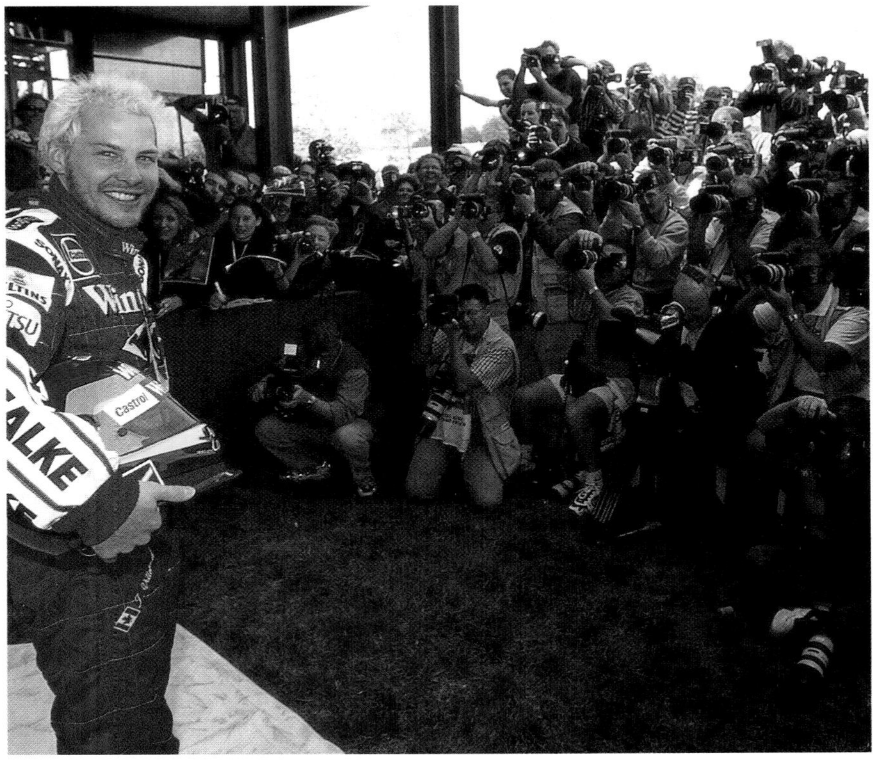

We
BRIDGESTONE

A perfect display

Both McLaren-Mercedes taught their rivals a sharp lesson at Interlagos, finishing over one minute ahead of their nearest competitor, Michael Schumacher.
The weekend had not actually got off to the best of starts for the silver arrows team. A storm of protest rained down on them before the cars had even turned a wheel. Several teams reckoned McLaren's braking system gave them an illegal advantage. It did not achieve much, as even without the system, the McLarens were still way out in front...

GRANDE PRÊMIO DO BRASIL
INTERLAGOS

Two days of political patter in the paddock at Interlagos.

Braking aids: McLaren lose out

Even before the grand prix weekend got underway, the temperature was rising in Interlagos and it had nothing to do with the sunny weather. Chronology of a legal weekend.

Only Thursday and it's raining protests

On Thursday, at exactly 15h40 Ferrari protested the McLaren, Williams and Jordan teams, claiming these three teams were using an illegal braking aid. *«We do not know exactly how these systems work,»* claimed Scuderia Ferrari spokesman Claudio Berro. *«But we have cause to think they are not legal. The aim of our protest is to clarify the situation.»*
Along with the Arrows team, Ferrari put in another protest against McLaren and Williams, while Minardi, Sauber and Tyrrell also protested McLaren.
It was then the turn of Brazil GP stewards to study all the protests. If the McLaren, Williams and Jordan cars were declared illegal, then they would have to hurriedly their braking system, or run under appeal. This last route ran the risk of the teams losing any points scored in the Brazilian GP, if the appeals were rejected.
The situation was even more edgy as, on Thursday, McLaren boss Ron Dennis had declared that there was no question of the team dismantling their braking system. *«It is completely legal and we have written proof from the FIA. Whatever the outcome we will use it here.»*
If the stewards in Interlagos found in favour of the three teams, then Ferrari was ready to go with the flow. *«In this case we have what is needed in our packing cases and we will also use an assisted braking system,»* confirmed the Scuderia.

The long wait on Friday

Night fell on the matter and as the sun rose the next day, the Brazilian stewards were still in the dark. They asked the three teams concerned to disconnect their brake systems for Friday's session, before the teams were convened to a meeting at half past four to explain their position.
On Friday, the plaintiffs were confident they would win. *«Apparently the McLaren system uses no special controls, nor a third pedal or button,»* explained Peter Sauber, one of those who had protested the McLarens. *«From what we know, it operates automatically depending on the angle of the steering wheel. So there is a direct relationship between the steering and the rear wheels. This constitutes four wheel steering, which is completely illegal.»*
Over at Minardi, who had also protested McLaren, another explanation was on offer. The McLaren device is a secondary braking system, independent of the normal braking and the rules forbid the use of two parallel braking systems.» McLaren were maintaining their belief that the device was in line with the regulations. *«Our device is activated by the position of the steering wheel, but it is mechanical and therefore perfectly legal,» insisted Ron Dennis.*
While building its car, McLaren asked the FIA's technical director Charlie Whiting if the device was legal, on several occasions and the answer was always yes. But Whiting is not able to make a decision, he can only give a clarification. As it happened, he advised Ferrari to protest McLaren after hearing the arguments put forward by the Scuderia.

Saturday: Peter beats Dennis

Sunglasses perched on his nose, a cultivated tan and faded jeans, Henri Peter sported a broad grin on Saturday at lunchtime. The protest which the lawyer had written on behalf of his client, Scuderia Ferrari, had done the trick.
The Brazilian GP stewards had decided the braking aid devices found on the McLarens, Williams and Jordans was illegal.
A professor of commercial and sports law at Geneva university, Henri Peter also runs a legal practice in Lugano and has worked in this capacity for Ferrari since 1984.
He wrote the protest handed in by the Scuderia on Thursday in Interlagos. *«McLaren had managed to convince the FIA of the legality of its system,»* explained Henri Peter. *«But we believed the device was illegal. We did not know how it worked, but we had seen its effect, which was to have a car with four wheel steering.»*
The F1 regulations actually state that four wheel steering is banned. To back up its argument, Ferrari provided drawings of all sorts of vehicles where steering is under the sole control of the rear wheel braking system.
On Saturday morning, after another night of deliberation, the stewards confirmed the analysis of Peter and declared the braking aid systems to be banned from now on. To everyone's surprise, the three teams concerned did not appeal and started the race without the systems being fitted. Ron Dennis was thinking about fitting them again for Argentina to test the water there.
Jean Todt meanwhile, refrained from crowing over his victory on Saturday afternoon. *«We never felt McLaren's superiority was down to their braking system. Their strength is in the overall package of their car. Today, the MP4/13 is a reference point and we have to fight hard to reach its level.»*

McLaren at the heart of the problem. Many of the rival teams felt the key to McLaren's superiority at Melbourne was in their steering brake system. Future events would prove that with or without it, Mika Hakkinen and David Coulthard were still out in front.

Mixed fortunes at Williams. On Saturday, Jacques Villeneuve had a huge shunt (see below.) He tackled qualifying with a stiff neck and was only tenth. Heinz-Harald Frentzen in the other Williams (below) somehow managed to get his car to third on the grid.

◁
Fourth on the grid, Michael Schumacher had third place wrested from him in the dying moments of the session, by Heinz-Harald Frentzen. «We changed the setting in the last few minutes and it did not work,» he explained. I think the McLarens will be unbeatable in the race, but we should be the best of the rest.»

With or without their steering brake, the McLarens are still out in front

With or without their braking aid, the McLarens still dominated. On Saturday, at the end of qualifying it was indeed once again Mika Hakkinen and David Coulthard who set the two fastest times. *«I have to say I love this track, as it really suits my style,»* remarked the Finnish driver.
Not having observed the yellow flags in the morning, Mika Hakkinen risked having his best qualifying time disallowed. He got round the problem by the simple expedient of setting two laps faster than any of his rivals. However, a few hours later, he and a host of other drivers were hauled over the coals for the same offence. They all said they could not see the flag in question.

Head: Ferrari is making a fool of itself

It did not take long for the Williams team to react. Having been humiliated by McLaren in Australia, Jacques Villeneuve, Heinz-Harald Frentzen and the Williams boys had been working flat out to get a braking system up and running in time for the Brazilian GP.
But, while Heinz-Harald loved it, Jacques said he did not want it. *«I tried the system, but I don't like it and I won't be using it here. In any case, next to the one McLaren has got, ours is a dinosaur.»* This remark got up Patrick Head's nose. *«I don't think Jacques understands how the McLaren system works,»* said the Williams technical director, before turning his tongue loose on Ferrari. *«Ferrari's protest is absurd. They have not the slightest idea how a Williams is built and they have made themselves look stupid by acting this way. If they have done it, I can only imagine it is simply to find an excuse for being off the pace.»* On Saturday, Head had to eat his words as Ferrari had definitely won the day.

Even allowing for Hakkinen's declaration that he loved this track, it was surprising that he was seven tenths quicker than team-mate David Coulthard. *«It's true, it is a big gap,»* he conceded. *«But really, I like this track as all the corners are a real challenge. I think a lot of people will go off the track during the race in the same way we saw it happen a lot in qualifying. It will be important not to push too hard in some corners.»*
Asked about his disappointment at no longer having the braking system, Hakkinen thought for a moment before replying. *«Yes, I am disappointed. The car is a whole package. We had a super car and now it has one part less.»*
In second place, David Coulthard also admitted surprise at the gap to his team- mate. *«I think Mika was quicker in the second sector, because when I add up my best sector times I am not so far behind him. He is making up two tenths just in the third corner. But I am not worried. The race is not a qualifying session. I intend winning tomorrow.»*

With 16.4 million inhabitants according to 1995 figures, Sao Paulo is a capital city of contrasts on a grand scale. While part of the population lives in sumptiously splendid villas, over a million still live in the favellas alongside the putrid River Tiete.
◁

STARTING GRID

		Mika HAKKINEN 1'17"092
David COULTHARD 1'17"757	-1-	
		Heinz-H. FRENTZEN 1'18"109
M. SCHUMACHER 1'18"250	-2-	
		Alexander WURZ 1'18"261
Eddie IRVINE 1'18"449	-3-	
		G. FISICHELLA 1'18"652
R. SCHUMACHER 1'18"735	-4-	
		Olivier PANIS 1'18"753
Jacques VILLENEUVE 1'18"761	-5-	
		Damon HILL 1'18"988
Jarno TRULLI 1'19"069	-6-	
		R. BARRICHELLO 1'19"344
Johnny HERBERT 1'19"375	-7-	
		Jean ALESI 1'19"449
Jan MAGNUSSEN 1'19"644	-8-	
		Toranosuke TAKAGI 1'20"203
Shinji NAKANO 1'20"390	-9-	
		Esteban TUERO 1'20"459
Mika SALO 1'20"481	-10-	
		Ricardo ROSSET 1'20"748
Pedro DINIZ 1'20"847	-11-	

Second consecutive double for Ron Dennis' team

Pure perfection from the McLarens

The two McLaren drivers showed no signs of effort after their display. At the end of a perfect race, Mika Hakkinen and David Coulthard had racked up another one-two finish which was free of any controversy. Team boss Ron Dennis' smile looked like an ear to ear banana.
Happy people have little to say and as Mika Hakkinen is not exactly a chatterbox by nature, the Finn did not have much to tell about his race, which had been perfect from start to finish, as he then confirmed: «*Yes, everything went well. My only worry came six laps from the end when I ran over some debris which had been blown across the track in the middle of the straight. I braked but I still hit it, luckily without doing any damage to my front wing. Before the race, I had been a bit worried about the start. When you are on pole, the track slopes away and there is a tendency to roll backwards. But in the end it all went off okay. It was a good race and I am very happy with the way it went.*»
Alongside him, David Coulthard could not say the same. «*I had planned to pass Mika at the first corner, but I made a complete mess of the start. I had chosen a traditional clutch with a foot pedal, while Mika used a clutch controlled on the steering wheel and with that slope going the wrong way, I found it difficult to hold the car and make a hill start.*»
Once fired off the line, the two silver arrows were not troubled again, especially as they had opted for a one stop strategy, which allowed them to run away from the Ferraris and Williams, which had chosen to stop twice.
When they crossed the line, the two McLarens led home their immediate pursuer, Michael Schumacher by over a minute. Right at the end of the race, Hakkinen therefore decided to slow down and let his team-mate close up so they could both finish in style. Two double from two starts for McLaren. It all looked so easy.

▷ *An impeccable start for the two McLarens as Mika Hakkinen does a magnificent job of exploiting his pole position, despite his place on the grid being on a slight slope. As they brake for the first turn, he already has a sizeable lead.*

With or without

At Interlagos, the two McLarens proved they could win without their steering brake. Following the Steward's decision, the team dismantled the system from all its cars. Or at least that was the official version.
Word on the street, or the pit-lane to be precise, opponents of Team Grey were less convinced. «*We are almost certain that McLaren raced today with their braking aid,*» said an anonymous Ferrari person.
On Thursday, some indiscrete remarks let it be known that McLaren could not dismantle their braking system in Brazil, whatever the result of the protest lodged by Ferrari.
It would seem that the electronic side of this apparatus was too closely linked to that of the rest of the car, for it to be simply switched off.
On Sunday, the post race scrutineering revealed no irregularities in this area when the two McLarens were checked. As Ferrari did not protest the race results, the matter ended there.
In theory, the whole affair would start all over again and intensify in two weeks time at the Argentinean Grand Prix. Ron Dennis had promised to re-install his steering brake system in Buenos Aires.

Holidays already

They had only completed two grands prix, but for the McLaren drivers, the two week break before Argentina was already an excuse for a holiday. «*I am off to Argentina tomorrow, to have a rest,*» said Mika Hakkinen. The opposition however could not afford to twiddle their collective thumbs. Both the Williams and Ferrari drivers were heading back to Europe on Sunday evening to crack on with some intensive testing. Usually, both Michael Schumacher and Jacques Villeneuve headed off for a few days of R & R in the north of Brazil before tackling the Argentinean Grand Prix. This time, they had to sacrifice their holidays in an effort to close the gap to the McLarens.

▷ *Giancarlo Fisichella in pensive mood. An accident on Sunday morning left the Italian with no time to set up the spare car for the race. He fought a car that oversteered for the first 35 laps and eventually came home sixth.*

IN THE POINTS

1.	Mika HAKKINEN	West McLaren Mercedes	1 h 37'11"747
2.	David COULTHARD	West McLaren Mercedes	at 1"102
3.	M. SCHUMACHER	Scuderia Ferrari Marlboro	at 1'00"550
4.	Alexander WURZ	Mild Seven Benetton Playlife	at 1'07"453
5.	Heinz-H. FRENTZEN	Winfield Williams	at 1 lap
6.	Giancarlo FISICHELLA	Mild Seven Benetton Playlife	at 1 lap

Fastest lap : Mika HAKKINEN, lap 64, 1'19"337, avg. 194.754 km/h

△
Champagne! Coulthard had their thirst showered away in Interlagos.

Ferrari makes the best of a bad job...

Jean Todt was best left alone on Sunday after the race. The Ferrari sporting director was asked by a journalist if he did not feel wiped out at seeing his car finish over a minute down on the McLarens. «It is listening to you journalists that wipes me out,» was the Frenchman's only comment after the result of the Brazilian Grand Prix had sunk in.

In the race, Michael Schumacher was no match for the incredible pace of the McLarens. *«It all began badly. I made a very poor start,»* explained the German. *«I was actually surprised that more cars did not pass me.»*

However, his biggest fright came during his second pit stop, when the engine stalled. *«I do not know what happened, as usually we have a procedure which prevents this sort of thing from happening. Luckily my mechanics got me going again very quickly and I did not lose my place.»*

In the week to come, the Scuderia had planned an intensive test programme in order to improve the F 300 in time for the Argentinean Grand Prix. For its part, Goodyear would have a new construction for Buenos Aires- in Interlagos, Ferrari felt it was losing a good second a lap because of the tyres.

Combined with the twisty layout of the Argentine track, this step forward might make the Ferraris much more of a menace for McLaren. At least, that was what Michael Schumacher was hoping for. *«We will certainly be closer to the grey cars in Buenos Aires,»* he suggested. *«I don't know if we will be able to attack them, but at least the gap between us should be smaller.»*

Jacques Villeneuve remains optimistic

One fifth place and one seventh. The Williams team had known better weekends than Interlagos.

Despite this, on Sunday night, there was no sign of depression in the camp. *«I enjoyed myself a lot in this race,»* commented Jacques Villeneuve after coming seventh and therefore failing to score any points. *«The car seemed to work a lot better than in qualifying and I am very happy with that. Unfortunately I started from too far back on the grid to have any chance of a good result. We lost too much time this weekend trying too many new things on the car and we paid the price. Overall, I think it will go better from Argentina. Our efforts should be rewarded.»*

Like Ferrari, Williams was about to start testing on the following Wednesday at Barcelona. In Brazil, the fact the team had to try new parts during a grand prix weekend, proved that they were at least working hard to catch the McLarens.

Alesi is satisfied

Qualified down on the eighth row, Jean Alesi knew this weekend held no hope of glory. In the race, he therefore settled for fighting off the advances of Olivier Panis, before bringing his Sauber home ninth. *«Actually, the car was better than I had hoped for. It was definitely better than in qualifying,»* he said. Dripping with sweat, but all smiles, even his mechanics rushed to cheer him.

In the other Sauber, Johnny Herbert had retired five laps from the flag, ordered to pit by his team. He had crashed on Saturday and his neck was still hurting. Peter Sauber felt it was better to call him in as soon as he done enough laps to be classified as a finisher.

Ninth place for Jean Alesi. Nothing to write home about, but it won him a hero's welcome from the Sauber team. His mechanics were impressed with his start. From 15th on the grid, he was up to ninth by the end of the opening lap.
▽

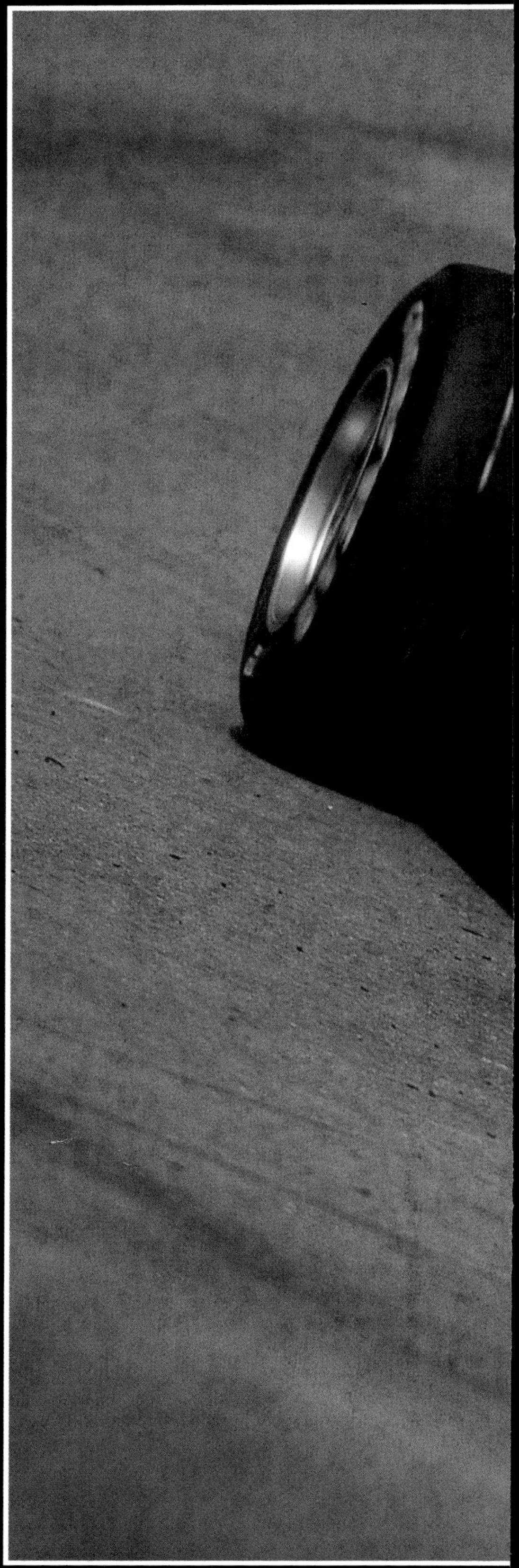

Michael Schumacher hard at work. On the Interlagos roller coaster, the German was powerless against the McLarens. He was having a hard enough time keeping his Ferrari pointing in the right direction.

Surprise decision from the World Council

Flashback to the lap 56 of the Australian Grand Prix: Lap 56 and after slowing down, David Coulthard lets his teammate Mika Hakkinen go past and take the chequered the flag. Some people saw it as a gesture of loyalty to an unlucky teammate, was not seen that way by many. In the days following the Australian Grand Prix, the FIA and the McLaren team were inundated with letters of protest, mainly from gamblers who had bet on Coulthard winning.

At Interlagos on Saturday, made a point of brushing aside this criticism. *«I have no sympathy for people who lost money because of our tactics in Australia,»* he declared. *«Formula 1 is not adapted to betting and those who risk it must first understand the way the sport works before betting sums they cannot afford to lose.»*

The number of Formula 1 races whose outcome was decided in the pit lane is significant, but from now on, all that was about to change. The week before the Brazilian race, the FIA had put out a statement declaring that teams could no longer arbitrarily decide the finishing order of their drivers.

The decision angered Ron Dennis. *«The FIA has decided to put a new interpretation on the regulations. So be it. We respect their wishes and will obey them to the letter. But I warn that we will continue to race as a team because that is the right thing to do. Tactics are a fundamental part of the spirit of F1. In Melbourne our drivers worked for the team and I see nothing wrong in that. If we had not made any plans and if David and Mika had battled for the lead and had broken their engines, it would have been our fault.»*

In any case, it seemed almost impossible to check if a team had employed a strategy for its drivers. It is very easy to slow down in an imperceptible manner or to artificially lengthen a pit stop, or on the pretext of a problem, to call a driver into the pits.

The FIA did not appear to have thought this through. In Interlagos, Bernie Ecclestone declared that the two McLarens would be disqualified if they adopted a similar tactic to the one used in Australia. In Interlagos, Coulthard made no attempt to attack Hakkinen. But how to tell if he held back or if his car's performance prevented him from doing so?

▷ *«The cream cake trick still works then.» David Coulthard was keen to share his 27th birthday cake with Mika Hakkinen.*

▽ *«I don't think I am out of the woods yet.» Having qualified only 11th, Damon Hill reflects on his future, having abandoned his broken Jordan. After an awful season with Arrows, the 1996 world champion would have to be patient before returning to the winner's enclosure five months later in Spa.*

David's cash

In Melbourne, the McLaren team's tactics worked in favour of Mika Hakkinen. But Ron Dennis was keen to insist that there was no favouritism towards the Finn. «We have never favoured one driver to the detriment of the other. The strategy was put in place to give the team the best overall result possible. In other circumstances, David would have had the advantage.»

On Sunday night, Ron Dennis assured David Coulthard that the tables would be turned at a later date. «David will also benefit from our strategy later in the season,» was his guarantee.

Damon Hill criticises McLaren

Damon Hill feels that banning team strategy is good news for the sport. *«McLaren's strategy is not good for the image of the team, of Mercedes or for F1 and for all the drivers,»* said the Englishman in Brazil. *«The spectators want to see real racing, not events where the result has been decided in advance. David* (Coulthard) *and Mika* (Hakkinen) *let themselves get dragged into this silly public relations exercise and these arguments to satisfy the sponsors. For me, their arrangement completely spoilt Melbourne.»*

These harsh words probably stemmed from some bad feeling towards McLaren. In the summer of 1997, negotiations between Hill and the team broke down because of his excessive financial demands.

PRACTICE TIMES

No	Driver	Car/Engine/Chassis	Practice Friday	Practice Saturday	Qualifying	Warm-up
1.	Jacques Villeneuve	Williams/Mecachrome/FW20/3 (G)	1'20"031	1'19"429	1'18"761	1'20"946
2.	Heinz-Harald Frentzen	Williams/Mecachrome/FW20/2 (G)	1'19"937	1'18"647	1'18"109	1'20"975
3.	Michael Schumacher	Ferrari/F300/184 (G)	1'20"164	1'18"974	1'18"250	1'20"578
4.	Eddie Irvine	Ferrari/F300/183 (G)	1'19"916	1'19"364	1'18"449	1'20"547
5.	Giancarlo Fisichella	Benetton/Playlife/198/5 (B)	1'20"777	1'18"674	1'18"652	1'21"712
6.	Alexander Wurz	Benetton/Playlife/198/4 (B)	1'19"936	1'18"879	1'18"261	1'21"009
7.	David Coulthard	McLaren/Mercedes/MP4-13/3 (B)	1'18"799	1'17"535	1'17"757	1'19"526
8.	Mika Hakkinen	McLaren/Mercedes/MP4-13/4 (B)	1'18"573	1'17"432	1'17"092	1'19"394
9.	Damon Hill	Jordan/Honda/198/3 (G)	1'20"527	1'19"329	1'18"988	1'21"521
10.	Ralf Schumacher	Jordan/Honda/198/4 (G)	1'19"721	1'18"738	1'18"735	1'21"651
11.	Olivier Panis	Prost/Peugeot/AP01/4 (B)	1'19"786	1'19"138	1'18"753	1'21"107
12.	Jarno Trulli	Prost/Peugeot/AP01/3 (B)	1'20"919	1'19"474	1'19"069	1'21"079
14.	Jean Alesi	Sauber/Petronas/C17/3 (G)	1'20"021	1'19"686	1'19"449	1'21"117
15.	Johnny Herbert	Sauber/Petronas/C17/1 (G)	2'06"081	1'19"867	1'19"375	1'21"192
16.	Pedro Diniz	Arrows/A19/2 (B)	1'21"298	1'21"042	1'20"847	1'22"654
17.	Mika Salo	Arrows/A19/3 (B)	1'21"116	1'20"771	1'20"481	1'21"374
18.	Rubens Barrichello	Stewart/Ford/SF2/1 (B)	1'20"010	1'20"299	1'19"344	1'20"620
19.	Jan Magnussen	Stewart/Ford/SF2/3 (B)	1'20"839	1'20"330	1'19"644	1'21"026
20.	Ricardo Rosset	Tyrrell/Ford/026/2 (G)	1'22"962	1'21"541	1'20"748	1'22"228
21.	Toranosuke Takagi	Tyrrell/Ford/026/1 (G)	1'21"598	1'20"760	1'20"203	1'21"584
22.	Shinji Nakano	Minardi/Ford/M198/1 (B)	1'21"938	1'21"242	1'20"390	1'21"681
23.	Esteban Tuero	Minardi/Ford/M198/3 (B)	1'21"901	1'21"040	1'20"459	1'22"542

LAP CHART

position:	1	2	3	4	5	6	7	8	9	10	11	12	13	14	15	16	17	18	19	20	21	22
start:	8	7	2	3	6	4	5	10	11	1	9	12	18	15	14	19	21	22	23	17	20	16
1	8	7	2	4	3	6	1	5	14	18	11	12	15	9	19	22	21	20	17	16	23	
2	8	7	2	4	3	6	1	5	18	14	11	12	15	9	19	22	21	20	17	23	16	
3	8	7	2	4	3	6	1	5	18	14	11	12	15	9	19	22	21	20	17	23	16	
4	8	7	2	4	3	6	1	5	18	14	11	12	15	9	19	21	20	17	23	16		
5	8	7	2	4	3	6	1	5	18	14	11	12	15	9	19	21	20	17	23	16		
6	8	7	2	4	3	6	1	5	18	14	11	12	15	9	19	21	20	17	23	16		
7	8	7	2	4	3	6	1	5	18	14	11	12	15	9	19	21	20	17	23	16		
8	8	7	2	4	3	6	1	5	18	14	11	12	15	9	19	21	20	17	23	16		
9	8	7	2	4	3	6	1	5	18	14	11	12	15	9	19	21	20	17	23	16		
10	8	7	2	3	4	6	1	5	18	14	11	12	15	9	19	21	20	17	23	16		
11	8	7	2	3	4	6	1	5	18	14	11	12	15	9	19	21	20	17	23	16		
12	8	7	2	3	4	6	1	5	18	14	11	12	15	9	19	21	20	17	23	16		
13	8	7	2	3	4	6	1	5	18	14	11	12	15	9	19	21	20	17	23	16		
14	8	7	2	3	4	6	1	5	18	14	11	15	12	9	19	21	20	17	23	16		
15	8	7	2	3	4	6	1	5	18	14	11	15	9	19	12	21	20	17	23	16		
16	8	7	2	3	4	6	1	5	18	14	11	15	9	19	12	21	20	17	23	16		
17	8	7	2	3	4	6	1	5	18	14	11	15	9	19	21	20	17	23	16	12		
18	8	7	2	3	4	6	1	5	18	14	11	15	9	19	21	20	17	23	16			
19	8	7	2	3	4	6	1	5	18	14	11	15	9	19	21	20	23	16				
20	8	7	2	3	4	6	1	5	18	14	11	15	9	19	20	23	16					
21	8	7	2	3	4	6	1	5	18	14	11	15	9	19	20	23	16					
22	8	7	2	3	4	6	1	5	18	14	11	15	9	19	23	16	20					
23	8	7	2	3	4	6	1	5	18	14	11	15	9	19	23	16	20					
24	8	7	2	3	4	6	1	5	18	14	11	15	9	19	23	16	20					
25	8	7	2	3	4	6	1	5	18	14	11	15	9	23	16	19	20					
26	8	7	2	3	4	6	1	5	18	14	11	15	9	23	16	19	20					
27	8	7	2	6	1	4	5	3	18	14	11	15	9	23	19	20						
28	8	7	6	1	5	3	2	18	14	11	4	15	9	23	19	20						
29	8	7	6	1	3	2	5	18	14	11	4	15	9	23	19	20						
30	8	7	6	3	2	5	18	14	11	4	15	1	9	19	23	20						
31	8	7	6	3	2	5	18	14	4	11	1	15	9	19	23	20						
32	8	7	6	3	2	5	18	14	4	11	1	15	9	19	23	20						
33	8	7	6	3	2	5	18	14	4	11	1	15	9	19	23	20						
34	8	7	6	3	2	5	18	14	4	11	1	15	9	19	23	20						
35	8	7	6	3	2	5	18	14	4	11	1	15	9	19	23	20						
36	8	7	6	3	2	5	14	4	11	1	18	15	9	19	23	20						
37	8	7	6	3	2	5	14	4	1	11	15	18	9	19	23	20						
38	8	7	6	3	2	5	14	4	1	11	15	18	19	9	23	20						
39	8	7	6	3	2	5	14	4	1	11	15	18	19	9	23	20						
40	8	7	6	3	2	5	14	4	1	11	15	118	19	9	23	20						
41	8	7	6	3	2	5	14	1	4	11	15	18	19	9	23	20						
42	8	7	6	3	2	5	1	4	11	14	18	15	19	9	23	20						
43	8	7	6	3	2	5	1	4	11	14	18	15	19	9	23	20						
44	8	7	6	3	2	5	1	4	14	11	18	15	19	9	23	20						
45	8	7	6	3	2	5	1	4	14	11	18	15	19	9	20							
46	8	7	3	6	5	1	4	2	14	11	18	15	19	9	20							
47	8	7	3	1	4	5	2	6	14	11	18	15	19	9	20							
48	8	7	3	4	1	2	6	5	14	11	18	15	19	9	20							
49	8	7	3	4	2	6	5	1	14	11	18	15	9	19	20							
50	8	7	3	4	2	6	5	1	14	11	18	15	9	19	20							
51	8	7	3	4	2	6	5	1	14	11	18	15	9	19	20							
52	8	7	3	4	2	6	5	1	14	11	18	15	9	19	20							
53	8	7	3	4	2	6	5	1	14	11	18	15	9	19								
54	8	7	4	3	6	2	5	1	14	11	18	15	9	19								
55	8	7	3	6	2	4	5	1	14	11	18	15	9	19								
56	8	7	3	6	2	5	1	4	14	11	15	18	9	19								
57	8	7	3	6	2	5	1	4	14	11	15	9	19									
58	8	7	3	6	2	5	1	4	14	11	15	9	19									
59	8	7	3	6	2	5	1	4	14	11	15	9	19									
60	8	7	3	6	2	5	1	4	14	11	15	9	19									
61	8	7	3	6	2	5	1	4	14	11	15	9	19									
62	8	7	3	6	2	5	1	4	14	11	15	9	19									
63	8	7	3	6	2	5	1	4	14	11	15	9	19									
64	8	7	3	6	2	5	1	4	14	15	9	19										
65	8	7	3	6	2	5	1	4	14	15	9	19										
66	8	7	3	6	2	5	1	4	14	15	9	19										
67	8	7	3	6	2	5	1	4	14	9	15	19										
68	8	7	3	6	2	5	1	4	14	9	19											
69	8	7	3	6	2	5	1	4	14	9	19											
70	8	7	3	6	2	5	1	4	14	9	19											
71	8	7	3	6	2	5	1	4	14													
72	8	7	3	6																		

BRIDGESTONE

Best result for a Bridgestone shod runner:

Mika Hakkinen, McLaren-Mercedes, *1st*

CHAMPIONSHIPS

(after two rounds)

Drivers :

1. Mika HAKKINEN 20
2. David COULTHARD 12
3. Heinz-Harald FRENTZEN 6
4. M. SCHUMACHER 4
5. Eddie IRVINE 3
6. Alexander WURZ 3
7. Jacques VILLENEUVE 2
8. Johnny HERBERT 1
   Giancarlo FISICHELLA 1

Constructors :

1. McLaren / Mercedes 32
2. Williams / Mecachrome 8
3. Ferrari 7
4. Benetton / Playlife 4
5. Sauber / Petronas 1

CLASSIFICATION & RETIREMENTS

Pos	Driver	Team	Time
1.	Hakkinen	McLaren Mercedes	in 1h37'11"747
2.	Coulthard	McLaren Mercedes	at 1"102
3.	M. Schum.	Ferrari	at 1'00"550
4.	Wurz	Benetton Playlife	at 1'07"453
5.	Frentzen	Williams Mecachrome	at 1 lap
6.	Fisichella	Benetton Playlife	at 1 lap
7.	Villeneuve	Williams Mecachrome	at 1 lap
8.	Irvine	Ferrari	at 1 lap
9.	Alesi	Sauber Petronas	at 1 lap
10.	Hill	Jordan Mugen Honda	at 2 laps
11.	Magnussen	Stewart Ford	at 2 laps
12.	Herbert	Sauber Petronas	physical problem

Lap	Driver	Team	Reason
1	R. Schum.	Jordan Mugen Honda	off
4	Nakano	Minardi Ford	off
18	Trulli	Prost Peugeot	fuel pump
19	Salo	Arrows	engine
20	Takagi	Tyrrell Ford	engine
27	Diniz	Arrows	gearbox
45	Tuero	Minardi Ford	throttle
53	Rosset	Tyrrell Ford	gearbox
57	Barrichello	Stewart Ford	gearbox
64	Panis	Prost Peugeot	gearbox

FASTEST LAPS

	Driver	Time	Lap
1.	Hakkinen	1'19"337	65
2.	M. Schum.	1'19"627	63
3.	Coulthard	1'19"646	59
4.	Wurz	1'19"863	63
5.	Fisichella	1'20"010	63
6.	Villeneuve	1'20"129	59
7.	Frentzen	1'20"271	59
8.	Irvine	1'20"378	61
9.	Panis	1'20"449	51
10.	Alesi	1'20"623	64
11.	Magnussen	1'20"991	27
12.	Hill	1'21"035	55
13.	Herbert	1'21"456	53
14.	Barrichello	1'21"758	39
15.	Trulli	1'22"933	10
16.	Diniz	1'22"969	18
17.	Takagi	1'23"226	20
18.	Tuero	1'23"293	39
19.	Rosset	1'23"342	16
20.	Salo	1'23"565	14
21.	Nakano	1'24"475	5

SECOND ROUND

GRANDE PRÊMIO DO BRASIL, INTERLAGOS

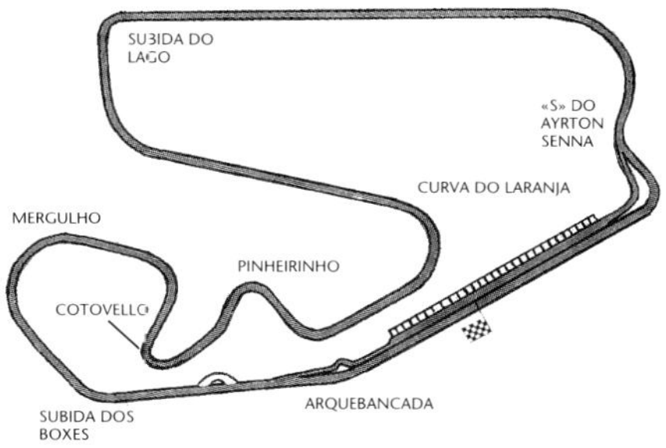

Date : March 29, 1998
Lenght : 4325 meters
Distance : 72 tours, 309.024 km
Weather : fine, 31 degrees

RACE SUMMARY

- As soon as the red lights went out, Mika Hakkinen stormed into the lead and took off for a long and lonely drive. He led every single lap of the race.
- After just one lap, the situation is calm. Mika Hakkinen leads Coulthard by over a second and is three seconds ahead of Heinz-Harald Frentzen in third. Eddie Irvine is ahead of a slow starting Michael Schumacher.
- After 18 laps, Hakkinen leads Coulthard by almost 5 seconds and the Frentzen-Schumacher duo by 23 seconds as the Ferrari driver has got past his team-mate Irvine.
- Michael Schumacher passes Frentzen at the first pit stops, but then he has to fight to make sure he does not suffer the supreme indignity of being lapped by both McLarens.
- The Bridgestone runners only make one pit stop, while the Goodyear users opt for two. The two McLarens are totally dominant.

WEEK-END GOSSIP

• Ron Dennis is very angry

On Saturday morning, David Coulthard's MP4/13 broke down out on the circuit. He decided to walk back to the pits and left his car to attract the attention of the photographers on that part of the track. Its a photo frenzy! They came from all around the track to snap away at their leisure: close ups of the gearbox, the steering wheel and the instrument panel and all sorts of other details that McLaren naturally wanted to keep secret, in view of the current steering brake drama.
As the TV cameras had filmed the photo-vultures snapping at the McLaren carcass, Ron Dennis went ballistic. He gave Coulthard a right royal ticking off for having abandoned his car, which is only what every other driver would do in this situation - and then complained about the behaviour of the photographers. Too late, the damage was done and lovely pictures of the McLaren were published around the world.

• Ferrari makes progress

Ferrari had solved part of the problem it suffered with its exhaust pipes in Melbourne. The Scuderia had thrown together a solution to stop the exhausts from overheating the gearbox. In Brazil, the F 300 were fitted with vertical exhausts which seemed to do the job.

• Goodyear hard at work

Goodyear had brought a new compound to Interlagos and promised a new construction for Buenos Aires. Bridgestone was worried about the American company catching up and was not resting on its laurels. It promised a new tyre for Imola.

• Alain Prost looks to the USA

Alain Prost put forward an argument for two day grand prix meetings instead of three, with the Friday to be cancelled, in order to accommodate up to 20 grands prix per season. «F1 needs races in the States and in China. These two countries would up the sport's viewing figures by 60 percent.

• Berger to Sauber?

Gerhard Berger's retirement, from the paddock at least, might be short lived. The Austrian was in Interlagos for the weekend and rumours had him replacing Max Welti, sacked at the end of 1997, as sporting director at Sauber.

• Ford with Benetton

It seemed that Ford was about to ink a deal with Benetton to supply the team with its V10 in 1999. The car company directors dropped the hint, letting it be known they wanted to start winning in F1 very soon.

The sky scraper builders of São Paulo must all be millionaires. The city skyline is a mess of building of all shapes and sizes, slashed through with huge avenues, most of them one way. ▽ Finding your way around is like driving through a maze.

Marlb
Aspr
TOMMY
prey

Revenge of the Reds

Just two weeks after the Brazilian Grand Prix had turned out to be a McLaren benefit, Scuderia Ferrari managed to buck the trend in Buenos Aires.
Having rather forcefully muscled David Coulthard out of the way and then flown off the track with the arrival of the first drops of rain, Michael Schumacher won an incident packed Argentine Grand Prix.
The victory was all the more appreciated by the tifosi as it stopped the rot in the championship after a bad start to the season.

GRAN PREMIO MARLBORO DE ARGENTINA
BUENOS AIRES

Schumacher the meat in the sandwich

For the first time this season, McLaren did not monopolise the front row of the grid. On Sunday in Buenos Aires, David Coulthard found Michael Schumacher lining up alongside him in his Ferrari. This proved that the silver arrows were not totally unbeatable. *«I am quite surprised to find myself here,»* admitted the German after qualifying. *«It is something of a miracle and I had expected to be third. Now that I am starting from the front row, everything is possible in the race.»*

Questioned as to the progress on his car, the double world champion confirmed that the new Goodyear tyres, (see page 110) had been the key to improvements on his F300. *«Having tried the new tyres in Barcelona, I was quite confident. They also allow us to use better settings for the chassis.»*

On a twisty track like Buenos Aires, overtaking is always very difficult in the race and so the start would be especially important. *«It will be crucial for me to get in the lead at the first corner,»* continued Schumacher. *«In Brazil, I had a slight problem with this, but we have sorted it out now. I did a lot of practice starts in Barcelona and it should be okay now.»*

On pole position for the first time this season, David Coulthard was also planning to be first into Turn 1. *«The weekend has started well, but the moment of truth comes when the lights go out on Sunday afternoon,»* explained the Scotsman.*»I am fairly confident, even though I know we are going to have to work hard to beat Ferrari.»*

Mika Hakkinen was only third. He was also disappointed. *«Everything went wrong today,»* he complained. *«I made a bad tyre choice and made a few mistakes on my two quickest laps. I could have done a lot better.»*

STARTING GRID

		David COULTHARD 1'25"852
M. SCHUMACHER 1'26"251	-1-	
		Mika HAKKINEN 1'26"632
Eddie IRVINE 1'26"780	-2-	
		R. SCHUMACHER 1'26"827
Heinz-H. FRENTZEN 1'26"876	-3-	
		Jacques VILLENEUVE 1'26"941
Alexander WURZ 1'27"198	-4-	
		Damon HILL 1'27"483
G. FISICHELLA 1'27"836	-5-	
		Jean ALESI 1'27"839
Johnny HERBERT 1'28"016	-6-	
		Toranosuke TAKAGI 1'28"811
R. BARRICHELLO 1'29"249	-7-	
		Olivier PANIS 1'29"320
Jarno TRULLI 1'29"352	-8-	
		Mika SALO 1'29"617
Pedro DINIZ 1'30"022	-9-	
		Shinji NAKANO 1'30"054
Esteban TUERO 1'30"158	-10-	
		Ricardo ROSSET 1'30"437
Jan MAGNUSSEN 1'31"178	-11-	

▷ *David Coulthard took pole in Buenos Aires. It was one of the rare times this season that he would line up ahead of Mika Hakkinen on the grid.*

Contrary to what the results sheets say, Riccardo Rosset and his Tyrrell did occasionally put on a fiery performance. ▷ ▽

Buenos Aires is one of the favourite legs of the F1 season. A view of «La Boca,» one of the most colourful areas of the «Federal Capital.» ▽ ▽

Michael Schumacher brushes aside the opposition and the tricky track

About face. After the first two races, it seemed that the pattern for the season had already been fixed and that we were in for a series of dull and predictable processions led by the two McLaren-Mercedes. Not so! The Argentinean Grand Prix was rich in excitement on its way to a result which even the most ardent tifosi could not have hoped for. Victory for Ferrari, as Michael Schumacher beat Mika Hakkinen fair and square in a McLaren which had been considered invincible.
The German had to fight hard for this win, especially as, once again, he messed up his start. *«We really have a problem with that,»* he explained after the race. Third at the first corner, the Ferrari driver took Mika Hakkinen on the second lap, before setting off in pursuit of David Coulthard. He took him with a controversial move that sent the McLaren waltzing into the grass. *«David went very wide into this corner,»* said Schumacher in justification of his actions. *«I went down the inside and I was much quicker than him, but he shut the door on me. He had already done it to me in Australia, but this time I decided he would not get away with it. The impact damaged my front wing and my car began to understeer through the right hand corners. Luckily it was not too serious.»* For David Coulthard, it was serious as the incident put an end to any thoughts of winning the race. The Scot rejoined in sixth place and was incapable of getting to the front.
Charging along in front, the German built up a big enough lead to allow him to refuel twice, once more than the McLarens. *«For my second stop, I had just enough of an advantage not to lose my position,»* he said. *«Everything depended on the mechanics and they were really great.»*
With this first win of the season, Michael Schumacher closed the gap to Mika Hakkinen to twelve points. It was good news for the tifosi, just two weeks before the San Marino Grand Prix. «We have a very busy test schedule over the next few days and we will introduce several new parts at Imola. I am optimistic and I think we are going to have a very exciting championship this season.» He did not know how prophetic those words would be...

Scary moment on lap 68

Michael Schumacher thought the race was already in his pocket, when it started to rain on the Buenos Aires circuit. With four laps to go, the track was like an ice rink and there were spins and slides galore.
The German did not escape the attentions of the rain and on the last corner his Ferrari went straight on into a gravel trap. *«There was one part where the track was particularly slippery and I got caught out. Luckily this morning I had seen Johnny (Herbert) get stuck in the sand at this point. I realised then that the best thing to do was to accelerate rather than brake, in order to get out.»*
In the morning, the Ferrari driver had actually taken the trouble of going to speak to Herbert to ask his advice as to what to do at the point and he even went to look at the perimeter service road at that point on the track. That allowed him to save his skin and the win in the afternoon. Professional or what?

What a shower! The champagne of course, not Jean Todt. The Frenchman was as happy as two cars on a podium. ▽

Lap 68: Michael Schumacher's off track excursion. The moment when the hearts of thousands of tifosi stopped beating. The incident ended happily, thanks to the German's clairvoyance. ◁▽

IN THE POINTS

1.	M. SCHUMACHER	Scuderia Ferrari Marlboro	1 h 48'36"175
2.	Mika HAKKINEN	West McLaren Mercedes	at 22"899
3.	Eddie IRVINE	Scuderia Ferrari Marlboro	at 57"745
4.	Alexander WURZ	Mild Seven Benetton Playlife	at 1'08"134
5.	Jean ALESI	Red Bull Sauber Petronas	at 1'18"286
6.	David COULTHARD	West McLaren Mercedes	at 1'19"751

Fastest lap : Alexander WURZ, lap 39, 1'28"179, avg. 173.878 km/h

△
Mika Hakkinen takes to the track during practice. By coming second, the Finn made the best of a bad job in the championship, even though he was powerless against Michael Schumacher in Buenos Aires.

McLaren takes a pasting

There was a change of mood in the McLaren-Mercedes camp. Smiling from ear to ear in Australia and Brazil, this time Ron Dennis could not get out of the Buenos Aires paddock fast enough after the race, officially in a hurry to make the flight home. For the Team Grey boss, Argentina was a failure, as he had set his heart on 16 wins from 16 grand prix starts in 1998. The plan had failed, much to everyone's surprise, especially that of Mika Hakkinen. «*I must say I am very surprised to see what the Ferraris managed to do here,*» admitted the Finn after the race. «*It was an excellent performance when compared to what I did. I think that things were a little bit better for David. I never managed to find a good set-up all weekend. So, in those circumstances, coming second is not too bad.*» Towards the end of the race, when it became apparent that Michael Schumacher would have to make a second refuelling stop, Hakkinen, who was only stopping once, allowed himself a moment of hope of retaking the lead. But he did not really believe it possible. «*I had hoped I might at least get back in front, but I came up behind some backmarkers and I lost a lot of time. Having said that, even if I had got the lead back, I think it would not have taken Michael long to pass me again. Then I just made sure of my place. It was raining, there was no point in* taking any risks.»

▷
Fourth place for Alexander Wurz. He could have been third, but for a small mistake which let Eddie Irvine slip by.

Was Ralf Schumacher facing his old demons again? After going off the track a lot in 1997, here he was racking up error number three from three races. In Buenos Aires, the German spun twice, the second time proving fatal for his suspension.
▽

Thanks to Goodyear

Michael Schumacher's success might have been down to his tyres. Goodyear had come along with a new front tyre which went some way to cutting out the understeer in high speed corners, which its teams were suffering with. Wider by 25 millimetres, this tyre also had a new construction. «*I think we have closed the gap to McLaren by a good second with this tyre,*» was Schumacher's analysis of the situation. Unlike Ferrari, McLaren had done no testing since Interlagos. «*We didn't need to. We are very happy with our car and our current tyres,*» *was the cocky comment from within the English team.* «*I think we still have the advantage in terms of performance, even if it is obvious that Goodyear has closed up,*» said Hiroshi Yasukawa, Bridgestone's motorsport director, after the race. «*Everyone is praising this new Goodyear tyre, but I would point out that we have been using this wider type of tyre since the start of the season. Actually, we are thinking now of reducing the width, to improve the car's aerodynamics.*»

PRACTICE TIMES

No	Driver	Car/Engine/Chassis	Practice Friday	Practice Saturday	Qualifying	Warm-up
1.	Jacques Villeneuve	Williams/Mecachrome/FW20/3 (G)	1'29"610	1'29"614	1'26"941	1'49"224
2.	Heinz-Harald Frentzen	Williams/Mecachrome/FW20/2 (G)	1'30"317	1'28"347	1'26"876	1'51"159
3.	Michael Schumacher	Ferrari/F300/184 (G)	1'29"114	1'27"737	1'26"251	1'48"501
4.	Eddie Irvine	Ferrari/F300/185 (G)	1'29"781	1'28"987	1'26"780	1'49"046
5.	Giancarlo Fisichella	Benetton/Playlife/198/5 (B)	1'30"963	1'29"781	1'27"836	1'49"030
6.	Alexander Wurz	Benetton/Playlife/198/4 (B)	1'31"850	1'29"842	1'27"198	1'49"735
7.	David Coulthard	McLaren/Mercedes/MP4-13/4 (B)	1'28"130	1'28"289	1'25"852	1'49"435
8.	Mika Hakkinen	McLaren/Mercedes/MP4-13/3 (B)	1'29"488	1'28"501	1'26"632	1'48"025
9.	Damon Hill	Jordan/Honda/198/3 (G)	1'30"645	1'28"701	1'27"483	1'51"240
10.	Ralf Schumacher	Jordan/Honda/198/4 (G)	1'29"845	1'29"633	1'26"827	1'52"048
11.	Olivier Panis	Prost/Peugeot/AP01/2 (B)	1'31"297	1'30"722	1'29"320	1'49"673
12.	Jarno Trulli	Prost/Peugeot/AP01/3 (B)	1'31"428	1'30"402	1'29"352	1'50"607
14.	Jean Alesi	Sauber/Petronas/C17/3 (G)	1'30"859	1'29"151	1'27"839	1'47"594
15.	Johnny Herbert	Sauber/Petronas/C17/1 (G)	1'31"081	1'30"808	1'28"016	9'19"807
16.	Pedro Diniz	Arrows/A19/2 (B)	1'32"660	1'31"509	1'30"022	1'53"294
17.	Mika Salo	Arrows/A19/3 (B)	1'32"257	1'32"563	1'29"617	1'49"314
18.	Rubens Barrichello	Stewart/Ford/SF2/1 (B)	1'31"727	1'30"432	1'29"249	1'49"568
19.	Jan Magnussen	Stewart/Ford/SF2/3 (B)	1'34"829	1'31"283	1'31"178	1'51"257
20.	Ricardo Rosset	Tyrrell/Ford/026/2 (G)	1'31"761	1'31"975	1'30"437	1'53"166
21.	Toranosuke Takagi	Tyrrell/Ford/026/1 (G)	1'30"054	1'33"299	1'28"811	1'51"150
22.	Shinji Nakano	Minardi/Ford/M198/1 (B)	1'33"390	1'33"675	1'30"054	1'52"483
23.	Esteban Tuero	Minardi/Ford/M198/3 (B)	1'33"731	1'32"883	1'30"158	1'52"824

LAP CHART

position:	1	2	3	4	5	6	7	8	9	10	11	12	13	14	15	16	17	18	19	20	21	22
start:	7	3	8	4	10	2	1	6	9	5	14	15	21	18	11	12	17	16	22	23	20	19
1	7	8	3	2	4	1	14	6	9	5	15	18	10	12	21	11	17	16	23	19	22	20
2	7	3	8	4	2	1	14	6	9	5	15	18	10	12	21	11	17	16	23	19	22	20
3	7	3	8	4	1	2	14	6	9	5	15	18	10	12	21	11	17	16	19	23	22	20
4	7	3	8	4	1	14	2	6	9	5	15	18	10	12	21	11	17	16	19	23	22	20
5	3	8	4	1	14	7	2	6	9	5	15	18	10	12	21	11	17	16	19	23	22	20
6	3	8	4	1	14	7	2	6	9	5	15	18	10	12	21	11	17	19	16	23	22	20
7	3	8	4	1	14	7	2	6	9	5	15	18	10	12	21	11	17	19	16	23	22	20
8	3	8	4	1	14	7	2	6	9	5	15	18	10	12	21	11	17	19	16	23	22	20
9	3	8	4	1	14	7	2	6	9	5	15	18	10	12	21	11	17	19	16	23	22	20
10	3	8	4	1	14	7	2	6	9	5	15	18	10	12	11	21	17	19	16	23	22	20
11	3	8	4	1	14	7	2	6	9	5	15	18	10	12	11	21	17	19	16	23	22	20
12	3	8	4	1	14	7	2	6	9	5	15	18	10	11	12	21	17	19	16	23	22	20
13	3	8	4	1	14	7	2	6	9	5	15	18	10	11	12	21	17	19	16	23	22	20
14	3	8	4	1	14	7	2	6	9	5	15	18	10	11	12	21	17	19	23	22	20	
15	3	8	4	1	14	7	2	6	9	5	15	18	10	11	12	21	17	19	23	22	20	
16	3	8	4	1	14	7	2	6	9	5	15	18	10	11	12	21	17	19	23	22	20	
17	3	8	4	1	14	7	2	6	9	5	15	18	10	11	12	21	17	23	22	19	20	
18	3	8	4	1	14	7	2	6	9	5	15	18	11	12	21	17	23	22	10	20		
19	3	8	4	1	14	7	2	6	9	5	15	18	11	12	21	23	22	20	10			
20	3	8	4	1	14	7	2	6	9	5	15	18	11	12	21	23	22	20	10			
21	3	8	4	1	14	7	2	6	9	5	15	18	11	12	21	23	22	20	10			
22	3	8	4	1	14	7	2	6	9	5	15	18	11	12	21	23	22	10	20			
23	3	8	4	1	14	7	2	6	9	5	15	18	11	12	21	23	22	20				
24	3	8	4	1	14	7	2	6	9	5	15	18	11	12	21	23	22	20				
25	3	8	4	1	14	7	2	6	9	5	15	18	11	12	21	23	22	20				
26	3	8	4	1	14	7	2	6	9	5	15	18	11	12	21	23	22	20				
27	3	8	4	1	7	14	2	6	5	9	15	18	11	12	21	23	22	20				
28	3	8	4	1	7	2	6	5	9	15	14	18	11	12	21	23	22	20				
29	8	3	4	1	7	2	6	5	15	14	18	9	11	12	21	23	22	20				
30	8	3	1	7	4	2	6	5	15	14	18	9	11	12	21	23	22	20				
31	8	3	1	7	4	2	6	5	15	14	18	9	11	12	21	23	22	20				
32	8	3	1	7	4	2	6	5	15	14	18	9	11	12	21	23	22	20				
33	8	3	1	4	2	6	5	15	14	7	18	9	11	12	21	23	22	20				
34	8	3	1	4	2	6	5	15	14	7	18	9	11	12	21	23	22	20				
35	8	3	1	4	2	6	5	14	15	7	18	9	11	12	21	23	22	20				
36	8	3	1	4	2	6	5	14	15	7	18	9	11	12	21	22	23	20				
37	8	3	1	4	2	6	5	14	15	7	18	9	11	12	21	22	23	20				
38	8	3	4	2	6	14	15	1	7	5	18	9	11	12	21	22	23	20				
39	8	3	4	6	14	15	1	7	5	18	11	9	2	12	21	22	23	20				
40	8	3	4	6	14	1	7	5	18	15	11	9	2	12	21	22	23	20				
41	8	3	4	14	6	1	7	5	15	11	9	2	18	12	21	22	23	20				
42	8	3	4	14	6	1	7	5	15	11	9	2	18	12	21	22	23	20				
43	3	8	4	14	6	1	7	5	15	9	2	11	18	12	21	22	23	20				
44	3	8	4	14	6	1	7	5	15	9	11	18	2	12	21	22	23	20				
45	3	8	4	14	6	1	7	5	15	9	11	18	2	12	21	22	23	20				
46	3	8	4	14	6	1	7	5	15	9	11	2	18	12	21	22	23	20				
47	3	8	4	14	6	1	7	5	11	9	2	18	12	21	22	23	20					
48	3	8	4	14	6	1	7	5	11	9	2	18	12	21	22	23	20					
49	3	8	4	14	6	1	7	5	11	9	2	18	12	21	22	23	20					
50	3	8	4	14	6	1	7	5	11	9	2	18	12	21	22	23	20					
51	3	8	4	6	14	1	7	5	11	9	2	18	12	21	22	23	20					
52	3	8	4	6	14	1	7	5	11	9	2	18	12	21	22	23	20					
53	3	8	4	6	14	5	7	11	9	2	18	12	21	22	23	20						
54	3	8	4	6	14	5	7	11	9	2	18	12	21	22	23	20						
55	3	8	4	6	14	5	7	11	9	2	18	12	21	22	23	20						
56	3	8	4	6	14	5	7	11	9	2	18	12	21	22	23	20						
57	3	8	4	6	14	5	7	11	9	2	18	12	21	22	23	20						
58	3	8	4	6	14	5	7	11	9	2	18	12	21	22	23	20						
59	3	8	4	6	14	5	7	11	9	2	18	12	21	22	23	20						
60	3	8	4	6	14	5	7	11	9	2	18	12	21	22	23	20						
61	3	8	4	6	14	5	7	11	9	2	18	12	21	22	23	20						
62	3	8	4	6	14	5	7	11	9	2	18	12	21	22	23	20						
63	3	8	4	6	14	5	7	11	9	2	18	12	21	22	23	20						
64	3	8	6	4	14	5	7	11	9	2	18	12	21	22	20							
65	3	8	6	4	14	5	7	11	9	2	18	12	21	22	20							
66	3	8	4	6	14	7	5	9	2	18	12	21	22	20								
67	3	8	4	6	14	7	5	9	2	18	12	21	22	20								
68	3	8	4	6	14	7	5	9	2	18	12	21	22	20								
69	3	8	4	6	14	7	5	9	2	18	12	21	22									
70	3	8	4	6	14	7	5	9	2	18	12	21										
71	3	8	4	6	14	7	5	9	2													
72	3	8	4	6	14	7	5															

Best result for a Bridgestone shod runner:

Mika Hakkinen, McLaren-Mercedes, 2nd

CHAMPIONSHIPS

(after three rounds)

Drivers :

1. Mika HAKKINEN 26
2. Michael SCHUMACHER 14
3. David COULTHARD 13
4. Eddie IRVINE................................... 7
5. Heinz-Harald FRENTZEN 6
   Alexander WURZ 6
7. Jean ALESI.. 2
   Jacques VILLENEUVE 2
9. Johnny HERBERT 1
   Giancarlo FISICHELLA 1

Constructors :

1. McLaren / Mercedes..................... 39
2. Ferrari.. 21
3. Williams / Mecachrome 8
4. Benetton / Playlife 7
5. Sauber / Petronas 3

CLASSIFICATION & RETIREMENTS

Pos	Driver	Team	Time
1.	M. Schum.	Ferrari	in 1h48'36"175
2.	Hakkinen	McLaren Mercedes	at 22"899
3.	Irvine	Ferrari	at 57"745
4.	Wurz	Benetton Playlife	at 1'08"134
5.	Alesi	Sauber Petronas	at 1'18"286
6.	Coulthard	McLaren Mercedes	at 1'19"751
7.	Fisichella	Benetton Playlife	at 1'28"438
8.	Hill	Jordan Mugen Honda	at 1 lap
9.	Frentzen	Williams Mecachrome	at 1 lap
10.	Barrichello	Stewart Ford	at 2 laps
11.	Trulli	Prost Peugeot	at 2 laps
12.	Takagi	Tyrrell Ford	at 2 laps
13.	Nakano	Minardi Ford	at 3 laps
14.	Rosset	Tyrrell Ford	at 4 laps
15.	Panis	Prost Peugeot	engine

Lap	Driver	Team	Reason
14	Diniz	Arrows	gearbox
18	Magnussen	Stewart Ford	transmission
19	Salo	Arrows	gearbox
23	R. Schum.	Jordan Mugen Honda	suspension
47	Herbert	Sauber Petronas	accident
53	Villeneuve	Williams Mecachrome	accident
64	Tuero	Minardi Ford	off

FASTEST LAPS

	Driver	Time	Lap
1.	Wurz	1'28"179	39
2.	Hakkinen	1'28"261	32
3.	M. Schum.	1'28"272	23
4.	Coulthard	1'28"468	57
5.	Fisichella	1'28"507	69
6.	Irvine	1'28"933	27
7.	Alesi	1'29"000	44
8.	Panis	1'29"201	57
9.	Hill	1'29"310	46
10.	Frentzen	1'29"592	37
11.	Villeneuve	1'29"694	35
12.	Herbert	1'29"857	30
13.	Barrichello	1'30"408	36
14.	Trulli	1'30"876	25
15.	Tuero	1'30"992	27
16.	Takagi	1'31"057	41
17.	Nakano	1'31"168	36
18.	R. Schum.	1'31"541	17
19.	Salo	1'32"519	12
20.	Magnussen	1'32"808	16
21.	Rosset	1'33"091	42
22.	Diniz	1'33"350	8

THIRD ROUND

GRAN PREMIO MARLBORO DE ARGENTINA, BUENOS AIRES

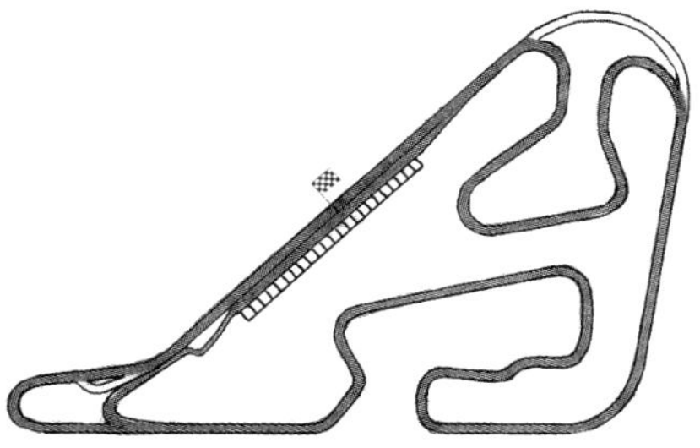

Date : April 12, 1998
Lenght: 4256 meters
Distance : 72 laps, 306.449 km
Weather : cloudy before the rain, 19 degrees

All results

RACE SUMMARY

- At the start, Michael Schumacher is caught out by Mika Hakkinen and David Coulthard maintains his first place.
- Michael Schumacher passes Mika Hakkinen at the start of second lap. A few moments later, Eddie Irvine does the same thing to Frentzen.
- By lap 4, Michael Schumacher has caught up with David Coulthard. One more lap and as the Scotsman gets the line wrong, the German slides by in his Ferrari. The two cars touch and Coulthard's McLaren slides off the track to rejoin in sixth place.
- Behind the leading trio, Jacques Villeneuve is under attack from Jean Alesi, who is coming under pressure from Coulthard.
- When Esteban Tuero comes in for his pit stop, one of the new wheels is missing. The mechanics find it in the garage.
- In the lead, M. Schumacher is heading for certain victory, even though he goes off the track when the rain comes down.

WEEK-END GOSSIP

• A dog day afternoon

Jacques Villeneuve arrived in Buenos Aires fresh from ten days piranha fishing in the Amazon jungle. «*It's really quite a nice fish....once it's cooked!*» he assured everyone.

On Thursday, the Canadian celebrated his 27th birthday, but come Sunday in the Williams pit, no one was in the mood to celebrate anything. Villeneuve had been forced to retire on lap 53 after a coming together with Coulthard, when he was fighting for a lowly sixth place. «*David tried to go round the outside,*» related the Canadian. «*But before he had got right ahead of me, he moved over and I had nowhere to go. I am not really sure whose fault it was, but given where we were in the order, it does not matter too much. I have not yet lost all hope of winning the championship. We know what is wrong with the car and what to do to solve our problems. I am still confident.*»

• Schumacher has fun

On Wednesday, as soon as he arrived in Argentina, Michael Schumacher played a soccer match with the junior squad of «Racing,» the famous Buenos Aires team. «*They gave me the chance to play with them and I had fun,*» said the Ferrari pilot. «*Anyway, I was very careful not to take any knocks.*» To everyone's general surprise, he managed to score three goals during the game; a reminder that football was his first love.

• ....and ups the bidding price

Michael Schumacher's money box is already a sight for sore eyes and it was about to overflow. Ferrari's parent company, Fiat, had allegedly offered the German 82 million dollars to stay with the Scuderia for three more years; his existing contract expiring at the end of 1999. With Mercedes also wanting to secure his services in the year 2000 «*at whatever price,*» the auction bidding had started.

• Viva Las Vegas

There was renewed talk of a grand prix in the United States. The Vegas project consisted of building a circuit in a park at the end of «The Strip» and it seemed to have the approval of Bernie Ecclestone. It would be partly financed by the «Paradise» complex, which would feature the biggest hotel in the world, boasting 14,000 rooms.

• Williams prepares for Le Mans

Contrary to habit, Patrick Head missed the start of practice. The Williams technical director was in France at the Castellet circuit, to finalise preparations of the car which the Williams team was entering in the Le Mans 24 Hours race.

A deserted road in Patagonia, between Bajo Caracoles and Calafate. The south of Argentina offers the traveller the beauty of wide open spaces.

David defeats Goliath

After their win in Argentina, Ferrari towered over the Imola circuit, boiling red with its tens of thousands of tifosi, like Goliath for the San Marino Grand Prix.

But every Goliath has to look out for his David and in this case his name was Coulthard, the Scot winning the San Marino Grand Prix in style. He did not have a big lead at the flag and had to nurse a sick McLaren across the line not long before the arrival of second placed Michael Schumacher. Hakkinen had to retire with similar problems to his team

GRAN PREMIO DI SAN MARINO
IMOLA

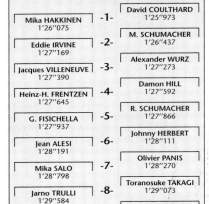

△ *Second consecutive pole for David Coulthard*

He's always in a hurry that Alexander Wurz. The Austrian did well to qualify in fifth place. ▷ ▽

STARTING GRID

	Row	
	-1-	David COULTHARD 1'25"973
Mika HAKKINEN 1'26"075		
	-2-	M. SCHUMACHER 1'26"437
Eddie IRVINE 1'27"169		
	-3-	Alexander WURZ 1'27"273
Jacques VILLENEUVE 1'27"390		
	-4-	Damon HILL 1'27"592
Heinz-H. FRENTZEN 1'27"645		
	-5-	R. SCHUMACHER 1'27"866
G. FISICHELLA 1'27"937		
	-6-	Johnny HERBERT 1'28"111
Jean ALESI 1'28"191		
	-7-	Olivier PANIS 1'28"270
Mika SALO 1'28"798		
	-8-	Toranosuke TAKAGI 1'29"073
Jarno TRULLI 1'29"584		
	-9-	R. BARRICHELLO 1'29"641
Pedro DINIZ 1'29"932		
	-10-	Esteban TUERO 1'30"649
Jan MAGNUSSEN 1'31"017		
	-11-	Shinji NAKANO 1'31"255
Ricardo ROSSET 1'31"482		

Ferrari makes do with an acceptable gap

«Four tenths, I think that is an acceptable gap.» On Saturday, Michael Schumacher was rather pleased with his performance in qualifying. *«After free practice this morning I thought we would be much further behind. In fact we are very close to the McLarens. Particularly as I made a mistake in my quickest lap when I had a slide through the last corner and I must have lost a couple of tenths.»*
To listen to the German, you would have thought that pole position had been in his grasp.
For the race, it therefore looked as though it was going to be tight at the top between the McLarens on the front row and both Ferraris which had monopolised the second row. *«It will all depend on the tyres,»* continued Schumacher. *«I think our Goodyear tyres will go the distance. We will see. We have a modification to make to our car overnight and we will try it out in tomorrow morning's warm-up. It might give us a small advantage.»* Michael would not be drawn further on the subject.
For McLaren, it was David Coulthard who took pole for the second consecutive race. Strange, as qualifying had not gone well for the Scotsman. He was even complaining about the handling of his chassis, which he felt was less well balanced than on Friday. *«I should not have got pole today,»* he admitted. *«We got the settings wrong for the second run and I made a mistake on the third one. Luckily, no one beat the time I did on my first flying lap.»*
In second spot, Mika Hakkinen was as disappointed as he had been in Argentina. The Finn was celebrating his 100th grand prix this weekend and he would have liked to have done so with a pole position. *«Yes I think it is a shame that I missed out on pole,»* he affirmed. *«My tyres were going off, even before the end of my first lap and there was nothing I could do. But I am not too worried. It will be a long hard race. The start will be particularly important and then anything can happen.»*
Ferrari did not seem to be facing an easy task in the race, even though the Scuderia could count on the unconditional support of over 100,000 tifosi who would only have eyes for the red cars.

Williams: something seriously wrong

The atmosphere was far from serene in the Williams motor home on Saturday afternoon. Jacques Villeneuve was sixth on the grid and his look said he was almost resigned to his fate, faced with the problems currently affecting the FW20. They seemed to be getting worse from race to race. *«I really fought hard, I gave it my best shot,»* he complained. *«I could not have gone any quicker as the car was well set up. But the result was that I had to fight it out with the Benettons and Jordans. It shows there is something seriously wrong with our chassis.»* Villeneuve said all he could hope for in the race was a few points, nothing more. At this point he was asked by an Italian journalist if Michael Schumacher could beat the McLarens and win the grand prix. *«Yes, if he steers at them hard,»* said the Canadian, who evidently had not yet forgotten last year's Jerez incident.

Coulthard does it...but only just

◁
David Coulthard savours his first taste of victory this season - at this stage he does not know it will also be his last! For the tifosi, the sight of two Ferrari drivers on the podium was some consolation for seeing a McLaren win.

Up to that point, the race had been positively soporific. At first, the two McLarens had taken off into the distance with such ease, that some of the tifosi, seated on the Imola grass had started to sunbathe or nod off under the warm Italian sun.

Mika Hakkinen's retirement on the eighteenth lap had revived their spirits slightly. The Finn was a solid second, when he suddenly slowed dramatically and pitted. This promoted Michael Schumacher's Ferrari to second place and after a while the crowd began once again to snore rather than roar. At half distance, David Coulthard had a very solid and tedious 26 second lead.

But then life got interesting again. Little by little, lap after lap, Coulthard began to lose ground to Schumacher who had not put down his weapons. After both drivers had made their second pit stop, the gap came down to 20 seconds and was getting smaller by a second a lap. The snoozers sat up and the end of the race promised some excitement.

Was Coulthard playing with Schumacher? So it seemed, as the Scotsman still had something in reserve and kept the lead to the flag. But it was close and only four seconds separated the McLaren from the Ferrari at the end. «*My only concern was to look after my engine and my car,*» explained Coulthard once out of the cockpit. «*I only had Michael to keep an eye on. He would not have got past.*»

He denied having suffered the slightest problem, putting his slowing pace down to caution. However, this was not strictly true. «We were getting worried towards the end,» confided a McLaren engineer. «*The telemetry indicated the David's gearbox was overheating and we told him to slow down in case he suffered the same failure as Mika. It's lucky the race was not three or four laps longer.*»

For that day's winner, victory at Imola meant a healthy climb back up the championship leader-board and Mika Hakkinen now only had a slender three point lead over his team-mate. «*I think everything is looking good for the rest of the season,*» concluded Coulthard.

Schumacher nether thought it was on

Try as he might, racking up fastest lap after fastest lap towards the end of the race, he never really tought he could catch David Coulthard. «It is my job never to give up until I take the chequered flag,» he insisted after the race. « *But I thought David was only slowing down to be careful. I did not beleive it.*» According to him, the race went as well as could be expected.«*Of course, we have not been able to give the tifosi the result they were waiting for. But we could not have done better. We made no mistakes when it came to tyre choice or race strategy. But to be honest, I should have finished third here, behind Mika Hakkinen. We must now take an enormous step forward if we want to beat the McLarens. Especially as Barcelona, in two weeks time, is not really a track that suits our car. We will have to work on the tyre side. That is the area where we must make a difference.*» And yet another nail of criticism in Goodyear's coffin!

Heinz-Harald Frentzen was fifth. Quite a change from last year when he won the San Marino Grand Prix. «I had a difficult race,» he said. «My settings were wrong and the car oversteered for the whole race.»
▽

IN THE POINTS

1. David COULTHARD	West McLaren Mercedes	1 h 34'24"593
2. M. SCHUMACHER	Scuderia Ferrari Marlboro	at 4"554
3. Eddie IRVINE	Scuderia Ferrari Marlboro	at 51"776
4. Jacques VILLENEUVE	Winfield Williams	at 54"590
5. Heinz-H. FRENTZEN	Winfield Williams	at 1'07"477
6. Jean ALESI	Red Bull Sauber Petronas	at 1 lap

Fastest lap : M. SCHUMACHER, lap 48, 1'29"345, avg. 198.645 km/h

Heinz-Harald Frentzen in mid-refuelling. On this track in 1997, the German had taken his first and only grand prix win to date. This time he was a long way off, finishing fifth. Complaining he had chosen the wrong set up, he had to fight an oversteering FW20 for the entire race.

GRAN PREMIO DI SAN MARINO

△ It was not Mika Hakkinen's weekend. He missed out on pole position on Saturday and then had to retire with a gearbox problem on Sunday. Two weeks later at the Spanish Grand Prix, Ron Dennis was talking of sabotage to explain the problem.

FIA in a flap over penguins

Disappointment for the tifosi. Scuderia Ferrari was due to turn up with its new high level exhaust system, reputedly worth a leap forward of about one second per lap, but on Thursday, Michael Schumacher said it was not to be. *«We are still experiencing too many reliability problems to use it this weekend,»* explained the German. *«But it should all be ready in time for the Spanish Grand Prix.»*
All the same, the Ferraris did have some new parts in Imola, most notably two winglets, known as «penguins» by the French in the paddock, which had begun to sprout on several of this season's cars and had been briefly given an outing on Eddie Irvine's Ferrari in Melbourne. These were not pretty penguins in the opinion of FIA President Max Mosley, who wanted to ban them immediately. *«I don't know what reason Max could have for this ban,»* declaimed Michael Schumacher. *«They have been authorised for the past two years and here we are in the middle of the season, we would have to change the rules. What right have they to do this?»*
FIA likes its cars neat and tidy and nothing fancy. At the start of 1983 these worthy body, then called FISA, banned from one day to the next, six wheeled F1 cars after Williams carried out extensive tests of a chassis with four rear wheels. These tests had produced such interesting results that other teams also looked at six wheelers and FISA opted for an immediate ban to avoid a soapbox championship.
Max Mosley appears to be an aesthete and does not like the penguin wings. In 1997, it was only Tyrrell who fitted them and that did not matter as they did not get much television time. But this time they were sprouting all down the pit lane. As banning them involved a mid-season rule change and it could not be seen as a safety issue, it needed the unanimous agreement of all the teams. On Friday, Ferrari Sporting Director Jean Todt let it be known that he might agree to the ban, but that he would not take a decision until after qualifying. Put another way, he wanted to wait and see if the penguins worked on the F300.
It seemed they did not, as FIA banned the penguins on Thursday 30th April, a few days after the San Marino Grand Prix. Strangely, none of the teams appealed against the decision, obviously being sold on the idea that these items were not suitable to the high-tech image of Formula 1. The sponsors were certainly in favour of the ban as the winglets hid some of their signage on the side pods and chassis.

Bridgestone does well out of Formula 1

In Imola, the McLaren team took its third win of the season and all the indications were that it was well on the way to winning the constructors' championship.
This success was of course due, in no particular order to the Mercedes engine, the MP4/12 chassis and maybe above all to its Bridgestone tyres.
Without doing a direct back to back test, it is impossible to tell exactly how much of an advantage came from the tyres. What was beyond doubt was that so far this season, Bridgestone had come up with some excellent tyres.
While McLaren could congratulate themselves for choosing Bridgestone tyres, Bridgestone themselves were very pleased with their decision to come into Formula 1. On Saturday, the president of Bridgestone Europe, Mr. Takeshi Uchiyama held a press conference to explain that the company's brand awareness had increased by 12% in the past year in the five major European markets: France, Germany, UK, Italy and Spain. Until now, brand awareness had only risen by 0.8% per year from 1992 to 1996. *«We believe this increase is due to our Formula 1 involvement,»* underlined Mr. Uchiyama. As far as sales were concerned, the president said these had experienced a 20% upturn in the replacement tyre market for road cars in the first quarter of 1997 alone.
Thanks to this year's association with McLaren and Benetton, there was no doubt that brand awareness would increase still further in 1998.

Denial from Jean Todt

Was Michael Schumacher on the verge of leaving Ferrari? That was the rumour doing the rounds in the Imola paddock. On Thursday, some Italian papers even announced that the German would be replaced by Jacques Villeneuve at Ferrari in 1999! On Friday, Jean Todt took pleasure in defusing the bomb. *«Since Michael's very first grand prix in our colours, the Italian press has said he is leaving,»* he joked. *«I think that above all, he like working with Ferrari and he feels at home in our team. These are just rumours.»* On Sunday, the German confirmed he had discussed the possibility of extending his stay with Ferrari and he also admitted he had been approached by Mercedes. *«Jurgen Hubbert helped me when I was much younger in 1989. I have known him for a long time and it is natural that we should speak to one another. Nothing more.»* Nothing more, but enough to get the Latin press fired up.

100,000 tifosi. That's a lot of people, especially when seen from a helicopter. ▽

PRACTICE TIMES

No	Driver	Car/Engine/Chassis	Practice Friday	Practice Saturday	Qualifying	Warm-up
1.	Jacques Villeneuve	Williams/Mecachrome/FW20/3 (G)	1'28"644	1'27"876	1'27"390	1'30"330
2.	Heinz-Harald Frentzen	Williams/Mecachrome/FW20/4 (G)	1'29"470	1'27"694	1'27"645	1'30"492
3.	Michael Schumacher	Ferrari/F300/186 (G)	1'28"088	1'27"056	1'26"437	1'29"434
4.	Eddie Irvine	Ferrari/F300/185 (G)	1'29"028	1'27"751	1'27"169	1'29"996
5.	Giancarlo Fisichella	Benetton/Playlife/198/6 (B)	1'28"963	1'27"653	1'27"937	1'29"891
6.	Alexander Wurz	Benetton/Playlife/198/4 (B)	1'29"864	1'27"959	1'27"273	1'30"216
7.	David Coulthard	McLaren/Mercedes/MP4-13/3 (B)	1'27"940	1'25"627	1'25"973	1'28"085
8.	Mika Hakkinen	McLaren/Mercedes/MP4-13/4 (B)	1'27"617	1'26"431	1'26"075	1'29"525
9.	Damon Hill	Jordan/Honda/198/3 (G)	1'29"246	1'27"318	1'27"592	1'30"275
10.	Ralf Schumacher	Jordan/Honda/198/4 (G)	1'28"891	1'27"421	1'27"866	1'31"321
11.	Olivier Panis	Prost/Peugeot/AP01/5 (B)	1'29"175	1'27"854	1'28"270	1'30"423
12.	Jarno Trulli	Prost/Peugeot/AP01/3 (B)	1'30"804	1'43"882	1'29"584	1'30"628
14.	Jean Alesi	Sauber/Petronas/C17/3 (G)	1'29"516	1'27"931	1'28"191	1'30"449
15.	Johnny Herbert	Sauber/Petronas/C17/4 (G)	1'30"223	1'28"291	1'28"111	1'30"662
16.	Pedro Diniz	Arrows/A19/2 (B)	1'30"795	1'29"954	1'29"932	1'32"345
17.	Mika Salo	Arrows/A19/3 (B)	1'29"828	1'28"130	1'28"798	1'29"428
18.	Rubens Barrichello	Stewart/Ford/SF2/1 (B)	1'30"849	1'28"712	1'29"641	1'32"092
19.	Jan Magnussen	Stewart/Ford/SF2/3 (B)	1'32"196	1'30"243	1'31"017	1'33"956
20.	Ricardo Rosset	Tyrrell/Ford/026/2 (G)	1'32"554	1'32"459	1'31"482	1'33"303
21.	Toranosuke Takagi	Tyrrell/Ford/026/1 (G)	1'30"190	1'29"628	1'29"073	1'30"991
22.	Shinji Nakano	Minardi/Ford/M198/4 (B)	1'32"052	1'30"349	1'31"255	1'30"948
23.	Esteban Tuero	Minardi/Ford/M198/3 (B)	1'31"954	1'31"182	1'30"649	1'32"087

LAP CHART

position:	1	2	3	4	5	6	7	8	9	10	11	12	13	14	15	16	17	18	19	20	21	22
start:	7	8	3	4	6	1	9	2	10	5	15	14	11	17	21	12	18	16	23	19	22	20
1	7	8	3	1	4	2	5	14	10	12	15	17	11	21	16	23	9	20	22	19	6	
2	7	8	3	1	4	2	5	14	10	12	15	17	11	21	23	16	20	22	9	19	6	
3	7	8	3	1	4	2	5	14	10	12	15	17	11	21	23	16	20	22	9	19	6	
4	7	8	3	1	4	2	5	14	10	12	15	17	11	21	23	16	20	22	9	19	6	
5	7	8	3	1	4	2	5	14	10	12	15	17	11	21	23	16	20	22	9	19	6	
6	7	8	3	1	4	2	5	14	10	12	15	17	11	21	23	16	20	22	9	19	6	
7	7	8	3	1	4	2	5	14	10	12	15	17	11	21	16	23	20	22	9	19	6	
8	7	8	3	1	4	2	5	14	10	12	15	17	11	21	16	23	20	22	9	19	6	
9	7	8	3	1	4	2	5	14	10	12	15	17	11	21	16	23	20	22	9	6		
10	7	8	3	1	4	2	5	14	10	12	15	17	11	21	16	23	20	22	9	6		
11	7	8	3	1	4	2	5	14	10	12	15	17	11	21	16	23	20	9	22	6		
12	7	8	3	1	4	2	5	14	10	12	17	11	15	21	16	23	20	9	22	6		
13	7	8	3	1	4	2	5	14	10	12	17	11	21	16	23	9	20	22	6			
14	7	8	3	1	4	2	5	14	10	12	17	11	21	16	9	23	20	22	6			
15	7	8	3	1	4	2	5	14	10	12	17	11	21	16	9	23	20	22	6			
16	7	8	3	1	4	2	5	14	10	12	17	11	21	16	9	23	20	22	6			
17	7	3	1	4	8	2	5	14	10	12	17	11	21	9	16	23	20	22	6			
18	7	3	1	4	2	14	10	12	17	11	21	9	23	16	20	22						
19	7	3	1	4	2	14	10	12	11	21	9	17	23	22	20							
20	7	3	1	4	2	14	10	12	11	21	9	17	23	22	20							
21	7	3	1	4	2	14	10	12	11	9	17	21	23	20	22							
22	7	3	1	4	2	14	11	12	10	9	17	21	23	20	22							
23	7	3	1	4	2	11	14	10	9	12	17	21	23	20	22							
24	7	3	1	4	2	14	10	11	9	12	17	21	23	20	22							
25	7	3	1	4	2	14	10	11	12	17	9	21	23	20	22							
26	7	3	1	4	2	14	10	11	12	17	9	21	23	20	22							
27	7	3	4	2	1	14	10	11	12	17	9	21	23	20	22							
28	7	3	4	1	14	2	10	11	12	9	21	17	23	20								
29	7	3	4	1	14	2	10	11	12	9	21	17	23	20								
30	7	3	4	1	14	2	10	11	12	9	21	23	20	17								
31	7	3	4	1	14	2	11	10	12	9	21	23	20	17								
32	7	3	4	1	14	2	11	10	12	9	21	23	20	17								
33	7	3	4	1	14	2	11	10	12	9	21	23	20	17								
34	7	3	4	1	14	2	11	10	9	12	21	23	20	17								
35	7	3	4	1	14	2	11	10	9	21	23	20	17									
36	7	3	4	1	14	2	11	10	9	21	23	20	17									
37	7	3	4	1	14	2	11	9	10	21	23	17	20									
38	7	3	4	1	14	2	11	9	10	21	23	17	20									
39	7	3	4	1	14	2	11	9	10	21	23	17	20									
40	7	3	4	1	14	2	11	9	10	21	23	17	20									
41	7	3	4	1	2	14	11	9	10	23	17	20										
42	7	3	4	1	2	14	11	9	10	23	17	20										
43	7	3	4	1	2	14	11	9	10	23	17	20										
44	7	3	4	1	2	14	11	9	10	23	17	20										
45	7	3	4	1	2	14	11	9	10	23	17	20										
46	7	3	4	1	2	14	11	9	10	23	17	20										
47	7	3	4	1	2	14	11	9	10	23	17	20										
48	7	3	4	1	2	14	11	9	10	23	17	20										
49	7	3	4	1	2	14	11	9	10	23	17											
50	7	3	4	1	2	14	11	9	10	23	17											
51	7	3	4	1	2	14	11	9	10	23	17											
52	7	3	4	1	2	14	11	9	10	23	17											
53	7	3	4	1	2	14	11	9	10	23	17											
54	7	3	4	1	2	14	11	9	10	23	17											
55	7	3	4	1	2	14	11	9	10	23	17											
56	7	3	4	1	2	14	11	9	10	23	17											
57	7	3	4	1	2	14	9	10	23	17												
58	7	3	4	1	2	14	10	23	17													
59	7	3	4	1	2	14	10	23	17													
60	7	3	4	1	2	14	10	23	17													
61	7	3	4	1	2	14																
62	7	3	4	1	2																	

CLASSIFICATION & RETIREMENTS

Pos	Driver	Team	Time
1.	Coulthard	McLaren Mercedes	in 1h34'24"593
2.	M. Schum.	Ferrari	at 4"554
3.	Irvine	Ferrari	at 51"776
4.	Villeneuve	Williams Mecachrome	at 54"590
5.	Frentzen	Williams Mecachrome	at 1'07"477
6.	Alesi	Sauber Petronas	at 1 lap
7.	R. Schum.	Jordan Mugen Honda	at 2 laps
8.	Tuero	Minardi Ford	at 2 laps
9.	Salo	Arrows	at 2 laps
10.	Hill	Jordan Mugen Honda	soupapes
11.	Panis	Prost Peugeot	moteur

Lap	Driver	Team	Reason
1	Barrichello	Stewart Ford	accident
9	Magnussen	Stewart Ford	gearbox
13	Herbert	Sauber Petronas	puncture
18	Wurz	Benetton Playlife	engine
18	Fisichella	Benetton Playlife	off
18	Hakkinen	McLaren Mercedes	gearbox
19	Diniz	Arrows	engine
28	Nakano	Minardi Ford	engine
35	Trulli	Prost Peugeot	throttle
41	Takagi	Tyrrell Ford	air pressure
49	Rosset	Tyrrell Ford	air pressure

FASTEST LAPS

	Driver	Time	Lap
1.	M. Schum.	1'29"345	46
2.	Coulthard	1'29"497	21
3.	Villeneuve	1'29"726	55
4.	Hakkinen	1'30"115	15
5.	Irvine	1'30"206	58
6.	Frentzen	1'30"283	39
7.	Alesi	1'30"391	23
8.	Panis	1'30"481	53
9.	Hill	1'30"859	53
10.	Salo	1'31"267	19
11.	Wurz	1'31"562	14
12.	R. Schum.	1'31"837	20
13.	Fisichella	1'31"969	15
14.	Herbert	1'32"215	9
15.	Trulli	1'32"361	9
16.	Takagi	1'32"430	21
17.	Diniz	1'32"988	11
18.	Tuero	1'33"443	53
19.	Nakano	1'33"889	22
20.	Rosset	1'34"491	9
21.	Magnussen	1'35"069	5

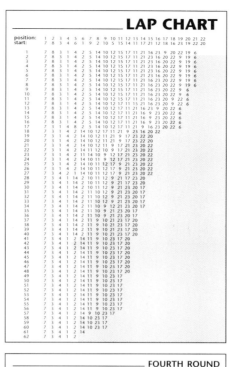

FOURTH ROUND

GRAN PREMIO DI SAN MARINO, IMOLA

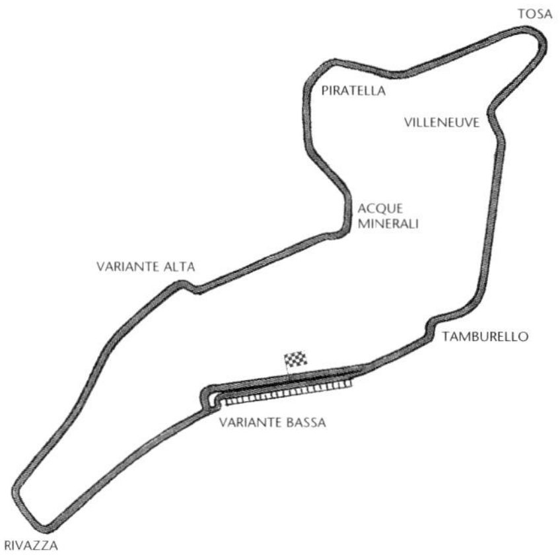

Date : April 26, 1998
Lenght : 4927 meters
Distance : 62 laps, 305.443 km
Weather : sunny, 23 degrees

CHAMPIONSHIPS

(after four rounds)

Drivers :

1. Mika HAKKINEN 26
2. David COULTHARD 23
3. Michael SCHUMACHER 20
4. Eddie IRVINE.................................11
5. Heinz-Harald FRENTZEN 8
6. Alexander WURZ 6
7. Jacques VILLENEUVE 5
8. Jean ALESI.......................................3
9. Johnny HERBERT 1
   Giancarlo FISICHELLA 1

Constructors :

1. McLaren / Mercedes.....................49
2. Ferrari...31
3. Williams / Mecachrome 13
4. Benetton / Playlife 7
5. Sauber / Petronas 4

RACE SUMMARY

- The two McLarens take off easily at the start.
- Alexander Wurz makes a good start, but his gearbox gets stuck in first gear and Damon Hill, caught unawares, cannot avoid him. Both men have to visit the pits at the end of the first lap.
- At the back, Rubens Barrichello is hit by his team mate, Jan Magnussen and loses his rear wing and a bit further on he spins the Stewart.
- Johnny Herbert retires on lap 13 in his pit. He had a puncture, but a misunderstanding with his team, meant they thought he had a suspension failure.
- On lap 18, Mika Hakkinen slows dramatically and further back, Giancarlo Fisichella spins. It is not a good lap for Benetton as Wurz retires with a broken engine.
- After the second pit stop, Michael Schumacher is pushing hard, while Coulthard slows. His lead had been reduced to 4.554s at the flag.

WEEK-END GOSSIP

• Uncle Willi is staying

The juicy contract which ties Michael Schumacher to his manager Willi Weber and gives him 20% of everything the driver earns, around 12 million dollars in 1997, was due to end in 1998.

It had been signed in 1988 for a ten year period at the time when Michael Schumacher was still a total unknown and paid 2000 D. Marks a month by Weber to drive in his German F3 championship team.

In Imola, Willi Weber extended this contract for another four years to the end of 2002, which meant that Michael was going to keep racing at least until then. *«It is not signed, but I am happy with Willi and anyway we are friends as well as partners. Actually, I don't think we really need a contract between us,»* said the driver on Saturday afternoon.

• Coulthard reckons he is in favour

David Coulthard explained in Imola that he thinks he can stay with McLaren in 1999. *«I know that Jurgen Hubbert* (Mercedes boss) *has approached Michael Schumacher. But I think I can be as quick as him and beat him when I am on top form. My problem is that I am less consistent than him, but I am working on it.»*

• Head optimistic

Williams technical director Patrick Head does not lack optimism. «I think we can still win the world championship this year,» he claimed in Imola. «Williams is not the sort of team to give up. It is too early to write us off.»

• Ford waits until Spain

Ford should have brought the Evolution 4 version of its Cosworth engine for the Stewart team here in San Marino. However, reliability problems meant its debut was delayed to the Spanish Grand Prix. It would no doubt have been a help to the Stewart boys as they qualified 17th and 20th. In the race, Rubens Barrichello was knocked out by Jan Magnussen. One more black mark on the Dane's report card.

• Makinen breaks the Williams

After Michael Doohan it was now the turn of world rally champion Tommi Makinen to try the Williams in Barcelona. Unfortunately, when on a quick lap, the Finn got his gears crossed. He wanted to go from 5th to 6th but selected 4th instead. The FW20 took off like a spinning top and crashed heavily into the barriers at 295 km/h. The driver was okay, the chassis less so. *«I will always remember this day,»* he said. *«It's a bit like sitting in a rocket going to the moon.»* No doubt that is where the Williams mechanics would have liked to send him.

The Holy of Holies for the tifosi is the entrance to the Ferrari factory at Maranello, a stones throw from the Imola circuit.

West

Mika in a world of his own

Yet another double for McLaren-Mercedes in the usual order of Hakkinen-Coulthard. This time the Finn had a 50 second lead over his championship rival Michael Schumacher.

It was rather a dull race, not to say totally boring. The only variation on the procession theme was the battle for third place. Eddie Irvine was doing such a good job on behalf of Michael Schumacher he could not avoid a collision with Giancarlo Fisichella.

GRAN PREMIO MARLBORO DE ESPAÑA
BARCELONA

Mika Hakkinen ahead of David Coulthard: the natural order of things

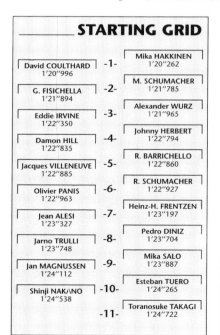

△

Once again Michael Schumacher was powerless against the McLaren hegemony in practice. Third place on the grid for the German.

His third pole position of the season seemed an effortless affair for Mika Hakkinen and he seemed as diffident as ever when talking about his exploit afterwards. «*You know, just because your name is on top of the time sheets for the past two days, it does not mean that everything is going well,*» he intoned. «*I had a few little problems but I guess everyone does. That's F1 for you.*»
To these momentous thoughts the Finn added that he was reasonably confident about the race itself. «*I think everything should go well and there should not be any nasty surprises. Actually, the track has been very consistent over the past two days and we have been able to set up the car well. Also, I have to say that the gap to David is a good psychological boost for me.*» On Saturday, Mika outpaced Coulthard by a crushing 0.7 seconds, a huge gap in F1 terms. «*I don't know how Mika did it,*» admitted the Scotsman. «*No doubt he feels more confident with his car than I do. On this track you really have to attack the corners and know what you are going to do without worrying about how the car will react. It's as simple as that.*» Once again, Michael Schumacher would referee the contest between the two McLarens, even though his Ferrari was giving away 1.5 seconds to Hakkinen. «*Of course it is a very big gap,*» conceded the Scuderia driver. «*And I really had to fight to do that time. Luckily we have our new exhaust system here, without which we would have been completely outpaced. I am not very optimistic about the race.*»

A helicopter shot of the Catalunya track and its quick corners which makes it one of the most demanding circuits for the chassis.

▷

Benetton clearly making progress

Since the start of the season, Giancarlo Fisichella had been slower than team mate Alexander Wurz, which surprised a lot of people in the paddock and confirmed the young Austrian's talent. However, at Barcelona, «Fisico» managed to qualify fourth, just ahead of Alexander Wurz, although the gap between them was only 71 thousandths of a second! «*This is a fantastic day for me,*» admitted Fisico. «*My aim was to qualify in the top six and I am fourth. I am delighted. The car is going well and I think we have a chance to get on the podium.*» Alexander Wurz was also satisfied with the performance of the Benetton in qualifying. «*We have managed to constantly improve our performance level and I am very pleased to have done a good job of setting up my car.*»

STARTING GRID

	-1-	Mika HAKKINEN 1'20"262
David COULTHARD 1'20"996	-1-	
	-2-	M. SCHUMACHER 1'21"785
G. FISICHELLA 1'21"894	-2-	
	-3-	Alexander WURZ 1'21"965
Eddie IRVINE 1'22"350	-3-	
	-4-	Johnny HERBERT 1'22"794
Damon HILL 1'22"835	-4-	
	-5-	R. BARRICHELLO 1'22"860
Jacques VILLENEUVE 1'22"885	-5-	
	-6-	R. SCHUMACHER 1'22"927
Olivier PANIS 1'22"963	-6-	
	-7-	Heinz-H. FRENTZEN 1'23"197
Jean ALESI 1'23"327	-7-	
	-8-	Pedro DINIZ 1'23"704
Jarno TRULLI 1'23"748	-8-	
	-9-	Mika SALO 1'23"887
Jan MAGNUSSEN 1'24"112	-9-	
	-10-	Esteban TUERO 1'24"265
Shinji NAKANO 1'24"538	-10-	
	-11-	Toranosuke TAKAGI 1'24"722

Another Sunday drive for the silver arrows

△ *Mika Hakkinen makes an impeccable start from pole position. The Finn cruised the race. Behind him, Michael Schumacher spins his wheels and drops a few places.*

Pole position, race fastest lap, in the lead from start to finish (apart from one lap during the pit stops) Mika Hakkinen did it all in Barcelona. Having dominated all the practice sessions, he made clear his intention to pull away in the championship. *«I had fun,»* was his comment after stepping off the podium. *«Yes, I think fun is the right word. I had to lap a lot of backmarkers, but it was all good fun! I have to say that for many years I have driven cars that did not allow me to fight and so now that I have a car I can overtake with, I like doing it.»*

Evidently the Finn had no problems, which was not the case for David Coulthard, second. *«I really had to go flat out all the time,»* he said. *«But there was nothing I could do against Mika here. I simply was not quick enough. Actually, I don't understand why not and it is hard to accept. Mika was the best today and he richly deserves the win. There can be no doubt about that.»*

A lonely third

Michael Schumacher was third. After making a very bad start, the German came round at the end of the first lap in fifth place and it was not until the first series of pit stops that he got past Fisichella and Irvine, his team-mate making life easier by backing off for his boss. However, Schumacher soon lost any advantage gained in this move, as he was hit with a ten second penalty for exceeding the pit lane speed limit (126.4 km/h in a 120 km/h zone.) «I switched on the speed limiter, but it did not work,» was his excuse. *«When I realised I was going too quickly, I braked but it was too late.»*

Overtaken by Wurz while he fumed in the sin bin, the German managed to reclaim third place at the second pit stops. *«It was lucky, because I would never have managed to overtake him on the track,»* concluded Michael Schumacher. *«I was already finding it difficult to get by the Minardis, so a Benetton would have been impossible.»* A difficult weekend that reaped only four points. It was better than nothing.

7500 dollar fine for Fisichella

Lap 29: Giancarlo Fisichella and Eddie Irvine tangle and end up in the gravel. The Italian tried to make his feelings known, but the Irishman was having nothing to do with it. ▽

Eddie Irvine and Giancarlo Fisichella had been fighting pretty much since the start of the race. At the start, the Irishman had managed to beat the Italian to the first corner and was running ahead of the Benetton and Michael Schumacher's Ferrari. When it was time for the first pit stops, Irvine decided to slow things down as much as possible, in order to let Schumacher get past both of them; a move which went off perfectly.

On lap 29, Fisichella had had enough of this little game and decided to deal with the Irish driver. He pulled alongside him on the straight and try to pass him, braking for the first corner. The Ferrari began to slide and both cars ended in the gravel. A very angry «Fisico» only just contained himself from thumping Irvine, who did not respond to his advances.

After the race, both men were ordered before the stewards to explain their behaviour. While Eddie Irvine walked out a free man, Giancarlo Fisichella was hit with a 7500 dollar fine for "HAVING CAUSED AN AVOIDABLE ACCIDENT". *«It is the right decision,»* agreed Irvine. *«But I think the fine is a bit steep, because what Giancarlo did was not so bad. He tried to pass me, but he did not take the outside line and moved back without giving me enough room. The crash was inevitable.»*

Not surprisingly, the little Italian saw things differently. *«Eddie moved over on me at the start. If I had not backed off we would both have been out of the race,»* said an outraged Fisichella. *«Then he blocked me so that Schumacher could pass us. I tried to go down the inside, but he shut the door, so I tried the outside. I was clearly ahead, but he came across. I did not see what happened then or if he made a mistake. His behaviour is really disgraceful. I tried to talk to him, but he did not even bother to reply.»*

Giancarlo Fisichella's frustration seemed genuine and his arguments made sense. Once again, Eddie Irvine accepted none of the blame and luckily for him the stewards agreed with his view of the incident.

IN THE POINTS

1.	Mika HAKKINEN	West McLaren Mercedes	1 h 33'37"621
2.	David COULTHARD	West McLaren Mercedes	at 9"439
3.	M. SCHUMACHER	Scuderia Ferrari Marlboro	at 47"094
4.	Alexander WURZ	Mild Seven Benetton Playlife	at 1'02"538
5.	R. BARRICHELLO	Stewart Ford	at 1 lap
6.	Jacques VILLENEUVE	Winfield Williams	at 1 lap

Fastest : Mika HAKKINEN, lap 25, 1'24"275, avg. 201.967 km/h

△ David Coulthard was never able to bother Mika Hakkinen in Barcelona. The Scotsman blamed a car that was a bit nervous at the back end, which he could not cope with.

Sabotage says McLaren

McLaren boss Ron Dennis certainly has a sense for the spectacular. During a press conference with around fifty journalists present, he said that Mika Hakkinen's retirement and David Coulthard's problems at Imola had been down to a form of sabotage.
«*After Mika's retirement, we looked into the problem,*» he explained in conspiratorial tones. «*And we discovered that certain bearings which we buy from a supplier to use in our gearbox were wrapped in a slightly different colour of paper than usual. It turned out these were not the parts we had ordered, but counterfeit parts from Asia. We are continuing our enquiries.*»
True counterfeit, sabotage or a simple mistake, it did not matter. Ron Dennis simply wanted to make it clear that the sacrosanct team was in no way to blame for its one and only mechanical failure of the season.

16th and last classified finisher, Olivier Panis was three laps down at the end of the Spanish Grand Prix. The only bright point in a bad weekend was his fourth place in the Sunday morning warm-up. ▽

Fifth place for Rubens Barrichello

Two points in the nick of time

Rubens Barrichello's fifth place in Barcelona could not have come at a better time for the Stewart team. Until then, the Scottish team had failed to score a single point, because of worrying reliability problems with SF02.
Technical director, Alan Jenkins had taken a risk this season by using a carbon gearbox. It caused enormous reliability problems in its development phase and caused several retirements in the early part of the season.
It got so bad that engine supplier and partner Ford was getting fed up with the situation. For several weeks, the rumour had been doing the rounds that the American firm wanted to start winning as soon as possible and was now considering doing a deal with the Benetton team. On Saturday, team boss Paul Stewart felt compelled to officially deny that Ford was thinking of breaking its contract with Stewart, which was to run until 2000.
In this rather tense atmosphere, the two points brought home by Rubens Barrichello in Barcelona arrived like a breath of fresh air. Throughout the race, the Brazilian had no problem keeping ahead of Jacques Villeneuve's Williams, proof of the competitiveness and new found reliability of the SF02.
After the race, the party under the Stewart motorhome awning was as rowdy as if the team had won! «*Yes, I think this is a new beginning for the team,*» rejoiced Rubens. «*It was a very tough race, but it is great to score two points. I think we all deserve this result.*»

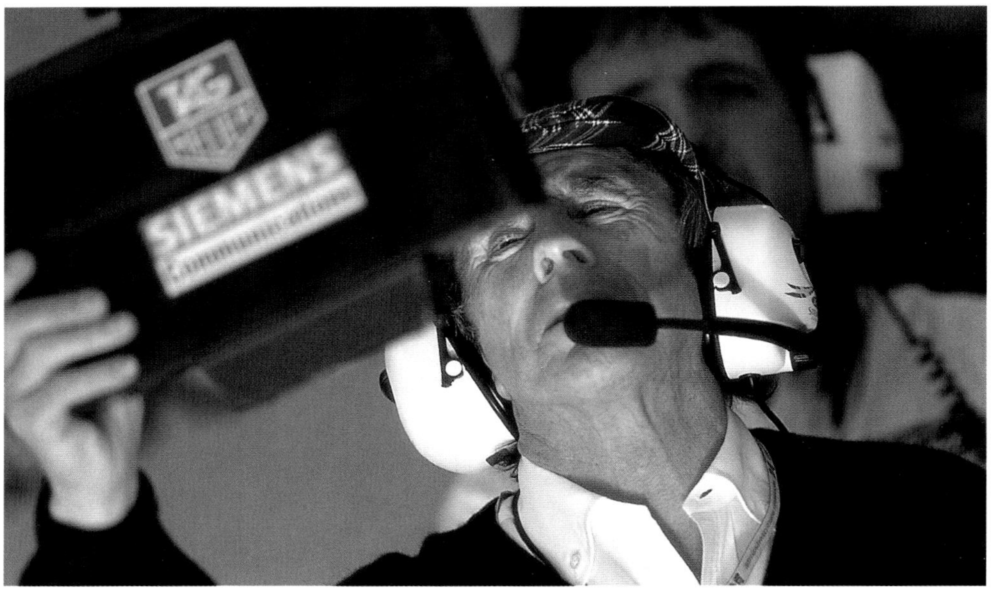

Bernie battles against boredom

In Germany, the papers were filled with stories about the imminent transfer of Michael Schumacher from Ferrari to McLaren for 1999. The German was under contract to Ferrari, but there was a clause which allowed him to leave the team if he did not win the title this year. As the chance of victory seemed to be slipping away from him in Barcelona, Mercedes were pushing to get the double world champion on board. At Imola, Mercedes board member Jurgen Hubbert had once again banged on about how much the three pointed star rated the German driver and wanted to work with him.
However, for Michael Schumacher, leaving the Scuderia without having once won a world title with it would be a defeat and he was not in the habit of giving up. If Schumacher did join McLaren, he would be behind the wheel of the best car on the grid and there was no doubt as to who would win the 1999 world championship. With a boring season therefore in prospect, Bernie Ecclestone entered the ring. Mr. Formula 1 could not accept a season crushed by a dominant Schumacher-McLaren partnership of no interest to anyone outside Germany. With this in mind, he publically advised Schumacher to stay with Ferrari and usually, what Bernie wants, Bernie gets.

Prost understands his problems

Alain Prost had nothing to smile about so far this season. On Saturday, a frown on his face, he explained the cause of the problems which were holding up his cars' performance and which prevented Olivier Panis and Jarno Trulli from qualifying any better than their 12th and 18th places on the Barcelona grid. «*We have had a series of problems since the winter,*» he began. «*At first it was reliability problems with the gearbox. Now we still have a traction problem. We have studied all the data and I can say we now understand the causes of our troubles.*»
This did not mean an immediate solution was to hand. «*The problem is linked to the rear suspension, which is not rigid enough. Psychologically, it is good that we have got to the bottom of it. Now we have to manufacture some new parts, which will take between four and six weeks.*»
The new rear suspension, which will include carbon parts will be sub-contracted out in England, to «B3 Technology,» the company owned by John Barnard. «*He will make the parts to our design,*» concluded Prost. «*We are using him simply to save time.*»

PRACTICE TIMES

No	Driver	Car/Engine/Chassis	Practice Friday	Practice Saturday	Qualifying	Warm-up
1.	Jacques Villeneuve	Williams/Mecachrome/FW20/5 (G)	1'24"198	1'23"483	1'22"885	1'26"370
2.	Heinz-Harald Frentzen	Williams/Mecachrome/FW20/4 (G)	1'23"843	1'23"083	1'23"197	1'25"536
3.	Michael Schumacher	Ferrari/F300/186 (G)	1'23"468	1'22"890	1'21"785	1'24"852
4.	Eddie Irvine	Ferrari/F300/185 (G)	1'23"421	1'22"497	1'22"350	1'25"176
5.	Giancarlo Fisichella	Benetton/Playlife/198/6 (B)	1'24"286	1'22"102	1'21"894	1'24"107
6.	Alexander Wurz	Benetton/Playlife/198/4 (B)	1'24"311	1'22"414	1'21"965	1'25"382
7.	David Coulthard	McLaren/Mercedes/MP4-13/3 (B)	1'22"965	1'21"223	1'20"996	1'23"270
8.	Mika Hakkinen	McLaren/Mercedes/MP4-13/4 (B)	1'22"147	1'20"791	1'20"262	1'22"460
9.	Damon Hill	Jordan/Honda/198/3 (G)	1'24"888	1'22"974	1'22"835	1'26"730
10.	Ralf Schumacher	Jordan/Honda/198/4 (G)	1'24"420	1'23"113	1'22"927	1'25"925
11.	Olivier Panis	Prost/Peugeot/AP01/5 (B)	1'24"272	1'23"317	1'22"963	1'24"677
12.	Jarno Trulli	Prost/Peugeot/AP01/3 (B)	1'24"897	1'24"680	1'23"748	1'25"541
14.	Jean Alesi	Sauber/Petronas/C17/3 (G)	1'24"257	1'23"397	1'23"327	1'26"698
15.	Johnny Herbert	Sauber/Petronas/C17/4 (G)	1'23"237	1'23"058	1'22"794	1'25"630
16.	Pedro Diniz	Arrows/A19/4 (B)	1'25"770	1'24"793	1'23"704	1'26"278
17.	Mika Salo	Arrows/A19/3 (B)	1'26"285	1'24"096	1'23"887	1'26"087
18.	Rubens Barrichello	Stewart/Ford/SF2/1 (B)	1'24"037	1'22"673	1'22"860	1'25"702
19.	Jan Magnussen	Stewart/Ford/SF2/3 (B)	1'26"606	1'24"862	1'24"112	1'26"425
20.	Ricardo Rosset	Tyrrell/Ford/026/2 (G)	1'26"371	1'25"885	1'25"946	not qualif.
21.	Toranosuke Takagi	Tyrrell/Ford/026/3 (G)	1'25"336	1'23"944	1'24"722	1'26"452
22.	Shinji Nakano	Minardi/Ford/M198/3 (B)	1'25"280	1'25"375	1'24"538	1'27"226
23.	Esteban Tuero	Minardi/Ford/M198/4 (B)	1'25"525	1'24"640	1'24"265	1'25"991

LAP CHART

position:	1	2	3	4	5	6	7	8	9	10	11	12	13	14	15	16	17	18	19	20	21
start:	8	7	3	5	6	4	15	9	18	1	10	11	2	14	16	12	17	19	23	22	21
1	8	7	4	5	3	6	18	1	15	9	12	11	19	17	21	22	10	23	14	2	16
2	8	7	4	5	3	6	18	1	15	9	11	12	19	17	21	22	10	23	14	2	16
3	8	7	4	5	3	6	18	1	15	9	11	12	19	17	21	22	10	23	14	2	16
4	8	7	4	5	3	6	18	1	15	9	11	12	19	17	21	22	10	23	14	2	16
5	8	7	4	5	3	6	18	1	15	9	11	12	19	17	21	22	10	23	14	2	16
6	8	7	4	5	3	6	18	1	15	9	11	12	19	17	21	10	22	23	14	2	16
7	8	7	4	5	3	6	18	1	15	9	11	12	19	17	21	10	22	14	23	2	16
8	8	7	4	5	3	6	18	1	15	9	11	12	19	17	21	10	22	14	23	2	16
9	8	7	4	5	3	6	18	1	15	9	11	12	19	17	21	10	22	14	23	2	16
10	8	7	4	5	3	6	18	1	15	9	11	12	19	17	21	10	14	22	23	2	16
11	8	7	4	5	3	6	18	1	15	9	11	12	19	17	21	10	14	22	23	2	16
12	8	7	4	5	3	6	18	1	15	9	11	12	19	17	21	10	14	22	23	2	16
13	8	7	4	5	3	6	18	1	15	9	11	12	19	17	21	10	14	22	23	2	16
14	8	7	4	5	3	6	18	1	15	9	11	12	19	17	21	10	14	22	23	2	16
15	8	7	4	5	3	6	18	1	15	9	11	12	19	17	21	10	14	22	23	2	16
16	8	7	4	5	3	6	18	1	15	9	11	12	19	17	21	10	14	22	23	2	16
17	8	7	4	5	3	6	18	1	15	9	11	12	19	17	21	10	14	22	23	2	16
18	8	7	4	5	3	6	18	1	15	9	11	12	19	17	21	10	14	22	23	2	16
19	8	7	4	5	3	6	18	1	15	9	12	19	17	11	21	14	10	22	23	2	16
20	8	7	4	5	3	6	18	1	15	9	12	17	11	21	14	22	23	2	19	10	16
21	8	7	4	5	3	6	18	1	15	9	12	17	11	14	21	22	19	23	2	10	
22	8	7	4	5	3	6	18	1	15	9	12	11	14	22	19	10	21	2	23		
23	8	7	4	5	3	6	1	18	12	15	9	11	14	22	19	10	21	2	23		
24	8	7	4	5	3	1	6	18	15	9	12	11	14	19	10	21	2	22	23		
25	8	7	4	3	5	1	6	18	15	9	11	12	19	14	10	21	2	22	23		
26	8	7	3	4	5	1	6	18	15	9	11	12	19	14	10	21	2	22	23		
27	7	8	3	4	5	1	6	18	15	9	11	12	19	14	10	21	2	22	23		
28	8	7	3	4	5	6	18	1	15	9	11	12	19	14	10	21	2	22	23		
29	8	7	3	6	18	1	15	9	11	12	14	19	10	21	2	22	23				
30	8	7	3	6	18	1	15	9	11	12	14	19	10	21	2	22	23				
31	8	7	3	6	18	1	15	9	11	12	14	19	10	21	2	22	23				
32	8	7	3	6	18	1	15	9	11	12	14	19	10	21	2	22	23				
33	8	7	3	6	18	1	15	9	11	12	14	19	10	21	2	22	23				
34	8	7	3	6	18	1	15	9	11	14	19	10	12	21	2	22	23				
35	8	7	3	6	18	1	15	9	11	19	10	12	14	21	2	22	23				
36	8	7	3	6	18	1	15	9	11	19	10	12	14	21	2	22	23				
37	8	7	3	6	18	1	15	9	11	19	10	12	14	21	2	22	23				
38	8	7	3	6	18	1	15	9	11	19	10	12	14	21	2	22	23				
39	8	7	3	6	18	1	15	9	11	10	19	12	14	2	21	22	23				
40	8	7	3	6	18	1	15	9	11	10	19	12	14	2	21	22	23				
41	8	7	6	3	18	1	15	9	11	10	19	12	14	2	21	23	22				
42	8	7	6	3	18	1	15	11	9	10	19	12	14	2	21	23	22				
43	8	7	6	3	18	1	15	9	11	12	14	10	19	2	21	22	23				
44	8	7	6	3	1	18	15	9	11	12	14	10	19	2	21	22	23				
45	8	7	6	3	1	18	15	11	9	12	14	10	19	2	21	22	23				
46	7	8	6	3	18	1	15	11	9	12	14	10	19	2	21	22	23				
47	8	7	3	6	18	1	15	11	12	14	10	19	2	21	22	23					
48	8	7	3	6	18	1	15	11	12	14	10	19	2	21	22	23					
49	8	7	3	6	18	1	15	11	12	14	10	2	19	21	22	23					
50	8	7	3	6	18	1	15	11	12	14	10	2	19	21	22	23					
51	8	7	3	6	18	1	15	11	12	14	10	2	19	21	22	23					
52	8	7	3	6	18	1	15	11	12	14	10	2	19	21	22	23					
53	8	7	3	6	18	1	15	11	12	14	10	2	19	21	22	23					
54	8	7	3	6	18	1	15	11	12	14	10	2	19	21	22	23					
55	8	7	3	6	18	1	15	11	12	14	10	2	19	21	22	23					
56	8	7	3	6	18	1	15	11	12	14	10	2	19	21	22	23					
57	8	7	3	6	18	1	15	11	12	14	10	2	19	21	22	23					
58	8	7	3	6	18	1	15	11	12	14	10	2	19	21	22	23					
59	8	7	3	6	18	1	15	11	12	14	10	2	19	21	22	23					
60	8	7	3	6	18	1	15	11	12	14	10	2	19	21	22	23					
61	8	7	3	6	18	1	15	12	14	10	2	19	21	22	23						
62	8	7	3	6	18	1	15	12	2	14	10	19	21	22	23						
63	8	7	3	6	18	1	15	2	12	14	10	19	21	22	23						
64	8	7	3	6	18	1	15														
65	8	7	3	6																	

Best result for a Bridgestone shod runner:

Mika Hakkinen, McLaren-Mercedes, 1st

CLASSIFICATION & RETIREMENTS

Pos	Driver	Team	Time
1.	Hakkinen	McLaren Mercedes	in 1h33'37"621
2.	Coulthard	McLaren Mercedes	at 9"439
3.	M. Schum.	Ferrari	at 47"094
4.	Wurz	Benetton Playlife	at 1'02"538
5.	Barrichello	Stewart Ford	at 1 lap
6.	Villeneuve	Williams Mecachrome	at 1 lap
7.	Herbert	Sauber Petronas	at 1 lap
8.	Frentzen	Williams Mecachrome	at 2 laps
9.	Trulli	Prost Peugeot	at 2 laps
10.	Alesi	Sauber Petronas	at 2 laps
11.	R. Schum.	Jordan Mugen Honda	at 2 laps
12.	Magnussen	Stewart Ford	at 2 laps
13.	Takagi	Tyrrell Ford	at 2 laps
14.	Nakano	Minardi Ford	at 2 laps
15.	Tuero	Minardi Ford	at 2 laps
16.	Panis	Prost Peugeot	hydraulic system
Lap	**Driver**	**Team**	**Reason**
21	Diniz	Arrows	engine
22	Salo	Arrows	engine
29	Fisichella	Benetton Playlife	accident
29	Irvine	Ferrari	accident
47	Hill	Jordan Mugen Honda	engine

FASTEST LAPS

	Driver	Time	Lap
1.	Hakkinen	1'24"275	25
2.	M. Schum.	1'24"625	47
3.	Coulthard	1'24"778	63
4.	Wurz	1'25"343	44
5.	Alesi	1'25"668	32
6.	Irvine	1'25"778	20
7.	Fisichella	1'25"851	18
8.	Frentzen	1'26"011	4
9.	Herbert	1'26"354	26
10.	Trulli	1'26"394	26
11.	Villeneuve	1'26"407	24
12.	Hill	1'26"501	38
13.	Panis	1'26"502	59
14.	Barrichello	1'26"532	24
15.	R. Schum.	1'26"533	41
16.	Magnussen	1'27"203	44
17.	Tuero	1'27"601	47
18.	Diniz	1'27"638	16
19.	Salo	1'27"767	21
20.	Nakano	1'27"767	25
21.	Takagi	1'28"066	34

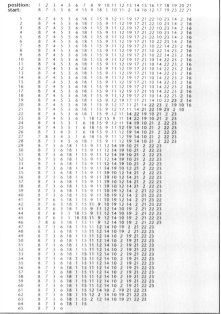

FIFTH ROUND

GRAN PREMIO MARLBORO DE ESPAÑA, BARCELONE

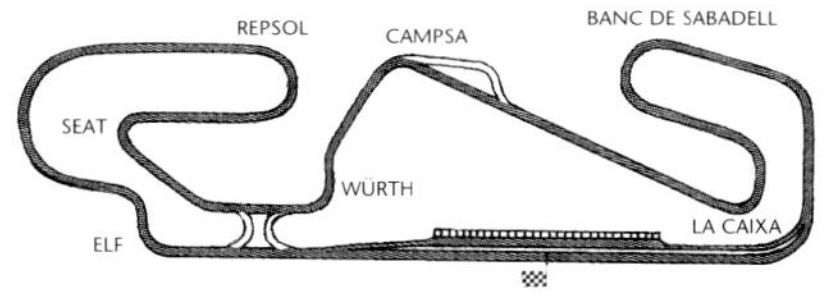

Date : May 10, 1998
Lenght : 4726 meters
Distance : 65 laps, 307.196 km
Weather : sunny, 21 degrees

CHAMPIONSHIPS

(after five rounds)

Drivers :

1. Mika HAKKINEN 36
2. David COULTHARD 29
3. Michael SCHUMACHER 24
4. Eddie IRVINE 11
5. Alexander WURZ 9
6. Heinz-Harald FRENTZEN 8
7. Jacques VILLENEUVE 6
8. Jean ALESI 3
9. Rubens BARRICHELLO 2
10. Johnny HERBERT 1
    Giancarlo FISICHELLA 1

Constructors :

1. McLaren / Mercedes 65
2. Ferrari 35
3. Williama / Mecachrome 14
4. Benetton / Playlife 10
5. Sauber / Petronas 4
6. Stewart / Ford 2

WEEK-END GOSSIP

- **Society page**

Several celebrities turned up in Barcelona: the King of Spain of course, but also the actor Anthony Quinn, looking good for his age and Spanish rally star, Carlos Sainz.

- **Villeneuve - bad loser**

Jacques Villeneuve seems to have had enough of Formula 1: *«I am not enjoying driving in these conditions,»* he declared. *«It is really frustrating to be so far back and it is no fun, starting the weekend knowing there is no chance of winning.»* In the race, he fought hard, trying to snatch fifth place from Rubens Barrichello. He failed!

- **Michael keeps pushing the wheels along**

Michael Schumacher is ceaselessly pushing the Goodyear people to work harder. *«In order to catch the McLarens, Goodyear has to move forward by two steps, not one,»* was his view in Spain. But the American engineers were not taking it easy and were trying a front tyre which was the same width as the rear.

- **Three pedals on the Prost**

The Prost team tried a three pedal set-up during private testing the week before this race. The extra brake pedal operated on the rear wheels only. It was not used during the grand prix.

- **Mercedes claim merger will not affect them**

Directors of Mercedes present in Barcelona denied that the merger of the Daimler- Benz group and the American Chrysler company would have any effect whatsoever on the three pointed star's racing activities. *«We will continue with both the Indy and F1 programmes,»* announced the German giant's motorsport boss, Norbert Haug.

- **1% is better than nothing**

Peugeot turned up here with a new evolution of its A16 engine; the A16 EV3. *«It put out around 1% more power and we will use it from Saturday,»* explained Peugeot Sport director Pierre-Michel Fauconnier. 1% is roughly equivalent to 7.5 horsepower.

- **Prost would like to be Ron Dennis**

Alain Prost said he would like to be in Ron Dennis' shoes. *«Ron is in an exceptional situation, but one which creates exceptional problems in terms of looking after his two drivers while keeping an eye on the Schumacher threat. It is a very interesting position.»*

RACE SUMMARY

- Mika Hakkinen makes the best start and already leads David Coulthard by almost two seconds at the end of the first lap. Further back, Eddie Irvine leads Giancarlo Fisichella dn Michael Schumacher, who once again messed up his start.
- In the early stages, Mika Hakkinen pulls away at the rate of around one second per lap from David Coulthard. It is a dull race, with no one apparently capable of making an overtaking move.
- The first series of pit stops do nothing to change the running order, which stays the same to the end. The two Arrows retire at almost the same time and at the same place, both with broken engines.
- On lap 29 Eddie Irvine and Giancarlo Fisichella collide at the first corner and are out. Michael Schumacher had already managed to pass both of them during the pit stops as Eddie Irvine had slowed right down to help his team mate.
- Hakkinen wins as he pleases, from David Coulthard and Michael Schumacher.

No, this picture is not printed back to front. Michael Schumacher's pit stop seen in the windows of the media centre.

The track of the silver stars

Once again, Mika Hakkinen had a trouble free run and ran away with the Monaco Grand Prix. David Coulthard had been second at the start of the race until his engine exploded, thus depriving McLaren of another one-two finish.
Michael Schumacher was out of contention after colliding with Alexander Wurz and Mika Hakkinen thus had almost twice as many points as the German after this race. It all seemed to be going the Finn's way, but that did not take into account the uncertainties of this sport.

GRAND PRIX DE MONACO MONTE-CARLO

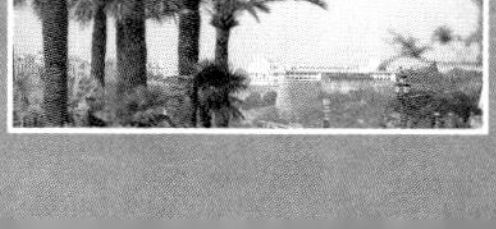

▷ Trouble-free qualifying for the silver arrows.

300 metres to sort themselves out

In Barcelona, Michael Schumacher had said he had no doubt that he would be closer to the McLarens in Monaco than on other circuits. However, once again it was Mika Hakkinen who took pole position ahead of David Coulthard. The German was only fourth. With the front row, yet again monopolised by McLaren-Mercedes, it seemed we might be in for a dull race. In fact, with overtaking being well nigh impossible here, the start of the race would probably be the only part of the race which would decide its outcome. Whichever McLaren held the advantage 300 metres into the race at the Sainte Devote chicane would then be hard to beat. Mika Hakkinen was well aware of that. *«The start will be very important as you cannot fit two cars through Sainte Devote at the same time. David and I will have to discuss that,»* suggested the Finn, adding that apart from his team mate, he feared no one. *«To be honest, at the moment, I cannot see who could beat us. It will be a long race, but it is pointless for me to worry about Michael* (Schumacher) *or Giancarlo* (Fisichella.)*»*

On Saturday, Hakkinen was spellbinding. It was exactly what he wanted, to prove that his wins were not simply down to the superiority of his car, but were also a result of his talent.

He put on a virtuoso performance for his four quick laps. *«The hardest is always the last one,»* he continued. *«I was not able to improve, because I did not want to take too many risks. The hardest thing here is to control yourself. Monaco is not so tiring physically, but mentally you must always stay calm, even when you are stuck in traffic.»*

Once more, Mika Hakkinen found David Coulthard alongside him on the front row. The team struggle between the two men was beginning to turn in the Finn's favour. *«Of course I am disappointed,»* said the Scot, who only missed out by 34 hundredths of a second. *«But tomorrow's race is another story and it will be above all a waiting game.»*

On Saturday, no sooner had qualifying ended, than a few drops of rain began to fall on Monaco. If the heavy rain forecast for Sunday did arrive, then the race might have some surprises up its sleeve.

Concorde Agreement: Peter Sauber's is the only abstention

On Friday, Peter Sauber was the only team boss who refused to put his name to the new Concorde Agreement and the only one not to pose in full suit and tie with Bernie Ecclestone and Prince Albert of Monaco for the photo souvenir of this long awaited event. It marked the end of the resistence of the McLaren, Williams and Tyrrell teams.

The Zurich man did not want to give his reasons, but it seemed that it had something to do with the European Union. The Sauber team is actually the only one not to be based within its jurisdiction, which caused a few incompatibilities with the documentation as it stood.

All the other team owners duly signed the Concorde Agreement, which would not control the commercial aspects of Formula 1 until 2008. It would most importantly define the distribution of the television rights money between the teams. *«I think this new agreement is very good for the sport,»* was Max Mosley's view. *«It brings the needed stability to Formula 1 and puts an end to the complex discussions we have had over the past four or five years.»*

It was true that, up until now, negotiations between the teams had been stormy. *«The text presented to the teams on Thursday was the 34th version of a 100 page document. I must admit I gave up reading all the small print after the third or fourth version,»* sighed Mosley.

From now on, with all the teams being in agreement, the last obstacle to floating Formula 1 on the Stock Exchange had been removed. Wait for the money to roll in!

A track for maximum downforce, big wings are the order of the day. This year the Prost team hold the record, with a tri-plane, worthy of the Red Baron. It was not much use for Olivier Panis, who only qualified 18th. ▷

Schumacher disappointing

Michael Schumacher had only managed to qualify in fourth place. It was a big disappointment for the thousands of Italian fans who had made the trip. *« I expected to be closer to the McLarens, but I got the maximum out of the car today. It is well balanced and there is nothing more to come. It seems obvious to me that the Bridgestone runners have got a definite advantage on this track, in terms of traction coming out of the corners. I think I will settle for a podium finish in this race.»*

Far too tight for the sophisticated modern day cars, the Monaco circuit has no place on today's Formula 1 calendar. But who can resist this backdrop? ▽▽

Super Fisico

The big surprise on Saturday was Giancarlo Fisichella's third place for Benetton. For a few minutes, the Italian was actually quickest, before seeing his time bettered by the two McLarens. «*But I am not at all disappointed, quite the contrary,*» affirmed Fisichella with a big smile.
At the start of the season, the Italian was regularly beaten by his team mate, Alexander Wurz. But since the Spanish Grand Prix, he seemed to have gained the upper hand. «I had a few problems in adapting to the Benetton chassis,» he admitted. «*Now I feel a lot more comfortable in the team. Here we have a new rear suspension which makes the car more stable.*»
All the same, Fisichella did not hold out too much hope for the race. «*I think the two McLarens will be too quick for me so I would be very happy to finish third.*» A statement which was not born of a lack of ambition but had more to do with a realistic attitude. Alexander Wurz was sixth in the other Benetton, confirming that the blue cars were on form at this track.

◁
Damon Hill seems pensive after qualifying. The Englishman could do no better than 15th place on the grid, just ahead of his team mate, Ralf Schumacher. The Jordan team was at all time low in Monaco.

A fuzzy foto of Frentzen. While the German qualified fifth, his team-mate Villeneuve had to make do with 13th spot. His worst grid position in Formula One.
◁

STARTING GRID

		Mika HAKKINEN 1'19"798
David COULTHARD 1'20"137	-1-	G. FISICHELLA 1'20"368
M. SCHUMACHER 1'20"702	-2-	Heinz-H. FRENTZEN 1'20"729
Alexander WURZ 1'20"955	-3-	Eddie IRVINE 1'21"712
Mika SALO 1'22"144	-4-	Johnny HERBERT 1'22"157
Jarno TRULLI 1'22"238	-5-	Jean ALESI 1'22"257
Pedro DINIZ 1'22"355	-6-	Jacques VILLENEUVE 1'22"468
R. BARRICHELLO 1'22"540	-7-	Damon HILL 1'23"151
R. SCHUMACHER 1'23"263	-8-	Jan MAGNUSSEN 1'23"411
Olivier PANIS 1'23"536	-9-	Shinji NAKANO 1'23"957
Toranosuke TAKAGI 1'24"024	-10-	Esteban TUERO 1'24"031
	-11-	

And they're off for 78 unrelenting laps and once again the two McLarens make a perfect getaway.

Mika's childhood dream comes true

Seven in the evening. The race has been over for a few hours already. Since stepping out of his silver arrow, Mika Hakkinen has not stopped shaking hands and being patted on the back.
He has also been at the champagne in a big way, drinking not only with his fiancee Erja Honkanen, but also with Mercedes-Benz top brass Jurgen Hubbert and Norbert Haug, Mercedes motor sport boss and of course with McLaren's Ron Dennis.
There are some who say that a win at Monaco is worth as much as a world championship on a driver's record. That Sunday night, Mika Hakkinen was in no mood to disagree. But it is time for him to return to his apartment in Fontvieille, drink some strong black coffee and get the dinner jacket out. For tonight, Mika is the host and Prince Rainier the guest, as tradition demands for the winner of the Monaco Grand Prix. The gala dinner is yet another part of Monaco's demands on the drivers. Mika has dreamt of all these events for so long, he can hardly believe it is actually happening. «*I cannot understand anything,*» he admitted after the race. «I think only this evening, or perhaps after this night will I fully understand what has happened to me and realise its importance.» As a demonstration his driving had been superb. Hakkinen kept the lead from start to finish, even when he made his pit stop he was not headed. After team mate David Coulthard had retired, he had such a big lead over the field, he could afford to go carefully. «*When you are leading by between 20 and 30 seconds, you certainly do not want to be attacking at 100% of your capability,*» explained the Finn. «*So you slow down to 90%. The tyre temperature drops and they start to pick up bits of rubber which have accumulated on the track and that starts to upset the handling. Then is the time to push hard again but maybe keeping a couple of tenths of a second in hand.*»
It was a delicate mission, but Mika accomplished it perfectly. It gave him a 17 point lead over David Coulthard and stretched the gap to Michael Schumacher to 22 points. From now it seemed the road to the championship was straight ahead.

Mika Hakkinen shared his joy with all his team, especially Ron Dennis and Norbert Haug (in background) before stepping up to the podium.

Giancarlo has but one ambition - victory

Fisichella finished a magnificent second in this Monaco Grand Prix and made only one slight mistake on his way when he nudged the barrier at Rascasse, which sent his Benetton into a slide. «*It was entirely my fault,*» admitted the Roman warrior. «*But apart from that, everything went well. I am very happy with this second place. I love the Monaco circuit.*» After the 1997 Belgian Grand Prix, this was Giancarlo's second ever second place in F1. Now his target was to win. «*I know I have to go one better now.*» He then turned to Hakkinen, sat beside him: Is that alright with you Mika? «*A win, just one win, please...*» There was no answer...

«Fisico» flies between the Monegasque barriers. Second place awaits him at the end of the road.

Alexander Wurz comes out of it well

Alexander Wurz had not yet refuelled when he had to fight off the advances of Michael Schumacher's Ferrari. The Austrian kept his provisional second place until the pit stop on lap 42, as the German came off worse, after the two men collided (see below.)
He had only just got going again, when he went straight on at the slight turn after the tunnel exit. He hit the barrier very hard. The two front wheels were torn off and Wurz was suddenly a helpless passenger in a missile doing 270 km/h. He ended up bouncing off the water barriers at the port chicane, which were installed after fellow Austrian Karl Wendlinger had his big accident at exactly the same spot back in 1994.
On Sunday evening, the driver had no idea whatsoever as to the cause of the accident. *«Maybe it is linked to my hitting Michael, or maybe something to do with my pit stop. We will have to examine the wreckage to find out,»* he said calmly.

A bad call from Michael Schumacher

△
Alexander Wurz' wrecked Benetton comes to rest. The Austrian had a narrow escape.

Considered by many to be a driving god, Michael Schumacher is nevertheless not infallible. On the twisty streets of Monaco he was guilty of the sin of impatience. When hê could have waited a few more laps until Alexander Wurz made his pit stop a few laps later, the German decided to chance his arm on a track where he knows better than most, just how hazardous overtaking can be.
Contrary to what he had hoped for, he did not make a good start. At the first corner he was fourth, in other words he had not improved on his grid position, behind the two McLarens and Giancarlo Fisichella, whom he tried to pass without success until the Italian pitted.
As usual the Ferrari mechanics were incredibly efficient, getting the German out on the track ahead of the Italian.
That still left Alexander Wurz to deal with in the other Benetton and he had yet to pit. The Ferrari was manifestly quicker than the Benetton and Michael Schumacher was losing his cool stuck behind the slower car, even though it seemed obvious that Wurz would have to refuel soon. As the two men approached the Loews hairpin, stuck behind a group of backmarkers, Schumi dived down the inside. Alex refused to be intimidated and did not back off, with the result that both cars touched front and back. Schumacher managed to get ahead in the muddle, but it was not for long. «Alex opened the door so I went for it,» explained the Ferrari driver after the race. «We touched but it was really nothing and I was sure my car was alright. But something broke at the back end and I had to come back to the pits. It is really strange.»
Michael Schumacher felt it was best to retire once he had inspected the damage. At that point the mechanics realised they could change the broken parts. *«I set off again,»* continued Schumacher. *«I was three laps down and there was nothing much to hope for from this race. But at Monaco, anything can happen. Sometimes there are only four finishers. What's more, the sky looked menacing and it could have started to rain. I could have tried to do something. I have to say that after it had been repaired the car did not feel as good as before.»*
His mount might have been wounded, but he was still doing quick laps, which took him from sixteenth to tenth, but he was a long way off a points finish. To add to his woes, a last minute move to get past Pedro Diniz, left him minus the front wing. All the evidence suggested Michael Schumacher was not on top form at Monaco.

The Monaco track must have something against Jacques Villeneuve. After a disastrous two days of practice, the Canadian ended the day in a modest fifth place.
▽

«Sarge, someone has nicked the squad car!» In Monaco, the police always turn out in impressive force, even if sometimes there are so many of them, they seem to be looking for one another.
◁▽

IN THE POINTS

1.	Mika HAKKINEN	West McLaren Mercedes	1 h 51'23"595
2.	Giancarlo FISICHELLA	Mild Seven Benetton Playlife	at 11"475
3.	Eddie IRVINE	Scuderia Ferrari Marlboro	at 41"378
4.	Mika SALO	Danka Zepter Arrows	at 1'00"363
5.	Jacques VILLENEUVE	Winfield Williams	at 1 lap
6.	Pedro DINIZ	Danka Zepter Arrows	at 1 lap

Fastest lap : Mika HAKKINEN, lap 29, 1'22"948, avg. 146.130 km/h

It was the final season for the Tyrrell team as it had been sold to the soon-to-be British American Racing team. While Riccardo Rosset was in difficulty - Monaco was the second time in a row he did not qualify, team mate Toranosuke Takagi was putting in some honourable performances. He finished 11th in the Principality.

PIAA

Max Mosley reckons everything is ship shape

By Monaco, the 1998 Formula 1 season was not exactly shaping up to be the most exciting one of the past few years. The constructors' title already seemed to be the property of McLaren and it was just a question of deciding which of its drivers would pick up the crown. What is more, the new regulations, aimed at making overtaking easier, appeared to have had the opposite effect. FIA President Max Mosley however, felt that all was Bristol fashion on the good ship Formula 1. «*Of course it is not good to see one team dominating as has been the case this year,*» he conceded on Saturday afternoon during a press conference. «*But one team trying to beat the others is what this sport is all about. It is the essence of F1. One has to admit that the people at McLaren have done a remarkable job this winter. Along with their partner Bridgestone, they have built a fantastic car. That is part of the game and it would be a grave error to try and intervene in this type of situation. It is up to the others to catch up with McLaren.*»
As for the regulations, Mosley claimed to be completely satisfied with the situation. «*All fans of 'traditional' motor racing would like to see more overtaking. However, thinking about it twice that the rarity of overtaking moves makes them more dramatic. Take the Argentinean Grand Prix for example. There was a very intense 30 minute period during the second run of pit stops. One did not know whether Hakkinen or Schumacher would come out of the pits in the lead. It was all the more exciting as whoever was second would be unable to overtake whoever was first. In F1 you cannot take your eyes off the television screen for a moment, because you might miss something. The motorcycle grands prix have so much overtaking that you can stop watching them for a while. One always knows it is only the final few laps which count. It is the same difference as between the number of baskets scored in a basketball game, sometimes over 100 points and a football game where sometimes no goals are scored. I prefer the football approach.*» It was a brilliant performance from Max, who nevertheless said he was looking into ways of making overtaking easier. «*We are studying several alternatives, but the main thing is we do not want to radically change the shape of the cars in order to achieve it. F1 must respect its spirit.*»

Alain Prost reckons the show must be changed

With the new technical regulations introduced in 1998, the F1 cars were slowed down by around two to three seconds per lap. On the other hand, they appear to be even more sensitive than before, from an aerodynamic point of view, which renders overtaking even more difficult.
If Max Mosley was happy with the situation, Alain Prost could not say the same in Monaco. «*It is imperative that we change the rules to improve the show,*» he remarked. «*For example, we could go back to very wide tyres as I think they are part of the magic of Formula 1 as far as the fans are concerned. Refuelling should also be banned. Before it was introduced, drivers started the race with 220 litres of fuel on board. The car's handling changed as the race progressed and they had to look after their tyres. Strange things could happen. At the moment there are no surprises. With refuelling, the cars are always on fresh tyres and have hardly any fuel on board. That means that the race order hardly changes from start to finish.*»
«The Professor» has often aired his opinions in the F1 Commission, to little effect. «*Unfortunately there is not much support for my ideas,*» continued Prost. «*Above all, I think that before any changes are made, their effect must be analysed in depth.*»
For 1999, nothing would change. «*Nothing should be changed for the time being as we have enough problems as it is,*» concluded the Frenchman. «*We must give careful thought to the long term. We have to be careful because change always favours the big teams as the others take longer to optimise their cars.*»

△

«Let me see now. I turn right here.» Eddie Irvine, with a map of the track stuck to his steering wheel, finished the race a lonely third.

More bad luck for David Coulthard. This time an exploding engine.

▷

Monaco often produces results never to be seen anywhere else. This time it was Arrows turn to surprise, with Mika Salo finishing 4th and Pedro Diniz 6th.

▽

Jacques Villeneuve: Monaco is great

Five o'clock. He has just picked up two points for fifth place and he is as happy as a kid with a new toy. It is not a great result for a reigning world champion but it is an honourable one, as Jacques Villeneuve started from 13th place on the grid and since the beginning of the year he has been fighting a Williams chassis which is not up to its reputation. With these two Monaco points the Canadian moves up to sixth in the championship, equal with his team mate!
«*It's the first time I have finished at Monaco and it feels great,*» enthused the Canadian. «*I am always pleased to see that Alexander Wurz was not frightened of standing up to Michael Schumacher. He did well!*»

PRACTICE TIMES

No	Driver	Car/Engine/Chassis	Practice Friday	Practice Saturday	Qualifying	Warm-up
1.	Jacques Villeneuve	Williams/Mecachrome/FW20/5 (G)	1'24"081	1'23"579	1'22"468	1'26"654
2.	Heinz-Harald Frentzen	Williams/Mecachrome/FW20/4 (G)	1'23"656	1'22"223	1'20"729	1'25"920
3.	Michael Schumacher	Ferrari/F300/186 (G)	1'23"685	1'22"890	1'20"702	1'24"107
4.	Eddie Irvine	Ferrari/F300/185 (G)	1'23"765	1'22"314	1'21"712	1'24"611
5.	Giancarlo Fisichella	Benetton/Playlife/198/6 (B)	1'22"205	1'21"145	1'20"368	1'25"151
6.	Alexander Wurz	Benetton/Playlife/198/1 (B)	1'23"946	1'22"683	1'20"955	1'24"493
7.	David Coulthard	McLaren/Mercedes/MP4-13/3 (B)	1'22"757	1'22"091	1'20"137	1'24"199
8.	Mika Hakkinen	McLaren/Mercedes/MP4-13/4 (B)	1'21"937	1'22"702	1'19"798	1'23"878
9.	Damon Hill	Jordan/Honda/198/3 (G)	1'25"947	1'24"698	1'23"151	1'27"602
10.	Ralf Schumacher	Jordan/Honda/198/4 (G)	1'27"160	1'24"312	1'23"263	1'26"348
11.	Olivier Panis	Prost/Peugeot/AP01/5 (B)	1'25"119	1'29"010	1'23"536	1'27"786
12.	Jarno Trulli	Prost/Peugeot/AP01/3 (B)	1'24"191	1'22"830	1'22"238	1'27"173
14.	Jean Alesi	Sauber/Petronas/C17/3 (G)	1'24"901	1'23"777	1'22"257	1'25"887
15.	Johnny Herbert	Sauber/Petronas/C17/4 (G)	1'23"914	1'25"110	1'22"157	1'27"118
16.	Pedro Diniz	Arrows/A19/4 (B)	1'24"735	1'24"759	1'22"355	1'26"650
17.	Mika Salo	Arrows/A19/3 (B)	1'25"400	1'22"171	1'22"144	1'24"896
18.	Rubens Barrichello	Stewart/Ford/SF2/4 (B)	1'25"863	1'23"100	1'22"540	1'25"688
19.	Jan Magnussen	Stewart/Ford/SF2/3 (B)	1'25"836	1'23"823	1'23"411	1'27"012
20.	Ricardo Rosset	Tyrrell/Ford/026/2 (G)	1'26"625	1'25"615	1'25"737	not qualif.
21.	Toranosuke Takagi	Tyrrell/Ford/026/3 (G)	1'26"761	1'24"456	1'24"024	1'25"861
22.	Shinji Nakano	Minardi/Ford/M198/4 (B)	1'28"652	1'25"512	1'23"967	1'26"433
23.	Esteban Tuero	Minardi/Ford/M198/3 (B)	1'27"844	1'24"250	1'24"031	1'28"287

CLASSIFICATION & RETIREMENTS

Pos	Driver	Team	Time
1.	Hakkinen	McLaren Mercedes	in 1h51'23"595
2.	Fisichella	Benetton Playlife	at 11"475
3.	Irvine	Ferrari	at 41"378
4.	Salo	Arrows	at 60"363
5.	Villeneuve	Williams Mecachrome	at 1 lap
6.	Diniz	Arrows	at 1 lap
7.	Herbert	Sauber Petronas	at 1 lap
8.	Hill	Jordan Mugen Honda	at 2 laps
9.	Nakano	Minardi Ford	at 2 laps
10.	M. Schum.	Ferrari	at 2 laps
11.	Takagi	Tyrrell Ford	at 2 laps
12.	Alesi	Sauber Petronas	gearbox

Lap	Driver	Team	Reason
1	Tuero	Minardi Ford	off
10	Frentzen	Williams Mecachrome	accident
12	Barrichello	Stewart Ford	suspension
18	Coulthard	McLaren Mercedes	engine
31	Magnussen	Stewart Ford	suspension
43	Wurz	Benetton Playlife	engine
45	R. Schum.	Jordan Mugen Honda	accident
50	Panis	Prost Peugeot	crewless wheel
57	Trulli	Prost Peugeot	gearbox

FASTEST LAPS

	Driver	Time	Lap
1.	Hakkinen	1'22"948	29
2.	Coulthard	1'22"955	17
3.	M. Schum.	1'23"189	65
4.	Fisichella	1'23"594	25
5.	Wurz	1'23"970	40
6.	Villeneuve	1'24"381	70
7.	Diniz	1'24"456	39
8.	Irvine	1'24"457	28
9.	Alesi	1'24"539	51
10.	Salo	1'24"582	38
11.	Panis	1'24"874	33
12.	Herbert	1'25"053	66
13.	Nakano	1'26"054	70
14.	Hill	1'26"091	69
15.	R. Schum.	1'26"228	23
16.	Trulli	1'26"501	25
17.	Takagi	1'26"506	60
18.	Magnussen	1'26"637	24
19.	Frentzen	1'26"777	5
20.	Barrichello	1'27"719	9

LAP CHART

position:	1	2	3	4	5	6	7	8	9	10	11	12	13	14	15	16	17	18	19	20	21
start:	8	7	5	3	2	6	4	17	15	12	14	16	1	18	9	10	19	11	22	21	23
1	8	7	5	3	6	2	4	17	14	12	15	16	18	1	19	9	10	21	11	22	
2	8	7	5	3	6	2	4	17	14	12	15	16	18	1	19	9	10	21	11	22	
3	8	7	5	3	6	2	4	17	14	12	15	16	18	1	19	9	10	21	11	22	
4	8	7	5	3	6	2	4	17	14	12	15	16	18	1	19	9	10	21	11	22	
5	8	7	5	3	6	2	4	17	14	12	15	16	18	1	19	9	10	21	11	22	
6	8	7	5	3	6	2	4	17	14	12	15	16	18	1	19	9	10	21	11	22	
7	8	7	5	3	6	2	4	17	14	12	15	16	18	1	19	9	10	21	11	22	
8	8	7	5	3	6	2	4	17	14	12	15	16	18	1	19	9	10	21	11	22	
9	8	7	5	3	6	2	4	17	14	12	15	16	18	1	19	9	10	21	11	22	
10	8	7	5	3	6	4	17	14	12	15	16	18	1	19	9	10	21	11	22		
11	8	7	5	3	6	4	17	14	12	15	16	18	1	19	9	10	21	11	22		
12	8	7	5	3	6	4	17	14	12	15	16	1	19	9	10	21	11	22			
13	8	7	5	3	6	4	17	14	12	15	16	1	19	9	10	21	11	22			
14	8	7	5	3	6	4	17	14	12	15	16	1	19	9	10	21	11	22			
15	8	7	5	3	6	4	17	14	12	15	16	1	19	9	10	21	11	22			
16	8	7	5	3	6	4	17	14	12	15	16	1	19	9	10	21	22	11			
17	8	7	5	3	6	4	17	14	12	15	16	1	19	9	10	21	22	11			
18	8	5	3	6	4	17	14	12	15	16	1	19	9	10	21	22	11				
19	8	5	3	6	4	17	14	12	15	16	1	19	9	10	21	22	11				
20	8	5	3	6	4	17	14	12	15	16	1	19	9	10	21	22	11				
21	8	5	3	6	4	17	14	12	15	16	1	19	9	10	21	22	11				
22	8	5	3	6	4	17	14	12	15	16	1	19	9	10	21	22	11				
23	8	5	3	6	4	17	14	12	15	16	1	19	9	10	21	22	11				
24	8	5	3	6	4	17	14	12	15	16	1	19	9	10	21	22	11				
25	8	5	3	6	4	17	14	12	15	16	1	19	9	10	21	22	11				
26	8	5	3	6	4	17	14	12	15	16	1	19	9	10	21	22	11				
27	8	5	3	6	4	17	14	12	15	16	1	19	9	10	21	22	11				
28	8	5	3	6	4	17	14	12	15	16	1	19	9	10	21	22	11				
29	8	5	3	6	4	17	14	12	15	16	1	19	9	10	21	22	11				
30	8	5	6	3	4	17	14	12	15	16	1	19	9	10	21	22	11				
31	8	6	3	5	4	17	14	12	15	16	1	9	10	21	22	11					
32	8	6	3	5	4	17	14	12	15	16	1	9	10	21	22	11					
33	8	6	3	5	4	17	14	12	15	16	1	9	10	21	22	11					
34	8	6	3	5	4	17	14	12	15	16	1	9	10	21	22	11					
35	8	6	3	5	4	17	14	12	15	16	1	9	10	21	22	11					
36	8	6	3	5	4	17	14	12	15	16	1	9	10	21	22	11					
37	8	6	3	5	4	17	14	15	16	1	9	10	12	21	22	11					
38	8	6	5	4	17	14	16	1	9	10	15	12	21	22	11	3					
39	8	6	5	4	17	14	16	1	9	10	15	12	21	22	11	3					
40	8	6	5	4	17	14	16	1	9	10	15	12	21	22	11	3					
41	8	6	5	4	17	14	16	1	9	10	15	12	21	22	11	3					
42	8	5	4	6	14	17	16	1	9	10	15	12	21	22	11	3					
43	8	5	4	14	17	1	16	10	15	9	12	22	21	11	3						
44	8	5	4	14	17	1	16	15	9	12	10	22	21	11	3						
45	8	5	4	14	17	1	16	15	9	12	22	21	11	3							
46	8	5	4	14	17	1	16	15	9	12	22	21	11	3							
47	8	5	4	14	17	1	16	15	9	12	22	21	11	3							
48	8	5	4	14	17	1	16	15	9	12	22	21	11	3							
49	8	5	4	14	17	1	16	15	9	12	22	21	11	3							
50	8	5	4	14	17	1	16	15	9	12	22	21	3								
51	8	5	4	14	17	1	16	15	9	12	22	21	3								
52	8	5	4	14	17	1	16	15	9	12	22	21	3								
53	8	5	4	14	17	1	16	15	9	12	22	21	3								
54	8	5	4	14	17	1	16	15	9	12	22	21	3								
55	8	5	4	17	14	1	16	15	9	12	22	21	3								
56	8	5	4	17	14	1	16	15	9	12	22	21	3								
57	8	5	4	17	14	1	16	15	9	22	21	3									
58	8	5	4	17	14	1	16	15	9	22	21	3									
59	8	5	4	17	14	1	16	15	9	22	21	3									
60	8	5	4	17	14	1	16	15	9	22	21	3									
61	8	5	4	17	14	1	16	15	9	22	21	3									
62	8	5	4	17	14	1	16	15	9	22	21	3									
63	8	5	4	17	14	1	16	15	9	22	21	3									
64	8	5	4	17	14	1	16	15	9	22	21	3									
65	8	5	4	17	14	1	16	15	9	22	21	3									
66	8	5	4	17	14	1	16	15	9	22	21	3									
67	8	5	4	17	14	1	16	15	9	22	21	3									
68	8	5	4	17	14	1	16	15	9	22	21	3									
69	8	5	4	17	14	1	16	15	9	22	21	3									
70	8	5	4	17	14	1	16	15	9	22	21	3									
71	8	5	4	17	14	1	16	15	9	22	3	21									
72	8	5	4	17	14	1	16	15	9	22	3	21									
73	8	5	4	17	1	16	15	9	22	3	21										
74	8	5	4	17	1	16	15	9	22	3	21										
75	8	5	4	17	1	16	15	9	22	3	21										
76	8	5	4	17	1	16	15	9	22	3	21										
77	8	5	4	17	1	16	15														
78	8	5	4	17																	

SIXTH ROUND

GRAND PRIX DE MONACO, MONTE CARLO

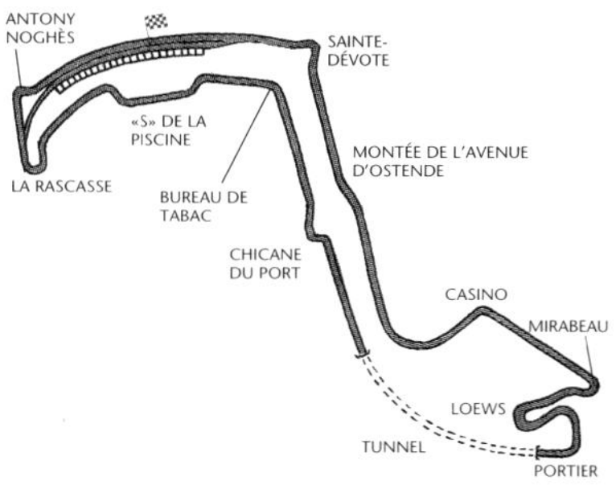

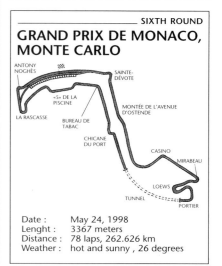

Date : May 24, 1998
Lenght : 3367 meters
Distance : 78 laps, 262.626 km
Weather : hot and sunny , 26 degrees

CHAMPIONSHIPS (after six rounds)

Drivers :
1. Mika HAKKINEN 46
2. David COULTHARD 29
3. Michael SCHUMACHER 24
4. Eddie IRVINE 15
5. Alexander WURZ 9
6. Heinz-Harald FRENTZEN......8
   Jacques VILLENEUVE 8
8. Giancarlo FISICHELLA 7
9. Mika SALO 3
   Jean ALESI 3
11. Rubens BARRICHELLO 2
12. Johnny HERBERT 1
    Pedro DINIZ 1

Constructors :
1. McLaren / Mercedes..........75
2. Ferrari................................39
3. Williams / Mecachrome.....16
   Benetton / Playlife 16
5. Arrows..................................4
   Sauber / Petronas 4
7. Stewart / Ford 2

WEEK-END GOSSIP

• **Michelin heading back**

Goodyear seems intent on pulling out at the end of the year, despite rumours to the contrary. *«At the moment, the management has not changed its mind,»* confirmed Goodyear's motor sport boss Perry Bell on Thursday. This decision could encourage Michelin to return to F1. A few months earlier the directors of the Clermont Ferrand company had decided against it, but in Barcelona, some of the French firms engineers were spotted snooping around the paddock in plain clothes. Pierre Dupasquier, their competitions boss was in the Prost garage and was not trying to hide. *«I was very interested to see Mr. Dupasquier here,»* commented Hiroshi Yasukawa, Bridgestone's motor sport director. *«I welcomed him and I hope Michelin will come into F1. I firmly believe that competition between manufacturers adds another dimension to the sport.»*

• **Bernie counter attacks**

Furious that the flotation of F1 on the stock market had failed, mainly because of critical remarks made by Karel van Miert, the EU man with a brief to look into competition, Bernie Ecclestone was preparing to take him to court for defamation, claiming 365 million pounds sterling in damages and interest. For its part, FIA would do the same and was asking for 180 million pounds.

• **Silver top**

Jean Alesi had a new design on his helmet for Monaco, with silver replacing the white. It was as much a surprise for the man himself as anyone else. *«I have an arrangement with Shoei helmets and they wanted to do something special. They sent me this helmet without even consulting me. I like these new colours.»*

• **Supertec has a good pedigree**

A rumour that had been doing the rounds for some time was confirmed: from now on, Flavio Briatore would look after the commercial side of the Mecachrome engine business. On Thursday, the French company signed an exclusive agreement with *«Super Performance Competition Engineering,»* a company run by Flavio Briatore, which will be the exclusive distributor of the Renault developed V10 engines. It was pointed out that Renault is working on a new generation of engines for the 1999 season, built by Mecachrome and supplied by Supertec.

• **A grand prix in India**

In Barcelona, Michael Taub and Anwar Saleem, representatives of an Indian Grand Prix consortium, met with Bernie Ecclestone to negotiate running the event. An Indian Grand Prix could be on the calendar in 2000.

RACE SUMMARY

- A perfect start from both McLarens sees them lead through the first corner, with Hakkinen ahead of Coulthard. Next up come Giancarlo Fisichella and Michael Schumacher.
- In the early stages the two McLarens pull away and net 12 fastest laps between them from laps 4 to 12. The pack stretches out behind them, while Frentzen succumbs to pressure from Irvine.
- On lap 18 Coulthard retires with a broken engine.
- Michael Schumacher is the first to refuel on lap 30. One lap later, Fisichella pits and comes out behind the Ferrari.
- Schumacher now comes up behind Wurz and tries to pass him at all costs at the Loews hairpin by going down the inside but the Austrian does not give way. The two cars touch. The damaged Ferrari stops in the pits for repairs and restarts three laps down on Hakkinen.
- Wurz, whose car seems unaffected by the accident, refuels. Shortly after he has a big accident coming out of the tunnel and ends up at the port chicane.
- Fisichella now finds himself second behind Hakkinen and ahead of Irvine. The order stays the same to the end.
- Jean Alesi is running fifth. Gearbox problems force him to pull out five laps from the finish.
- On the last lap, still trying to climb through the field, Michael Schumacher slides in the port chicane, hits Pedro Diniz and breaks his front wing. He finishes 10th.

The luxury yachts in the harbour are part of the charm of Monaco. Some of them have lounges of such excessive beauty that it seems a crime to sail these palaces.

PlayStation
GAULOISES
AGFA
ALCATEL
CANAL+
BRIDGESTONE
TRULLI
GAULOISES
E
Agfa
BiC
10028347
POTENZA
BRIDGESTONE
BBS
BRIDGESTONE

Canada's crazy crashes

Two starts, loads of accidents, three appearances from the safety car, Jacques Villeneuve in the lead for all of 300 metres and Michael Schumacher barging Heinz-Harald Frentzen into the grass - just some of the amazing events which marked the Canadian Grand Prix as a mad afternoon of motor racing.

At the final bell, it was Michael Schumacher who took the top honours, despite a ten second penalty for his bully boy tactics on Frentzen. What a day!

GRAND PRIX PLAYER'S DU CANADA MONTREAL

Saturday morning: the start of a slide and big fright for Mika Hakkinen on the Gilles Villeneuve circuit. It is rare for a photographer to capture an off track excursion so clearly and completely.

STARTING GRID

		David COULTHARD 1'18"213
Mika HAKKINEN 1'18"282	-1-	
		M. SCHUMACHER 1'18"497
G. FISICHELLA 1'18"826	-2-	
		R. SCHUMACHER 1'19"242
Jacques VILLENEUVE 1'19"588	-3-	
		Heinz-H. FRENTZEN 1'19"614
Eddie IRVINE 1'19"616	-4-	
		Jean ALESI 1'19"693
Damon HILL 1'19"717	-5-	
		Alexander WURZ 1'19"765
Johnny HERBERT 1'19"845	-6-	
		R. BARRICHELLO 1'19"953
Jarno TRULLI 1'20"188	-7-	
		Olivier PANIS 1'20"303
Toranosuke TAKAGI 1'20"328	-8-	
		Mika SALO 1'20"536
Shinji NAKANO 1'21"230	-9-	
		Pedro DINIZ 1'21"301
Jan MAGNUSSEN 1'21"62[illegible]	-10-	
		Esteban TUERO 1'21"822
Ricardo ROSSET 1'21"824	-11-	

Again and always the two McLarens, but in the wrong order

In Montreal, David Coulthard pulled off his third pole of the season. The Scotsman managed to do the fastest time right at the end of the session with a truly awesome lap. *«Yes, I had to take some risks to beat Mika. I really went for broke,»* he recounted. *«I have to say I had more confidence in the car in my car on this circuit than I did in Spain or Monaco. That meant I could push for those last few tenths.»* Mika Hakkinen was not too disappointed with second place. The Finn had encountered a lot of traffic on his quick laps. *«Actually, pole position is in a strange place on this circuit. Sometimes it can be better to start second. We will see.»*

Michael Schumacher was third and was happily surprised with what he saw on the stopwatch. *«The McLarens are now only a whisker ahead of us. It proves that Goodyear's new tyres are working.»*

The night before qualifying, Eddie Irvine had declared that the Canadian Grand Prix would be crucial for Ferrari. The double world champion was of the same opinion.

«We have various reasons to think we can go well here. If it turns out not be the case, then our championship chances are looking pretty thin. Today we can see that we are now very close to the McLarens. I am very optimistic for the championship.»

The «evolution» Williams is disappointing

Lengthened by ten centimetres with repositioned gearbox and exhausts, with the rear wing and driver's position pushed back, the *«B»* spec. Williams FW20 did not have much in common with its early season version.

The team's two drivers had not stopped complaining that their car was unstable, that the rear end lacked balance and now it seemed that this FW20B was finally to their satisfaction. Heinz-Harald Frentzen had even confided in a friend that he felt as though he was driving a Rolls Royce. However, in practice in Montreal the *«evolution»* Williams were a disappointment as neither Jacques Villeneuve nor Heinz-Harald Frentzen could get nowhere near the McLarens. On Saturday, the local boy was 1.3 seconds off pole position. Easily enough to worry the sixty thousand spectators around the course. *«The car is better than the one we had at the start of the season, but I was unable to set it up to my liking,»* lamented Villeneuve.

Schumacher survives the mayhem and madness

What a race! A host of cars going off the track, accidents, three appearances by the Safety Car, two starts: the Canadian Grand Prix was by far the most incident packed of the season. Michael Schumacher finally emerged the winner of this afternoon of torment. Thanks partly to the cool weather which suited his new tyres, but also thanks to the retirement of the two McLarens. Starting with the intention of only making one pit stop, David Coulthard was leading when his Mercedes engine lost half its power because of a throttle problem. Meanwhile, Mika Hakkinen did not even make it to the end of the first lap because of a gearbox problem.
With the two McLarens out of the way, Michael Schumacher was easily the quickest man on the track. His journey was not without incident however, thanks to his incident with Heinz-Harald Frentzen (see opposite) which cost him a ten second penalty. *«I asked the team over the radio to tell my why I had been penalised,»* explained the German. *«They said something about Frentzen, but I did not understand anything.»*
Rejoining the race in third place, behind Giancarlo Fisichella and Damon Hill, the German had one more worrying moment as he tried to pass the Englishman. *«What Damon did was unacceptable. There is an understanding and an agreement between the drivers: you can change line once, but you must not zig-zag. I hope the stewards will do something about it.»* Hill did not agree (see page 143.) Once he had dispensed with Hill, Schumacher was on his way to his second win of the season.

◁
Michael Schumacher's jump for joy is as high as the tension that reigned during this crazy race.

«Can someone tell me what happened?» Violently «taken out» by Michael Schumacher, Heinz-Harald Frentzen was still trying to work out what had happened as he stepped from the car.
◁▽

Schumacher takes Frentzen out of the race

An incident that made waves

Lap 21. The Safety Car is on the track so the Canadian Grand Prix is temporarily «neutralised» for a third time. Michael Schumacher dives into the pits to refuel-in itself this is theoretically an illegal move as the pit lane entrance is supposed to be closed each time the Safety Car is on the track, but this time it was not. As he goes back onto the track and while the yellow flags are being waved so that all overtaking is forbidden, the Ferrari shoots across to the outside of the track and forces Frentzen onto the grass to avoid it. *«I apologise to Heinz-Harald. As I came out of the pits, I looked in the mirrors but I did not see him as he was in my blind spot.»*
The poor Williams driver was thus knocked out of the race, having suffered a similar fate in Monaco, two weeks earlier, when Eddie Irvine pushed him at the Loews hairpin. *«Heinz Harald is too nice. He should have taken Schumacher out of the race,»* commented a Williams engineer. After the press conference, Schumacher went to the Williams garage to apologise in person to Frentzen, who replied he was not interested in listening.
In the paddock, there were many who agreed with the Williams driver, especially as Ferrari technical director Ross Brawn had warned his driver over the radio that Frentzen was coming. Indeed, Frank Williams lodged a protest about Schumacher's behaviour.
This forced Schumacher to have to explain his actions. Unsurprisingly, the whole incident was glossed over. The sporting power was not about to disqualify a driver who had just relit the championship fire.

Jacques Villeneuve led the race.....for 300 metres until he tried to pass Giancarlo Fisichella. It was an optimistic move and he went off the road immediately. Before the race, the local paper, «La Presse,» had run a survey which found that 61% percent of those asked, thought that the new version of the Williams would allow Villeneuve to challenge the McLarens. They were to be disappointed.
▽

IN THE POINTS

1.	M. SCHUMACHER	Scuderia Ferrari Marlboro	1 h 40'57"355
2.	Giancarlo FISICHELLA	Mild Seven Benetton Playlife	at 16"662
3.	Eddie IRVINE	Scuderia Ferrari Marlboro	at 1'00"058
4.	Alexander WURZ	Mild S. Benetton Playlife	at 1'03"232
5.	R. BARRICHELLO	Stewart Ford	at 1'21"512
6.	Jan MAGNUSSEN	Stewart Ford	at 1 lap

Fastest lap : M. SCHUMACHER, lap 48, 1'19"379, avg. 200.501 km/h

AGFA
BIC
CANAL+
POTENZA
BRIDGESTONE
MILD SEVEN
KOREAN
FedEx

1

AGFA
BIC
CANAL+
POTENZA
BRIDGESTONE
LVS
KOREAN
FedEx

2

3

«Let me out!»
First start and first scare for Alexander Wurz, here trapped in his Benetton which had rolled three times before stopping the right way up. Perfectly calm, the Austrian returned to his pit to climb into the spare car to line up for the second start.

Jacques Villeneuve has not given up hope

«Don't be bullied Michael. If you see a driver in your way, push him onto the grass.» On the grid, Sylvester Stallone gives Schumacher some good advice.

Making the most of all the retirements, both Stewarts finished in the points. However, sixth place was not enough to save Jan Magnussen's job. The Dane would be replaced as from the next race.

Third place for Eddie Irvine after a very quiet race.

Were the Quebecois going off Jacques Villeneuve already? On Wednesday, at his annual Canadian Grand Prix press conference there were no more than sixty people door stepping the «Box Office,» the bar where the young champion was due to put in an appearance at two o'clock.
It was a long way off the thousands of fans who had showed up to greet him at the Molson Centre when he had just won the world championship title. This season's lack of results - not one podium from six grands prix obviously had something to do with this strange lack of interest.
The sixty or so fans were to be disappointed. Villeneuve arrived at the prescribed hour in a black limo and crept in through the tradesman's entrance without spending even a few seconds with those who had turned up to see him. The Canadian was protected by about twenty bodyguards wearing black leather jackets, who stopped anyone getting over the barriers.
The conference itself lasted almost two hours and was attended by around two hundred local journalists. Jacques Villeneuve talked about everything from his personal life to his season so far. Thanks to the society writer from the *«Journal de Montreal,»* Monelle Saindon, we learned that the Canadian driver does not have time for a personal relationship, serious or otherwise. *«As long as I am racing I am forced to be selfish,»* he theorised. *«But later when the time comes to settle down and have a family, I know I want a wife who has character and aspirations.»*
Even though this 1998 season already looks compromised, the Canadian has not given up hope of winning more races and more titles. *«As long as there are Fangio's five championships, Prost's 51 victories and Senna's 65 pole positions, there is still much to accomplish. I am only 27, with several years of racing left and a lot of championships to win.»*
The night before, Villeneuve had been presented with the *«Canadian Athlete Par Excellence 1997.»* He beat the athlete Larry Walker to the trophy. The runner up was not impressed. *«I've been beaten by a car,»* he declared. Jacques took exception to the remark. *«It's a shame that my selection has upset him. He is probably just bitter. In sport you have to give your all, and I reckon I have done that. I train two hours a day and my discipline is very physical. Yes there is a machine between me and the track, but that also applies to skiers. If Walker had won the title, I would have congratulated him.»*

Poor Peter Sauber!

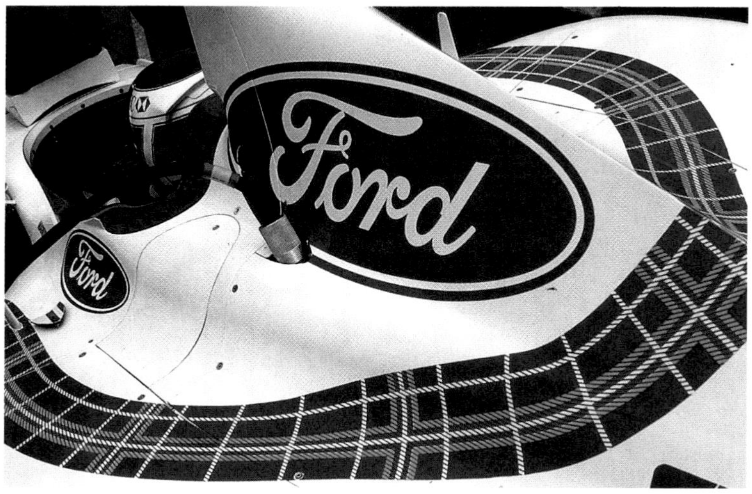

A bit too tight, the first corner at Montreal is always a problem. This year it was the scene of two serious accidents, luckily without injury.
At the first start it was Alexander Wurz who caused the pile up. He was squeezed by other cars and forced to cut across the grass in his Benetton, which meant he could not brake and the Austrian crashed into Jean Alesi's Sauber, as well as Johnny Herbert's and Jarno Trulli's Prost. His Benetton rolled over three times, before he climbed out unhurt.
At the second start, it was Ralf Schumacher who pushed a bit too hard. He also went across the grass and spun in the middle of the track, causing mayhem in the chasing pack, with Trulli's Prost mounting Alesi's Sauber. Ralf Schumacher showed a certain style by claiming his spin was caused by a transmission problem which left him without any engine braking. He simply forgot to mention the bit where he shot across the grass.
Johnny Herbert was lucky that his mechanics were able to repair his C17 after the first incident - it was only a twisted suspension arm. The only Sauber driver still in the running, his race came to an end on lap 19, when he spun trying to pass Jan Magnussen's Stewart. *«I could have stayed behind him, but it's my job to try and overtake him,»* said the Englishman with a broad grin. Peter Sauber did not see the joke and did not want to comment after the race.

PRACTICE TIMES

No	Driver	Car/Engine/Chassis	Practice Friday	Practice Saturday	Qualifying	Warm-up
1.	Jacques Villeneuve	Williams/Mecachrome/FW20/5 (G)	1'21"597	1'19"898	1'19"588	1'22"622
2.	Heinz-Harald Frentzen	Williams/Mecachrome/FW20/4 (G)	1'20"622	1'19"512	1'19"614	1'21"940
3.	Michael Schumacher	Ferrari/F300/187 (G)	1'19"999	1'19"198	1'18"497	1'22"360
4.	Eddie Irvine	Ferrari/F300/185 (G)	1'20"821	1'19"979	1'19"616	1'30"685
5.	Giancarlo Fisichella	Benetton/Playlife/198/6 (B)	1'20"480	1'19"414	1'18"826	1'22"351
6.	Alexander Wurz	Benetton/Playlife/198/5 (B)	1'21"274	1'20"956	1'19"765	1'24"577
7.	David Coulthard	McLaren/Mercedes/MP4-13/3 (B)	1'20"316	1'18"741	1'18"213	1'22"281
8.	Mika Hakkinen	McLaren/Mercedes/MP4-13/4 (B)	1'19"613	1'18"741	1'18"282	1'22"065
9.	Damon Hill	Jordan/Honda/198/3 (G)	1'21"069	1'20"350	1'19"717	1'23"086
10.	Ralf Schumacher	Jordan/Honda/198/4 (G)	1'21"294	1'19"362	1'19"242	1'23"583
11.	Olivier Panis	Prost/Peugeot/AP01/5 (B)	1'21"191	1'20"671	1'20"303	1'23"052
12.	Jarno Trulli	Prost/Peugeot/AP01/3 (B)	1'21"282	1'20"170	1'20"188	1'22"931
14.	Jean Alesi	Sauber/Petronas/C17/3 (G)	1'20"252	1'19"623	1'19"693	1'23"647
15.	Johnny Herbert	Sauber/Petronas/C17/4 (G)	1'21"239	1'19"990	1'19"845	1'22"447
16.	Pedro Diniz	Arrows/A19/1 (B)	1'22"100	1'21"251	1'21"301	1'23"801
17.	Mika Salo	Arrows/A19/3 (B)	1'21"962	1'20"075	1'20"536	1'23"537
18.	Rubens Barrichello	Stewart/Ford/SF2/4 (B)	1'20"937	1'21"196	1'19"953	1'23"051
19.	Jan Magnussen	Stewart/Ford/SF2/3 (B)	1'23"146	1'22"875	1'21"629	1'26"337
20.	Ricardo Rosset	Tyrrell/Ford/026/2 (G)	1'23"011	1'21"505	1'21"824	1'25"859
21.	Toranosuke Takagi	Tyrrell/Ford/026/1 (G)	1'21"370	1'21"281	1'20"328	1'24"774
22.	Shinji Nakano	Minardi/Ford/M198/4 (B)	1'22"137	1'21"361	1'21"230	1'24"801
23.	Esteban Tuero	Minardi/Ford/M198/3 (B)	1'22"425	1'21"700	1'21"822	1'26"042

LAP CHART

position:	1	2	3	4	5	6	7	8	9	10	11	12	13	14	15	16	17	18	19	20	21	22
start:	7	8	3	5	10	1	2	4	14	9	6	15	18	12	11	21	17	22	16	19	23	20
1	7	3	5	1	2	18	9	19	16	20	22	15	11	17	23	6	4					
2	7	3	5	1	2	18	9	19	16	20	22	15	11	17	23	6	4					
3	7	3	5	1	2	18	9	19	16	20	22	15	11	17	23	6	4					
4	7	3	5	1	2	18	9	19	16	20	22	15	11	17	23	6	4					
5	7	3	5	1	2	18	9	19	16	20	22	15	11	17	23	6	4					
6	7	3	5	1	18	2	9	19	16	20	22	15	11	17	23	6	4					
7	7	3	5	1	18	2	9	19	16	20	22	15	11	17	23	6	4					
8	7	3	5	18	1	2	9	19	16	20	22	15	11	17	23	6	4					
9	7	3	5	18	1	2	9	19	16	20	15	22	11	17	23	6	4					
10	7	3	5	18	1	2	9	19	16	20	15	22	11	17	23	6	4					
11	7	3	5	1	2	9	18	19	16	20	15	22	11	17	23	6	4					
12	7	3	5	1	2	9	18	19	16	15	20	22	11	17	23	6	4					
13	7	3	5	1	2	9	18	19	15	20	22	11	17	23	6	4	16					
14	7	3	5	1	2	9	18	19	15	20	22	11	17	23	6	4	16					
15	7	3	5	1	2	9	18	19	15	22	11	17	23	6	4	20	16					
16	7	3	5	1	2	9	18	19	15	22	11	17	23	6	4	20	16					
17	7	3	5	1	2	9	18	19	15	22	11	17	23	6	4	20	16					
18	7	3	5	1	2	9	18	19	15	22	11	17	23	6	4	20	16					
19	3	5	1	2	18	9	19	22	11	23	6	4	20	16								
20	5	1	3	2	18	9	19	22	11	23	6	4	20	16								
21	5	1	3	9	19	22	11	23	6	4	18	20	16									
22	5	1	3	9	19	22	11	23	6	4	18	20	16									
23	5	3	9	19	22	11	6	4	18	20	23	16	1									
24	5	3	9	19	11	22	6	4	18	20	23	16	1									
25	5	3	9	19	11	22	6	4	18	20	23	16	1									
26	5	3	9	19	11	22	6	4	18	20	23	16	1									
27	5	3	9	19	11	22	6	4	18	20	23	16	1									
28	5	3	9	19	11	22	6	4	18	20	23	16	1									
29	5	3	9	19	11	6	4	22	18	20	23	16	1									
30	5	3	9	19	11	6	4	22	18	20	23	16	1									
31	5	3	9	19	11	6	4	22	18	20	16	23	1									
32	5	3	9	19	11	6	4	22	18	20	16	23	1									
33	5	3	9	19	11	6	4	22	18	20	16	23	1									
34	5	3	9	19	11	6	4	22	18	20	16	23	1									
35	5	9	3	11	6	4	22	18	19	20	16	23	1									
36	5	9	3	11	6	4	22	18	19	20	16	23	1									
37	5	9	3	11	6	4	22	18	19	20	23	16	1									
38	5	3	9	11	6	22	18	4	19	20	23	16	1									
39	5	3	11	6	18	9	4	19	22	20	23	16	1									
40	5	3	18	9	6	4	19	22	20	23	16	1										
41	5	3	18	4	6	19	22	20	9	23	16	1										
42	5	3	18	4	6	19	22	20	23	16	9	1										
43	5	3	18	4	6	19	22	20	23	16	1											
44	3	5	18	4	6	19	22	20	23	16	1											
45	3	5	18	4	6	19	22	20	23	16	1											
46	3	5	18	4	6	19	22	20	23	16	1											
47	3	5	18	4	6	19	22	20	23	16	1											
48	3	5	4	18	6	19	22	20	23	16	1											
49	3	5	4	6	18	19	22	20	23	16	1											
50	3	5	4	6	18	19	22	20	23	16	1											
51	3	5	4	6	18	19	22	20	23	16	1											
52	3	5	4	6	18	19	22	20	23	16	1											
53	3	5	4	6	18	19	22	20	23	16	1											
54	3	5	4	6	18	19	22	20	16	1												
55	3	5	4	6	18	19	22	20	16	1												
56	3	5	4	6	18	19	22	20	16	1												
57	3	5	4	6	18	19	22	20	16	1												
58	3	5	4	6	18	19	22	20	16	1												
59	3	5	4	6	18	19	22	20	16	1												
60	3	5	4	6	18	19	22	20	16	1												
61	3	5	4	6	18	19	22	20	16	1												
62	3	5	4	6	18	19	22	20	16	1												
63	3	5	4	6	18	19	22	20	16	1												
64	3	5	4	6	18	19	22	20	16													
65	3	5	4	6	18	19	22	20	16													
66	3	5	4	6	18	19	22	20	16													
67	3	5	4	6	18	19	22	20	16													
68	3	5	4	6	18	19	22	20	16													
69	3	5	4	6	18																	

CLASSIFICATION & RETIREMENTS

Pos	Driver	Team	Time
1.	M. Schum.	Ferrari	in 1h40'57"355
2.	Fisichella	Benetton Playlife	at 16"662
3.	Irvine	Ferrari	at 1'00"058
4.	Wurz	Benetton Playlife	at 1'03"232
5.	Barrichello	Stewart Ford	at 1'21"512
6.	Magnussen	Stewart Ford	at 1 lap
7.	Nakano	Minardi Ford	at 1 lap
8.	Rosset	Tyrrell Ford	at 1 lap
9.	Diniz	Arrows	at 1 lap
10.	Villeneuve	Williams Mecachrome	at 6 laps
Lap	**Driver**	**Team**	**Reason**
1	Takagi	Tyrrell Ford	transmission
1	Trulli	Prost Peugeot	accident
1	Alesi	Sauber Petronas	accident
1	R. Schum.	Jordan Mugen Honda	accident
1	Hakkinen	McLaren Mercedes	gearbox
19	Salo	Arrows	understeer
19	Herbert	Sauber Petronas	off
19	Coulthard	McLaren Mercedes	transmission
21	Frentzen	Williams Mecachrome	accident
40	Panis	Prost Peugeot	engine
43	Hill	Jordan Mugen Honda	engine
54	Tuero	Minardi Ford	accident

FASTEST LAPS

	Driver	Time	Lap
1.	M. Schum.	1'19"379	48
2.	Coulthard	1'20"852	11
3.	Fisichella	1'20"942	34
4.	Villeneuve	1'21"233	61
5.	Irvine	1'21"327	54
6.	Panis	1'21"669	39
7.	Wurz	1'21"694	66
8.	Diniz	1'21"814	67
9.	Hill	1'21"933	25
10.	Barrichello	1'22"239	44
11.	Frentzen	1'22"430	12
12.	Magnussen	1'22"867	32
13.	Nakano	1'22"907	67
14.	Tuero	1'22"939	53
15.	Rosset	1'23"418	60
16.	Herbert	1'23"466	10
17.	Salo	1'24"451	8

SEVENTH ROUND

GRAND PRIX PLAYER'S DU CANADA, MONTRÉAL

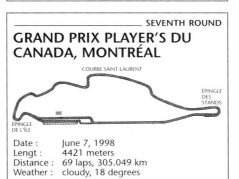

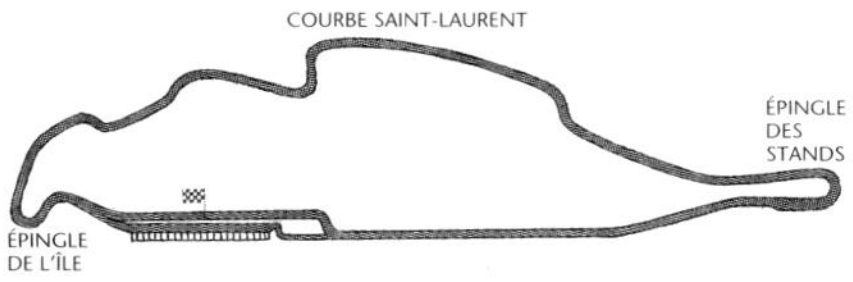

Date : June 7, 1998
Lengt : 4421 meters
Distance : 69 laps, 305.049 km
Weather : cloudy, 18 degrees

CHAMPIONSHIPS

(after seven rounds)

Drivers :

1.	Mika HAKKINEN	46
2.	Michael SCHUMACHER	34
3.	David COULTHARD	29
4.	Eddie IRVINE	19
5.	Giancarlo FISICHELLA	13
6.	Alexander WURZ	12
7.	Heinz-Harald FRENTZEN	8
	Jacques VILLENEUVE	8
9.	Rubens BARRICHELLO	4
10.	Mika SALO	3
	Jean ALESI	3
12.	Johnny HERBERT	1
	Pedro DINIZ	1
	Jan MAGNUSSEN	1

Constructors :

1.	McLaren / Mercedes	75
2.	Ferrari	53
3.	Benetton / Playlife	25
4.	Williams / Mecachrome	16
5.	Stewart / Ford	5
6.	Arrows	4
	Sauber / Petronas	4

WEEK-END GOSSIP

- **Damon Hill pumped up**

Damon Hill had taken a major tongue lashing from Michael Schumacher in the post race press conference. Told of the German's comments, the 1996 World Champion hit back just as hard. «*You should pay no attention to what Michael says,*» he blasted. «*You only have to look at what he has done in the past to see that he is not in a position to speak. He should not be blaming anyone. In fact he does it too often, no doubt feeling that attack is the best form of defence.*»

- **Drama and scandal**

Bernie Ecclestone withdrew the VIP guest pass that Jacques Villeneuve and all the drivers are entitled to use for a «friend.» The pretext for this was the Canadian is going out with someone who works in F1 and therefore already has a pass. From then on, all the local papers were deep in conjecture as to who this lucky lady could be. A magazine even published a picture of Jacques on a yacht surrounded by various beauties. The mystery remained unsolved.

- **Problem solved**

Following the introduction by the Canadian parliament of the C-71 law banning all tobacco advertising, the Canadian Grand Prix almost did not take place in 1997. But the authorities had then decided to suspend the introduction of the law for two years, which allowed the event to run in 1997 and 1998. Then, the future of the grand prix became clearer. An amendment to the law was proposed by the health minister, which would allow F1 teams sponsored by tobacco companies to keep their liveries.

- **Congratulations**

Betise, the wife of Patrick Head, the Williams technical director had just given birth to their first child, Luke.

- **Verstappen in prison**

The Benetton test driver, Jos Verstappen was jailed in Belgian. He got into a brawl in kart circuit bar with the father of a 14 year old lad who had been quicker than the Dutchman.

- **Ken is back**

The great Ken Tyrrell made his first visit of the season to the Montreal paddock as a guest, now that he has sold his team to BAT.

- **Ladies, dry your tears**

Mika Hakkinen got married to his fiancee Erja, in great secrecy in Monaco, the week after the grand prix. A public church ceremony was due to take place later in Finland.

RACE SUMMARY

- At the start, Wurz goes off on the grass and collides with Alesi and Trulli. The Benetton rolls three times, but the driver is uninjured. Herbert is also involved.
- The race is stopped and Alesi, Wurz and Trulli take the re-start in their spare cars. Herbert's car is brought back to the pits and the Englishman takes the second start from the pit lane.
- At the second start, Hakkinen's gearbox jams. Further back, Ralf Schumacher gets it sideways and causes another pile up, in which Trulli and Alesi are yet again eliminated.
- Michael Schumacher overtakes Fisichella just before the Safety Car comes out for five laps.
- As the race gets underway again, Coulthard and Schumacher pull away from the field. Diniz goes off and as he comes back on, he spreads so much grass all over the track, that the Safety Car comes out again on lap 14.
- Underway again and Coulthard retires, leaving Schumacher in the lead. Salo and Herbert crash at the hairpin bringing out the Safety Car for the third time. Schumacher takes the opportunity to refuel and as he exits the pit, he fails to see Frentzen and pushes him off the track.
- For the fourth start, Villeneuve goes round the outside of Fisichella at the first corner. He gets it all wrong, goes off and breaks his rear wing.
- Schumacher is given a ten second stop-go penalty for having caused Frentzen's retirement. He rejoins in third and does not take long to get past Hill, who has tried to block him.
- After Fisichella's only pit stop, Schumacher takes the lead and extends it. Then it is his turn to refuel and he just keeps the lead ahead of the Italian, who finishes second.

Montreal city centre, seen from Ile Notre-Dame. With the delights of downtown so close at ▽ *hand, the Canadian Grand Prix is a big hit with the F1 folk.*

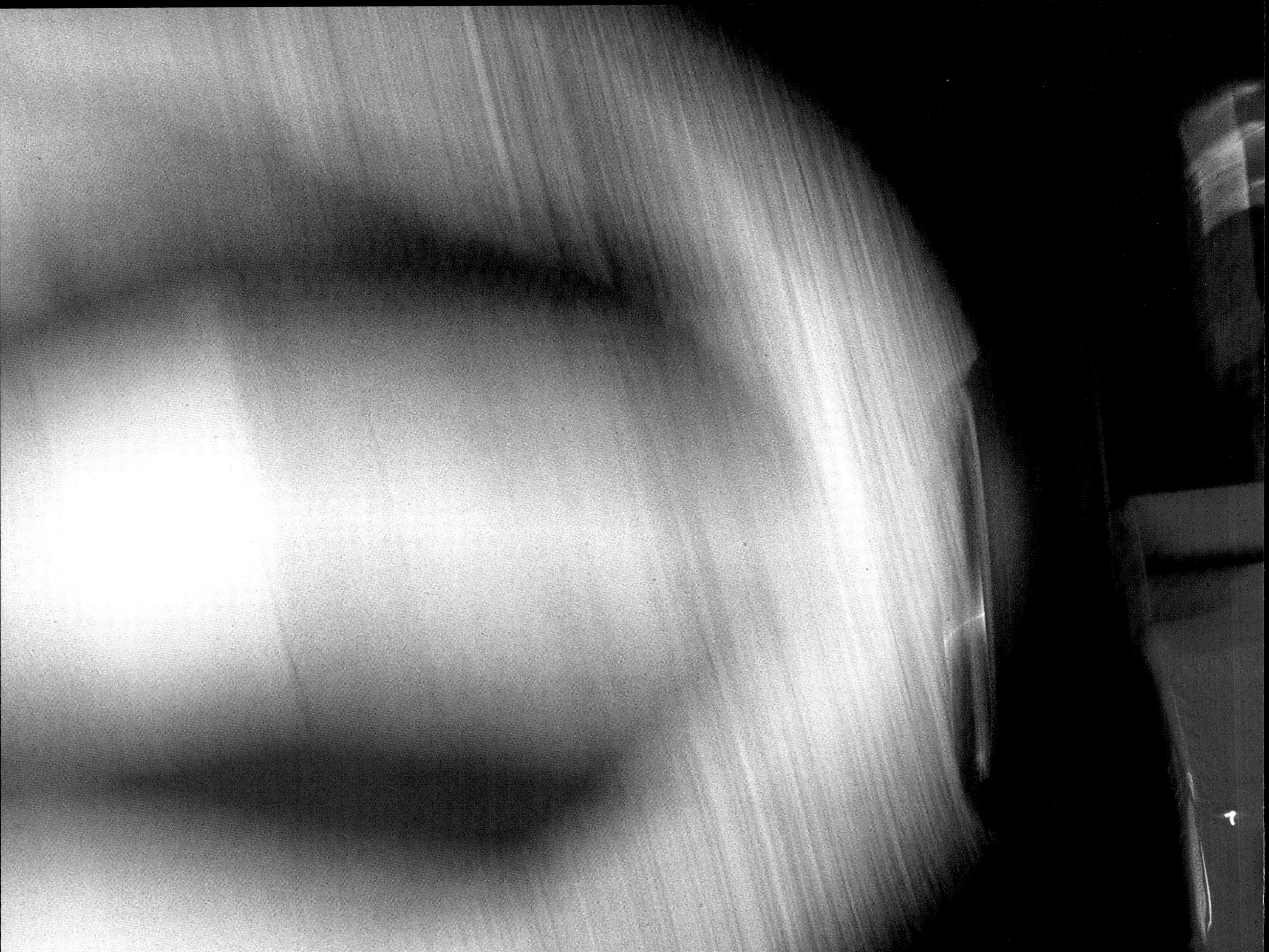

Ferrari turns the tables

After an early part of the season which saw Ferrari completely crushed by the dominance of the McLarens, Scuderia Ferrari managed to reverse the trend in Magny Cours.

Its two drivers got a stranglehold on the race, scoring Ferrari's first one-two finish since 1990 and only leaving McLaren the crumbs off the table - a third place for Hakkinen and a sixth place for Coulthard. The race could have turned out differently if the first start, at which both McLarens took off into the lead, had not been aborted.

GRAND PRIX MOBIL 1 DE FRANCE
MAGNY-COURS

Schumacher thinks everything is possible

This time, Jean Todt was finally smiling. On Friday, the Ferrari sporting director said he wanted to wait for the qualifying session before deciding whether or not his cars had closed the gap to the McLarens. On Saturday, that confirmation was forthcoming. Throughout the qualifying session, Mika Hakkinen and Michael Schumacher traded fastest times until the McLaren took the pole by just two tenths of a second. David Coulthard in the second McLaren was incapable of beating the Ferrari and had to settle for third.

On Saturday, no less than six drivers had qualified in the same second. This is a long way off the total domination seen from McLaren so far this season. *«Yes it's true, we are all very close,»* commented Michael Schumacher. *«And unlike the situation in Canada or Argentina, it is not down to cool weather or any other unusual circumstances. I think this time we have really caught up with McLaren. I think we can even fight for the world championship now. On Sunday, even if Mika wins and I finish second, the gap will only be 16 points. We will then have eight grands prix to play with and everything is still possible.»*

In the McLaren camp, David Coulthard did not agree with the Ferrari driver. *«I don't think we have lost our advantage,»* suggested the Scot. *«This circuit suits the Ferrari particularly well because there is only one fast and demanding corner for the chassis. The rest is just slow corners and chicanes. I think at Silverstone, in two weeks time, we should find that we are a long way in front again.»*

△ And here's Jos Verstappen again. On Wednesday 17th June, the Dutchman had taken part in a test session where it was decided he would replace Jan Magnussen from now on. The man who Jackie Stewart had rated as the most talented F3 driver he had ever seen, including Ayrton Senna, was thus out on his ear. One wondered what Jos Verstappen had that merited this change.

STARTING GRID

		Mika HAKKINEN 1'14"929
M. SCHUMACHER 1'15"159	-1-	
		David COULTHARD 1'15"333
Eddie IRVINE 1'15"527	-2-	
		Jacques VILLENEUVE 1'15"630
R. SCHUMACHER 1'15"925	-3-	
		Damon HILL 1'16"245
Heinz-H. FRENTZEN 1'16"319	-4-	
		G. FISICHELLA 1'16"375
Alexander WURZ 1'16"460	-5-	
		Jean ALESI 1'16"627
Jarno TRULLI 1'16"892	-6-	
		Johnny HERBERT 1'16"977
R. BARRICHELLO 1'17"024	-7-	
		Jos VERSTAPPEN 1'17"604
Olivier PANIS 1'17"671	-8-	
		Pedro DINIZ 1'17"880
Ricardo ROSSET 1'17"908	-9-	
		Mika SALO 1'17"970
Toranosuke TAKAGI 1'18"221	-10-	
		Shinji NAKANO 1'18"273
Esteban TUERO 1'19"146	-11-	

Disappointment for Sauber and Prost

During testing the previous week at Magny Cours, when all the teams were in action, Jean Alesi had ended the week quickest overall. He attributed this performance to the new long wheelbase Sauber chassis, which seemed to work wonders.

After that performance, the Frenchman was no doubt hoping for better than his eleventh place on the grid. Unfortunately neither of the two Saubers was able to use the new engine which they had been counting on for qualifying. On Saturday morning, Jean Alesi and Johnny Herbert both had their Petronas-Ferraris go bang, even though they had only just been fitted to the cars. They were out of action for the rest of the morning and the mechanics had to make two lightning changes. The two C-17s were ready in time for qualifying, but with the old engine. *«We lacked power and the car is much too slow down the straights,»* complained Jean Alesi by way of explanation.

The Prost camp was equally down in the dumps. For his home race, Olivier Panis was hoping for better than 16th on the grid.

Last year at this time, he was recovering from his Canadian GP accident, which had robbed him of the chance of a pole position at this track - in those days, the Prost factory was just across the road. Since then, Prost GP had moved to Guyancourt near Paris and the AP01 had major problems.

An unreliable gearbox which was also too heavy and thus affected the handling of the car. The week before, following the fashion, the team had tested a long wheelbase chassis. But the recipe which had worked for other teams only aggravated the situation in the Prost team and they went back to the conventional car.

On Saturday, Trulli managed to haul himself up to 12th place, but Panis had to settle for 16th. He was not in a good mood: *«A very difficult day for me.»*

▷ Idyllic France. The Nievre region is a rural paradise full of second homes that are the envy of all.

△ Damon Hill qualified in seventh place in Magny Cours, just behind team mate Ralf Schumacher.

△ *We've won! The mechanics' joy when Michael Schumacher crossed the line was the result of weeks of hard work.*

Ferrari one - two: the Reds strike it rich in Magny Cours

«*Eddie! Eddie!*» The race finished half an hour ago. Under the Ferrari motorhome awning, thirty or so Ferrari mechanics are tucking into rigatoni with tomatoes - their first proper meal since seven o'clock that morning. When Eddie Irvine appears, dripping with sweat, to a man, they all stand up and chant his name. For the workers, he is the hero of the hour.
In Magny Cours, Eddie Irvine did indeed show an exceptional mastery at the wheel of a car which had serious gearbox problems.
The race went like a dream for the Scuderia who landed their first one-two finish since the 1990 Spanish Grand Prix. «*This is a very special day for us*» confirmed Michael Schumacher. «*It prove we really are very close to the McLarens. Frankly, after the huge amount of work we have done, it is very welcome. We have improved the aerodynamics on our car and at the same time, Goodyear has made a huge step forward. It was not easy for them.*»
The Scuderia did have one piece of good luck in the shape of a scrubbed first start. Jos Verstappen had stalled the Stewart on the grid when Mika Hakkinen had already flown into the lead. At the second start, the Finn got it wrong, allowing both Ferraris to take off in front. «**I did not get my first start wrong,**» said Schumacher. «*In fact I was worried about having a worst one the second time, as happened in Canada, but everything was fine.*»
With Eddie Irvine riding shotgun in second place, the German's task consisted in bringing his F300 home. «*I had no problems,*» he concluded. «*Apart from my radio which was making so much noise, I had to switch it off so as not to lose concentration.*»
For his part, Eddie Irvine had a busy day keeping Mika Hakkinen behind him to the end. «*I had gearbox problems,*» explained the Irishman, «*and my wheels were locking up in the hairpin onto the pit straight. That is why Hakkinen nearly got past me. And in the last corner on the last lap, it was a disaster. I must have lost a second just there.*»
Under acceleration though, the Irishman managed to keep his second place by 172 thousandths of a second. Ferrari's double finish now brought them to within eleven points of McLaren in the constructors' championship.

Four points is better than nothing

For Mika Hakkinen, it was all over at the start. «*I got it completely wrong,*» humbly admitted the Finn after the race. «*I selected first too early and I let the clutch out too suddenly. With these grooved tyres it is difficult to stop getting wheelspin.*»
Stuck behind Eddie Irvine, Mika Hakkinen was resigned to following the Irishman who was putting the seal on his team leader's escape. «*When I moved up to third I knew it would not be easy. Overtaking is a nightmare on this track unless you take a huge risk. I tried that once and had a spin, so I decided to play it safe for four points rather than have an accident.*»
The Finn was not really that disappointed. «*I would have been really disappointed if we had finished out of the points today. But this third place has limited the damage. Of course, I would rather have kept going after the first start. I did not understand why the race was stopped. When I got back to the grid and saw Verstappen's car, I thought, 'What Just for that?' In my opinion there was no danger.*»
He was not too worried about the rest of the championship. «*We will work flat out, but I think this track suited the Ferrari really well. We will see at Silverstone,*» concluded Hakkinen.

First lap, Adelaide hairpin. Michael Schumacher has already gone and Eddie Irvine leads the rest of the field. The Scuderia had produced their dream scenario.
◁▽

Last corner and last try for Mika Hakkinen to get past Eddie Irvine, slowing with gearbox problems.
▽

IN THE POINTS

1.	M. SCHUMACHER	Scuderia Ferrari Marlboro	1 h 34'45"026
2.	Eddie IRVINE	Scuderia Ferrari Marlboro	at 19"575
3.	Mika HAKKINEN	West McLaren Mercedes	at 19"747
4.	Jacques VILLENEUVE	Winfield Williams	at 1'06"965
5.	Alexander WURZ	Mild Seven Benetton Playlife	at 1 lap
6.	David COULTHARD	West McLaren Mercedes	at 1 lap

Fastest lap : D. COULTHARD, lap 59, 1'17"523, avg. 197.360 km/h

Seen from a helicopter, grand prix grids are always impressive. Here, a few seconds before the second start, Jos Verstappen's Stewart is being pushed aside.

FORMULA ONE
PADDOCK
Club
FORMULA ONE
PADDOCK
Club

△ «No, I'm not sulking. Everything is fine.» At Magny Cours, Jean Alesi just missed out on the points as he finished seventh in his new long wheelbase Sauber.

Jean Todt to stay

Usually not very chatty, Jean Todt was in rather voluble mood at the end of the French Grand Prix. He had good reason as the Frenchman had just experienced the first Ferrari one-two finish since he took over the running of the Scuderia. «*We will celebrate this evening,*» he announced with a big smile. «*This was a perfect day. On Monday we can wake up and tell ourselves we did a good job. We have taken 30 points out of McLaren's lead in the Constructors championship.*» (It was actually 25 points and the Frenchman had obviously got carried away with his optimism.) When he came down to earth, Jean Todt admitted the rest of the championship would not be so easy. «*We must not think we are going to do the double every weekend. But when you look at what we have achieved since Melbourne, it has to be said we have achieved an incredible amount of work.*»
It was exactly five years since Jean Todt had arrived at Ferrari to take over the team. On Sunday, the Frenchman announced that he had just signed a new three year contract, which would keep him in the job until July 2001.

David Coulthard had his usual run of bad luck at Magny Cours. He could have finished fourth but for a problem with his refuelling hose which prevented the mechanics putting the right amount of fuel in. He therefore had to stop four times- his second stop lasted nearly 37 seconds without a single drop of fuel going in the tank! ▽

Magny Cours scuppered by the World Cup

One could almost call the spectators by name as on Friday, the number of spectators at Magny Cours only reached a few thousand. It was going to be a tough weekend for the Nievre track. However, on Sunday Guy Mourot, the grand prix press officer put out a release which mentioned a figure of 75,000 or 5000 more than in 1997. The increase was mainly in the general enclosures where ticket prices were cheapest.
When the French Grand Prix was put back on the calendar, only in March after legal problems linked to television rights - it was too late for a ticket sales push. The organisers used to sell around 15,000 tickets to large French companies. This year, they did not bother to wait and shifted their funds to purchase tickets for the football World Cup. This year only 300 of these tickets were sold.
At this point, the organisers offered 11,000 free tickets to schools for underprivileged children. The local councils financed coaches which brought in children from all four corners of France. It was a generous move, but it did nothing to fill the coffers.
To crown it all, the vagaries of the calendar meant that the French soccer team were playing in the tournament on exactly the same day as the grand prix. As a further incentive to draw the crowds to motor racing, Roland Hodel, the promoter- organiser of the event, arranged to transmit the France-Paraguay match, which started one hour after the end of the race, on the giant screens around the track. It did not do the trick and on Sunday evening, only a few spectators in the main grandstand stayed on for the soccer.
The 1998 French Grand Prix was in danger of ending up with a loss of several millions of francs, a loss which would have to be soaked up by the local region. It also appeared that Bernie Ecclestone sensed future problems and had already made a move, by financing the rebuilding of the Le Castellet circuit, in order to move the grand prix there from 1999. The World Cup might just have been the death of Magny Cours.

King Leo rules the waves

Several teams had made the most of the three week gap between the Canadian and French races and modified their chassis. Thus the Sauber team arrived at the French GP with a completely modified C17, that sported a long wheelbase chassis, a new rear suspension and a tweaked front wing. The modifications bore fruit on the French track in private testing the week before the race, as Jean Alesi was quickest overall (see page 146.)
Sauber was not the only team to turn up in France with a long wheelbase. Stewart and Minardi also slavishly followed the fashion. «*When we saw that McLaren had brought out a car with a very long wheelbase, we though about it and decided it was probably a good way of sorting out the weight distribution,*» was the word from Sauber. «*Above all, it allows the front end to work better on the turn in to corners.*» Once the decision to modify the C17 was made, it took only five weeks for the men of Hinwil to build the new Sauber. «*It is a big modification which will be particularly useful on the many quick tracks coming up this summer,*» they said.
Having designed the new car, Leo Ress, the team's technical director did not attend the Magny Cours to see his new creation perform. Instead, he went off to Greece for his annual two weeks summer holiday! «*He is mad keen on windsurfing,*» said the team's press officer Gustav Busing. «*He decided to take a complete break from F1. Peter Sauber offered to fax him the results of testing at his hotel, but Leo declined. He wants to clear his head and he needed to.*»
Leo Ress made but one request to Peter Sauber. When he returned from his holiday at the beginning of July, he wanted to know exactly which engine the team would be using next season, so that he could start work immediately on the new C18.
For the moment, the boss was hesitation between renewing his Ferrari contract (very expensive) or making the switch to Mecachrome (less expensive but shared with British American Racing, Benetton and maybe Williams.)

PRACTICE TIMES

No	Driver	Car/Engine/Chassis	Practice Friday	Practice Saturday	Qualifying	Warm-up
1.	Jacques Villeneuve	Williams/Mecachrome/FW20/5 (G)	1'19"008	1'16"782	1'15"630	1'18"442
2.	Heinz-Harald Frentzen	Williams/Mecachrome/FW20/4 (G)	1'17"026	1'16"745	1'16"319	1'18"466
3.	Michael Schumacher	Ferrari/F300/187 (G)	1'17"429	1'15"738	1'15"159	1'17"189
4.	Eddie Irvine	Ferrari/F300/185 (G)	1'16"597	1'15"870	1'15"527	1'17"628
5.	Giancarlo Fisichella	Benetton/Playlife/198/6 (B)	1'17"664	1'17"106	1'16"375	1'18"545
6.	Alexander Wurz	Benetton/Playlife/198/2 (B)	1'17"706	1'17"205	1'16"460	1'18"607
7.	David Coulthard	McLaren/Mercedes/MP4-13/3 (B)	1'16"707	1'15"909	1'15"333	1'16"483
8.	Mika Hakkinen	McLaren/Mercedes/MP4-13/6 (B)	1'16"515	1'15"613	1'14"929	1'16"718
9.	Damon Hill	Jordan/Honda/198/3 (G)	1'17"895	1'17"426	1'16"245	1'18"819
10.	Ralf Schumacher	Jordan/Honda/198/4 (G)	1'17"505	1'16"678	1'15"925	1'18"790
11.	Olivier Panis	Prost/Peugeot/AP01/5 (B)	1'18"367	1'18"706	1'17"671	1'18"729
12.	Jarno Trulli	Prost/Peugeot/AP01/3 (B)	1'18"036	1'17"711	1'16"892	1'19"442
14.	Jean Alesi	Sauber/Petronas/C17/3 (G)	1'18"172	1'18"893	1'16"627	1'18"611
15.	Johnny Herbert	Sauber/Petronas/C17/4 (G)	1'17"977	1'17"873	1'16"977	1'19"092
16.	Pedro Diniz	Arrows/A19/1 (B)	1'19"023	1'18"389	1'17"880	1'20"240
17.	Mika Salo	Arrows/A19/5 (B)	1'18"656	1'18"075	1'17"970	1'19"733
18.	Rubens Barrichello	Stewart/Ford/SF2/4 (B)	1'18"703	1'18"170	1'17"024	1'19"097
19.	Jos Verstappen	Stewart/Ford/SF2/3 (B)	1'20"286	1'18"451	1'17"604	1'19"641
20.	Ricardo Rosset	Tyrrell/Ford/026/2 (G)	1'18"649	1'18"405	1'17"908	1'22"160
21.	Toranosuke Takagi	Tyrrell/Ford/026/3 (G)	1'19"057	1'17"847	1'18"221	1'19"788
22.	Shinji Nakano	Minardi/Ford/M198/4 (B)	1'20"445	1'19"324	1'18"273	1'19"835
23.	Esteban Tuero	Minardi/Ford/M198/5 (B)	1'20"871	1'19"475	1'19"146	1'21"376

LAP CHART

position:	1	2	3	4	5	6	7	8	9	10	11	12	13	14	15	16	17	18	19	20	21	22
start:	8	3	7	4	1	10	9	2	5	6	14	12	15	18	19	11	16	20	17	21	22	23
1	3	4	8	7	1	10	9	6	14	5	12	2	18	11	15	19	20	21	16	22	17	23
2	3	4	8	7	1	10	9	6	14	5	2	18	11	15	19	20	21	12	16	22	17	23
3	3	4	8	7	1	10	9	6	14	5	2	18	11	15	19	20	21	16	22	17	23	12
4	3	4	8	7	1	10	9	6	14	5	2	18	11	15	19	20	21	16	22	17	23	12
5	3	4	8	7	1	10	9	6	14	5	2	18	15	11	19	20	21	16	22	17	23	12
6	3	4	8	7	1	10	9	6	14	5	2	15	18	11	19	20	21	16	22	17	23	12
7	3	4	8	7	1	10	9	6	14	5	2	15	18	11	19	21	20	16	22	17	23	12
8	3	4	8	7	1	10	9	6	14	5	2	15	18	11	19	21	20	16	17	22	23	12
9	3	4	8	7	1	10	9	6	14	5	2	15	18	11	19	21	20	16	17	22	23	12
10	3	4	8	7	1	10	9	6	14	5	2	15	18	11	19	21	20	16	17	22	23	12
11	3	4	8	7	1	10	9	6	14	5	2	15	18	11	19	21	20	16	17	22	23	12
12	3	4	8	7	1	10	9	6	14	5	2	15	18	11	19	21	20	16	17	22	23	12
13	3	4	8	7	1	10	9	6	14	5	2	15	18	11	19	21	20	16	17	22	23	12
14	3	4	8	7	1	10	9	6	14	5	2	15	18	11	19	21	20	16	17	22	23	12
15	3	4	8	7	1	10	6	14	9	5	2	15	18	11	19	21	20	16	17	22	23	12
16	3	4	8	7	1	6	10	14	5	2	9	15	18	11	19	16	17	22	20	21	23	12
17	3	4	8	7	1	6	14	5	2	15	10	18	9	11	19	16	17	22	21	23	12	
18	3	4	8	7	1	14	5	2	15	6	18	11	19	9	16	17	22	21	23	10	12	
19	3	4	8	7	1	14	2	15	6	18	5	11	19	9	16	17	22	21	23	12	10	
20	3	4	7	8	1	14	2	15	6	18	5	11	19	16	17	22	21	23	12	10		
21	3	4	7	8	1	14	15	6	18	5	11	2	19	16	17	21	22	23	12	10		
22	3	4	7	1	14	8	15	6	5	18	11	2	16	17	21	19	22	23	12	10		
23	4	3	1	8	14	7	15	6	5	2	18	11	16	17	21	19	22	23	12	10		
24	3	1	4	8	7	6	15	14	5	2	11	18	16	17	21	19	22	12	23	10		
25	3	4	8	7	1	6	14	5	2	11	18	15	16	17	21	19	22	23	12	10		
26	3	4	8	7	1	6	14	5	2	11	18	15	16	17	21	19	22	23	12	10		
27	3	4	8	7	1	6	14	5	2	11	18	15	16	17	21	19	22	23	12	10		
28	3	4	8	7	1	6	14	5	2	11	18	15	16	17	21	19	22	23	12	10		
29	3	4	8	7	1	6	14	5	2	11	18	15	16	17	21	19	22	23	12	10		
30	3	4	8	7	1	6	14	5	2	18	15	11	16	17	21	19	22	23	12	10		
31	3	4	8	7	1	6	14	5	2	18	15	11	16	21	17	19	22	23	12	10		
32	3	4	8	7	1	6	14	5	2	18	15	11	16	21	19	17	22	23	12	10		
33	3	4	8	7	1	6	14	2	5	18	15	11	16	21	19	17	22	12	23	10		
34	3	4	8	7	1	6	14	2	5	18	15	11	16	21	19	17	22	12	23	10		
35	3	4	8	7	1	14	6	2	15	18	11	5	16	19	21	17	22	12	23	10		
36	3	4	8	7	1	14	6	2	15	18	11	5	16	19	17	21	22	12	23	10		
37	3	4	8	7	1	14	6	2	15	18	11	5	16	19	17	21	22	12	23	10		
38	3	4	8	7	1	14	6	2	15	18	11	5	16	19	17	21	22	12	23	10		
39	3	4	8	7	1	14	6	2	15	18	11	5	19	16	21	17	22	12	23	10		
40	3	4	8	7	1	14	6	2	15	18	11	5	19	21	17	16	22	12	23	10		
41	3	4	8	7	1	14	6	2	15	18	11	5	19	21	17	16	22	12	23	10		
42	3	4	8	7	1	14	6	2	15	18	11	5	19	21	17	16	22	12	10			
43	3	4	8	7	1	14	6	2	15	18	11	5	19	21	17	16	12	22	10			
44	3	8	7	4	1	14	6	2	15	18	11	5	19	21	17	16	12	22	10			
45	3	8	7	4	1	14	6	2	15	18	5	11	19	21	17	16	12	22	10			
46	3	8	7	4	1	6	14	2	15	18	5	11	21	19	17	16	12	22	10			
47	3	8	7	4	1	6	2	14	15	5	18	11	21	19	17	16	12	22	10			
48	3	8	7	4	1	6	2	14	5	15	18	11	21	19	17	16	12	22	10			
49	3	8	7	4	1	6	2	14	5	15	18	11	21	19	17	16	12	22	10			
50	3	8	7	4	1	6	2	14	5	15	18	11	21	19	17	16	12	22	10			
51	3	8	7	4	1	2	6	14	5	15	18	11	19	21	17	16	12	22	10			
52	3	8	7	4	1	6	14	2	5	15	18	11	19	17	16	21	12	22	10			
53	3	8	7	4	1	6	14	2	15	5	18	11	19	17	16	21	12	22	10			
54	3	8	7	4	1	6	14	2	15	5	18	11	19	17	21	16	12	22	10			
55	3	7	4	8	1	6	14	2	15	5	18	11	19	17	21	16	12	22	10			
56	3	4	8	1	7	6	14	2	15	5	18	11	19	17	21	16	22	10				
57	3	4	8	1	6	14	7	2	15	5	18	11	19	17	21	16	22	10				
58	3	4	8	1	6	7	14	2	15	5	18	11	19	17	21	16	22	10				
59	3	4	8	1	6	7	14	2	15	5	18	11	19	17	21	16	22	10				
60	3	4	8	1	6	7	14	2	15	5	18	11	19	17	21	16	22	10				
61	3	4	8	1	7	6	14	2	15	5	18	11	19	17	16	22	10					
62	3	4	8	1	7	6	14	2	15	5	18	11	19	17	16	22	10					
63	3	4	8	1	7	6	14	2	15	5	18	11	19	17	16	22	10					
64	3	4	8	1	6	14	2	7	15	5	18	11	19	17	16	22	10					
65	3	4	8	1	6	14	2	7	15	5	18	11	19	17	16	22	10					
66	3	4	8	1	6	14	2	7	15	5	18	11	19	17	16	10						
67	3	4	8	1	6	14	7	2	15	5	18	11	19	17	16	10						
68	3	4	8	1	6	14	7	2	15	5	18	11	19	17	16	10						
69	3	4	8	1	6	14	7	15	5	18	11	19	17	16								
70	3	4	8	1	6	7	14	15	5													
71	3	4	8	1																		

BRIDGESTONE

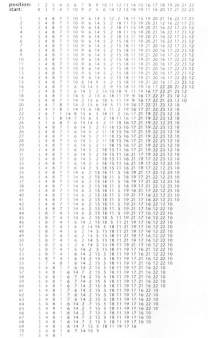

Best result for a Bridgestone shod runner:

Mika Hakkinen, McLaren-Mercedes, *3rd*

CLASSIFICATION & RETIREMENTS

Pos	Driver	Team	Time
1.	M. Schum.	Ferrari	in 1h34'45"026
2.	Irvine	Ferrari	at 19"575
3.	Hakkinen	McLaren Mercedes	at 19"747
4.	Villeneuve	Williams Mecachrome	at 66"965
5.	Wurz	Benetton Playlife	at 1 lap
6.	Coulthard	McLaren Mercedes	at 1 lap
7.	Alesi	Sauber Petronas	at 1 lap
8.	Herbert	Sauber Petronas	at 1 lap
9.	Fisichella	Benetton Playlife	at 1 lap
10.	Barrichello	Stewart Ford	at 2 laps
11.	Panis	Prost Peugeot	at 2 laps
12.	Verstappen	Stewart Ford	at 2 laps
13.	Salo	Arrows	at 2 laps
14.	Diniz	Arrows	at 2 laps
15.	Frentzen	Williams Mecachrome	accident
16.	R. Schum.	Jordan Mugen Honda	at 3 laps
17.	Nakano	Minardi Ford	engine

Lap	Driver	Team	Reason
17	Rosset	Tyrrell Ford	engine
20	Hill	Jordan Mugen Honda	engine
42	Tuero	Minardi Ford	gearbox
56	Trulli	Prost Peugeot	off
61	Takagi	Tyrrell Ford	engine

FASTEST LAP

	Driver	Time	Lap
1.	Coulthard	1'17"523	59
2.	M. Schum.	1'17"770	4
3.	Hakkinen	1'18"493	52
4.	Villeneuve	1'18"913	42
5.	Irvine	1'18"956	25
6.	R. Schum.	1'19"052	56
7.	Frentzen	1'19"229	48
8.	Fisichella	1'19"307	48
9.	Wurz	1'19"320	36
10.	Hill	1'19"490	4
11.	Alesi	1'19"660	48
12.	Herbert	1'19"771	51
13.	Trulli	1'19"869	6
14.	Panis	1'19"953	32
15.	Takagi	1'20"299	37
16.	Barrichello	1'20"651	43
17.	Verstappen	1'20"849	47
18.	Salo	1'21"502	61
19.	Diniz	1'21"765	38
20.	Nakano	1'21"883	42
21.	Rosset	1'22"435	3
22.	Tuero	1'22"761	34

EIGHTH ROUND

GRAND PRIX MOBIL 1 DE FRANCE, MAGNY-COURS

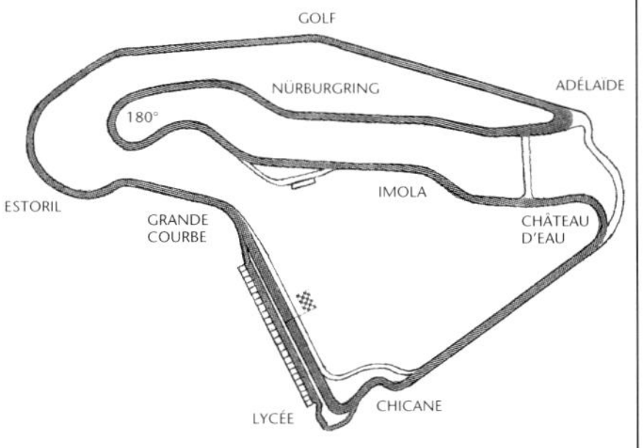

Date : June 28, 1998
Lenght : 4247 meters
Distance : 71 laps, 301.564 km
Weather : fine, 25 degrees

CHAMPIONSHIPS

(after eight rounds)

Drivers :

1. Mika HAKKINEN 50
2. Michael SCHUMACHER 44
3. David COULTHARD 30
4. Eddie IRVINE................................25
5. Alexander WURZ 14
6. Giancarlo FISICHELLA 13
7. Jacques VILLENEUVE 11
8. Heinz-Harald FRENTZEN 8
9. Rubens BARRICHELLO.....................4
10. Mika SALO......................................3
    Jean ALESI.......................................3
12. Johnny HERBERT.............................1
    Pedro DINIZ 1
    Jan MAGNUSSEN..............................1

Constructors :

1. McLaren / Mercedes 82
2. Ferrari...69
3. Benetton / Playlife 27
4. Williams / Mecachrome 19
5. Stewart / Ford 5
6. Arrows..4
   Sauber / Petronas 4

RACE SUMMARY

- Jos Verstappen stalls his Stewart Ford on the grid and a second start is called for.
- At the second attempt, Hakkinen messes up his start and is overtaken by Schumacher and Irvine.
- Schumacher pulls away in the early stages at the rate of one second a lap, while Irvine does his job and delays the two McLarens.
- Hakkinen tries a suicidal passing move on Irvine and spins. He manages not to stall but has to pit for tyres.
- There are no changes until the second set of pit stops. With a fuel filling problem, David Coulthard has to stop twice to take on fuel. He finishes sixth.
- At the head of the field, after all the pit stops, Hakkinen tries to pass Irvine without success. The Irishman hangs on to second to the flag.

WEEK-END GOSSIP

• Heinz-Harald on form

After a big accident in private testing at Magny Cours the week before the race, it was not certain that Heinz-Harald Frentzen would be fit enough to race in the French Grand Prix. *«I feel perfectly well,»* he told us on Thursday, adding that he had every intention of talking to Schumacher about their Canadian GP accident. *«I have not had the chance to do it yet, but it will in any case be a private discussion.»*

• Business is booming

Michael Schumacher's manager Willi Weber disclosed details of his little star's 1998 salary, around 75 million sterling all in. That included his salary from Ferrari, his personal sponsors and the sale of items from the *«Michael Schumacher Collection,»* a range of goods bearing his name. It was the highest amount ever earned by a European sportsman.

• Indianopolis in the running

Indianapolis is hoping to organise a grand prix in 2000. The week before, circuit owner Tony George, went to London for talks with Bernie Ecclestone to discuss the possibility. The F1 cars would use part of the famous oval, but most of the track would be new and built inside the speed bowl.

• Still no agreement

Peter Sauber had still not signed the new Concorde Agreement which linked all the other teams in the paddock in commercial terms. If he did not sign, it would cost the Swiss team a fortune as it would not receive its share of the television rights money. However, for the time being, Fritz Kaiser, the team's co-owner said they still had to wait before signing. *«The problems that are likely to arise between the European Union and Formula 1 must be taken very seriously. They have to be analysed before we commit ourselves,»* explained the Austrian.

• Half a Villeneuve

The transfer market began to wake up in Magny Cours. Craig Pollock, director of the future British American Racing team declared he had a 50% chance of getting Jacques Villeneuve to drive for his team. In the meantime, he announced the signing of a contract with Mecachrome for the supply of engines in 1999.

• A good deal

The Formula 1 TV rights for China, Russia, India and most Asian countries, with the exception of Japan, have been secured by PPG1, a French-Canadian television production company connected to British American Tobacco, the owner of the BAR team.

Luxury, calm and style of a Loire chateau. This is the type of property many spectators stay in during the grand prix, as the locals higher out accommodation if they have room, which is definitely the case here.

Schumacher the «Regenmeister»

It was a soaking Silverstone, especially during the second half of the race. In these conditions it was hardly surprising to find the «Regenmeister (the rain master) on the top step of the podium.

However, it was an action packed race for the German. He was hit with a ten second penalty for having lapped a backmarker under a yellow flag. Notified too late for the sanction to be applied correctly, Schumacher ended up taking the chequered flag in the pit lane!

THE 1998 RAC BRITISH GRAND PRIX
SILVERSTONE

Mika versus Michael, Act 2

«No, I swear I am not Damon Hill, I am Mr. Bean.» The 1996 world champion is still a hero at home and signed autographs non-stop at Silverstone.

At Magny Cours, two weeks earlier, the Ferraris had made the McLarens look silly as they notched up their first one-two finish in eight years. At Silverstone, the McLarens were playing at home and had every intention of taking their revenge.
On Saturday, Hakkinen got the first part of the job done, by taking pole position. *«We have done an awful lot of work on the car in the past few days and we have made a noticeable improvement,»* said the Finn at the end of the session. *«But I am still a bit worried. At the start of the season, our Bridgestone tyres gave us a definite advantage. Today, I think Goodyear has caught up. The Bridgestone engineers will have to work harder.»*
Within McLaren, it was really Hakkinen who made the difference, as team mate David Coulthard had to settle for fourth place, over a second down on the Finn.
Michael Schumacher was delighted to have qualified on the front row. *«I messed up my quickest lap, going too wide at the chicane, but I do not think I could have beaten Mika anyway,»* commented the German. *«I think the start will be very tight.»*
On Saturday, the clouds were low over Silverstone and it began to rain after the end of qualifying, while a genuine storm was expected in the area for Sunday. It turned up true to form.
As a rule, racing in the rain could favour Michael Schumacher, recognised as the rain master. On Saturday though, he played down this reputation. *«I don't see why I would have an advantage over Mika if it rained,»* he said. *«All the drivers can deal with their cars in any conditions.»*
Mika Hakkinen duly confirmed that rain did not bother him either. *«It is not a worry. All you have to do is set up the car properly.»* Sunday's race would teach him it is not just a question of getting the right settings.

The Benettons had a big traction problem at the exit to corners on this track. Giancarlo Fisichella and Alexander Wurz (pictured here) could qualify no better than 11th and 12th.

Always looking for a new gimmick, even if he pretends not to like playing the star, Jacques Villeneuve decided to dye his hair purple this summer. It did not hinder him from qualifying in third place.

Jacques is back

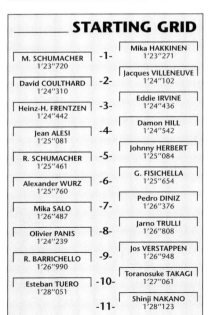

Since the end of the previous season, Jacques Villeneuve had failed to finish in the top three, either in the race or in qualifying.
At Silverstone, the Canadian finally managed it, setting a surprising third quickest time in qualifying. *«This shows the progress made with our car,»* he explained. *«We have some new aerodynamic parts here and they seem to be working very well.»*
His team mate Heinz-Harald Frentzen was only sixth, unable to improve at the end of the session. *«I really like the improvements to the car, but I lost time on my best lap. It's a shame because I know I could have been on the second row.»*
Another disappointed customer was David Coulthard, the local hero as the only British driver who had a reasonable chance of victory. The Scotsman was pleased with himself and his quickest time on Friday. That night, at the now traditional British Grand Prix ball, held at Stowe school, he told any camera crew who stuck a mike under his nose that he intended winning the British GP in order to make up some of the 20 point gap, separating him from Mika Hakkinen.
On Saturday after qualifying, that hope was beginning to fly out the window as the Scotsman was only fourth on the grid. *«I don't know what happened today. It is incomprehensible»* he lamented. *«I was slower this afternoon than in the morning. Now we will have to study the telemetry with my engineers to understand why. There must be a good reason for it. We will find it, but of course I am very disappointed.»*

STARTING GRID

		Mika HAKKINEN 1'23"271
M. SCHUMACHER 1'23"720	-1-	
		Jacques VILLENEUVE 1'24"102
David COULTHARD 1'24"310	-2-	
		Eddie IRVINE 1'24"436
Heinz-H. FRENTZEN 1'24"442	-3-	
		Damon HILL 1'24"542
Jean ALESI 1'25"081	-4-	
		Johnny HERBERT 1'25"084
R. SCHUMACHER 1'25"461	-5-	
		G. FISICHELLA 1'25"654
Alexander WURZ 1'25"760	-6-	
		Pedro DINIZ 1'26"376
Mika SALO 1'26"487	-7-	
		Jarno TRULLI 1'26"808
Olivier PANIS 1'24"239	-8-	
		Jos VERSTAPPEN 1'26"948
R. BARRICHELLO 1'26"990	-9-	
		Toranosuke TAKAGI 1'27"061
Esteban TUERO 1'28"051	-10-	
	-11-	Shinji NAKANO 1'28"123

Controversy: Michael Schumacher wins the race in the pits

It does not happen often but Michael Schumacher got his tactics all wrong before the start. On the grid, when the time came to make a last minute decision about settings for the race the «*Regenmeister*» as they call the rain master back home in Germany, opted for dry settings. «*The skies seemed to be clearing,*» he explained after the race. «*I thought the track would dry. It was a big mistake. When it started to rain really hard, the car was almost undriveable.*»
Overtaken by David Coulthard, right from lap five, Michael Schumacher was already losing ground to the McLarens. And when the downpour became a real monsoon, the German was losing around four seconds per lap to Hakkinen. «*I really could not go any quicker,*» he went on. «*I nearly went off several times and I told myself all I could do was wait.*»
Given the force of the downpour and the high number of crashes, including David Coulthard's, the race director decided to neutralise the race with the safety car. At that moment, the Ferrari driver was over 40 seconds behind Hakkinen, but the gap came down to nothing as the pack queued up behind the safety car. «*Of course I was lucky,*» he admitted. «*But I think even Mika would agree that the safety car had to come out as the conditions were too difficult. In fact this intervention should have taken place earlier.*»
As the rain eased, the safety car went in after six laps and the race was on again. The track was drying and Michael Schumacher and his dry settings made short work of Mika Hakkinen; his life made easier as the Finn's car was damaged. Just a few laps later and Michael Schumacher won his third consecutive victory ahead of Mika Hakkinen. The Finn's lead in the world championship was now down to just two little points, with seven races to go. It was going to be a hot summer on the tracks.

The Stewards get it wrong

After Michael Schumacher passed Alexander Wurz under waved yellow flags, the stewards decided to hit him with a ten second penalty. As the German's radio was not working the Ferrari pit hung out a board to tell their driver to come in on lap 59. «*I don't understand,*» said the driver. «*I knew the race was ending on lap 60, but I did as I was told and came in.*» He then spent 10 seconds in the pit lane and drove out again. «*I could see the McLaren mechanics jumping for joy on the pit wall and I was scared that Mika had won,*» he added. Finally, the stewards knocked ten seconds off Michael Schumacher's lead over Mika Hakkinen. The McLaren team protested Ferrari's win, arguing that the yellow flag incident had taken place 12 laps before the finish, which means the guilty party is supposed to actually sit out the 10 seconds in the pit, rather than have them added to his time. The protest was rejected, as the delay was down to the stewards (see below.) McLaren appealed but to no avail.

Different lines for Mika Hakkinen and Michael Schumacher as the track dries.

◁ ▽

When the race was run under the Safety Car, when the rain was at its hardest, visibility was almost zero.

▽

Chronology of errors

15h15: It is raining harder than ever. While lapping Alexander Wurz, Michael Schumacher fails to see the waved yellow flags and passes the Austrian.

15h16: Because of the terrible weather and the number of cars sliding off the track, the race director decides to bring out the Safety Car. All the drivers close up behind it and Mika Hakkinen loses his 38 second lead over Michael Schumacher.

15h39: Schumacher is given a ten second penalty.

15h46: The Ferrari team is notified of this decision. 31 minutes have elapsed since Schumacher committed the crime, while the rules state that this decision should have been given within 25 minutes. The piece of paper handed to Jean Todt is handwritten and difficult to read. «Are we being asked to apply article 57, section «c» or «e» asks Todt. «No idea,» replies the marshal. It is a major problem as section «c» states the driver must come into the pit lane for a 10 second stop-go penalty, while section «e» affirms that 10 seconds will be added to his total final time.

15h48: Not sure, the Scuderia calls its driver in - he has a 20 second lead in any case over Mika Hakkinen. It is the final lap and Michael Schumacher thus crosses the line in the pit lane.

◁

Last lap: the Scuderia calls Schumacher in to serve his 10 second stop-go penalty. It did not happen as the Ferrari pit is situated past the finish line.

IN THE POINTS

1.	M. SCHUMACHER	Scuderia Ferrari Marlboro	1 h 47'12"450
2.	Mika HAKKINEN	West McLaren Mercedes	at 12"465
3.	Eddie IRVINE	Scuderia Ferrari Marlboro	at 19"199
4.	Alexander WURZ	Mild Seven Benetton Playlife	at 1 lap
5.	Giancarlo FISICHELLA	Mild Seven Benetton Playlife	at 1 lap
6.	Ralf SCHUMACHER	B&H Jordan Mugen Honda	at 1 lap

Fastest lap : M. SCHUMACHER, lap 12, 1'35"704, avg. 193.346 km/h

Schweppes
Mobil

Mika Hakkinen did not really shine at Silverstone. Having led for the first 50 laps, he went off the track at high speed, damaging the floor of his car. This let Michael Schumacher charge off into the lead and Hakkinen made the best of a bad job by coming second.

△ «No problem Martin» Max Mosley looks fresh as a daisy even though he has just stepped out of the McLaren two seater, having done a few laps chauffeured round by Martin Brundle, who do not stint in his efforts to frighten the FIA President.

A very angry David Coulthard

On Thursday, David Coulthard looked like a winner. He was telling anyone who cared to listen that the British Grand Prix would be the chance to close some of the gap to Mika Hakkinen.
On Saturday, after he could manage no better than fourth, the Scotsman described his day as *«The worst of my career.»* And yet the worst was yet to come. At the start of the race, he was looking good. On lap 29 he was lying second, less than a second behind Mika Hakkinen. He had no intention of staying meekly behind either. But when the rain got worse he could not avoid spinning off the track.
On Monday, the British tabloid press like the Daily Star was full of scandal concerning the Scot and did not even bother mentioning Michael Schumacher's performance! *«I am very disappointed and very angry,»* declared Coulthard to the English press. *«I find it incredible that the team gave Mika rain tyres and put me on intermediates. Do we not have the same weather forecast? Maybe the weather forecast was unclear and they wanted to hedge their bets, but it did not work in my case. I was at a definite disadvantage and I would like to know if it is a question of favouritism. I want to find out just how the decision to put me on intermediates was taken.»*
With that, he went to cool off in the McLaren motorhome. By then the damage was done.

Another McLaren failure

While in the lead, Mika Hakkinen suffered the same fate as his team mate; Coulthard going off at the righthander at Bridge, Hakkinen straight over the grass at frightening speed. *«I will not forget that accident in a hurry,»* he admitted after the race. *«I think it was one of the worst moments of my career. But, when I got to that point on the track, I did not feel I was going too quickly.»*
His McLaren spun like a top and part of his front wing was torn off. Unlike his team mate, the Finn was able to continue, but the handling of his MP4/13 had suffered. *«Part of the wing broke, as well as a deflector and part of the nose. I decided to slow down, but when Michael (Schumacher) came up behind me, there was nothing I could do.»*
Sure enough, once the safety car had pulled off the track, (see page 155) the Ferrari closed dramatically on the McLaren. In the Becketts complex, Mika Hakkinen was unable to avoid cutting across the grass once again, handing the lead to his rival. *«In the fast corners, the car was not too bad,»* continued the Finn. *«But at Becketts it would not turn in and I could not avoid going straight on.»*
Then having to fight off Eddie Irvine, Hakkinen finished second. *«Obviously this is a very disappointing day,»* he concluded. *«It could have been worse. I could have ended up with zero points.»*
This had been a serious failure for Ron Dennis' team and on home ground at that. It was also the third failure in a row after Montreal and Magny Cours.

▷ Lap 28. With the rain at its worst, Johnny Herbert goes off and is stuck in the gravel. A few moments earlier the Englishman had been fighting off Jean Alesi, who had not appreciated being attacked by his team mate. From this moment on, their relationship at Sauber turned sour.

Jacques Villeneuve and Eddie Irvine let McLaren have it with both barrels

After two bad grands prix for McLaren, Ron Dennis and his team were heavily criticised by some drivers. On Thursday, Jacques Villeneuve tore the team's management apart. *«Given the spectacular way McLaren started the season, it looked likely they would walk away with the championship and that no one would get near them. I think the McLaren is still the best car, but the team is not doing a good job with it. In one way they are messing up everything.»* The Canadian therefore felt the championship might possibly go to Ferrari.
Eddie Irvine was of the same opinion and said so even more forcefully. *«The championship is over,»* claimed the Irishman. *«It's finished and McLaren have missed the boat. They had the chance to pull out a huge lead at the start of the season and they did not manage it. Now they will be made to pay. From now on, Michael will be hard to beat and I can also give them a hard time in the next few races.»*
Although a McLaren driver himself, David Coulthard also had some criticisms to bring to the party. *«In Magny Cours, Mika could not pass Eddie Irvine, which is his job. If he is incapable of playing the role of lead driver then I will do it.»*
Faced with this verbal assault, the grey team's boss Ron Dennis remained impassive. *«I don't care what Eddie Irvine thinks,»* he replied. *«Ferrari has always made these sorts of statement ever since I have been in Formula 1. I have never lost sleep over them and I will not start now.»*
On Friday afternoon, it just so happened that Eddie Irvine and Ron Dennis were seated side by side in a press conference. The Irishman did not miss the opportunity to keep at it by adding further criticism of McLaren. *«If I had to bet on the outcome of the championship I would put all my money on Michael,»* he declared. *«McLaren has made so many tactical errors that we have closed the gap having been completely left behind at the beginning of the season.»*
Ron Dennis replied by saying he had a lot of respect for the drivers, but that the Irishman was wrong. And that he would do better to concentrate on his own job rather than criticise others.

Eddie Irvine: *«Damon is a sad old man»*

To say that Eddie Irvine was angry with Damon Hill would be an understatement. After a very bad start because of gearbox problems, Irvine was working his way up through the field until he came up behind Hill on lap four. And there he stayed. *«Damon is nothing but a sad old man and a bad loser to boot,»* blasted the Irishman after the race. *«To stop me passing, he was up to his old tricks. He was zig-zagging and using all the road. It is useless talking to him. It is the stewards who should do something about it. He had his punishment when he went off the track.»*
With Damon Hill out, Eddie continued on his way and finished third. Towards the end of the race, he gave up on attacking Hakkinen when his car unaccountably started to lose grip.

A spectator decides to put on his own show after the race. Crazy English! And ugly at that! ▽

PRACTICE TIMES

No	Driver	Car/Engine/Chassis	Practice Friday	Practice Friday	Qualifying	Warm-up
1.	Jacques Villeneuve	Williams/Mecachrome/FW20/5 (G)	1'26"114	1'24"791	1'24"102	1'42"133
2.	Heinz-Harald Frentzen	Williams/Mecachrome/FW20/4 (G)	1'26"107	1'25"187	1'24"442	1'41"620
3.	Michael Schumacher	Ferrari/F300/187 (G)	1'26"884	1'24"260	1'23"720	1'40"296
4.	Eddie Irvine	Ferrari/F300/185 (G)	1'26"791	1'24"834	1'24"436	1'40"127
5.	Giancarlo Fisichella	Benetton/Playlife/198/6 (B)	1'26"840	1'25"822	1'25"654	1'39"802
6.	Alexander Wurz	Benetton/Playlife/198/7 (B)	1'27"121	1'25"904	1'25"760	1'40"917
7.	David Coulthard	McLaren/Mercedes/MP4-13/3 (B)	1'25"640	1'24"233	1'24"310	1'37"910
8.	Mika Hakkinen	McLaren/Mercedes/MP4-13/6 (B)	1'25"764	1'23"639	1'23"271	1'37"921
9.	Damon Hill	Jordan/Honda/198/3 (G)	1'27"667	1'24"683	1'24"542	1'43"797
10.	Ralf Schumacher	Jordan/Honda/198/4 (G)	1'27"460	1'24"496	1'25"461	1'43"738
11.	Olivier Panis	Prost/Peugeot/AP01/2 (B)	1'29"193	1'26"881	1'26"847	1'41"762
12.	Jarno Trulli	Prost/Peugeot/AP01/6 (B)	1'28"685	1'27"002	1'26"808	1'44"526
14.	Jean Alesi	Sauber/Petronas/C17/2 (G)	1'28"136	1'25"769	1'25"081	1'42"369
15.	Johnny Herbert	Sauber/Petronas/C17/4 (G)	1'27"978	1'25"949	1'25"084	1'42"908
16.	Pedro Diniz	Arrows/A19/1 (B)	1'29"375	1'26"929	1'26"376	1'41"938
17.	Mika Salo	Arrows/A19/5 (B)	1'29"262	1'26"947	1'26"487	1'41"582
18.	Rubens Barrichello	Stewart/Ford/SF2/4 (B)	1'28"339	1'27"323	1'26"990	1'42"530
19.	Jos Verstappen	Stewart/Ford/SF2/3 (B)	1'28"983	1'27"690	1'26"948	1'43"305
20.	Ricardo Rosset	Tyrrell/Ford/026/2 (G)	1'29"664	1'28"650	1'28"608	1'48"865
21.	Toranosuke Takagi	Tyrrell/Ford/026/3 (G)	1'28"258	1'26"521	1'27"061	1'46"189
22.	Shinji Nakano	Minardi/Ford/M198/4 (B)	1'30"090	1'28"317	1'28"123	1'42"510
23.	Esteban Tuero	Minardi/Ford/M198/5 (B)	1'30"266	1'28"224	1'28"051	1'42"779

LAP CHART

position:	1	2	3	4	5	6	7	8	9	10	11	12	13	14	15	16	17	18	19	20	21	22
start:	8	3	1	7	4	2	9	14	15	5	6	16	17	12	19	18	21	23	22	20	10	11
1	8	3	7	14	1	2	9	15	6	4	5	17	16	10	12	21	19	20	11	23	22	18
2	8	3	7	14	1	2	9	15	4	6	5	17	16	10	12	21	11	20	19	23	22	18
3	8	3	7	14	1	2	9	15	4	6	5	17	10	16	21	12	11	20	19	23	22	18
4	8	3	7	14	1	2	9	4	15	6	5	17	10	16	21	11	20	12	19	23	22	18
5	8	7	3	14	2	1	9	4	15	6	5	10	17	16	21	11	20	12	19	23	22	18
6	8	7	3	14	2	1	9	4	15	6	5	10	17	16	21	11	20	12	19	23	22	18
7	8	7	3	14	2	1	9	4	15	6	5	10	17	16	21	11	20	12	19	22	18	23
8	8	7	3	14	2	4	1	9	15	6	5	10	17	16	21	11	20	12	19	18	22	23
9	8	7	3	14	2	4	1	9	15	6	5	10	17	16	21	11	20	19	12	18	22	23
10	8	7	3	14	2	4	1	9	15	6	5	10	17	16	21	11	20	19	18	12	22	23
11	8	7	3	14	2	4	1	9	15	6	5	10	17	16	21	11	20	19	18	12	22	23
12	8	7	3	14	4	2	1	9	15	6	5	10	17	16	21	11	20	19	18	12	22	23
13	8	7	3	14	4	2	1	9	15	6	5	10	17	16	21	11	20	19	18	22	12	23
14	8	7	3	14	4	2	1	15	6	5	17	16	10	21	11	20	19	18	22	12	23	
15	8	7	3	14	4	2	1	15	6	5	17	16	10	21	11	20	19	18	2	12	23	
16	8	7	3	14	4	1	15	6	5	17	16	10	21	11	20	18	19	22	12	23		
17	8	7	3	14	4	1	15	6	5	16	17	10	11	21	20	22	12	18	19	23		
18	8	7	3	14	4	1	15	6	5	17	16	10	11	21	20	22	12	19	23	18		
19	8	7	3	14	4	15	1	6	17	10	5	16	11	21	22	20	12	19	23	18		
20	8	7	14	4	3	15	10	17	1	6	5	16	11	21	22	20	12	19	23	18		
21	8	7	14	4	3	15	10	1	6	5	17	16	11	22	12	20	19	21	23	18		
22	8	7	3	14	4	15	10	1	6	5	17	16	11	22	12	19	20	21	23	18		
23	8	7	3	15	4	14	10	1	6	5	17	16	11	22	19	12	20	21	18	23		
24	8	7	3	4	15	14	10	1	6	5	17	16	11	22	19	20	18	21	23	12		
25	8	7	3	4	15	14	10	1	6	5	17	16	11	22	19	18	20	21	23	12		
26	8	7	3	4	15	14	10	1	6	5	17	16	11	22	19	18	21	20	23	12		
27	8	7	3	4	14	10	1	6	5	15	17	16	11	22	19	18	21	20	23	12		
28	8	7	3	4	14	10	1	6	5	16	11	22	19	18	21	20	23	12				
29	8	7	3	4	14	10	1	6	5	16	11	22	19	18	21	20	23	12				
30	8	7	3	4	14	10	1	6	5	16	11	19	18	22	21	12						
31	8	7	3	4	14	10	1	6	5	16	11	19	18	22	21	12						
32	8	7	3	4	14	10	1	5	6	16	11	19	18	22	21	12						
33	8	7	3	4	14	10	1	5	6	16	11	19	18	22	21	12						
34	8	7	3	4	14	10	1	5	6	16	11	19	18	22	21	12						
35	8	7	3	4	14	1	10	5	6	16	11	19	18	22	12	21						
36	8	7	3	4	14	1	5	6	10	16	11	19	18	22	12	21						
37	8	7	3	4	14	1	5	6	10	16	11	19	18	22	12	21						
38	8	3	4	14	1	5	6	10	16	11	19	18	22	21								
39	8	3	4	14	5	6	1	10	16	11	18	22	21									
40	8	3	4	14	5	6	1	10	11	22	21	16										
41	8	3	4	5	14	6	1	10	22	21	16											
42	8	3	4	14	5	6	10	1	22	21	16											
43	8	3	4	14	5	6	10	1	22	21	16											
44	8	3	4	14	5	6	10	1	22	21	16											
45	8	3	4	14	5	6	10	1	22	21	16											
46	8	3	4	14	5	6	10	1	22	21												
47	8	3	4	14	5	6	10	1	22	21												
48	8	3	4	14	5	6	10	1	22	21												
49	8	3	4	14	5	6	10	1	22	21												
50	8	3	4	14	5	6	10	1	22	21												
51	3	8	4	14	5	6	10	1	22	21												
52	3	8	4	14	5	6	10	1	22	21												
53	3	8	4	14	5	6	10	1	22	21												
54	3	8	4	5	6	10	1	22	21													
55	3	8	4	6	5	10	1	22	21													
56	3	8	4	6	5	10	1	22	21													
57	3	8	4	6	5	10	1	22														
58	3	8	4	6	5	10	1	22														
59	3	8	4	6	5	10	1															
60	3	8	4																			

CLASSIFICATION & RETIREMENTS

Pos	Driver	Team	Time
1.	M. Schum.	Ferrari	in 1h47'12"450
2.	Hakkinen	McLaren Mercedes	at 12"465
3.	Irvine	Ferrari	at 19"199
4.	Wurz	Benetton Playlife	at 1 lap
5.	Fisichella	Benetton Playlife	at 1 lap
6.	R. Schum.	Jordan Mugen Honda	at 1 lap
7.	Villeneuve	Williams Mecachrome	at 1 lap
8.	Nakano	Minardi Ford	at 2 laps
9.	Takagi	Tyrrell Ford	at 4 laps

Lap	Driver	Team	Reason
14	Hill	Jordan Mugen Honda	spin
16	Frentzen	Williams Mecachrome	off
28	Salo	Arrows	throttle
28	Herbert	Sauber Petronas	spin
30	Tuero	Minardi Ford	accident
30	Rosset	Tyrrell Ford	accident
38	Trulli	Prost Peugeot	spin
38	Coulthard	McLaren Mercedes	off
39	Verstappen	Stewart Ford	engine
40	Barrichello	Stewart Ford	off
41	Panis	Prost Peugeot	spin
46	Diniz	Arrows	spin
54	Alesi	Sauber Petronas	gearbox

FASTEST LAPS

	Driver	Time	Lap
1.	M. Schum.	1'35"704	12
2.	Hakkinen	1'35"961	2
3.	Coulthard	1'36"120	3
4.	Irvine	1'36"530	12
5.	Frentzen	1'36"884	2
6.	Villeneuve	1'37"199	12
7.	Alesi	1'37"202	11
8.	Hill	1'37"223	12
9.	Herbert	1'37"343	12
10.	R. Schum.	1'37"389	9
11.	Diniz	1'37"887	10
12.	Wurz	1'37"982	12
13.	Salo	1'38"160	9
14.	Fisichella	1'38"424	9
15.	Barrichello	1'40"097	11
16.	Rosset	1'40"948	10
17.	Verstappen	1'41"114	12
18.	Takagi	1'41"629	4
19.	Panis	1'42"346	11
20.	Nakano	1'43"755	33
21.	Trulli	1'44"083	29
22.	Tuero	1'44"700	3

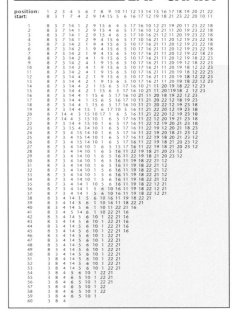

NINTH ROUND

THE 1998 RAC BRITISH GRAND PRIX, SILVERSTONE

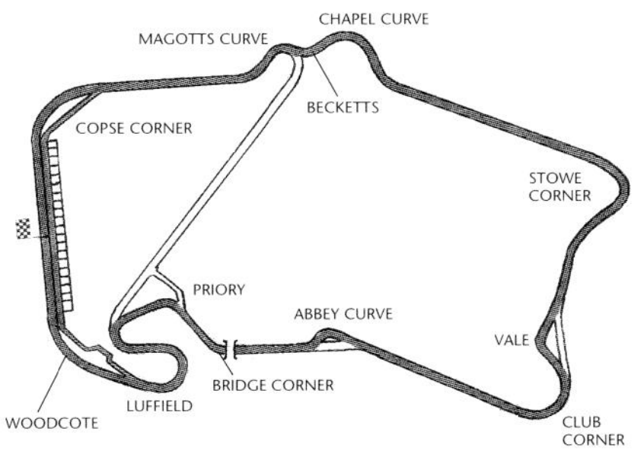

Date : July 12, 1998
Lenght : 5138 meters
Distance : 60 laps, 308.296 km
Weather : rain, 15 degrees

CHAMPIONSHIPS

(after nine rounds)

Drivers :

1. Mika HAKKINEN 56
2. Michael SCHUMACHER 54
3. David COULTHARD 30
4. Eddie IRVINE.................................29
5. Alexander WURZ 17
6. Giancarlo FISICHELLA 15
7. Jacques VILLENEUVE 11
8. Heinz-Harald FRENTZEN 8
9. Rubens BARRICHELLO....................4
10. Mika SALO......................................3
    Jean ALESI.......................................3
12. Johnny HERBERT............................1
    Pedro DINIZ 1
    Jan MAGNUSSEN.............................1
    Ralf SCHUMACHER..........................1

Constructors :

1. McLaren / Mercedes.....................86
2. Ferrari...83
3. Benetton / Playlife 32
4. Williams / Mecachrome 19
5. Stewart / Ford 5
6. Arrows...4
   Sauber / Petronas 4
8. Jordan / Mugen Honda...................1

WEEK-END GOSSIP

- **No presents at Ferrari**

Michael Schumacher will not be giving Eddie Irvine any presents. The Irishman told the English papers he was hoping for a small favour at his home race, but the German driver dismissed the idea. *«I am fighting for the championship so I cannot do anything for Eddie. It would not make sense.»*

- **Benetton join BAR**

On Friday, the Benetton team announced they had just signed a contract with Supertec Sport for the supply of Mecachrome engines in 1999 and 2000. Benetton will therefore have the same power units as BAR. For his part, Frank Williams refused to confirm that his team would also be using these engines.
It seemed he was still in conflict with Flavio Briatore, the Supertec boss, as to the number of teams using these power plants. Frank Williams had a deal with Renault which specified that no more than two teams would use the ex-Renault V10 and was furious the contract had been broken.

- **Coulthard sins again**

Both McLaren drivers are in too much of a hurry. On Friday, both were fined for exceeding the pit lane speed limit (fixed at 80 km/h.) As this was not David Coulthard's first offence he was fined 8000 dollars for his 96 km/h. Hakkinen tripped the radar beam at 92.9 km/h and had to cough up 3250 dollars.

- **Too late to be any use**

French company Mecachrome, which supplies both Williams and Benetton was hoping to have a new engine for qualifying for the Italian Grand Prix at the start of September. Much too late to give Williams any chance of hanging on to their championship title.

- **Take it to the Max**

As planned, Max Mosley the FIA president was given four laps of the Silverstone circuit as a passenger in the McLaren MP4-98T two seater. Martin Brundle driving, did not spare the horses through Silverstone's high speed corners. A stoic Mosley emerged from the cockpit looking in fine form and with a steady gait. *"After that, I am sure Max will be even more in favour of reducing speeds in F1,"* joked Michael Schumacher. When Jacques Villeneuve was asked who he would like to take for a ride in the car, the Canadian replied: *"I do not hate anyone enough to put them through that!"* Sylvester Stallone was also due to have a ride, but he failed the medical.

At Silverstone, a lot of the spectators camp on site. They have a good time and do not take themselves too seriously.
▽

RACE SUMMARY

- At the start, the cars stay pretty much in grid order, apart from Jean Alesi who makes up four places from his grid position.
- On lap 5, David Coulthard passes Michael Schumacher, who cannot match the pace of the McLarens.
- Light rain is falling on some part of the circuit and some people are already sliding off the track: Damon Hill on lap 14, Heinz-Harald Frentzen on lap 16. David Coulthard closes on Mika Hakkinen.
- Round lap 26 the rain gets heavier. Johnny Herbert and Mika Salo go off, as does David Coulthard, spinning three times.
- On lap 41, the rain has hit monsoon levels. Panis, Verstappen and Barrichello are all caught out, while Mika Hakkinen goes off but keeps going.
- The rain is so heavy that the safety car is brought out. Hakkinen, who had a 38 second lead over Michael Schumacher, sees it reduced to nothing.
- Six laps later and the safety car pulls off the track. Schumacher closes on Hakkinen and passes him on lap 51.
- Michael Schumacher is given a 10 second penalty which he comes in for on the last lap. He therefore takes the chequered flag in the pit lane - a first in Formula 1.

Mika back on track

After three barren grands prix, Mika Hakkinen spared anyone else the bother of having to try and win the Austrian Grand Prix, by making it his own almost from beginning to end.
David Coulthard, who was last at the end of the first lap, confirmed the superiority of the silver arrows, by carving his way through the field to finish second.
Michael Schumacher was third, powerless to challenge his rivals. He went off the track and had to change his front wing and came very close to losing his third place.

GROSSER PREIS VON ÖSTERREICH SPIELBERG

△ Giancarlo Fisichella en route to pole position.

The moment he stepped from the cockpit it was Giancarlo party time in the Benetton garage. ▷ ▽

The flamboyant Jean Alesi put on a great show in practice for the Austrian Grand Prix. He also made the most of the weather conditions to give Sauber its first ever front row qualifying position. ▽

Giancarlo Fisichella and Jean Alesi are shrewdest in the showers

In Austria, the weather services like to be very specific. They had predicted rain for the middle of the day and bang on midday the first drops fell on the Spielberg region. The shower was very heavy at first, before abating at the start of qualifying and stopping completely mid way through the session.

As the cars put in their laps, it became clear the track was drying and the fastest times would come right at the end of the hour. The chequered flag had actually been waved, on his last flying lap when Giancarlo Fisichella set the fastest time, more than seven tenths of a second ahead of Jean Alesi, who had seconds earlier set the what was then the quickest time.

Of course, it is highly unlikely that Fisichella would have set the fastest time in normal conditions, but that should not detract from his achievement. In these tricky conditions, it was important to be on top of one's game. *«Before the session I was a bit worried,»* recounted «Fisico.» *«The car was well set up for the dry and I was not sure what it would be like in the wet. At first, I fitted 100% rain tyres, but they were not working well. I went off twice and I slightly damaged the car.»*

Back in his pit to repair the damage, Fisichella went back out to try and improve on his fourth place. *«Right at the end of the session, my team called me in to fit new tyres and instructed me to stay out until the end of the session. It was a good idea as the car worked better on the new tyres and the track was also definitely quicker on the last lap.»*

Giancarlo Fisichella thus scored his first ever pole position and stole the thunder of the leading players in the championship. *«I am really very happy,»* he added. *«But I am not under any illusions. The race will be difficult and I would be happy simply to get on the podium.»*

Alesi superstar

For the first time in Peter Sauber's F1 career, one of his cars would start a grand prix from the front row. Thanks to the weather and the talents of the acrobatic Jean Alesi. At 13h59 minutes and 49 seconds, he set the fastest time, before seeing himself knocked off the perch a few seconds later by Fisichella. It did not matter, Alesi was on the front row. *«The front row changes everything. Maybe I can do a few laps in the lead. It will depend on the start. I'll just grit my teeth and hope!»*

A strategy typical of the man.

STARTING GRID

		G. FISICHELLA 1'29''598
Jean ALESI 1'30''317	-1-	
		Mika HAKKINEN 1'30''517
M. SCHUMACHER 1'30''551	-2-	
		R. BARRICHELLO 1'31''005
Mika SALO 1'31''028	-3-	
		Heinz-H. FRENTZEN 1'31''515
Eddie IRVINE 1'31''651	-4-	
		R. SCHUMACHER 1'31''917
Olivier PANIS 1'32''081	-5-	
		Jacques VILLENEUVE 1'32''083
Jos VERSTAPPEN 1'32''099	-6-	
		Pedro DINIZ 1'32''206
David COULTHARD 1'32''399	-7-	
		Damon HILL 1'32''718
Jarno TRULLI 1'32''906	-8-	
		Alexander WURZ 1'33''185
Johnny HERBERT 1'33''205	-9-	
		Esteban TUERO 1'33''399
Toranosuke TAKAGI 1'34''090	-10-	
		Shinji NAKANO 1'34''536
Ricardo ROSSET 1'34''910	-11-	

◁
The start. On the front row, Giancarlo Fisichella and Jean Alesi are caught napping by Mika Hakkinen.

First corner and first carnage: the two Minardis, both Tyrrells and Johnny Herbert are involved, but only Toranosuke Takagi stay stuck there.
▽

Mika back in the driving seat

Mika Hakkinen was jumping for joy. He walked onto the podium, both fists held high, visibly relieved to have put an end to a string of defeats since the Monaco Grand Prix. *«I have to say this has been the most enjoyable win of the season,»* he admitted once off the podium. *«I am very happy and I think Ron Dennis is too. A one-two was exactly what we had expected from this race. We had done a huge amount of work before coming here and I think we deserved this win. We definitely have the best car in the pit lane. Of course, there is still room for improvement, but I can't complain.»*
On a high, the Finn was quick to praise his team. *«It was an excellent race from start to finish. The decision to only refuel once was the right one and I was able to attack from start to finish without any problems.»*
In fact, Mika Hakkinen was out on his own throughout the race. After a demon start, which took him from third on the grid into the lead, he only ever came under some pressure in the first third of the race, when he had to deal with the pressing attentions of Michael Schumacher. *«At the start of the race I had a brake balance problem. I could not brakes as hard as usual, which allowed Michael to catch me. In any case, it is very hard to overtake on this track. You have to take risks and I do not think Michael would have got past. Then my brake trouble disappeared and when Michael went off, no one else got close, which did not surprise me.»*
Thanks to the rain, qualifying had been a lottery.
David Coulthard did not get a winning ticket, as he started from 14th place. Hit by Mika Salo's Arrows after the first few hundred metres, he had to pit for a new nose, which did not lose him too much time as the safety car was on the track at the time. *«Then the car just got better and better. It was really perfect for overtaking and I must say a thank you to all the other drivers I passed. They all moved over in a sporting manner.»*
David Coulthard finally came home second, five seconds adrift of Hakkinen.

IN THE POINTS

1.	Mika HAKKINEN	West McLaren Mercedes	1 h 30'44"086
2.	David COULTHARD	West McLaren Mercedes	at 5"289
3.	M. SCHUMACHER	Scuderia Ferrari Marlboro	at 39"093
4.	Eddie IRVINE	Scuderia Ferrari Marlboro	at 43"977
5.	Ralf SCHUMACHER	B&H Jordan Mugen Honda	at 50"655
6.	Jacques VILLENEUVE	Winfield Williams	at 53"202

Fastest lap : D. COULTHARD, lap 30, 1'12"878, avg. 213.348 km/h

△◁
Second corner: the two Arrows involve David Coulthard in their coming together. The Scotsman, whose only aim was to stay out of trouble for the first lap, is forced to pit for a new front wing.

◁
Another black day for the Prost team: while Jarno Trulli finishes 10th, Olivier Panis did not even make it off the grid, thanks to a blocked gearbox.

Ralf Schumacher says a big hello. After a disastrous start to the season, characterised by several crashes, the little brother secured his second consecutive points finish in Austria. His popularity is on the increase among the team owners.

sparco
BENSON &

Storm over a point

«Yabadabadoo!» Mika Hakkinen was overjoyed on the Spielberg circuit podium. He put a hat-trick of defeats to an end.

Lap 55. Having dealt with brother Ralf, Michael Schumacher has moved up to fourth, 15.3 seconds behind team-mate Eddie Irvine. At first the gap between the two Ferraris hardly alters. Then suddenly on lap 59, the Irishman slows down and loses up to two and half seconds per lap. It would seem that Eddie Irvine is once again being the dutiful team player. Having been lapping in the 1m 14s, he is suddenly the slowest car out there.

With four laps to go to the flag, under cover of running a bit wide at the first corner, he lets Schumacher pass. Only a few months ago, this behaviour would have been perfectly normal between team mates. The only problem is that FIA has now outlawed all team tactics.

In order to justify Eddie Irvine's actions, Scuderia Ferrari had to think up a suitably rational explanation, which Schumacher supplied with a certain aplomb. «*Eddie and me had brake problems,*» he claimed after the race. «*The pits told him to slow down, which allowed me to catch him.*»

It was certainly a major catch up and the press office burst out laughing to a man and woman when this theory was put forward. It was all the more unbelievable, as the moment Michael swept past, Irvine's speed picked up again. Officially, this was because he had to fight off Ralf Schumacher, who was actually a whopping ten seconds behind.

Eddie Irvine did not have the opportunity to give his version of the story. Once out of the car, he was called to the Ferrari motorhome where he was briefed by Jean Todt. Once in the paddock again, he spouted the official version.

Some Ferrari insiders reckoned the brake problem was just a pack of lies, invented just to get one extra point for Schumacher. Faced with this ridiculous scenario , FIA President Max Mosley explained three days later that teams could ask one of their drivers to move over if the other driver was in the running for the championship. «*The new rules banning team tactics are only in place to protect the interests of the sport,*» declared Mosley, as was the case of McLaren in Australia no doubt! In Austria, the McLaren did not consider even for a second, protesting Ferrari. «*I think it is normal that my team mate does not make my life difficult when I try to pass him,*» was Michael Schumacher's final remark on the subject. Basically, he was not wrong. It was just a shame that the rules had forced him to lie to cover up a strategy that has always been part of motor racing and contributed to the history of Formula One.

«And do you think this will disguise what we are doing and go unnoticed.» Jean Todt in conversation with Michael Schumacher during practice. Maybe they are discussing team tactics?

The hills are alive with the sound of....racing cars. The decor in Austria is the stuff of picture postcards.

Giancarlo Fisichella spoils it all

Giancarlo Fisichella and Jean Alesi were unable to exploit their advantage of starting from the front row when the lights went out. They were instantly overhauled by Mika Hakkinen and Michael Schumacher. After that, Fisichella was rolling on in third place while Alesi was passed by Eddie Irvine. When he rushed back onto the track after his first pit stop, Fisichella came alongside Alesi. The Frenchman braked late, and was taking the usual line round the corner. Stuck on the inside, Fisichella went onto the grass and the two cars touched. The Sauber stayed on the track but the Frenchman had stalled and that was the end of his race. Fisichella was to blame for the incident, having come from a long way back in his Benetton on the run to the corner.

However, back in the pits, «Fisico» denied all responsibility. «*Normally, Jean is very fair play,*» he said through gritted teeth «*and I do not want to complain about him. But I had got past him and then I glanced across and saw him coming over on my left and he cut across me. It is a shame as the car was going really well until then.*»

Jean Alesi was not even angry.

He went back to the Sauber motorhome, watched the race on television and then went home. «*I had less fuel on board than Giancarlo, which meant I could brake later than him. He went out of my field of vision and then suddenly he drove into me. I hate being the victim of a collision, but it is worse when it is the fault of someone I like and Giancarlo is a great guy!*»

PRACTICE TIMES

No	Driver	Car/Engine/Chassis	Practice Friday	Practice Saturday	Qualifying	Warm-up
1.	Jacques Villeneuve	Williams/Mecachrome/FW20/5 (G)	1'14″820	1'13″354	1'32″083	1'16″159
2.	Heinz-Harald Frentzen	Williams/Mecachrome/FW20/4 (G)	1'15″345	1'12″673	1'31″515	1'15″376
3.	Michael Schumacher	Ferrari/F300/188 (G)	1'14″411	1'12″690	1'30″551	1'14″307
4.	Eddie Irvine	Ferrari/F300/185 (G)	1'14″523	1'12″569	1'31″651	1'14″350
5.	Giancarlo Fisichella	Benetton/Playlife/198/6 (B)	1'13″704	1'13″074	1'29″598	1'14″941
6.	Alexander Wurz	Benetton/Playlife/198/7 (B)	1'14″397	1'13″671	1'33″185	1'14″942
7.	David Coulthard	McLaren/Mercedes/MP4-13/4 (B)	1'13″703	1'11″655	1'32″399	1'13″602
8.	Mika Hakkinen	McLaren/Mercedes/MP4-13/6 (B)	1'13″746	1'11″819	1'30″517	1'13″301
9.	Damon Hill	Jordan/Honda/198/3 (G)	1'14″535	1'13″010	1'32″718	1'15″162
10.	Ralf Schumacher	Jordan/Honda/198/4 (G)	1'15″117	1'13″259	1'31″917	1'15″086
11.	Olivier Panis	Prost/Peugeot/AP01/5 (B)	1'14″755	1'13″966	1'32″081	1'16″006
12.	Jarno Trulli	Prost/Peugeot/AP01/6 (B)	1'14″685	1'13″396	1'32″906	1'15″097
14.	Jean Alesi	Sauber/Petronas/C17/6 (G)	1'14″627	1'12″789	1'30″317	1'14″474
15.	Johnny Herbert	Sauber/Petronas/C17/1 (G)	1'14″103	1'13″421	1'33″205	1'15″368
16.	Pedro Diniz	Arrows/A19/4 (B)	1'16″303	1'13″999	1'32″206	1'15″638
17.	Mika Salo	Arrows/A19/5 (B)	1'15″696	1'13″802	1'31″028	1'15″574
18.	Rubens Barrichello	Stewart/Ford/SF2/4 (B)	1'14″302	1'13″887	1'31″005	1'14″881
19.	Jos Verstappen	Stewart/Ford/SF2/3 (B)	1'15″231	1'14″070	1'32″099	1'15″702
20.	Ricardo Rosset	Tyrrell/Ford/026/2 (G)	1'18″469	1'14″351	1'34″910	1'16″309
21.	Toranosuke Takagi	Tyrrell/Ford/026/3 (G)	1'15″158	1'13″730	1'34″090	1'14″480
22.	Shinji Nakano	Minardi/Ford/M198/4 (B)	1'16″171	1'14″906	1'34″536	1'16″142
23.	Esteban Tuero	Minardi/Ford/M198/5 (B)	1'16″582	1'14″738	1'33″399	1'15″788

LAP CHART

position:	1	2	3	4	5	6	7	8	9	10	11	12	13	14	15	16	17	18	19	20	21	22
start:	5	14	8	3	18	17	2	4	10	11	1	19	16	7	9	12	6	15	23	21	22	20
1	8	3	5	18	14	4	2	10	9	19	6	12	1	20	16	22	7	15	23	17		
2	8	3	5	18	14	4	2	10	9	19	6	12	23	1	20	16	22	15	7			
3	8	3	5	18	14	4	2	10	9	19	6	12	1	20	22	15	7	16	23			
4	8	5	3	18	14	4	2	10	9	12	1	19	20	7	22	15	6	23				
5	8	3	5	18	14	4	2	10	9	12	1	19	20	7	22	15	6	23				
6	8	3	5	18	14	4	2	10	9	12	1	19	7	20	22	15	6	23				
7	8	3	5	18	14	4	2	10	9	12	1	19	7	20	22	15	6	23				
8	8	3	5	4	14	2	10	9	18	12	1	7	19	20	15	22	6	23				
9	8	3	5	4	14	2	10	9	12	7	1	19	20	15	6	22	23					
10	8	3	5	4	14	2	10	9	7	12	1	19	20	15	6	22	23					
11	8	3	5	4	14	2	10	9	7	12	1	19	20	15	6	22	23					
12	8	3	5	4	14	2	10	9	7	12	1	19	20	15	6	22	23					
13	8	3	5	4	14	2	10	9	7	12	1	19	20	15	6	22	23					
14	8	3	5	4	14	2	10	7	9	12	1	19	20	15	6	22	23					
15	8	3	5	4	14	2	10	7	9	12	1	19	20	15	6	22	23					
16	8	3	5	4	14	2	7	10	9	12	1	19	20	15	6	22	23					
17	8	5	3	4	14	7	10	9	12	1	19	15	6	20	22	23						
18	8	5	4	14	7	10	9	3	12	1	19	15	6	20	22	23						
19	8	5	4	7	14	10	9	12	1	19	15	6	20	22	23	3						
20	8	5	4	7	14	10	12	1	19	15	6	9	20	22	23	3						
21	8	5	4	7	14	10	12	1	19	15	6	9	20	22	23	3						
22	8	4	7	10	12	1	19	15	9	6	22	23	3	20								
23	8	4	7	10	12	1	19	15	9	22	3	23	6	20								
24	8	4	7	10	12	1	19	15	9	3	22	23	6	20								
25	8	4	7	10	12	1	15	9	19	3	22	23	6	20								
26	8	4	7	10	12	1	15	9	3	22	23	19	6	20								
27	8	4	7	10	12	1	15	9	3	22	19	6	20	23								
28	8	7	4	10	12	1	15	9	3	22	19	6	20	23								
29	8	7	4	10	12	1	15	9	3	22	19	6	20	23								
30	8	7	4	10	12	1	15	3	9	22	19	6	20	23								
31	8	7	4	10	12	1	15	3	9	22	19	6	20									
32	8	7	4	10	12	1	3	15	9	22	19	6	20									
33	8	7	4	10	12	1	3	15	9	22	6	19	20									
34	8	7	4	10	12	3	1	15	9	22	6	19	20									
35	7	8	4	10	3	1	12	15	9	22	6	19	20									
36	7	8	4	10	3	1	12	15	9	22	6	19	20									
37	8	7	4	10	3	1	12	9	15	22	6	19	20									
38	8	7	4	10	3	1	9	12	22	6	15	19	20									
39	8	7	4	10	3	1	9	6	15	12	19	22	20									
40	8	7	4	10	3	1	9	6	15	12	19	22	20									
41	8	7	4	10	3	1	9	6	15	12	19	22	20									
42	8	7	4	10	3	1	9	6	15	12	19	22	20									
43	8	7	4	10	1	9	3	6	15	12	19	22	20									
44	8	7	4	10	9	3	1	6	15	12	19	22	20									
45	8	7	4	10	9	3	1	6	15	12	19	22	20									
46	8	7	4	10	3	1	6	9	15	12	19	22	20									
47	8	7	4	10	3	1	6	9	15	12	22	19	20									
48	8	7	4	10	3	1	6	9	15	12	22	19	20									
49	8	7	4	10	3	1	9	15	6	12	22	19	20									
50	8	7	4	10	3	1	9	15	6	12	22	19	20									
51	8	7	4	10	3	1	9	15	6	12	22	19	20									
52	8	7	4	10	3	1	9	15	6	12	22	20										
53	8	7	4	10	3	1	9	15	6	12	22	20										
54	8	7	4	10	3	1	9	15	6	12	22	20										
55	8	7	4	3	10	1	9	15	6	12	22	20										
56	8	7	4	3	10	1	9	15	6	12	22	20										
57	8	7	4	3	10	1	9	15	6	12	22	20										
58	8	7	4	3	10	1	9	15	6	12	22	20										
59	8	7	4	3	10	1	9	15	6	12	22	20										
60	8	7	4	3	10	1	9	15	6	12	22	20										
61	8	7	4	3	10	1	9	15	6	12	22	20										
62	8	7	4	3	10	1	9	15	6	12	22	20										
63	8	7	4	3	10	1	9	15	6	12	22	20										
64	8	7	4	3	10	1	9	15	6	12	22	20										
65	8	7	4	3	10	1	9	15	6	12	22	20										
66	8	7	4	3	10	1	9	15	6	12	22	20										
67	8	7	4	3	10	1	9	15	6	12	22	20										
68	8	7	3	4	10	1	9	15	6	12	22	20										
69	8	7	3	4	10	1	9	15	6	12	22	20										
70	8	7	3	4	10	1	9	15	6	12	22											
71	8	7	3	4	10	1	9															

CLASSIFICATION & RETIREMENTS

Pos	Driver	Team	Time
1.	Hakkinen	McLaren Mercedes	in 1h30'44″086
2.	Coulthard	McLaren Mercedes	at 5″289
3.	M. Schum.	Ferrari	at 39″093
4.	Irvine	Ferrari	at 43″977
5.	R. Schum	Jordan Mugen Honda	at 50″655
6.	Villeneuve	Williams Mecachrome	at 53″202
7.	Hill	Jordan Mugen Honda	at 1'13″624
8.	Herbert	Sauber Petronas	at 1 lap
9.	Wurz	Benetton Playlife	at 1 lap
10.	Trulli	Prost Peugeot	at 1 lap
11.	Nakano	Minardi Ford	at 1 lap
12.	Rosset	Tyrrell Ford	at 2 laps

Lap	Driver	Team	Reason
1	Takagi	Tyrrell Ford	accident
1	Panis	Prost Peugeot	clutch
2	Salo	Arrows	accident
4	Diniz	Arrows	accident
9	Barrichello	Stewart Ford	brakes
17	Frentzen	Williams Mecachrome	engine
22	Alesi	Sauber Petronas	accident
22	Fisichella	Benetton Playlife	accident
31	Tuero	Minardi Ford	spin
52	Verstappen	Stewart Ford	engine

FASTEST LAPS

	Driver	Time	Lap
1.	Coulthard	1'12″878	30
2.	M. Schum.	1'13″029	41
3.	Hakkinen	1'13″412	31
4.	Villeneuve	1'13″730	66
5.	R. Schum.	1'13″972	69
6.	Wurz	1'14″040	70
7.	Fisichella	1'14″044	20
8.	Irvine	1'14″066	58
9.	Hill	1'14″135	63
10.	Herbert	1'14″639	63
11.	Alesi	1'14″791	21
12.	Frentzen	1'15″446	16
13.	Nakano	1'15″575	37
14.	Verstappen	1'15″610	43
15.	Trulli	1'15″709	59
16.	Tuero	1'15″769	19
17.	Rosset	1'16″100	28
18.	Barrichello	1'16″822	5
19.	Diniz	2'02″090	2

TENTH ROUND

GROSSER PREIS VON ÖSTERREICH, SPIELBERG

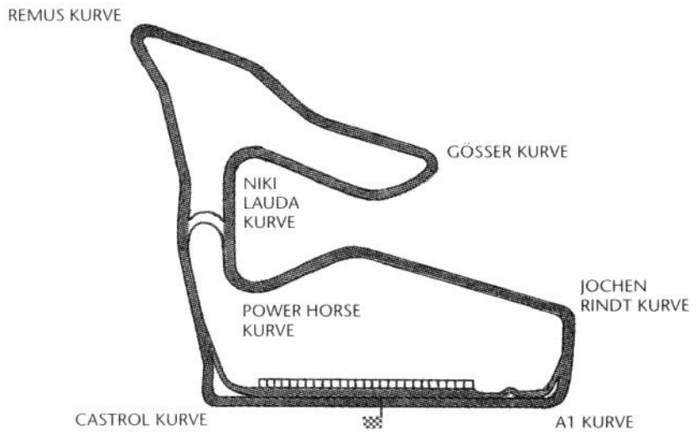

Date :	July 26, 1998
Lenght :	4319 meters
Distance :	71 laps, 306.649 km
Weather :	sunny, 21 degrees

CHAMPIONSHIPS

(after ten rounds)

Drivers :

1. Mika HAKKINEN 66
2. Michael SCHUMACHER 58
3. David COULTHARD 36
4. Eddie IRVINE 32
5. Alexander WURZ 17
6. Giancarlo FISICHELLA 15
7. Jacques VILLENEUVE 12
8. Heinz-Harald FRENTZEN 8
9. Rubens BARRICHELLO 4
10. Ralf SCHUMACHER 3
    Mika SALO 3
    Jean ALESI 3
13. Johnny HERBERT 1
    Pedro DINIZ 1
    Jan MAGNUSSEN 1

Constructors :

1. McLaren / Mercedes 102
2. Ferrari 90
3. Benetton / Playlife 32
4. Williams / Mecachrome 20
5. Stewart / Ford 5
6. Arrows 4
   Sauber / Petronas 4
8. Jordan / Mugen Honda 3

RACE SUMMARY

- Jean Alesi and Giancarlo Fisichella mess up their start, allowing Hakkinen to lead. Schumacher is second after passing Fisichella at the second corner.
- At the second corner, both Arrows spin off. Coulthard manages to avoid them, but as Salo tries to get going he hits the McLaren, breaking its front wing.
- The race director sends out the safety car to get all the wrecks towed off the track, giving Coulthard time to pit for a new nose and catch up with the pack.
- When the safety car pulls off on lap 3, Michael Schumacher attacks Mika Hakkinen on the outside under braking for the Gosser curve. It was an impossible move which did not work. Both men trade fastest lap times.
- On lap 18, Michael Schumacher runs too wide in the Rindt corner. He gets back on the track minus his front wing. He pits for a replacement and rejoins in 16th and last place.
- On lap 21, Giancarlo Fisichella makes his pit stop. Back on the track he tangles with Jean Alesi.
- Schumacher refuels on lap 43 and is back on the track in 7th spot. He moves up the order, enjoying a scrap with brother Ralf, passing him on lap 55. Eddie Irvine is now ahead of him. The Irishman slows down, allowing his team mate past and into third place.

WEEK-END GOSSIP

- **Villeneuve is called to the BAR**

It was not a big surprise. Just before the Austrian Grand Prix, Jacques Villeneuve announced he would be joining British American Racing in 1999, the team which has announced its intention of winning the first race of that season. *«Why wouldn't we win our first grand prix?»* asked Villeneuve with a big smile. *«You have to dream in life and if I have signed with BAR, it is because I think they can do it.»*

- **McLaren accuses Ferrari**

The McLaren team claimed to have proof that Ferrari uses an illegal anti-spin control. *«We have evaluated data which proves the Ferrari car comes out of corners at a speed which it is impossible to obtain by simple mechanical means, by acting on the suspension,»* declared Ron Dennis. However, he then went on to say he was sure that no teams were cheating. He therefore had no immediate plans to lodge a protest.
In Austria on Saturday morning, Ron Dennis went to see Jean Todt to advise him of this proof held by McLaren. Ferrari's sporting director immediately asked the scrutineers to check his cars. Nothing illegal was found. He then told the Italian press about this which put Dennis in a seriously bad mood.

«Someone should tell Karl that Gerhard is not racing in Formula 1 anymore.» As far as the public was concerned, the local hero is still not called Alexander Wurz, but is still Gerhard Berger. The joys of camping, except when it rains.

Winners, but only just

McLaren notched up another one-two finish in Hockenheim, but not with their usual crushing dominance, as only 13 seconds covered the first five finishers.

In fact, the McLarens' Mercedes V10s were suffering from excessive fuel consumption and the drivers were ordered to slow the pace. This was not enough to help Michael Schumacher, who was never on the pace throughout the weekend. The German finished fifth and saw the gap in the championship open up to 16 points.

GROSSER MOBIL 1 PREIS VON DEUTSCHLAND
HOCKENHEIM

STARTING GRID

David COULTHARD 1'42"347	-1-	Mika HAKKINEN 1'41"838
R. SCHUMACHER 1'42"994	-2-	Jacques VILLENEUVE 1'42"365
Eddie IRVINE 1'43"270	-3-	Damon HILL 1'43"183
G. FISICHELLA 1'43"369	-4-	Alexander WURZ 1'43"341
Heinz-H. FRENTZEN 1'43"467	-5-	M. SCHUMACHER 1'43"459
Johnny HERBERT 1'44"599	-6-	Jean ALESI 1'43"663
Jarno TRULLI 1'44"844	-7-	R. BARRICHELLO 1'44"776
Olivier PANIS 1'45"197	-8-	Toranosuke TAKAGI 1'44"961
Pedro DINIZ 1'45"588	-9-	Mika SALO 1'45"276
Shinji NAKANO 1'46"713	-10-	Jos VERSTAPPEN 1'45"623
	-11-	Esteban TUERO 1'47"265

McLarens on parade

It was no great surprise that Mika Hakkinen set the fastest time in the qualifying session for the German Grand Prix. In fact, it was the first time that the 1997 qualifying times were bettered this season, despite the introduction of grooved tyres and the reduction in car width, modifications which actually made the cars quicker in a straight line. David Coulthard was clocked at 356 km/h on Friday, just before the Clark chicane. It was an absolute record for Hockenheim.

Mika Hakkinen himself was not very surprised at his performance. However, he was amazed at what Jacques Villeneuve had done in qualifying third. *«What Jacques has done today prove he has talent. He did a very good job, as did the Jordans.»*

Once again, David Coulthard had to settle for second on the grid. *«Of course I am a bit disappointed to have been beaten by Mika. But I was unlucky during my last two laps which spoilt it all. Otherwise I think I could have been very close to Mika's time. I am confident for the race. I will be racing for the team. One always races for the team.»*

Third on the grid, Jacques Villeneuve could not get over the shock of having done so well. *«Since I have been driving for Williams, this is the first time the car has gone well at this circuit. But I am too far behind the McLarens to have a hope of winning.»*

9th: the worst result at the worst time

The klaxons were not so loud and the fireworks were packed away again. On Saturday, the Hockenheim stadium lacked the usual atmosphere, because Schumacher had a very black day. In the morning, when he had only just started the free practice session, he went off at the Ostkurve. Over enthusiastic, he had forgotten his tyres were still cold. As use of the spare car is banned in free practice, he lost precious time, while his car was brought back to the pits. Once underway again, his engine expired.

The German had lost too much time to have a hope of setting up his car correctly and he finally ended up ninth. *«I am very disappointed,»* he said on Saturday evening. *«It is not really the time or the place to have my worse qualifying of the season. We are not quick enough on this track and even without this morning's problems I would have been a long way back.»*

△ *Yet another pole for Mika Hakkinen. Whatever type of circuit, twisty or high speed, over the summer, the Finn made pole position his personal property.*

▷ *The German fans were distraught. In qualifying, Michael Schumacher had got it all wrong and was to be found languishing down in ninth place on the grid. He had not managed to find the right set up for his Ferrari and the long wheelbase chassis, tried on Friday, did not give satisfaction.*

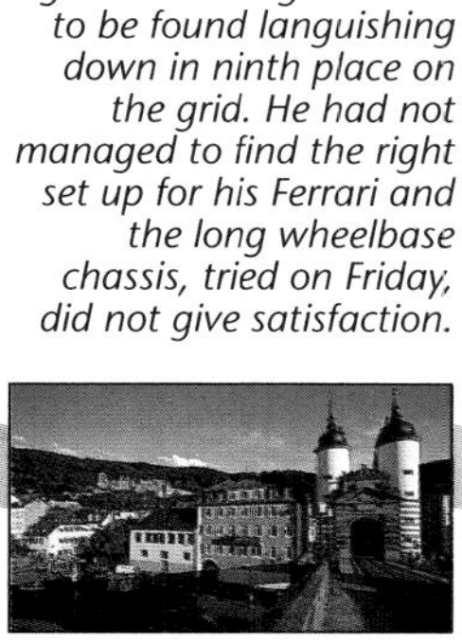

16 points ahead: Mika Hakkinen is running away with the championship

Mika Hakkinen has just won the German Grand Prix, but his stern impression makes it seem as though he was forced to retire on the first lap. It was proof of the pressure the Finn had been under. «*Mika did not have it easy today,*» explained his manager Didier Coton. «*In these situations, he takes several hours to unwind. For now he is going over and over the race in his mind.*»
Seen from the outside, Hakkinen's win looked pretty easy. But inside the cockpit of McLaren Number 8, life was different. «*I knew I had no need to worry about David, even if he was very close behind. He is a real professional and I knew he would not put us in a risky situation. Then, towards the end of the race, my engine started to lose power. It was slow down the straights. I thought something was leaking from somewhere.*»
McLaren explained that Mika's problems had more to do with fuel consumption trouble (see page 174) although a team engineer did admit there was also a leak. The chequered flag could not come soon enough for the Finn. «*I am very happy. I know I have a good lead in the championship, but no way am I thinking about it. Anything can still happen and I will keep concentrating right to the end.*»

△
A victory that no doubt looked easier from the outside than from within. But the result was the same. Mika Hakkinen had a serious option on the world championship after Hockenheim.

Fourth place and first points of the season for Damon Hill. The Englishman had a quiet race, eclipsed by the brio of his team mate Ralf Schumacher, who had proved capable of sticking with the McLarens in the early part of the race.
▽

Schumi nowhere

Michael Schumacher was nowhere all weekend. Having qualified ninth, he had an uneventful race to finish fifth.
He had just lost a further eight points to Hakkinen in the championship race. «*While there is still hope I will not give up,*» he commented. Starting from ninth, I could not expect much more than fifth place. Ferrari sporting director Jean Todt could not hide his unhappiness. «*I am very disappointed. We simply could not find the right set up this weekend. It turned out that on this track, in low downforce configuration, the car lacked grip and traction.*»

IN THE POINTS

1.	Mika HAKKINEN	West McLaren Mercedes	1 h 20'47"984
2.	David COULTHARD	West McLaren Mercedes	at 0"427
3.	Jacques VILLENEUVE	Winfield Williams	at 2"578
4.	Damon HILL	B&H Jordan Mugen Honda	at 7"185
5.	M. SCHUMACHER	Scuderia Ferrari Marlboro	at 12"613
6.	Ralf SCHUMACHER	B&H Jordan Mugen Honda	at 29"739

Fastest lap : David COULTHARD, lap 17, 1'46"116, avg. 231.471 km/h

GROSSER MOBIL 1 PREIS VON DEUTSCHLAND

Revitalised, Jacques Villeneuve?
At Hockenheim, the Canadian had his best race of the season, finishing on the podium for the first time this season. He even claimed he could have chased after the McLarens if his FW20 had not been affected by differential problems.

McLaren on the limit... of their fuel consumption

A modest eighth place for Eddie Irvine at Hockenheim. The Irishman explained he had fought hard all race, to no avail. «I carried on pushing hard, because I am not paid to cruise around,» he said.

The two Schumacher brothers wave to the crowd. Both finished in the points at Hockenheim.

The loneliness of the long distance straights at Hockenheim.

The McLaren-Mercedes team knows how to party when it wins. One hour after the finish at Hockenheim, there was still a huge crowd in front of the three Anglo-German team motorhomes. Rivers of champagne flowed and the PA system played a Finnish pop song written in Mika Hakkinen's honour. Those without a knowledge of Finnish - almost everyone- could only understand the cries of «Mika» which served as the riff to the tune. Most of the Mercedes directors were there to celebrate doing the double on home turf. Mario Illien, the designer of the Mercedes engine was in seventh heaven. It was his 49th birthday that very day and this win was a great present.
In the midst of all this jollity, one man looked serious: Ron Dennis. One could be forgiven for thinking that the McLaren boss had his smile surgically removed. *«We made all the right choices and we obtained a fantastic result at the end of a fantastic weekend,»* he intoned, before admitting the race had been no picnic. While the two silver arrows led the pack on the track, the team engineers realised they were using more fuel than predicted and that there was a risk they would not make it to the flag.
It was shortly after the pit stop that the problem became apparent. *«We did some calculations and realised that Mika and David had used more fuel than planned and that we had not put enough in to get them to the chequered flag,»* continued Dennis. *«We did not panic, but we had to rethink very quickly, because the longer we took the worse it got. We asked both drivers to change the fuel settings, something we very rarely do. They slowed down to gradually improve the situation.»* Dennis denied that Hakkinen had any sort of engine problem, as the Finn had suggested. *«Mika is not used to this sort of situation and he did not understand what was happening. If you reduce fuel consumption, you reduce power; that is normal.»* He seemed to be taking his driver for an ass.

PRACTICE TIMES

No	Driver	Car/Engine/Chassis	Practice Friday	Practice Saturday	Qualifying	Warm-up
1.	Jacques Villeneuve	Williams/Mecachrome/FW20/5 (G)	1'44"928	1'43"444	1'42"365	1'45"741
2.	Heinz-Harald Frentzen	Williams/Mecachrome/FW20/4 (G)	1'45"186	1'44"084	1'43"467	1'47"188
3.	Michael Schumacher	Ferrari/F300/188 (G)	1'44"757	1'45"038	1'43"459	1'46"002
4.	Eddie Irvine	Ferrari/F300/185 (G)	1'44"780	1'44"655	1'43"270	1'46"035
5.	Giancarlo Fisichella	Benetton/Playlife/198/6 (B)	1'46"005	1'44"129	1'43"369	1'46"513
6.	Alexander Wurz	Benetton/Playlife/198/7 (B)	1'45"943	1'45"153	1'43"341	1'46"988
7.	David Coulthard	McLaren/Mercedes/MP4-13/4 (B)	1'44"138	1'43"006	1'42"347	1'44"812
8.	Mika Hakkinen	McLaren/Mercedes/MP4-13/6 (B)	1'43"946	1'43"175	1'41"838	1'45"691
9.	Damon Hill	Jordan/Honda/198/3 (G)	1'44"294	1'43"746	1'43"183	1'46"460
10.	Ralf Schumacher	Jordan/Honda/198/4 (G)	1'45"511	1'44"114	1'42"994	1'45"271
11.	Olivier Panis	Prost/Peugeot/AP01/5 (B)	1'46"484	-	1'45"197	1'47"588
12.	Jarno Trulli	Prost/Peugeot/AP01/6 (B)	1'45"611	1'45"343	1'44"844	1'48"133
14.	Jean Alesi	Sauber/Petronas/C17/6 (G)	1'44"546	1'44"399	1'43"663	1'46"936
15.	Johnny Herbert	Sauber/Petronas/C17/1 (G)	1'45"364	1'48"128	1'44"599	1'47"279
16.	Pedro Diniz	Arrows/A19/6 (B)	1'46"903	1'46"677	1'45"588	1'48"496
17.	Mika Salo	Arrows/A19/5 (B)	1'46"163	1'45"535	1'45"276	1'47"878
18.	Rubens Barrichello	Stewart/Ford/SF2/4 (B)	1'46"257	1'45"537	1'44"776	1'47"003
19.	Jos Verstappen	Stewart/Ford/SF2/3 (B)	1'47"086	1'46"543	1'45"623	1'47"461
20.	Ricardo Rosset	Tyrrell/Ford/026/2 (G)	1'49"986	1'48"652	forfeited	
21.	Toranosuke Takagi	Tyrrell/Ford/026/3 (G)	1'46"743	1'45"533	1'44"961	1'48"961
22.	Shinji Nakano	Minardi/Ford/M198/4 (B)	1'48"832	1'47"366	1'46"713	1'48"572
23.	Esteban Tuero	Minardi/Ford/M198/5 (B)	1'48"175	1'48"299	1'47"265	1'49"001

LAP CHART

	1	2	3	4	5	6	7	8	9	10	11	12	13	14	15	16	17	18	19	20	21
position:	1	2	3	4	5	6	7	8	9	10	11	12	13	14	15	16	17	18	19	20	21
start:	8	7	1	10	9	4	6	5	3	2	14	15	18	12	21	11	17	16	19	22	23
1	8	7	10	1	9	4	3	5	2	14	15	18	12	11	19	17	6	21	16	22	23
2	8	7	10	1	9	4	3	5	2	14	18	15	12	11	19	17	6	21	16	22	23
3	8	7	10	1	9	4	3	5	2	14	18	15	12	11	19	17	6	21	22	23	
4	8	7	10	1	9	3	4	5	2	14	18	15	12	11	19	6	17	21	22	23	
5	8	7	10	1	9	3	4	5	2	14	18	15	12	11	19	6	17	21	22	23	
6	8	7	10	1	9	3	4	5	2	14	18	15	12	11	6	19	17	21	22	23	
7	8	7	10	1	9	3	4	5	2	14	18	15	12	6	19	11	17	21	22	23	
8	8	7	10	1	9	3	4	5	2	14	18	15	12	6	19	17	21	22	23	11	
9	8	7	10	1	9	3	4	5	2	14	18	15	12	6	19	17	21	22	23	11	
10	8	7	10	1	9	3	4	5	2	14	18	15	12	6	19	17	21	22	23	11	
11	8	7	10	1	9	3	4	5	2	14	18	15	6	12	19	17	21	22	23	11	
12	8	7	10	1	9	3	4	5	2	14	18	15	6	12	19	17	21	22	23	11	
13	8	7	10	1	9	3	4	5	2	14	18	15	6	12	19	17	21	22	23	11	
14	8	7	1	10	9	3	4	5	2	14	18	15	6	12	19	17	21	22	11	23	
15	8	7	1	9	3	4	5	2	10	14	15	18	6	12	19	17	21	22	11	23	
16	8	7	1	9	3	4	5	2	10	14	15	6	12	19	18	17	21	22	11	23	
17	8	7	1	9	3	4	5	2	10	14	15	6	12	18	19	17	21	22	11	23	
18	8	7	1	9	3	4	5	2	10	14	15	6	12	18	19	17	21	22	11	23	
19	8	7	1	9	3	4	5	2	10	14	15	6	12	18	19	17	21	22	11	23	
20	8	7	1	9	3	4	5	2	10	14	15	6	12	18	19	17	21	22	11	23	
21	8	7	1	9	3	4	5	2	10	14	15	6	12	18	19	17	22	11	21	23	
22	8	7	1	9	3	4	10	5	2	6	15	12	14	18	19	17	22	11	21	23	
23	8	7	1	9	3	4	10	6	5	2	14	12	18	15	17	19	22	21	11	23	
24	8	7	3	4	1	10	9	5	2	14	18	15	6	12	17	22	19	21	11	23	
25	8	7	1	4	10	9	3	5	2	14	18	15	6	12	21	17	22	11	23		
26	7	8	1	10	9	3	5	4	2	14	18	15	6	12	21	17	22	11	23		
27	7	8	1	10	9	3	5	4	2	14	15	6	18	12	21	17	22	11	23		
28	8	7	1	10	9	3	5	4	2	14	15	6	12	21	17	22	11	23			
29	8	7	1	10	9	3	5	4	2	14	15	6	12	21	17	22	11	23			
30	8	7	1	9	3	10	5	4	2	14	15	6	12	21	17	22	11	23			
31	8	7	1	9	3	10	5	4	2	14	15	6	12	21	17	22	11	23			
32	8	7	1	9	3	10	5	4	2	14	15	6	12	21	17	22	11	23			
33	8	7	1	9	3	10	5	4	2	14	15	6	12	21	17	22	11	23			
34	8	7	1	9	3	10	5	4	2	14	15	6	12	21	17	22	11	23			
35	8	7	1	9	3	10	5	4	2	14	15	6	12	21	17	22	11	23			
36	8	7	1	9	3	10	5	4	2	14	15	6	12	21	17	22	11	23			
37	8	7	1	9	3	10	5	4	2	14	15	6	12	21	17	11	23				
38	8	7	1	9	3	10	5	4	2	14	6	12	21	17	11	23					
39	8	7	1	9	3	10	5	4	2	14	6	12	21	17	11	23					
40	8	7	1	9	3	10	5	4	2	14	6	12	21	17	11	23					
41	8	7	1	9	3	10	5	4	2	14	6	12	21	17	11	23					
42	8	7	1	9	3	10	5	4	2	14	6	12	21	17	11	23					
43	8	7	1	9	3	10	5	4	2	14	6	12	17	21	11	23					
44	8	7	1	9	3	10	5	4	2	14	6	12	21	17	11						
45	8	7	1	9	3	10	5	4	2	14	6										

Best result for a Bridgestone shod runner:

Mika Hakkinen, McLaren-Mercedes, 1st

CLASSIFICATION & RETIREMENTS

Pos	Driver	Team	Time
1.	Hakkinen	McLaren Mercedes	in 1h20'47"984
2.	Coulthard	McLaren Mercedes	at 0"427
3.	Villeneuve	Williams Mecachrome	at 2"578
4.	Hill	Jordan Mugen Honda	at 7"185
5.	M. Schum.	Ferrari	at 12"613
6.	R. Schum.	Jordan Mugen Honda	at 29"739
7.	Fisichella	Benetton Playlife	at 31"027
8.	Irvine	Ferrari	at 31"650
9.	Frentzen	Williams Mecachrome	at 32"785
10.	Alesi	Sauber Petronas	at 48"372
11.	Wurz	Benetton Playlife	at 57"995
12.	Trulli	Prost Peugeot	at 1 lap
13.	Takagi	Tyrrell Ford	at 1 lap
14.	Salo	Arrows	at 1 lap
15.	Panis	Prost Peugeot	at 1 lap
16.	Tuero	Minardi Ford	at 2 laps
Lap	**Driver**	**Team**	**Reason**
3	Diniz	Arrows	throttle
25	Verstappen	Stewart Ford	transmission
28	Barrichello	Stewart Ford	gearbox
37	Nakano	Minardi Ford	gearbox
38	Herbert	Sauber Petronas	gearbox

FASTEST LAPS

	Driver	Time	Lap
1.	Coulthard	1'46"116	17
2.	Hakkine	1'46"252	17
3.	Villeneuve	1'46"274	35
4.	Hill	1'46"317	37
5.	R. Schum.	1'46"350	37
6.	M. Schum.	1'46"381	37
7.	Irvine	1'46"459	36
8.	Fisichella	1'46"831	15
9.	Wurz	1'46"880	16
10.	Frentzen	1'46"890	32
11.	Alesi	1'46"964	43
12.	Herbert	1'47"345	15
13.	Barrichello	1'47"544	17
14.	Panis	1'47"775	41
15.	Trulli	1'48"446	27
16.	Takagi	1'48"608	22
17.	Salo	1'48"899	34
18.	Verstappen	1'49"147	5
19.	Nakano	1'49"424	17
20.	Tuero	1'50"314	12
21.	Diniz	1'51"259	2

ELEVENTH ROUND

GROSSER MOBIL 1 PREIS VON DEUTSCHLAND, HOCKENHEIM

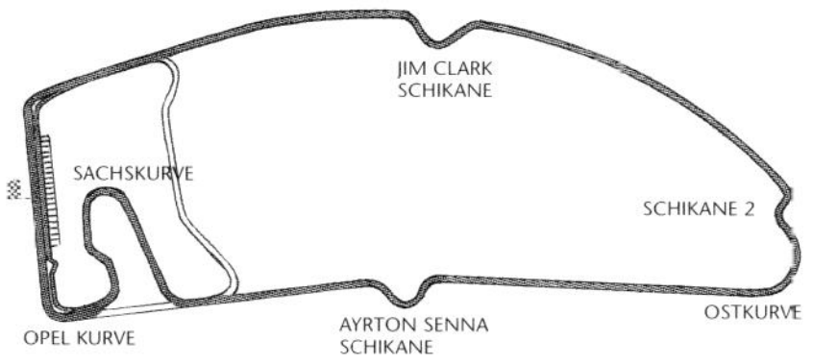

Date : August 2, 1998
Lenght : 6823 metres
Distance : 45 laps, 307.035 km
Weather : sunny and hot, 27 degrees

CHAMPIONSHIPS

(after eleven rounds)

Drivers :

1. Mika HAKKINEN 76
2. Michael SCHUMACHER 60
3. David COULTHARD 42
4. Eddie IRVINE 32
5. Alexander WURZ 17
6. Jacques VILLENEUVE 16
7. Giancarlo FISICHELLA 15
8. Heinz-Harald FRENTZEN 8
9. Rubens BARRICHELLO 4
   Ralf SCHUMACHER 4
11. Mika SALO 3
   Damon HILL 3
   Jean ALESI 3
14. Johnny HERBERT 1
   Pedro DINIZ 1
   Jan MAGNUSSEN 1

Constructors :

1. McLaren / Mercedes 118
2. Ferrari 92
3. Benetton / Playlife 32
4. Williams / Mecachrome 24
5. Jordan / Mugen Honda 7
6. Stewart / Ford 5
7. Arrows 4
   Sauber / Petronas 4

WEEK-END GOSSIP

- **One does not change a winning team**

The news was announced on Saturday, from the lips of Jurgen Hubbert, the president of the Daimler-Benz group, who was at Hockenheim. Mika Hakkinen and David Coulthard were confirmed as McLaren drivers for 1999. «*Hockenheim is our home grand prix,*» explained Hubbert. «*Therefore we wanted to announce our 1999 driver line-up. Mika and David have more than proved their worth in the past. They are supported and admired by all employees of the Daimler-Benz group.*»

- **Trulli: I give the AP01 4 out of 10**

In the early part of the race, Jarno Trulli was in fifth place and had hopes of scoring the Prost team's first points of the season. However, after thirty or so laps, the handling of his car started to deteriorate. Gradually slipping down the field, the Italian finally finished tenth. When the mechanics dismantled the car they found a broken rear shock absorber. If they had found the problem in the morning, the damper could have been changed before the race and Jarno would no doubt have scored some points. For the Italian it was just one more disappointment in a season that had been full of them. «*Yes, it has been a difficult year,*» he admitted. «*The car is not very good in every area. On a scale of 1 to 10 I would give it 4 and no more. There is no specific point that needs changing. The whole package has to improve.*»

- **Bridgestone brings special tyres**

With its long straights and tight chicanes, Hockenheim is particularly hard on the brakes. That prompted Bridgestone to bring a specially designed tyre for this track. «There are four very hard braking points on this track,» explained the Japanese company's technical director Hirohide Hamashima on the Thursday. «*The cars reach them at speed of up to 300 km/h and so it is important to have tyres with good traction in order to optimise the braking.*»

- **We don't want «HH» any more**

Williams technical director Patrick Head had some harsh words to say on the subject of Heinz-Harald Frentzen. «Heinz tends to go to sleep during the races,» was one of his more cutting remarks. Thus, the German driver could consider himself to be working his notice for the rest of the season. «HH» immediately investigated the possibility of going back to Sauber, although he was not excluding a career move to the United States, as he had always liked the Indycar series.

RACE SUMMARY

- At the start, the grid order is maintained. Mika Hakkinen is ahead of David Coulthard, while Ralf Schumacher gets the better of Damon Hill. Alexander Wurz gets it all wrong and brings up the rear.
- In the early laps, the McLarens whizz round in formation and Ralf Schumacher tries to catch them. Just when the Jordan is looking threatening, it makes its first pit stop.
- All the other drivers have opted to make only one refuelling stop. The McLarens are among the last to pit: lap 26 for Hakkinen and 27 for Coulthard.
- After the pit stops the positions remain the same. The McLarens slow down and are gradually caught by Villeneuve, Hill and Michael Schumacher. The top five are covered by 13 seconds at the flag.

◁ *On the Wednesday before the German GP, Michael Schumacher was captain of the F1 All-stars in a soccer match at Mannheim. The organised counted 27,000 paying spectators and the profits all went to charity.*

GYAR
DIJ
Marlboro
Shell
GOODYEAR
Asprey
TECHNOGYM
Marlboro
OMP
M. Schumacher

Abracadabra in Budapest

How do you overtake two McLarens that are just a bit slower than you on a track where it is reputedly impossible to overtake? Ferrari technical director Ross Brawn organised a bit of magic to make it happen in the middle of the Hungarian Grand Prix, by etting Michael Schumacher to refuel three times instead of two.
The strategy worked perfectly. Suffering from handling problems, Mika Hakkinen eventually finished a very distant sixth. The Scuderia had won in style.

MARLBORO MAGYAR NAGYDÍJ BUDAPEST

Statu quo in qualifying

▷

«You cannot even go off the road in private now.» Giancarlo Fisichella parks his Benetton in front of a wall of photographers. The Budapest track was the scene of many off-track excursions during practice, mainly because the surface was very dusty.

«I am very optimistic. Our car is set up perfectly for the race and we should be competitive, whether it is wet or dry.» Listening to that confident prediction, one could be forgiven for thinking Michael Schumacher had just put his Ferrari on pole for the Hungarian Grand Prix.

He was not of course, as yet again the two McLarens had made the front row their own private property. Until now, Schumacher had never been on pole this season, which had not prevented him from winning four grands prix. «Our car always works better in the race than in qualifying,» he continued. *«Which makes me confident, especially as the gap to the McLarens is very small, so third place is not a surprise. Now we must concentrate on setting up the car for the race.»*

Although blocked by Heinz-Harald Frentzen who was on his slowing down lap, Schumacher had given his all during the session, locking his wheels far more often than usual. *«Yes, I locked the brakes a lot. During qualifying it is not so important because you change the tyres for each run. I tried to get on the front row and at the end of the day, we are not far off.»*

If he was to get out in front, the Ferrari driver would first have to get the jump on the McLarens in this race which was crucial for the championship. Because if Mika Hakkinen finished ahead of the German once again, the latter's chances of getting the title would hypothetically be much slimmer.

It was however, the most likely scenario, if the McLarens got away cleanly. *«I am very happy to be back on pole as it is almost impossible to overtake on this track,»* was Mika Hakkinen's comment at the end of the session. *«Only the racing line is useable. Once you go off it, your tyres pick up dust and two or three laps are needed to clean them up. As you have to move off line to overtake, this makes passing almost non-existent.»*

In fact, the Finn had hoped to have a bigger lead over the German. *«We have modified the car since yesterday and I did not think Michael would be this close. At the end of the session the ambient temperature dropped by five or six degrees and the win started to blow against the traffic down the main straight. I think that for the last ten minutes, this must have cost a good tenth per lap. I could not improve without taking unnecessary risks.»*

In second spot, David Coulthard had once again been unable to beat his team mate and yet again the gap between them was tiny. *«I made a complete mess of my third run,»* said the Scotsman. *«I wanted to be running just before the end and when I arrived at the second last hairpin, I asked how much time was left. I was told '10 seconds.' There was someone going slowly in front of me and I could not cross the line before the flag.»*

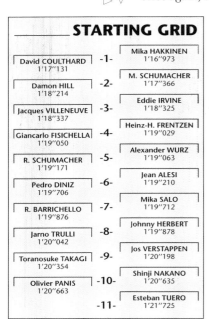

(Left)
David Coulthard breaks down during practice. But unlike at the Brazilian race, where the Scotsman returned on foot, this time he did not leave his car unattended for a second. He had been given such a dressing down by Ron Dennis at Interlagos (see page 105) he swore he would not be caught out again.
(Right)
...and he makes it clear to the photographers. «You will not photograph the car's back end. You will have to make do with mine!»

▷ ▽

STARTING GRID

David COULTHARD 1'17"131	-1-	Mika HAKKINEN 1'16"973
Damon HILL 1'18"214	-2-	M. SCHUMACHER 1'17"366
Jacques VILLENEUVE 1'18"337	-3-	Eddie IRVINE 1'18"325
Giancarlo FISICHELLA 1'19"050	-4-	Heinz-H. FRENTZEN 1'19"029
R. SCHUMACHER 1'19"171	-5-	Alexander WURZ 1'19"063
Pedro DINIZ 1'19"706	-6-	Jean ALESI 1'19"210
R. BARRICHELLO 1'19"876	-7-	Mika SALO 1'19"712
Jarno TRULLI 1'20"042	-8-	Johnny HERBERT 1'19"878
Toranosuke TAKAGI 1'20"354	-9-	Jos VERSTAPPEN 1'20"198
Olivier PANIS 1'20"663	-10-	Shinji NAKANO 1'20"635
	-11-	Esteban TUERO 1'21"725

Schumacher piles on the pressure

◁ *They're off! For now, everything is going well for Mika Hakkinen after another perfect start from pole position.*

What a talent! If proof were still needed that the double world champion has real class, then his win in Budapest provided it yet again. It also confirmed the tactical genius of Ross Brawn, Ferrari's technical director.

On the talent and tactics front, the Schumacher - Ferrari team had to pull out all the stops to beat McLaren-Mercedes in Budapest, such was the apparent superiority of the Anglo-German cars on this track. Practice had gone according to plan for them and another one-two finish looked on the cards, which would have also served to pretty much bury any hopes Michael Schumacher had of winning the title.

However, one hour later, the silver arrows were off-target. *«At first we had planned two pit stops,»* explained Jean Todt, the Scuderia's sporting director. *«But when Michael got stuck behind the two McLarens, we had two alternatives: stick to our original plan and finish third or try and gamble on three stops. It was Ross who pushed for this second solution and he was right. As it meant the car could take on less fuel, it meant we gained two seconds during the stops.»*

Told over the radio of this change of plan, at first Michael Schumacher could not see the genius behind the idea. *«At that time, I was fourth and stuck behind Jacques* (Villeneuve). *When we decided to stop three times it would have been better to be out in front and pulling away.»*

The German found himself leading after the second set of pit stops, with about 30 laps remaining. But unlike his rivals, he still had to refuel for a third and final time. *«When I left the pits, Ross told me I had 19 laps to pull out 25 seconds on Hakkinen. I said that I would do my best thank you!»*

And his best is what he did. He lapped quicker and quicker, sometimes increasing his lead by as much as two seconds per lap, except when he had a little off-track excursion which had not been part of the plan. Sliding with all four wheels, he let the Ferrari take him onto the grass before bringing it nicely back onto the track. «From the pit wall we could see the car was not damaged,» stated Jean Todt. *«But we were worried the incident might have cost us the three decisive seconds four our plan to work.»*

Putting in some mind-blowing lap times, the German somehow won his engineers' crazy bet. With fifteen laps to go, he made one last stop, without losing the lead, thus taking a victory which was as astonishing as it was unexpected. *«To be honest it is one of the best wins of my career,»* admitted the German. *«But it was also one of the hardest. Apart from the last part of the race I was flat out all the time. It was like doing 60 qualifying laps. An extraordinary day.»*

Sylvester Stallone continues research into his future film about Formula 1. On the grid, he did not yet know he was taking a picture of the eventual third placed man. ▽

IN THE POINTS

1.	M. SCHUMACHER	Scuderia Ferrari Marlboro	1 h 45'25"550
2.	David COULTHARD	West McLaren Mercedes	at 9"433
3.	Jacques VILLENEUVE	Winfield Williams	at 44"444
4.	Damon HILL	B&H Jordan Mugen Honda	at 55"075
5.	Heinz-H. FRENTZEN	Winfield Williams	at 56"510
6.	Mika HAKKINEN	West McLaren Mercedes	at 1 lap

Fastest lap : M. SCHUMACHER, lap 60, 1'19"286, avg. 180.349 km/h

Formula 1 can occasionally be aesthetically pleasing as demonstrated by these suspension mounting problems.

Jacques Villeneuve bad loser

There are no two ways about it, Jacques Villeneuve still harbours a grudge against Michael Schumacher and never misses a chance to make it known. In Budapest, the Canadian went so far as to say the German's win had been down to luck. «*It was the performance of the Goodyear tyres on this track which gave him the win. He was lucky, but it will not happen again. The Bridgestone people won't make the same mistake twice.*»
Commenting on Michael Schumacher's trip onto the grass when the German was in full attack mode, Villeneuve added that: «*It was Michael's typical off-track excursion when he is leading. No doubt it is a way of making it look more spectacular when he knows he is going to win.*» This ill feeling was enough to leave most listeners speechless.
Having finished third, the Canadian was nevertheless pleased with his day. «*The car was working very well, except that the power steering packed up after 10 laps. Luckily, I am in good physical shape which allowed me to keep going until the end. I have had power steering for the past two years and I am not used to putting so much effort into the steering wheel. Apart from that I had strange lights flashing in the cockpit. I asked the team by radio what it meant, but they did not answer. I thought it was better not to know.*»
This was the Canadian's second successive visit to the podium.

Schumacher deflates his critics

Not only is Michael Schumacher gifted with a magic touch at the wheel, he is also the most at ease of the current crop of drivers, when it comes to dealing with press conferences. Sure of himself, he never loses his cool and patiently puts forward his arguments.
On Thursday, after an official press conference, the German decided to stay in the press office to vent his anger about accusations that the Ferrari was not legal - rumours initiated by McLaren boss Ron Dennis (see page 167.)
More loquacious than ever, Michael Schumacher produced a string of arguments to prove the legality of his F300. «*I am literally shocked by the rumours put out about our car. Rather than accusing us in this way, Mr. Dennis should lodge an official protest. That way we would know where we stand. At Hockenheim I asked him to do it, but he did not deem it necessary.*»
And the reason for this was that Ron Dennis and technical director Adrian Newey, the technical director of the team, reckoned it was possible to produce anti-spin which is impossible to detect during scrutineering. This argument in no way satisfied Michael Schumacher. «*If he says that it is because they know exactly how to do it. They could therefore show the scrutineers exactly how they think we are cheating.*»
What angers the Ferrari driver the most, is the criticism placed on his own performance. «Not everyone is pleased when I win. And people are happy to believe rumours they want to believe, even if there is not the slightest proof. Our car has been checked an incredible number of times and it has never been found illegal.»
Then came the counter-attack. «*If you watch Mika Hakkinen's starts, you will see that last year he messed up 10 out of 17. This year however he has made excellent starts. The man has not changed, which means his car controls wheelspin much better. I am not claiming McLaren is cheating. On the contrary, I reckon their system is legal. I am convinced no teams are cheating in F1. The stakes are far too high. We are supported by Marlboro and Shell, two companies of international repute. Imagine the way these companies would be discredited if we were found to be cheating. It is impossible to take such a risk.*»
Convinced? Everyone has to decide for themselves.

Still not a single point in sight and soon there will be nails left to chew. It was a killer summer for the Prosts. In Budapest on Saturday, the team announced that both drivers had re-signed with the team for 1999. On Sunday, Jarno Trulli retired on lap 29, while Olivier Panis finished 12th (photo on right.) ▽

PRACTICE TIMES

No	Driver	Car/Engine/Chassis	Practice Friday	Practice Saturday	Qualifying	Warm-up
1.	Jacques Villeneuve	Williams/Mécachrome/FW20/5 (G)	1'20"441	1'19"016	1'18"337	1'20"580
2.	Heinz-Harald Frentzen	Williams/Mécachrome/FW20/4 (G)	1'21"218	1'19"107	1'19"029	1'19"967
3.	Michael Schumacher	Ferrari/F300/188 (G)	1'20"439	1'18"588	1'17"366	1'20"325
4.	Eddie Irvine	Ferrari/F300/185 (G)	1'20"778	1'19"252	1'18"325	1'20"935
5.	Giancarlo Fisichella	Benetton/Mécachrome/198/4 (B)	1'21"110	1'18"792	1'19"050	1'21"334
6.	Alexander Wurz	Benetton/Mécachrome/198/7 (B)	1'22"297	1'19"286	1'19"063	1'21"924
7.	David Coulthard	McLaren/Mercedes/MP4-13/7 (B)	1'19"989	1'17"495	1'17"131	1'19"555
8.	Mika Hakkinen	McLaren/Mercedes/MP4-13/5 (B)	1'20"186	1'17"337	1'16"973	1'18"694
9.	Damon Hill	Jordan/Honda/198/3 (G)	1'20"779	1'19"091	1'18"214	1'20"906
10.	Ralf Schumacher	Jordan/Honda/198/4 (G)	1'21"198	1'19"183	1'19"171	1'20"385
11.	Olivier Panis	Prost/Peugeot/AP01/5 (B)	1'22"442	1'20"920	1'20"663	1'22"344
12.	Jarno Trulli	Prost/Peugeot/AP01/7 (B)	1'25"700	1'21"585	1'20"042	1'2"920
14.	Jean Alesi	Sauber/Petronas/C17/6 (G)	1'21"990	1'19"449	1'19"210	1'2"799
15.	Johnny Herbert	Sauber/Petronas/C17/7 (G)	1'21"571	1'19"800	1'19"878	1'2"441
16.	Pedro Diniz	Arrows/A19/1 (B)	1'23"450	1'20"589	1'19"706	1'23"231
17.	Mika Salo	Arrows/A19/5 (B)	1'22"145	1'20"552	1'19"712	1'22"119
18.	Rubens Barrichello	Stewart/Ford/SF2/4 (B)	1'21"414	1'19"936	1'19"876	1'22"095
19.	Jos Verstappen	Stewart/Ford/SF2/3 (B)	1'21"903	1'20"883	1'20"198	1'22"961
20.	Ricardo Rosset	Tyrrell/Ford/026/4 (G)	1'25"611	1'23"279	1'23"140	not qualif.
21.	Toranosuke Takagi	Tyrrell/Ford/026/5 (G)	1'23"261	1'21"634	1'20"354	1'22"704
22.	Shinji Nakano	Minardi/Ford/M198/4 (B)	1'22"940	1'21"373	1'20"635	1'22"991
23.	Esteban Tuero	Minardi/Ford/M198/5 (B)	1'23"671	1'22"008	1'21"725	1'23"685

LAP CHART

position:	1	2	3	4	5	6	7	8	9	10	11	12	13	14	15	[illegible]	17	18	19	20	21
start:	8	7	3	9	4	1	2	5	6	10	14	16	17	18	15	[illegible]	19	[illegible]	22	11	23
1	8	7	3	4	9	1	2	6	14	5	16	17	10	15	12	[illegible]	19	[illegible]	22	21	11
2	8	7	3	4	9	1	2	6	14	5	16	17	10	15	12	[illegible]	19	[illegible]	22	21	11
3	8	7	3	4	9	1	2	6	14	5	16	17	10	15	12	[illegible]	19	[illegible]	22	21	11
4	8	7	3	4	9	1	2	6	14	5	16	17	10	15	12	[illegible]	19	[illegible]	22	21	11
5	8	7	3	4	9	1	2	6	14	5	16	17	10	15	12	[illegible]	19	[illegible]	21	23	11
6	8	7	3	4	9	1	2	6	14	5	16	17	10	15	12	[illegible]	19	[illegible]	21	23	11
7	8	7	3	4	9	1	2	6	14	5	16	17	10	15	12	[illegible]	19	[illegible]	21	23	11
8	8	7	3	4	9	1	2	6	14	5	16	17	10	15	12	[illegible]	19	[illegible]	21	23	11
9	8	7	3	4	9	1	2	6	14	5	16	17	10	15	12	[illegible]	19	[illegible]	21	23	11
10	8	7	3	4	9	1	2	6	14	5	16	17	10	15	12	[illegible]	19	[illegible]	21	23	11
11	8	7	3	4	9	1	2	6	14	5	16	17	10	15	12	[illegible]	19	[illegible]	21	23	11
12	8	7	3	4	9	1	2	6	14	5	16	17	10	15	12	[illegible]	19	[illegible]	21	23	11
13	8	7	3	9	4	1	2	6	14	5	16	17	10	15	12	[illegible]	19	[illegible]	21	23	11
14	8	7	3	9	1	2	6	14	5	16	17	10	15	12	18	[illegible]	22	[illegible]	11		
15	8	7	3	9	1	2	6	14	5	16	17	10	15	12	18	[illegible]	22	[illegible]	11		
16	8	7	3	9	1	2	6	14	5	16	17	10	15	12	18	[illegible]	22	[illegible]	11		
17	8	7	3	9	1	2	6	14	5	16	17	10	15	12	18	[illegible]	22	[illegible]	11		
18	8	7	3	9	1	2	6	14	5	16	17	10	15	12	18	[illegible]	22	[illegible]	21		
19	8	7	3	9	1	2	6	14	5	16	10	15	12	18	19	[illegible]	11	2			
20	8	7	3	9	1	2	6	14	5	16	10	15	12	18	19	[illegible]	11	2			
21	8	7	3	9	1	2	6	5	14	10	16	15	12	18	19	[illegible]	11	2			
22	8	7	3	9	1	2	6	5	14	10	16	15	12	18	19	[illegible]	22	2			
23	8	7	3	9	1	2	6	5	14	10	16	15	12	18	19	[illegible]	22	2			
24	8	7	3	1	9	2	6	5	14	10	15	16118	19	11	[illegible]	22	2				
25	8	7	3	1	2	6	5	14	9	10	15	16	19	11	12	[illegible]	22	2			
26	8	7	1	3	2	6	5	14	9	10	15	16	19	12	11	[illegible]	22	2			
27	8	7	1	3	2	6	5	14	9	15	10	12	16	18	19	[illegible]	22	2			
28	8	7	1	3	2	5	6	14	9	15	10	12	16	18	19	[illegible]	22	2			
29	8	7	1	3	2	5	14	9	6	15	10	16	18	19	11	[illegible]	21				
30	8	7	1	3	9	14	2	6	5	15	10	16	18	19	11	[illegible]	21				
31	8	7	3	1	9	2	6	5	14	15	10	16	18	19	11	[illegible]	21				
32	8	7	3	9	1	2	6	5	14	15	10	16	18	19	11	[illegible]	21				
33	8	7	3	9	1	2	6	5	14	10	15	16	18	19	11	[illegible]	21				
34	8	7	3	9	1	2	6	5	14	10	15	16	18	19	11	[illegible]	21				
35	8	7	3	9	1	2	6	5	14	10	15	16	18	19	11	[illegible]	21				
36	8	7	3	9	1	2	6	5	14	10	15	16118	19	11	[illegible]	21					
37	8	7	3	9	1	2	6	5	14	10	15	16	18	19	11	[illegible]	21				
38	8	7	3	9	1	2	6	5	14	10	15	16	18	19	11	[illegible]	21				
39	8	7	3	9	1	2	6	5	14	10	15	16	18	19	11	[illegible]	21				
40	8	7	3	9	1	2	6	5	14	10	15	16	18	19	11	[illegible]	21				
41	8	7	3	9	1	2	6	5	14	10	15	16	18	19	11	[illegible]	21				
42	8	7	3	9	1	2	6	5	14	10	15	16	18	19	11	[illegible]	21				
43	8	7	3	9	1	2	6	5	14	10	15	16	18	19	11	[illegible]	21				
44	8	7	3	9	1	2	6	5	14	10	15	16	18	19	11	[illegible]	21				
45	8	3	7	9	1	2	6	5	14	10	15	16	18	19	11	[illegible]	21				
46	8	3	7	9	1	2	6	5	14	10	15	16	18	19	11	[illegible]	21				
47	3	8	7	9	1	2	6	5	14	10	15	18	16	19	11	[illegible]	21				
48	3	8	7	9	1	2	6	5	14	10	15	18	19	11	16	[illegible]	21				
49	3	8	7	9	1	2	6	5	14	10	15	19	11	16	18	21	22				
50	3	8	7	9	1	2	14	5	6	10	15	19	11	16	18	21	22				
51	3	8	7	1	9	2	14	6	10	5	15	11	16	18	19	21	22				
52	3	7	8	1	2	9	6	14	5	10	15	16	18	19	11	21	22				
53	3	7	8	1	2	9	6	14	5	15	10	16	18	19	11	21	22				
54	3	7	8	1	2	9	6	14	5	15	10	16	19	11	18	21	22				
55	3	7	8	1	9	2	6	14	5	15	10	16	19	11	21	22					
56	3	7	8	1	9	2	6	14	5	15	10	16	19	11	21	22					
57	3	7	8	1	9	2	6	14	5	15	10	16	19	11	21	22					
58	3	7	8	1	9	2	6	14	5	15	10	16	19	11	21	22					
59	3	7	8	1	9	2	6	14	5	15	10	16	19	11	21	22					
60	3	7	8	1	9	2	6	14	5	15	10	16	11	19	21	22					
61	3	7	8	1	9	2	6	14	5	15	10	16	11	19	21	22					
62	3	7	8	1	9	2	6	14	5	15	10	16	11	19	21	22					
63	3	7	8	1	9	2	6	14	5	15	10	16	11	19	21	22					
64	3	7	8	1	9	2	6	14	5	15	10	16	11	19	21	22					
65	3	7	8	1	9	2	6	14	5	15	10	16	11	19	21	22					
66	3	7	8	1	9	2	6	14	5	15	10	16	11	19	21	22					
67	3	7	1	8	9	2	6	14	5	15	10	16	11	19	21	22					
68	3	7	1	8	9	2	6	14	5	15	10	16	11	19	21	22					
69	3	7	1	8	9	2	6	14	5	15	10	16	11	19	21	22					
70	3	7	1	8	9	2	14	5	15	10	16	11	19	21	22						
71	3	7	1	9	2	8	14	5	15	10	16	11	19	21	22						
72	3	7	1	9	2	8	14	5	15	10	16	11	19	21	22						
73	3	7	1	9	2	8	14	5	15	10	16	11	19	21	22						
74	3	7	1	9	2	8	14	5	10	15	16	11	19	21	22						
75	3	7	1	9	2	8	14	5	10	15											
76	3	7	1	9	2	8	14	5	10	15											
77	3	7	1	9	2																

CHAMPIONSHIPS

(after twelve rounds)

Drivers :

1.	Mika HAKKINEN	77
2.	Michael SCHUMACHER	70
3.	David COULTHARD	48
4.	Eddie IRVINE	32
5.	Jacques VILLENEUVE	20
6.	Alexander WURZ	17
7.	Giancarlo FISICHELLA	15
8.	Heinz-Harald FRENTZEN	10
9.	Damon HILL	6
10.	Rubens BARRICHELLO	4
	Ralf SCHUMACHER	4
12.	Mika SALO	3
	Jean ALESI	3
14.	Johnny HERBERT	1
	Pedro DINIZ	1
	Jan MAGNUSSEN	1

Constructors :

1.	McLaren / Mercedes	125
2.	Ferrari	102
3.	Benetton / Playlife	32
4.	Williams / Mecachrome	30
5.	Jordan / Mugen Honda	10
6.	Stewart / Ford	5
7.	Arrows	4
	Sauber / Petronas	4

CLASSIFICATION & RETIREMENTS

Pos	Driver	Team	Time
1.	M. Schum.	Ferrari	in 1h45'25"550
2.	Coulthard	McLaren Mercedes	at 9"433
3.	Villeneuve	Williams Mecachrome	at 44"444
4.	Hill	Jordan Mugen Honda	at 55"075
5.	Frentzen	Williams Mecachrome	at 56"510
6.	Hakkinen	McLaren Mercedes	at 1 lap
7.	Alesi	Sauber Petronas	at 1 lap
8.	Fisichella	Benetton Playlife	at 1 lap
9.	R. Schum.	Jordan Mugen Honda	at 1 lap
10.	Herbert	Sauber Petronas	at 1 lap
11.	Diniz	Arrows	at 3 laps
12.	Panis	Prost Peugeot	at 3 laps
13.	Verstappen	Stewart Ford	at 3 laps
14.	Takagi	Tyrrell Ford	at 3 laps
15.	Nakano	Minardi Ford	at 3 laps
16.	Wurz	Benetton Playlife	gearbox

Lap	Driver	Team	Reason
14	Tuero	Minardi Ford	engine
14	Irvine	Ferrari	gearbox
19	Salo	Arrows	gearbox
29	Trulli	Prost Peugeot	engine
55	Barrichello	Stewart Ford	gearbox

FASTEST LAPS

	Driver	Time	lap
1.	M. Schum.	1'19"286	60
2.	Villeneuve	1'20"078	57
3.	Frentzen	1'20"356	57
4.	Hakkinen	1'20"545	30
5.	Coulthard	1'20"546	28
6.	Hill	1'20"680	75
7.	R. Schum.	1'20"875	71
8.	Irvine	1'20"984	11
9.	Fisichella	1'21"060	48
10.	Herbert	1'21"329	37
11.	Alesi	1'21"439	35
12.	Wurz	1'21"479	48
13.	Takagi	1'22"495	48
14.	Panis	1'22"538	17
15.	Barrichello	1'23"294	50
16.	Trulli	1'23"318	25
17.	Diniz	1'23"429	43
18.	Nakano	1'23"573	50
19.	Verstappen	1'23"644	48
20.	Salo	1'23"716	18
21.	Tuero	1'25"450	7

TWELTH ROUND

MARLBORO MAGYAR NAGYDÍJ, BUDAPEST

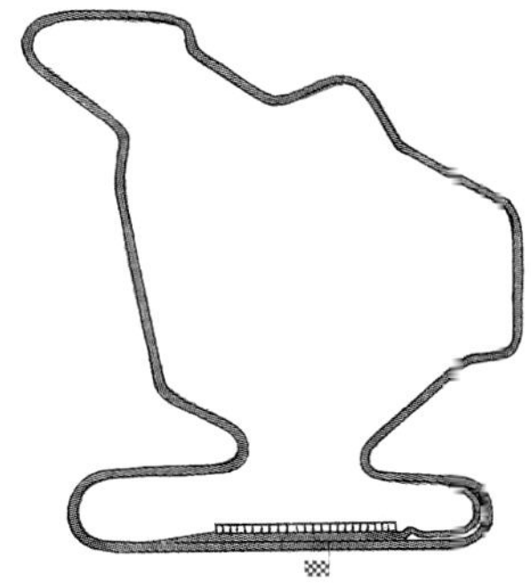

Date : August 16, 1998
Lenght : 3972 meters
Distance : 77 laps, 305.844 km
Weather : hot and sunny, 32 degrees

RACE SUMMARY

- When the red lights go out, Mika Hakkinen makes an impeccable start ahead of David Coulthard and Michael Schumacher.
- The Ferrari driver manages to hang onto the McLarens in the early stages. In fourth place, Eddie Irvine is soon left behind and when he retires, Damon Hill is there to inherit fourth place.
- It is only after the first fuel stops that Michael Schumacher steps up the pace. He appears to be taking about one second a lap off the McLarens.
- After the second set of pit stops, Michael Schumacher is in the lead and pushes very hard. He manages to pull out a big enough advantage to make a third pit stop without losing the lead, which he keeps to the end.
- Further back, Hakkinen's car is crippled and he finishes one lap down in 6th place.

WEEK-END GOSSIP

- **The cavalry are coming**

Was it panic mode at Goodyear? On Thursday, Bridgestone's sporting director declared that the Japanese company would not supply a single extra team in 1999 for technical reasons. This was unsettling news to say the least. It was probably to put out this fire that the American company's competitions director, Stu Grant made a lightning visit to the paddock on Saturday morning. He had not come to many races this year and his decision to pop over had only been taken on Friday. He spent Saturday in discussion with several teams.

- **The return of the steering brake?**

Faced with the difficulties of policing traction control devices, there were many voices from within the teams who asked for these to be legalised in the regulations. FIA President Max Mosley was considering doing just that in 1999. «Max advised me he was thinking of opening up the regulation,» admitted Ron Dennis on Saturday. «We immediately asked for a clarification as to the proposed changes as far as brakes are concerned.» It seemed the silver arrows might yet again be authorised to use the steering brake which permits the rear brakes to be applied independently of one another under acceleration to reduce wheelspin.

- **Jacques beats Michael.....on the motorway**

By chance, Jacques Villeneuve and Michael Schumacher found themselves side by side at traffic lights after leaving the Kempinski hotel on Friday morning. The former in a Mercedes, and the latter in an Alfa Romeo. They then had a mad duel to see who would be first to get to the track. Cutting through traffic, Michael Schumacher was the first to get to the motorway that leads from the city centre to the Hungaroring, which meant he was very surprised to find Villeneuve's Mercedes already parked when he got to the track. The Canadian was delighted with the trick he had played by asking for a police escort to cut through the traffic jams.
Not everyone appreciated this behaviour. After qualifying, an English journalist asked the German if his drive had been compatible with his work for the FIA promoting road safety. «Were you there to see what went on?» asked Schumacher. «I did not put anyone in danger and I certainly was driving less dangerously than most Hungarians.» It has to be said that on the wide Budapest avenues, street racing seems to be the national sport.

Budapest is a popular race on the calendar ▽ and not just because of the majorettes.

MILD SEVEN
6
Safra

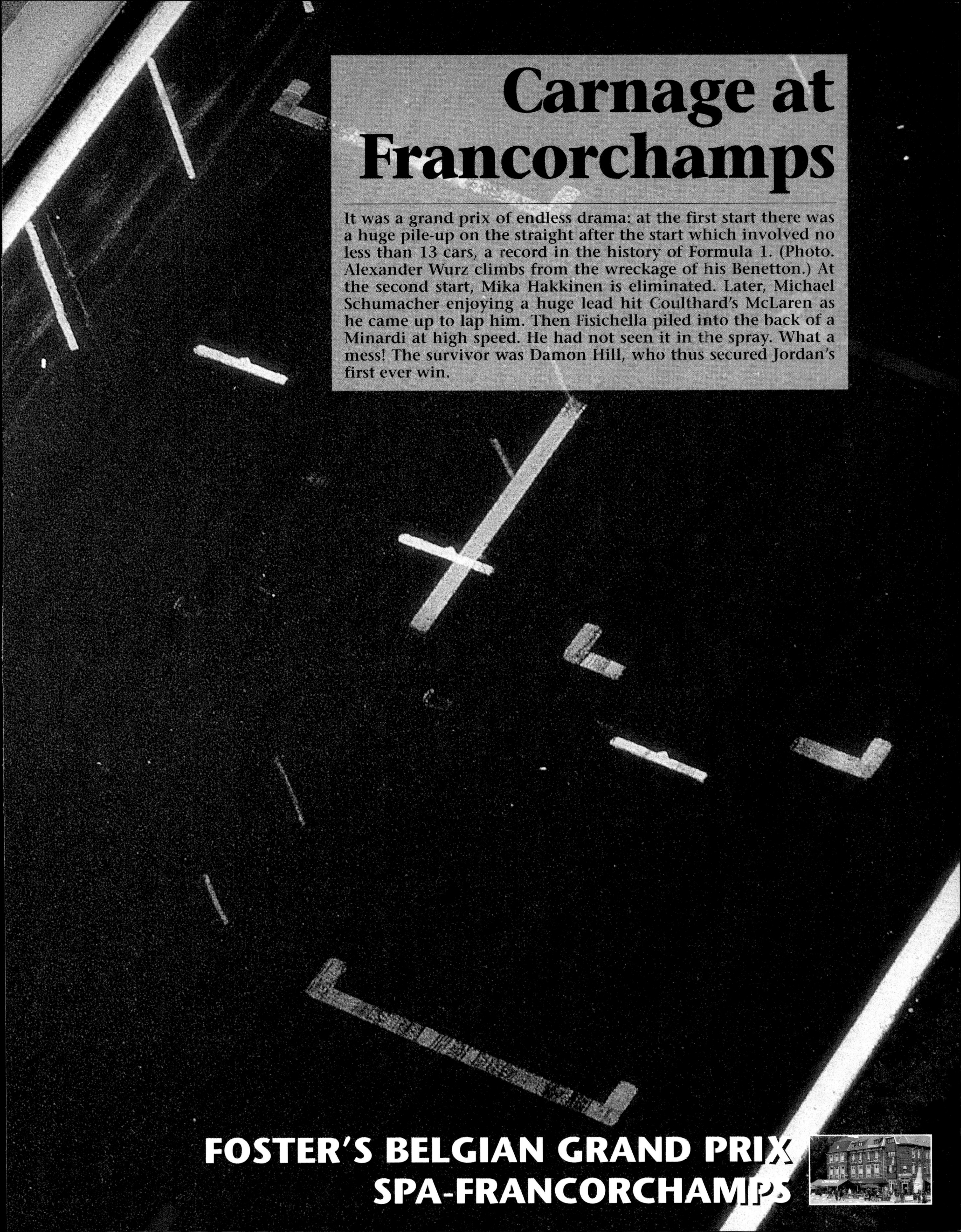

Carnage at Francorchamps

It was a grand prix of endless drama: at the first start there was a huge pile-up on the straight after the start which involved no less than 13 cars, a record in the history of Formula 1. (Photo. Alexander Wurz climbs from the wreckage of his Benetton.) At the second start, Mika Hakkinen is eliminated. Later, Michael Schumacher enjoying a huge lead hit Coulthard's McLaren as he came up to lap him. Then Fisichella piled into the back of a Minardi at high speed. He had not seen it in the spray. What a mess! The survivor was Damon Hill, who thus secured Jordan's first ever win.

FOSTER'S BELGIAN GRAND PRIX SPA-FRANCORCHAMPS

A cloud of dust is kicked up by Mika Salo's accident. During practice, the Raidillon at Spa had claimed yet more victims. On Friday, Jacques Villeneuve had a scary moment there. «It was the best accident of my F1 career,» he joked. On Saturday it was the turn of his mate, Mika Salo to lose control of his car at this daunting spot. It was a bigger impact than the Canadian's and the Finn had to be taken to hospital in Liege by helicopter. He was suffering from severe headaches. Once back at the track, Salo bravely took part in the qualifying session and hauled himself to 18thplace on the grid. Tough these F1 guys!

Never mind how, as long as we are on pole

The two McLarens lived up to their reputation. At the end of Saturday's qualifying session, the two silver arrows monopolised the front row of the grid for the ninth time this season; Mika preceding David as usual.
This was business as usual, but the surprise came from the stopwatch rather than the order: Mika Hakkinen had qualified in a time eight tenths quicker than Jacques Villeneuve's pole from last year. On a circuit like Spa, such progress is surprising to say the least, given modifications introduced to the technical regulations. With the reduction in car width and the introduction of grooved tyres, it seemed unbelievable that the cars could go quicker here than the previous year.
«It's true, I cannot understand how it happened,» said a surprised Hakkinen. *«I think it is because the drivers have improved this year!»* Basically the Finn did not care about it as long as he was on pole. When it was pointed out to him that he was over a second quicker than his main rival Michael Schumacher, Mika was no longer surprised. *«I am not surprised with the gap but it means nothing to me. I am here to win and score the maximum number of points for the championship and I am not really interested about what is happening at Ferrari.»*
No doubt the Finn's nose grew a few centimetres after such a remark.

Damon Hill is delighted with third on the grid

Jarno Trulli qualified 13th at Spa. «We made good progress this afternoon. For the first time, I passed through the "Raidillon" flat-out. Quite impressive!

Judging by the atmosphere under the Jordan motorhome awning on Saturday afternoon, one could believe the team had just won the Belgian Grand Prix. After 126 attempts, it was still looking for its first F1 win. But, truth was, the champagne flowing into the glasses was to celebrate Damon Hill's third place in qualifying- his best performance of the season. *«It's absolutely fantastic,»* he rejoiced. *«I am not happy, I am super-happy. For me this is almost as good as a win, because we are coming from a long way back. At the start of the season, our car was a disaster and now we have completely turned the situation around. It has cost a lot and made a big hole in the budget. We had to work like mad. The Jordan boys and those at Mugen-Honda have put in an enormous effort. This is the result.»*
From now on, Damon Hill reckoned his car was near perfect. *«I found just the right set up,»* he said happily. *«But I have to say I was good. I really drove well. It was great fun this afternoon.»* Having twice finished fourth in Hockenheim and Budapest, the Englishman was hoping to get on the podium on Sunday.

STARTING GRID

David COULTHARD 1'48"845	-1-	Mika HAKKINEN 1'48"682
M. SCHUMACHER 1'49"797	-2-	Damon HILL 1'49"728
Jacques VILLENEUVE 1'50"204	-3-	Eddie IRVINE 1'50"189
R. SCHUMACHER 1'50"501	-4-	G. FISICHELLA 1'50"462
Jean ALESI 1'51"189	-5-	Heinz-H. FRENTZEN 1'50"686
Johnny HERBERT 1'51"851	-6-	Alexander WURZ 1'51"648
R. BARRICHELLO 1'52"670	-7-	Jarno TRULLI 1'52"572
Pedro DINIZ 1'53"037	-8-	Olivier PANIS 1'52"784
Mika SALO 1'53"207	-9-	Jos VERSTAPPEN 1'53"149
Ricardo ROSSET 1'54"850	-10-	Toranosuke TAKAGI 1'53"237
Esteban TUERO 1'55"520	-11-	Shinji NAKANO 1'55"084

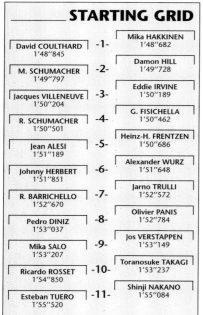

The Englishman survived the terrible weather conditions

A Hill emerges through the waves

Of course Damon Hill profited from the misfortune of others to take this race, but this is not take anything away from his performance. At Spa, you needed talent but also consistency and speed to triumph in the deluge.
Always a front runner throughout the race, the Englishman only had to give best to Michael Schumacher. *«It is an extraordinary race of course,»* he congratulated himself. *«I think we deserved it. We were competitive all weekend and this one-two finish proves it. Actually, we thought the weather would improve and I took the start with dry settings, which did not make life easy. The car would often aquaplane and that is why I had to let Michael by.»*
For Hill, the chequered flag could not come quickly enough. «It was really a very tough grand prix,» he continued. *«At one point I touched Trulli's Prost, luckily not seriously and I lost count of how many slides I had. The rain varied in strength at different points on the track. You had to be very careful.»*

Ralf wanted to win

Lap 32. With the debris from Fisichella's Benetton having been cleared away, the safety car went in and the race restarted for one last short spring to the finish. The field had closed up behind the safety car and the gaps were down to nothing. But Damon Hill was ahead of his team mate, Ralf Schumacher, so it seemed logical that there would be no change at the front.
This did not suit Ralf who attacked right from *the braking point at the first corner. «My plan was to attack Damon at this point as soon as the safety car had gone in,»* revealed the German as he stepped down from the podium. *«But you do not always get what you want and the team decided otherwise.»*
According to a Jordan engineer, Ralf got a real pasting over the radio from Eddie Jordan. *«After all, it was logical for Damon to win. He was quicker than me all weekend.»*

IN THE POINTS

1.	Damon HILL	B&H Jordan Mugen Honda	1 h 43'47"407
2.	Ralf SCHUMACHER	B&H Jordan Mugen Honda	at 0"932
3.	Jean ALESI	Red Bull Sauber Petronas	at 7"240
4.	Heinz-H. FRENTZEN	Winfield Williams	at 32"242
5.	Pedro DINIZ	Danka Zepter Arrows	at 51"682
6.	Jarno TRULLI	Gauloises Prost Peugeot	at 2 laps

Fastest lap : M. SCHUMACHER, lap 9, 2'03"766, avg. 202.679 km/h

△
«Gosh, I was thirsty.» Eddie Jordan had waited 126 grands prix to taste the winners champagne.

Eddie Jordan appeals to the courts to keep Ralf

The Williams team appeared to have its full complement of drivers for 1999. It seemed that Ralf Schumacher had just signed a contract with the reigning world champions to partner Alessandro Zanardi next season. Although not even the arrival of the Italian had yet been officially confirmed. For Ralf Schumacher, a move to Williams constituted a definite promotion in the F1 hierarchy, even if one should not expect too much from them in 1999. The job also came with nice accessories, like a much bigger salary than the 1.2 million sterling he was reputedly paid by Jordan.

◁
No need to describe Damon Hill's feelings after this win. One glance at the podium said it all.

Frank Williams is not in the habit of paying a king's ransom for his drivers, but the many German sponsors with the team, notably Falke clothing and Veltins beer, were ready to part finance the purchase of their countryman. Not to mention the fact that BMW, who would provide the engines from the year 2000, were also keen to have a German driver. In these circumstances, young Ralf looked like an ideal candidate for Frank Williams.
The problem was that Eddie Jordan saw things differently. Initially, the Irishman had signed a two year deal with Ralf, due to expire at the end of 1998. Things got complicated when Eddie Jordan reckoned he had signed a new deal for 1999 with Willi Weber, Ralf and Michael Schumacher's manager, on 31st July.
When he learnt his little lad was trying to do a runner, Jordan wrote to Frank Williams, informing him Ralf was already under contract to him. The driver's lawyers then sent Jordan letters accusing him of sending «lying» letters which were prejudicial to their client. From then on, the matter passed into the hands of the British courts, something Jordan is well used to, having gone there to dispute the loss of other drivers, including Michael Schumacher in 1991 and Giancarlo Fisichella in 1997. It now looked more than likely he was about to lose Ralf Schumacher as well.
History just goes on repeating itself.

Lap 27. For quite some time, troubled by the rain and spray, Giancarlo Fisichella was pretty much driving «on instruments.» Then he caught up with Shinji Nakano's Minardi, without even realising it, just as they came up to the braking point for the Bus Stop chicane. It was a huge impact and the Italian was lucky to walk away uninjured.
▽

The accident at the first start, seen from a helicopter. Images which need no comment.

Controversy: a mistake from Coulthard and Schumacher is eliminated

Lap 26. Michael Schumacher has the race in his pocket. With more than a thirty second lead over Damon Hill, it was hard to see how the German could lose the Belgian Grand Prix. Mika Hakkinen having retired, the Ferrari driver was getting ready to end the weekend with a seven point lead in the championship. An ideal scenario for the Scuderia.
But it was when he attempted to lap David Coulthard that a grain of sand slipped into the smooth running of his red car. Stuck behind the Scotsman's McLaren, the German was unable to avoid ramming it, when Coulthard slowed on the straight, precisely to let him pass. It was a very hard knock. The right front wheel of the Ferrari was ripped off and Schumacher limped back to the pits. The suspension was too badly damaged to be repaired and he retired.
The German was furious and leapt out of his cockpit to storm over to the McLaren garage where he had to be restrained by mechanics from both teams from hitting Coulthard. As far as Schumacher was concerned, Coulthard had deliberately caused the accident. *«It is obvious. David was lapping in the 2m 11s before I caught him. Once I was right behind him, he started doing 2m 16s. I do not think this difference is a coincidence,»* thundered Michael Schumacher to anyone who would listen. *«What is more, he slowed down at a point where we are normally flat out. I was not expecting it at all. David has enough experience to know that in this rain, there was no way I would realise he was slowing down and have enough time to react.»* Naturally, Coulthard on the other hand, felt it was Schumacher's fault. *«My engineer told me over the radio to let Michael through, so I stuck to the right hand side of the track,»* he explained. *«All I know is he drove into me. What was I supposed to do? I cannot drive looking behind me all the time. It was not my responsibility to watch him. It was up to him to be careful.»* Coulthard was not impressed with what happened once the Ferrari driver had stepped out of his cockpit and he described Schumacher as *«an animal.»* Having listened to both drivers, the stewards decided to right off the coming together as a racing incident.
How could they rule otherwise? Coulthard had made a mistake, nothing more.

After the collision with David Coulthard in the Pouhon downhill section, Michael Schumacher finishes his lap with three wheels on his wagon before regaining his pit. From where he stormed over to the McLaren garage to vent his anger at the Scot.

A misunderstanding rich in consequences

As Formula 1 becomes more and more of a media circus, capturing the world championship takes on an ever greater importance. For Ferrari as for McLaren, there were heavy financial consequences resting on the attribution of the title. If Mika Hakkinen won, then Mercedes, Mobil, West and Bridgestone all had major international advertising campaigns raring to go, hooked onto the world title. However, if it turned out to be Michael Schumacher who wore the supreme crown at the end of the seasons, then it would be Marlboro, Fiat, Shell and Goodyear reaping the benefits. Today, the budgets invested by these companies are so big that the sporting side of Formula 1 takes on a secondary importance behind the value of the investment. If you buy the best driver and the best equipment at a high price, then that is fine as long as the results follow.
The tension this situation creates was more noticeable than in the past this season. Nobody is in F1 to have fun any more. The mechanics do not whistle while they work anymore and the drivers have long since sacrificed their disco nights on the alter of efficiency.
This year, thanks to the mano a mano between McLaren and Ferrari, the tension had shot up a notch. In the Spa paddock after the race, once could almost feel the electricity flying between the motorhomes of the two teams. On the one hand, there was David Coulthard, still in his race suit, saying he could not drive while constantly looking in his mirrors. Barely thirty metres away, there was Michael Schumacher, wrapped up in a coat against the elements, convinced it was a deliberate act from the Scotsman.
The image of Michael Schumacher's reaction after his retirement, shown on televisions around the whole world, did not do much for his cause. Schumacher himself is well known for his strong arm tactics. Even so, it is possible to understand his immediate anger at seeing certain victory snatched from him so suddenly. In F1, the sport has become a spectacle and then a business. It is a unique formula that is hard to match. We must wait and see how long the lucrative situation can last.

A Sauber on the podium. Hurray for Jean but poor Johnny

A Sauber on the podium. This had not happened since the 1997 Hungarian Grand Prix. It was also the first one since Jean Alesi had driven for the team from Zurich. The result was all the more extraordinary as Alesi finished in the wheel tracks of the first two finishers. For the last part of the race, Alesi was glued to the back of the Jordans and even appeared to be pushing them hard, to such an extent, that at one point it looked as though Jean was trying to win the Belgian Grand Prix. *«No, that would have been impossible,»* he corrected. *«I could go as quick as the Jordans but no more. I could never have overtaken them as the visibility was too bad. I was just trying to concentrate and not make any mistakes. Also, Peter Sauber was shouting 'slow, slow' into my radio. It was very funny!»* For the team these four points from third place were more important than risking them all to gain one position. «We really needed these points,» agreed Alesi. *«This season the car has often been good but the level of the whole field is very high and that is why we are not scoring points. Today, all I could think about was those four points.»*
As soon as the post race press conference was over, Jean Alesi dashed to the team motorhome so as not to miss out on any of the party, nor on Peter Sauber's radiant smile. *«Finally we have a good result. I think it is well deserved,»* said the Swiss team owner. *«It is a shame Johnny had to retire. But at least it meant there was one more person with their fingers crossed in the garage while waiting for the chequered flag.»* Indeed, it had not been a very positive day for Johnny Herbert.
At the first start, the Englishman was caught up in the huge shunt caused by David Coulthard. *«I could see something strange was happening through the spray, when a tyre flew over my head and someone hit me from behind.»*
At the second start, history repeated itself. *«Mika Hakkinen got it sideways. He tried to straighten up the car too quickly and I could not avoid him.»*

Third place for Jean Alesi who finishes just a few seconds behind the winner. It's party time at Sauber.

PRACTICE TIMES

No	Driver	Car/Engine/Chassis	Practice Friday	Practice Saturday	Qualifying	Warm-up
1.	Jacques Villeneuve	Williams/Mecachrome/FW20/6 (G)	1'53"589	1'51"859	1'50"204	2'13"781
2.	Heinz-Harald Frentzen	Williams/Mecachrome/FW20/4 (G)	1'53"534	1'52"136	1'50"686	2'11"860
3.	Michael Schumacher	Ferrari/F300/188 (G)	1'51"895	1'52"058	1'50"027	2'07"839
4.	Eddie Irvine	Ferrari/F300/185 (G)	1'53"601	1'51"972	1'50"189	2'08"608
5.	Giancarlo Fisichella	Benetton/Playlife/198/3 (B)	1'54"171	1'52"542	1'50"462	2'09"127
6.	Alexander Wurz	Benetton/Playlife/198/7 (B)	1'54"158	1'53"020	1'51"648	2'10"917
7.	David Coulthard	McLaren/Mercedes/MP4-13/7 (B)	1'52"629	1'50"702	1'48"845	2'10"258
8.	Mika Hakkinen	McLaren/Mercedes/MP4-13/5 (B)	1'51"906	1'50"319	1'48"682	2'09"120
9.	Damon Hill	Jordan/Honda/198/3 (G)	1'53"100	1'51"368	1'49"728	2'10"076
10.	Ralf Schumacher	Jordan/Honda/198/4 (G)	1'54"116	1'52"346	1'50"501	2'09"539
11.	Olivier Panis	Prost/Peugeot/AP01/7 (B)	1'55"182	1'53"933	1'52"784	2'26"065
12.	Jarno Trulli	Prost/Peugeot/AP01/6 (B)	1'54"878	1'55"049	1'52"572	2'14"680
14.	Jean Alesi	Sauber/Petronas/C17/6 (G)	1'53"660	1'52"102	1'51"189	2'11"546
15.	Johnny Herbert	Sauber/Petronas/C17/1 (G)	1'54"130	1'53"379	1'51"851	2'14"147
16.	Pedro Diniz	Arrows/A19/1 (B)	1'56"431	1'55"302	1'53"037	2'13"853
17.	Mika Salo	Arrows/A19/5 (B)	1'55"730	1'54"814	1'53"207	2'16"139
18.	Rubens Barrichello	Stewart/Ford/SF2/3 (B)	1'54"433	1'54"071	1'52"670	2'11"374
19.	Jos Verstappen	Stewart/Ford/SF2/3 (B)	1'55"263	1'55"451	1'53"149	2'17"733
20.	Ricardo Rosset	Tyrrell/Ford/026/4 (G)	1'58"178	1'56"604	1'54"850	2'16"174
21.	Toranosuke Takagi	Tyrrell/Ford/026/5 (G)	1'56"080	1'53"898	1'53"237	2'14"038
22.	Shinji Nakano	Minardi/Ford/M198/4 (B)	1'57"682	1'56"329	1'55"084	2'16"217
23.	Esteban Tuero	Minardi/Ford/M198/5 (B)	1'57"014	1'57"000	1'55"520	2'20"842

LAP CHART

position:	1	2	3	4	5	6	7	8	9	10	11	12	13	14	15	16	17	18	19	20	21	22
start:	8	7	9	3	4	1	5	10	2	14	6	15	12	18	11	16	19	17	21	20	22	23
1	9	3	4	14	1	2	10	5	16	19	21	22	12	23	7							
2	9	3	4	14	1	2	10	5	16	19	21	22	12	23	7							
3	9	3	4	1	2	14	10	5	16	19	21	22	12	7	23							
4	9	3	4	1	2	14	10	5	16	19	21	22	12	7	23							
5	9	3	4	2	14	1	10	5	16	19	21	22	12	7	23							
6	9	3	4	2	14	1	10	5	16	19	21	22	12	7	23							
7	9	3	4	2	14	1	10	5	16	19	21	22	12	7	23							
8	3	9	4	2	14	1	10	5	16	19	21	22	12	7	23							
9	3	9	4	2	14	1	10	5	16	21	22	12	7	23								
10	3	9	2	14	1	10	4	5	16	21	12	22	7	23								
11	3	9	2	14	1	10	5	16	4	12	22	7	23									
12	3	9	2	14	1	5	10	16	4	12	22	7	23									
13	3	9	2	14	1	5	10	16	4	12	22	7	23									
14	3	9	14	2	1	5	10	16	4	12	22	7	23									
15	3	9	14	2	1	5	10	16	4	12	22	7	23									
16	3	9	14	1	2	5	10	16	4	12	22	7	23									
17	3	9	10	14	2	4	16	5	12	22	7	23										
18	3	9	10	14	2	4	16	5	12	7	22											
19	3	9	10	14	2	4	5	16	12	7	22											
20	3	9	10	14	2	4	5	16	12	7	22											
21	3	9	10	14	2	4	5	16	7	12	22											
22	3	9	10	14	2	4	5	7	16	12	22											
23	3	9	10	14	2	4	5	7	16	12	22											
24	3	9	10	14	2	4	5	16	7	12	22											
25	3	9	10	14	2	5	4	16	12	22	7											
26	9	10	14	2	5	16	12	22	7													
27	9	10	14	2	16	12	7	22														
28	9	14	10	2	16	12	7	22														
29	9	10	14	2	16	12	7	22														
30	9	10	14	2	16	12	7	22														
31	9	10	14	2	16	12	7	22														
32	9	10	14	2	16	12	7	22														
33	9	10	14	2	16	12	7	22														
34	9	10	14	2	16	12	7	22														
35	9	10	14	2	16	12	7	22														
36	9	10	14	2	16	12	7	22														
37	9	10	14	2	16	12	7	22														
38	9	10	14	2	16	12	7	22														
39	9	10	14	2	16	12	7	22														
40	9	10	14	2	16	12																
41	9	10	14	2	16	12																
42	9	10	14	2	16	12																
43	9	10	14	2	16																	
44	9	10	14	2	16																	

BRIDGESTONE

Best result for a Bridgestone shod runner:

Pedro Diniz, Arrows, 5th

CHAMPIONSHIPS

(after thirteen rounds)

Drivers :

1.	Mika HAKKINEN	77
2.	Michael SCHUMACHER	70
3.	David COULTHARD	48
4.	Eddie IRVINE	32
5.	Jacques VILLENEUVE	20
6.	Alexander WURZ	17
7.	Damon HILL	16
8.	Giancarlo FISICHELLA	15
9.	Heinz-Harald FRENTZEN	13
10.	Ralf SCHUMACHER	10
11.	Jean ALESI	7
12.	Rubens BARRICHELLO	4
13.	Mika SALO	3
	Pedro DINIZ	3
15.	Johnny HERBERT	1
	Jan MAGNUSSEN	1
	Jarno TRULLI	1

Constructors :

1.	McLaren / Mercedes	125
2.	Ferrari	102
3.	Williams / Mecachrome	33
4.	Benetton / Playlife	32
5.	Jordan / Mugen Honda	26
6.	Sauber / Petronas	8
7.	Arrows	6
8.	Stewart / Ford	5
9.	Prost / Peugeot	1

CLASSIFICATION & RETIREMENTS

Pos	Driver	Team	Time
1.	Hill	Jordan Mugen Honda	in 1h43'47"407
2.	R. Schum.	Jordan Mugen Honda	at 0"932
3.	Alesi	Sauber Petronas	at 7"240
4.	Frentzen	Williams Mecachrome	at 32"242
5.	Diniz	Arrows	at 51"682
6.	Trulli	Prost Peugeot	at 2 laps
7.	Coulthard	McLaren Mercedes	at 5 laps
8.	Nakano	Minardi Ford	at 5 laps

Lap	Driver	Team	Reason
1	Panis	Prost Peugeot	accident 1st start
1	Rosset	Tyrrell Ford	accident 1st start
1	Salo	Arrows	accident 1st start
1	Barrichello	Stewart Ford	accident 1st start
1	Herbert	Sauber Petronas	accident 2nd start
1	Wurz	Benetton Playlife	accident 2nd start
1	Hakkinen	McLaren Mercedes	accident 2nd start
9	Verstappen	Stewart Ford	engine
11	Takagi	Tyrrell Ford	spin
17	Villeneuve	Williams Mecachrome	spin
18	Tuero	Minardi Ford	battery
26	Irvine	Ferrari	spin
26	M. Schum.	Ferrari	accident
27	Fisichella	Benetton Playlife	accident

FASTEST LAPS

	Driver	Time	Lap
1.	M. Schum.	2'03"766	9
2.	Hill	2'05"630	7
3.	Frentzen	2'06"284	7
4.	Irvine	2'06"561	6
5.	Alesi	2'07"597	7
6.	Villeneuve	2'07"825	8
7.	R. Schum.	2'08"399	7
8.	Fisichella	2'09"528	5
9.	Coulthard	2'10"950	33
10.	Diniz	2'11"331	5
11.	Trulli	2'11"701	13
12.	Takagi	2'12"327	6
13.	Verstappen	2'12"425	8
14.	Nakano	2'13"230	12
15.	Tuero	2'19"996	5

THIRTEENTH ROUND

FOSTER'S BELGIAN GRAND PRIX, SPA-FRANCORCHAMPS

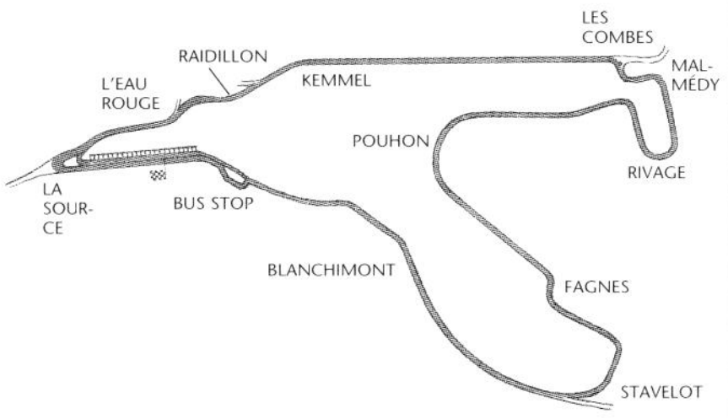

Date : August 30, 1998
Lenght : 6967 meters
Distance : 44 laps, 306.577 km
Weather : rain, 14 degrees

RACE SUMMARY

- At the first start, Mika Hakkinen leads at the La Source hairpin from Jacques Villeneuve and Michael Schumacher. Behind them, David Coulthard and Eddie Irvine touch. The Scots' McLaren steps out of line and causes a truly gigantic crash. The cars are running down the hill towards Eau Rouge and no less than 13 cars are eliminated: the two Arrows, the two Prosts, the two Tyrrells, the two Stewarts, as well as Alexander Wurz, Shinji Nakano, Johnny Herbert, David Coulthard and Eddie Irvine. The race is stopped.
- There are only 18 cars on the grid for the second start. As their teams have only one spare car, Panis, Barrichello, Salo and Rosset sit out the race.
- Hill makes an excellent start ahead of Michael Schumacher. Hakkinen clips the German's Ferrari, slides before being hit by Johnny Herbert. Further on, Wurz and Coulthard collide.
- The safety car comes out for just one lap, while the wreck of Hakkinen's car is cleared away.
- On lap 5, Villeneuve makes a mistake and is passed by Frentzen and Alesi. On the 17th lap he goes off the track.
- The rain gets worse from lap five. Schumacher passes Hill and takes off into the lead.
- Schumacher has a 37 second lead over Hill, when he catches Coulthard to lap him. The Ferrari slams into the back of the McLaren and both are forced to pit. Five laps later Coulthard rejoins the race in the hope of picking up a point.
- One lap later on lap 26, Fisichella fails to see Nakano's Minardi through the rain and spray and hits it full pelt. The safety car is out again while the Benetton debris is cleared away.
- When the safety car goes in, there are just 12 laps left. Hill wins ahead of Ralf Schumacher and Alesi.

WEEK-END GOSSIP

- **Ecclestone goes sailing ....in Gstaad**

Formula 1's Mr. Moneymaker, Bernie Ecclestone loves Gstaad. He has acquired a superb residence there, where he likes to spend his winters. At Spa, we learnt he intended forming a yacht club there with Marco Piccinini, the former Scuderia Ferrari boss. Among the honorary members we already had King Constantine of Greece and his brother in law, King Juan-Carlos of Spain. The only thing missing to justify a yacht club in the middle of the mountains, was the sea.

- **A plethora of publicity**

The Geneva based Allsport Management S.A. which holds the rights to circuit signage around the tracks, was reeling under the demand. As there is a physical limit to how many panels one can fit around a race track, Bernie Ecclestone plans to use an electronic system which allowed the message to be displayed by these panels when viewed on television, to be changed. The main advantage is that different countries and therefore different markets could be shown different advertisements. It was also a way of selling the same panel several times over.

- **The Concorde Agreement still not signed**

After the Sauber team finally signed the Concorde Agreement, shortly before the Belgian Grand Prix, it was assumed that everyone agreed with the document, which controls the commercial aspects of the sport. However, it seemed it was now Max Mosley, the FIA President, who was not in agreement with the final version of the document. Since Mosley had signed it, at the Monaco Grand Prix, it had undergone several modifications and the FIA president was no longer in agreement with those changes- notably as far as these relate to the European Union, which has accused FIA of running a monopoly situation.

- **Islamic fundamentalists threaten Spa**

The news was a banner headline across a Belgian daily paper, «le Jour.» An Islamic group had allegedly threatened to disrupt the Belgian Grand Prix if Bernie Ecclestone did not «donate» around 160,000 pounds to the medical organisation, «*Medecins sans frontiere Sudan*.» The money was supposed to help with repairs in the wake of America's bombing of the country not long before. An anonymous message sent to the newspaper stated that if the money was not handed over, then the grand prix would not start. The Belgian police took this matter seriously, even if the ransom amount, ridiculously small when viewed in the context of Ecclestone's fortune, made it seem that the whole incident might have been a hoax.

Second start: hit by Johnny Herbert, Mika Hakkinen appears to have some problems with his front suspension

BRIDGESTONE
BRIDGESTONE
GIRI 52
BRIDGESTONE
Agip
Marlboro
Marlboro
Shell
Marlboro
Shell
Marlboro
Shell

Monza and its tifosi see red

Italy saw the dream scenario become fact at Monza: the Ferraris finished first and second and Mika Hakkinen finished in a McLaren which was on its last legs.
Having started badly for them, the race finished in apotheosis as the podium was surrounded by a sea of humanity the like of which had never been seen before in the history of the tifosi. Michael Schumacher and Mika Hakkinen were now level pegging in the championship. There were two grands prix to go and Ferrari had the wind in their sails.

GRAN PREMIO CAMPARI D'ITALIA MONZA

Villeneuve on the front row

For the first time this season, both Prost-Peugeot cars managed to qualify in the top ten on the starting grid. «We have progressively improved the car,» explained Alain Prost. «Our positions today are not down to luck.» ▷ ▽

The Coulthard and Hakkinen ladies in their usual role, which consists for the most part, of waiting for their men to finish driving around in circles on the race tracks. ▽

Making the most of the strange weather conditions which affected the qualifying session, Jacques Villeneuve managed to stick his Williams on the front row of the grid for the first time this season. «*We completely changed the settings on the car overnight and we had not quite fine tuned it yet,*» explained the Canadian. «*It's a shame, because if we had been able to set it up correctly, I could have had a go at attacking Michael for pole position.*»

Sandwiched on the grid between Michael Schumacher and Mika Hakkinen, Jacques Villeneuve was well aware he ran the risk of interfering with the fight between these two. He was cool on the subject: «*Michael and Mika will be fighting for the title and I will simply be trying to win the race, without concerning myself about them.*»

Rain affects qualifying

Schumi masters the conditions

«*As I got to the fist chicane I immediately realised I had set the quickest time. I only had to see the crowd waving from the grandstand.*» On Saturday, Michael Schumacher did not need to wait to hear Jean Todt's voice on the radio. All around the Monza autodrome, the tifosi were ecstatic after it was announced that the German had got pole position.

The time he set was good enough to last right to the end of an extraordinary qualifying session. Having virtually flooded the track during the morning session, the showers abated slightly around midday and a weak and timid sun spread its rays over the track for the qualifying session.

All the same, the track was still very damp and would only dry after the cars had been out to dry the racing line for a while. The adverse conditions meant that not one single car took to the track in the first half hour of the session and the track was only really dry for the last few minutes. This meant there was a huge traffic jam as cars jostled for position and qualifying became something of a lottery.

This game of chance allowed Michael Schumacher, Ferrari and Goodyear to record their first pole position of the season. «*For sure, the strange weather conditions helped us today,*» admitted Michael Schumacher after qualifying. «*Even under normal circumstances, I think we would have been well placed. Actually we have made a lot of progress with the car since last week. Now it is quick and above all, very reliable.*»

Adopting a cautious approach, the German made his first run on rain tyres, in order to check out the track conditions. «*It was important to know where the puddles of standing water were. It was better to go out once on wets, rather than risk spinning and getting stuck in a gravel trap.*»

The German was reasonably optimistic about the race. «*We should have got this pole much earlier in the season. We have done an enormous amount of work and we have finally done it. This time, I think it is reasonable to think we can win the race.*»

STARTING GRID

		M. SCHUMACHER 1'25"280
Jacques VILLENEUVE 1'25"561	-1-	Mika HAKKINEN 1'25"679
David COULTHARD 1'25"987	-2-	Eddie IRVINE 1'26"159
R. SCHUMACHER 1'26"309	-3-	Alexander WURZ 1'26"567
Jean ALESI 1'26"637	-4-	Olivier PANIS 1'26"681
Jarno TRULLI 1'26"794	-5-	G. FISICHELLA 1'26"817
Heinz-H. FRENTZEN 1'26"836	-6-	R. BARRICHELLO 1'27"247
Damon HILL 1'27"362	-7-	Johnny HERBERT 1'27"510
Mika SALO 1'27"744	-8-	Jos VERSTAPPEN 1'28"212
Ricardo ROSSET 1'28"286	-9-	Toranosuke TAKAGI 1'28"346
Pedro DINIZ 1'28"387	-10-	Shinji NAKANO 1'29"101
Esteban TUERO 1'29"417	-11-	

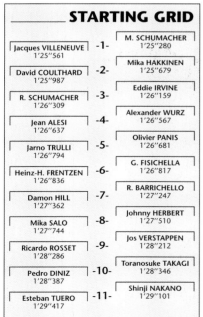

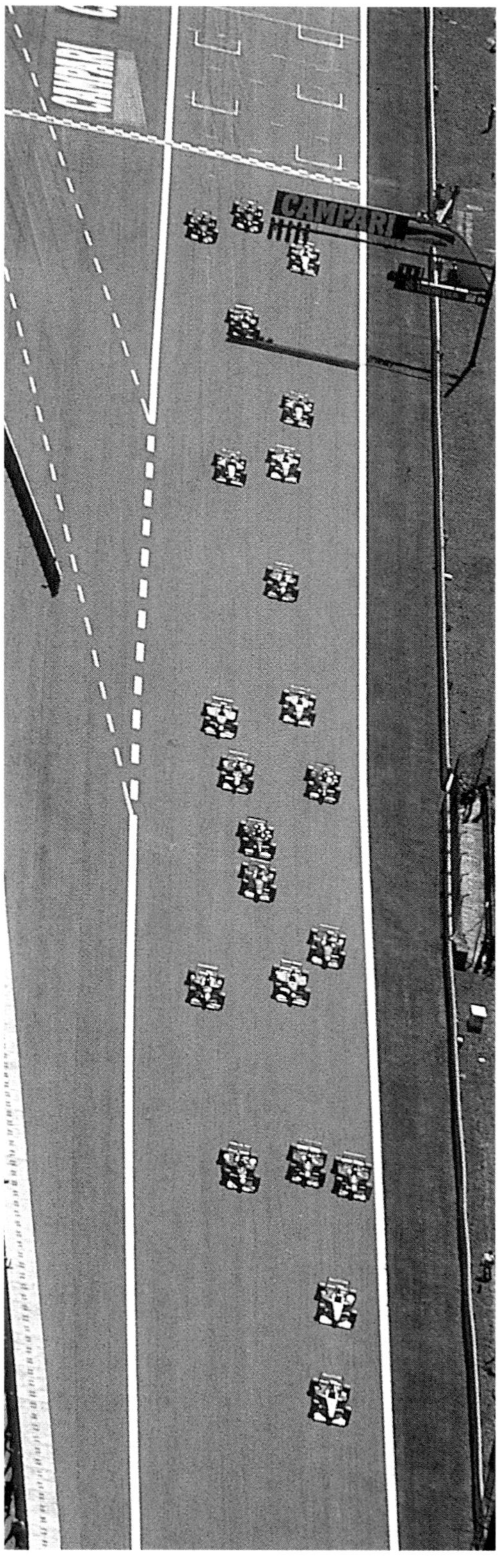

Ferrari sets Monza alight

What a race! Having taken pole position and then wasted it by missing his start, Michael Schumacher then vanquished a floundering Mika Hakkinen. This was vintage Schumacher; a man at the peak of his art. While this track had seemed to be purpose built to gift McLaren another grand prix win, the German took it from them and wiped out his deficit in the championship.

Michael Schumacher did not have it all his own way as he thought all was lost when the lights went out at the start: «*It was as though I was going off for a walk not a race,*» he recalled after the finish. «*It was awful. Everything that could go wrong did go wrong.*»

Fifth at the first corner, the German managed to get past Jacques Villeneuve, who had also made a bad start, at the second chicane and Eddie Irvine two laps later, the Irishman naturally putting up little resistance. «*So then I was third, but a long way behind the McLarens,*» continued Michael Schumacher. «*I did not think I could catch them, but to my great surprise, I was going quicker than them. Then David passed Mika and I understood he had problems.*»

Gradually closing on the Finn, the German finally overtook him on lap 17, at exactly the same moment that David Coulthard's engine gave out in a cloud of smoke. It all took a moment and the Ferrari was in the lead. «*It was a bit close with Mika. There was smoke from David's car and we could not see anything. I saw him go onto the grass at the chicane. That was my chance. He tried to close the door on me but he had lost momentum and I was able to get past.*»

From then on, the Ferrari driver had the race in his pocket. He pulled out a six second lead, which came down slightly once Hakkinen had stopped for fresh tyres. «*Mika was gaining two or three tenths per lap, but I was not worried. Our top speeds were very close and he would not have been able to pass me,*» added Schumacher.

With Eddie Irvine coming second, the Scuderia had done it all at Monza, in a race which had been expected to be very difficult for them. «*It is thanks to the work we have done on the chassis,*» concluded Michael Schumacher. «*We did all we could to make it ride the kerbs without losing its balance and it payed off. We will celebrate tonight and then it will be back to work.*»

With two grands prix remaining to the end of the championship, the trip had been reset to zero between Michael Schumacher and Mika Hakkinen.

The end of the season looked like being a stunner.

△ *Aren't they sweet, the two Schumacher brothers? It was the first time in the history of Formula 1 that two brothers shared the podium.*

Grandma said

Michael Schumacher loves his grandmother. On the evening of every grand prix or the following day at the latest, she rings him to give her impressions of the race. «*She is 74 years old, but she is still very sharp,*» said Schumacher. «*She never misses a race on television and always gives me her advice. After the disaster at Spa two weeks ago, she told me I had been very unlucky in that race and that destiny would redress the situation in Monza. She was right and I will ring her this evening to tell her.*»

Ralf is happy

Ralf Schumacher came through to take third place. As the season drew to a close the other one's brother was making less mistakes than in the beginning.

Monza was in any case the first time there had been two brothers on the podium in Formula1. «*Damon and I were running completely different strategies,*» explained Schumacher Minor. «*As he was starting from a long way back on the grid, he had decided to stop twice, while I was only doing one pit stop. When he caught up with me, the team called me on the radio and asked me to let him pass and I did, two laps later, as I knew I would overtake him again later.*» Ralf was one of the few drivers not to experience brake problems in the race.

◁ *Start: Michael Schumacher and Jacques Villeneuve completely flunked their starts, allowing the two McLarens to take the lead.*

IN THE POINTS

1.	M. SCHUMACHER	Scuderia Ferrari Marlboro	1 h 17'09"672
2.	Eddie IRVINE	Scuderia Ferrari Marlboro	at 37"977
3.	Ralf SCHUMACHER	B&H Jordan Mugen Honda	at 41"152
4.	Mika HAKKINEN	West McLaren Mercedes	at 55"671
5.	Jean ALESI	Red Bull Sauber Petronas	at 1'01"872
6.	Damon HILL	B&H Jordan Mugen Honda	at 1'06"688

Fastest lap : Mika HAKKINEN, lap 45, 1'25"139, avg. 243.977 km/h

◁ *Thanks to an excellent start, Jean Alesi found himself glued to Michael Schumacher's gearbox at the first corner. He started from eighth on the grid and managed to finish fifth, picking up two more points.*

Johnny Herbert attacks the daunting «Parabolica.» The Italian Grand Prix had been a nightmare for the Englishman, after one of his mechanics left a wrench in the footwell. The tool crashed about, finally coming to rest under the brake pedal, sending him flying off the track. How angry was he? When he got back to the pits, he packed his bag and left it at the Stewart motorhome, the team he is joining for 1999.

△ The tifosi are delirious after waiting years for this Ferrari one-two finish. It was all the more emotional as it put the Scuderia back in the running for the championship.

Madness and mayhem beneath the podium

The chequered flag has just fallen on Michael Schumacher's victory. All along the pit wall, in all the team garages the panic button is pressed and the mechanics pack up their equipment as quickly as possible. Too late. The invading crowd is already there and it is all the mechanics can do to stop the more daring of the spectators from acquiring a nice grand prix souvenir. At Ferrari, hundreds of passionate fans are beginning to make life difficult and the mechanics form a human wall in front of the garage and have to get heavy to prevent the braver members of the crowd from getting into the garage. Still stunned by the win, Jean Todt, helped by press officer Claudio Berro is finding it difficult to fight his way through the crowd and get to the podium, already surrounded by a mass of tifosi.
Things were getting tense in front of the Ferrari garage. The fans who were just arriving, were pressing on those in front and the pressure was getting unbearable. The mechanics can hold the crowd no longer and run for cover inside the garage. At this point the security service stepped in and things got nasty and blows rained down. Caught up in the euphoria of their favourite team's one-two finish, some fans went completely mad and started pushing and shoving an English cameraman caught up in the middle of the crowd. On the podium, the drivers were unaware of the situation. At their feet, a human sea all singing along to the Italian national anthem, was an unbelievable sight.
Monza has often lived through exciting times, but such collective hysteria had never been seen before - the last time Ferrari did the double here was in 1988, but the championship was not up for grabs then.
The Monza organisers ran the risk of being heavily fined by FIA after what was effectively a near riot in front of the podium. The tifosi do not care. Whatever fences are put up to keep them off the track, they will always manage to get over them if a Ferrari wins. If it were not for them, Monza would not be in Italy.

McLaren gets it wrong all down the line

On Saturday afternoon, Ron Dennis seemed incredibly confident. For the first time this season, neither one of his cars was qualified on the front row, but this did not prevent the Englishman from being more confident than ever of victory. «*I am convinced that in race trim we are the quickest,*» he insisted.
The early phase of the Italian Grand Prix seemed to bear out his theory, as David Coulthard tore off into the distance, making it all look easy. The same could not be said of Mika Hakkinen. «*I think I made the best start of my career today. I was laughing about it into my helmet and I was so happy, thinking about the tifosi. But immediately afterwards, I realised something was not quite right with my first set of tyres.*» Gradually slowing, the Finn was passed by Michael Schumacher at the exact moment when David Coulthard had to retire the other McLaren in a cloud of smoke with a broken engine. In a matter of seconds, Ron Dennis watched as both his cars lost the lead.
Mika Hakkinen talked through his race with the same detachment he uses after a win. This pilot from a cold land always manages to keep his cool and control his emotions under all circumstances. «*After my pit stop, it was the brakes which started to get worse. The pedal was getting soft and I could not avoid the spin.*» He actually got severely out of shape at the second chicane and it could have all been much worse for the McLaren driver, as he managed to rejoin the track without losing his place. «*I was lucky,*» he admitted. «*Because at that point, you are doing over 300 km/h.*»
And so it was that Mika Hakkinen nursed a sick car to the finish of the Italian Grand Prix, powerless to stop first Eddie Irvine and then Ralf Schumacher slip by. «*I am disappointed,*» he continued. «*But what can you do when you have reliability problems? It's better not to think about it.*» He still believed in his first world championship title - «*of course I am going to fight for it.*»

▷ *Mika Hakkinen lights up his brakes at the Ascari chicane. At half distance, when he refuelled, the McLaren mechanics noticed that the Finn's discs were already practically worn out. The Ferrari supplier, Carbone Industrie had anticipated this problem and provided the Scuderia with a new type of disc. «These discs are the same size as the old ones, but they are made from a completely different material with a slower wear rate,» explained Philippe Rerat, a Carbone Industrie engineer. «We have been working on it since June, but we have only just produced enough parts to supply the two Ferraris. It is the first time for years that we risk not supplying the championship winning car and we are doing everything to help Michael Schumacher.»*

▷ *Lap 11: Michael Schumacher (foreground) closes on Mika Hakkinen. He will soon pass the Finn, making the most of the smoke screen from Coulthard's broken engine.*

All results

PRACTICE TIMES

No	Driver	Car/Engine/Chassis	Practice vendredi	Practice samedi	Qualifying	Warm-up
1.	Jacques Villeneuve	Williams/Mecachrome/FW20/6 (G)	1'26"053	1'40"364	1'25"561	1'27"238
2.	Heinz-Harald Frentzen	Williams/Mecachrome/FW20/7 (G)	1'26"528	1'39"479	1'26"836	1'27"481
3.	Michael Schumacher	Ferrari/F300/186 (G)	1'25"246	1'40"656	1'25"289	1'26"924
4.	Eddie Irvine	Ferrari/F300/184 (G)	1'24"987	1'40"508	1'26"159	1'27"041
5.	Giancarlo Fisichella	Benetton/Playlife/198/6 (B)	1'26"885	1'40"261	1'26"817	1'27"845
6.	Alexander Wurz	Benetton/Playlife/198/4 (B)	1'26"886	1'40"588	1'26"567	1'27"571
7.	David Coulthard	McLaren/Mercedes/MP4-13/6 (B)	1'25"690	1'40"295	1'25"987	1'25"632
8.	Mika Hakkinen	McLaren/Mercedes/MP4-13/4 (B)	1'26"159	1'40"321	1'25"679	1'25"965
9.	Damon Hill	Jordan/Honda/198/3 (G)	1'26"838	1'41"437	1'27"362	1'27"052
10.	Ralf Schumacher	Jordan/Honda/198/4 (G)	1'27"079	1'39"955	1'26"309	1'27"054
11.	Olivier Panis	Prost/Peugeot/AP01/7 (B)	1'27"676	1'41"307	1'26"681	1'27"975
12.	Jarno Trulli	Prost/Peugeot/AP01/3 (B)	1'26"748	1'43"564	1'26"794	1'27"485
14.	Jean Alesi	Sauber/Petronas/C17/6 (G)	-	1'40"827	1'26"637	1'27"712
15.	Johnny Herbert	Sauber/Petronas/C17/2 (G)	1'27"541	1'41"372	1'27"510	1'27"667
16.	Pedro Diniz	Arrows/A19/7 (B)	1'53"671	1'43"515	1'28"387	1'28"582
17.	Mika Salo	Arrows/A19/6 (B)	1'29"603	1'42"402	1'27"744	1'28"219
18.	Rubens Barrichello	Stewart/Ford/SF2/2 (B)	1'28"066	1'40"613	1'27"247	1'27"974
19.	Jos Verstappen	Stewart/Ford/SF2/3 (B)	1'28"606	1'41"435	1'28"212	1'28"523
20.	Ricardo Rosset	Tyrrell/Ford/026/2 (G)	1'28"098	1'48"985	1'28"286	1'29"917
21.	Toranosuke Takagi	Tyrrell/Ford/026/5 (G)	1'28"135	1'40"697	1'28"346	1'27"021
22.	Shinji Nakano	Minardi/Ford/M198/3 (B)	1'28"849	1'44"820	1'29"101	1'29"339
23.	Esteban Tuero	Minardi/Ford/M198/5 (B)	1'28"847	1'44"279	1'29"417	1'29"273

LAP CHART

position:	1	2	3	4	5	6	7	8	9	10	11	12	13	14	15	16	17	18	19	20	21	22
start:	3	1	8	7	4	10	6	14	11	12	5	2	18	9	15	17	19	20	21	16	22	23
1	8	7	4	3	1	14	10	6	5	12	9	2	15	18	11	19	16	23	17	21	22	20
2	8	7	4	3	1	10	14	6	5	12	9	2	15	18	11	19	16	17	21	23	22	20
3	8	7	3	4	1	10	14	6	9	5	12	2	15	18	11	19	16	17	21	23	22	20
4	8	7	3	4	1	10	14	9	6	5	12	2	15	18	11	19	16	17	21	23	22	20
5	8	7	3	4	1	10	9	14	6	5	12	2	18	15	19	11	16	17	21	22	20	23
6	8	7	3	4	1	10	9	14	6	5	12	2	18	15	19	11	17	16	21	22	20	23
7	8	7	3	4	1	10	9	14	6	5	12	2	18	15	19	11	17	21	16	22	20	23
8	7	8	3	4	1	10	9	14	6	5	12	2	18	15	19	17	21	16	11	22	20	23
9	7	8	3	4	1	10	9	14	6	5	12	2	18	15	19	17	21	16	22	20	23	11
10	7	8	3	4	1	10	9	14	6	5	12	2	18	15	17	19	21	16	22	20	23	11
11	7	8	3	4	1	9	10	14	6	5	12	2	18	15	17	19	21	22	20	23	11	
12	7	8	3	4	1	9	10	14	6	5	12	2	18	15	17	19	21	22	20	23	11	
13	7	8	3	4	1	9	10	14	6	5	12	2	18	17	19	21	22	20	23	11		
14	7	8	3	4	1	9	10	14	6	5	12	2	18	17	19	20	21	23	11			
15	7	8	3	4	1	10	14	6	5	12	2	18	9	17	19	20	21	23	11			
16	7	8	3	4	1	10	14	6	5	2	18	9	17	12	19	21	20	23				
17	3	8	4	1	10	14	6	5	2	9	17	18	12	19	21	20	23					
18	3	8	4	1	10	14	6	5	2	9	17	12	19	21	18	20	23					
19	3	8	4	1	10	14	6	5	2	9	17	12	19	21	18	20	23					
20	3	8	4	1	10	14	6	5	2	9	17	12	19	21	18	20	23					
21	3	8	4	1	10	14	6	5	2	9	17	12	19	21	18	20	23					
22	3	8	4	1	10	14	6	5	2	9	17	12	19	21	18	20	23					
23	3	8	4	1	10	14	6	5	2	9	12	17	19	21	18	20	23					
24	3	8	4	1	10	14	6	5	2	9	17	19	21	18	20	23	12					
25	3	8	4	1	10	14	5	2	9	17	19	21	18	23	20	12						
26	3	8	4	1	10	14	5	2	9	17	19	21	18	23	20	12						
27	3	8	4	1	10	14	5	2	9	17	19	18	21	23	20	12						
28	3	8	4	1	10	14	5	2	9	17	19	18	21	23	20	12						
29	3	8	4	1	10	14	5	2	9	17	19	18	21	23	20	12						
30	3	8	4	1	10	14	5	2	9	17	19	18	21	23	20	12						
31	3	8	4	1	14	10	5	2	9	17	19	18	21	23	20	12						
32	8	3	4	1	14	10	5	2	9	17	19	18	21	23	20	12						
33	8	3	1	4	10	5	2	9	14	19	18	21	23	20	12							
34	8	3	4	1	10	5	2	9	14	19	18	21	23	20	12							
35	3	8	4	1	10	9	5	2	14	19	21	18	23	20	12							
36	3	8	4	1	10	9	14	2	5	19	21	18	23	20	12							
37	3	8	4	1	10	14	9	2	5	19	21	18	23	20	12							
38	3	8	4	10	14	9	2	5	19	21	18	23	20	12								
39	3	8	4	10	14	9	2	5	19	21	18	23	20	12								
40	3	8	4	10	14	9	2	5	21	18	23	20	12									
41	3	8	4	10	14	9	2	5	21	18	23	20	12									
42	3	8	4	10	14	9	2	5	21	18	23	20	12									
43	3	8	4	10	14	9	2	5	21	18	23	20	12									
44	3	8	4	10	14	9	2	5	21	18	23	20	12									
45	3	8	4	10	14	9	2	5	21	18	23	20	12									
46	3	8	4	10	14	9	2	5	21	18	23	20	12									
47	3	8	4	10	14	9	2	5	21	18	23	20	12									
48	3	8	4	10	14	9	2	5	21	18	23	20	12									
49	3	4	8	10	14	9	2	5	21	18	23	20	12									
50	3	4	8	10	14	9	2	5	21	18	23	20	12									
51	3	4	10	8	14	9	2	5	21	18	23	20										
52	3	4	10	8	14	9	2	5	21	18												
53	3	4	10	8	14	9																

CLASSIFICATION & RETIREMENTS

Pos	Driver	Team	Time
1.	M. Schum.	Ferrari	in 1h17'09"672
2.	Irvine	Ferrari	at 37"977
3.	R. Schum.	Jordan Mugen Honda	at 41"152
4.	Hakkinen	McLaren Mercedes	at 55"671
5.	Alesi	Sauber Petronas	at 1'01"872
6.	Hill	Jordan Mugen Honda	at 1'06"688
7.	Frentzen	Williams Mecachrome	at 1 lap
8.	Fisichella	Benetton Playlife	at 1 lap
9.	Takagi	Tyrrell Ford	at 1 lap
10.	Barrichello	Stewart Ford	at 1 lap
11.	Tuero	Minardi Ford	at 2 laps
12.	Rosset	Tyrrell Ford	at 2 laps
13.	Trulli	Prost Peugeot	at 3 laps
Lap	**Driver**	**Team**	**Reason**
11	Diniz	Arrows	off
13	Herbert	Sauber Petronas	brakes
14	Nakano	Minardi Ford	engine
16	Panis	Prost Peugeot	vibrations
17	Coulthard	McLaren Mercedes	engine
25	Wurz	Benetton Playlife	gearbox
33	Salo	Arrows	throttle
38	Villeneuve	Williams Mecachrome	spin
40	Verstappen	Stewart Ford	gearbox

FASTEST LAPS

	Driver	Time	Lap
1.	Hakkinen	1'25"139	45
2.	M. Schum.	1'25"483	26
3.	Coulthard	1'25"959	14
4.	R. Schum.	1'26"194	49
5.	Trulli	1'26"285	50
6.	Irvine	1'26"359	48
7.	Villeneuve	1'26"479	29
8.	Frentzen	1'26"656	40
9.	Fisichella	1'26"659	41
10.	Hill	1'26"730	52
11.	Alesi	1'26"840	52
12.	Wurz	1'27"620	24
13.	Takagi	1'27"726	46
14.	Barrichello	1'27"770	46
15.	Salo	1'27"866	25
16.	Panis	1'28"395	10
17.	Verstappen	1'28"583	32
18.	Herbert	1'29"092	10
19.	Tuero	1'29"093	51
20.	Diniz	1'29"124	9
21.	Rosset	1'29"393	50
22.	Nakano	1'29"853	13

FOURTEENTH ROUND

GRAN PREMIO CAMPARI D'ITALIA, MONZA

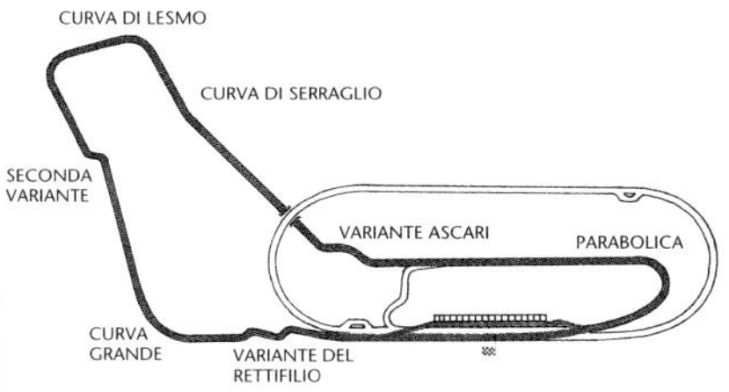

Date : September 13, 1998
Lenght : 5765 meters
Distance : 53 laps, 305.548 km
Weather : sunny, 24 degrees

CHAMPIONSHIPS

(after fourteen rounds)

Drivers :

1	Mika HAKKINEN	80
	Michael SCHUMACHER	80
3	David COULTHARD	48
4	Eddie IRVINE	38
5	Jacques VILLENEUVE	20
6	Damon HILL	17
	Alexander WURZ	17
8	Giancarlo FISICHELLA	15
9	Ralf SCHUMACHER	14
10	Heinz-Harald FRENTZEN	13
11	Jean ALESI	9
12	Rubens BARRICHELLO	4
13	Mika SALO	3
	Pedro DINIZ	3
15	Johnny HERBERT	1
	Jan MAGNUSSEN	1
	Jarno TRULLI	1

Constructors :

1	McLaren / Mercedes	128
2	Ferrari	118
3	Williams / Mecachrome	33
4	Benetton / Playlife	32
5	Jordan / Mugen Honda	31
6	Sauber / Petronas	10
7	Arrows	6
8	Stewart / Ford	5
9	Prost / Peugeot	1

WEEK-END GOSSIP

- **Very subtle**

The Italian public had not exactly forgiven David Coulthard for the accident during the Belgian Grand Prix. On Sunday, the main grandstands opposite the pits displayed banners which read: «Danger, Coulthard on track.» However, the previous week, during testing, the messages were far nastier: *«Coulthard assassin,»* or even *«Ron Dennis pays, Coulthard kills.»* Monza is not always very subtle.

- **Minardi poaches from Prost**

Giancarlo Minardi has decided to embark on a whole new investment programme. In Monza the team announced that it had signed several contracts: with Ford for a 1999 supply of engines; with Fondmetal technologies for use of their wind tunnel and finally with Cesare Fiorio, currently sporting director at Prost GP. Fiorio would be leaving the Prost team at the end of the season to take up the same position with Minardi in 1999.

- **Michael and David make up**

A few moments after their collision in Belgium it was hatred. Michael Schumacher had gone over to the McLaren pit to accuse David Coulthard of having tried to kill him. The Scotsman accused the German of acting like an animal. This situation was tense between the two drivers. Max Mosley, the FIA president had to intervene by asking both drivers to work out their differences before the Italian Grand Prix.

It was on Thursday on neutral ground, the Williams motorhome, that the meeting took place. Dead on three o'clock Michael Schumacher and David Coulthard sat down to talk. *«Neither of us has apologised,»* reported the German. *«But it was essential that we have a talk. Now there is no problem at all between us.»*

The Ferrari driver admitted he had got rather carried away in Belgium, admitting that Coulthard had not caused the accident deliberately.

- **Frentzen signs for Jordan**

Eddie Jordan announced in Monza that Heinz-Harald Frentzen would be driving alongside Damon Hill in 1999. *«Just a few years ago, it would have been unthinkable for Jordan to be in F1 without the budget that often accompanies two young drivers,»* commented Eddie Jordan. *«But we have progressed and today we are in a position to employ two experienced drivers, both past grand prix winners. I no longer want my team to be regarded as a kindergarten.»*

RACE SUMMARY

- Michael Schumacher gets the start all wrong. Same problem for Jacques Villeneuve alongside him. The two McLarens move into the lead from the second row.
- Michael Schumacher manages to overtake Jacques Villeneuve, braking for the second chicane. He passes Eddie Irvine two laps later.
- The McLarens are already a long way out in front and have a 2.8s advantage over Irvine after just one lap. One lap later the gap is 3.9s.
- When Michael Schumacher moves up to third place, he starts to catch the McLarens, putting in several fastest laps.
- On lap 7, Coulthard passes Hakkinen and pulls away. Hakkinen seems to have problems and Schumacher catches him.
- Coulthard retires on lap 17 with a broken engine. In the smoke and confusion, Schumacher slips past Hakkinen.
- After the pit stops, the order is the same. Schumacher has a six second advantage over Hakkinen, who is beginning to close the gap.
- On lap 45, Hakkinen sets the fastest race lap, but he pushes too hard. One lap later he spins off, but manages to keep going, but his car is wounded. Irvine passes him with five laps to go and then Ralf Schumacher gets by two laps later.

The calm of a Milan suburb at dawn. Situated to the north of the city, the Monza circuit is not that far from the Alps. Many of the drivers choose to reside at Lake Como during the ▽ grand prix weekend.

Hakkinen
BOSS
HUGO BOSS
Mobil 1
E
Mercedes-Benz

His best race

At the Nurburgring, Mika Hakkinen scored the greatest win of his career. Just when his supremacy in the championship was being brought into question and under constant pressure from Michael Schumacher, the Finn steered the perfect course from the front, all the way to the chequered flag. It was a demonstration of cool headedness which gave him a small cushion of points and a large psychological advantage going into the last race.
For Ferrari, the Nurburgring had been a failure and the Scuderia would have to work very hard before Japan.

GROSSER WARSTEINER PREIS VON LUXEMBURG, NÜRBURGRING

Part one of the job is done. For the second and consecutive time this season Michael Schumacher took pole position in qualifying.

A Ferrari front row: red trumps silver on Mercedes' home turf

McLaren boss Ron Dennis had good cause to pull his hair out, not that he had much to start with. While the McLaren-Mercedes MP4/13 is the car to beat, he has seen his supremacy melt away in Monza and now it was being turned into inferiority in qualifying for the Luxembourg Grand Prix. As the time had now come to fight for the title against the very determined Michael Schumacher, this was a somewhat irritating situation.

On Saturday, during the qualifying session, the Ferraris did not hang around and got down to business immediately. Michael Schumacher very quickly set the quickest time, which was good enough to annihilate the opposition, while team mate Eddie Irvine waited until the very last minute, before joining him on the front row. It was a Ferrari feast with only the crumbs left for McLaren; third place for Hakkinen and fifth for Coulthard.

From a Ferrari point of view, the ideal scenario had Michael Schumacher charging off into the distance while Eddie Irvine locks the door behind him. The strategy still had to be carried out and it was not a foregone conclusion as Schumacher had fluffed his last three starts. *«Making a good start is not as easy for us as it is for McLaren,»* claimed the German. *«My car has a bit of a problem in this area. We have been working on it since Monza and I hope we have solved it.»* The German declared that he was actually very surprised at the gap to the McLaren-Mercedes. *«We had a few small modifications on the car here, but I did not think they would make such a difference.»*

Mika Hakkinen was equally surprised. *«I did not expect to be so far back on the grid,»* regretted the Finn. *«But things did not go as I would have wished.»*

Ron Dennis is not worried

His cars' poor performance - it was the first time there had not been a McLaren on the front row this season -did not seem to unduly worry Ron Dennis. *«Of course we are a bit frustrated,»* was his analysis. *«But we are convinced that we cannot lose the championship. The race is on Sunday, not Saturday and we will mount an attacking strategy.»*

Dennis suggested it was the weather which had not suited his team. *«I have to admit that Goodyear has done a lot of work since the Italian Grand Prix. We expected to come here having upper hand and that is not the case, probably because it is cooler. Our Bridgestone tyres seem to work better when it is hot. But as I often tell the people in my team, at the circuits and back at the factory, that is Formula 1. It is a world championship and it is hard.»*

Eddie on a high

For the first time in his Formula 1 career, Eddie Irvine qualified on the front row. *«I am a bit surprised. I think that the McLarens could have done better. It will be strange not to have anyone to look at in front of me on the grid. The car is going well and I was able to dial out the understeer. I cannot stand understeer, it kills me.!»*

A bad session for David Coulthard as he was only fifth on the grid. His worst qualifying result of the season apart from the Austrian GP.

STARTING GRID

		M. SCHUMACHER 1'18"561
Eddie IRVINE 1'18"907	-1-	
		Mika HAKKINEN 1'18"940
G. FISICHELLA 1'19"048	-2-	
		David COULTHARD 1'19"169
R. SCHUMACHER 1'19"455	-3-	
		Heinz-H. FRENTZEN 1'19"522
Alexander WURZ 1'19"569	-4-	
		Jacques VILLENEUVE 1'19"631
Damon HILL 1'19"807	-5-	
		Jean ALESI 1'20"493
R. BARRICHELLO 1'20"530	-6-	
		Johnny HERBERT 1'20"650
Jarno TRULLI 1'20"709	-7-	
		Olivier PANIS 1'21"048
Mika SALO 1'21"120	-8-	
		Pedro DINIZ 1'21"258
Jos VERSTAPPEN 1'21"501	-9-	
		Toranosuke TAKAGI 1'21"525
Shinji NAKANO 1'22"078	-10-	
		Esteban TUERO 1'22"146
Ricardo ROSSET 1'22"822	-11-	

Here comes Mika again

«I feel good. To be honest I am happy. The situation is now completely different to the way it was a few hours ago.» A few minutes after the end of the race, Hakkinen was no chattier than usual. However, he had just pulled off a master stroke, winning the Luxembourg Grand Prix after 67 faultless laps, at the same time as fighting off Michael Schumacher every inch of the way.

Showing signs of the effort expended, he did not quite realise what he had done and could only just squeeze a smile at the finish. This grand prix had run to the beat of his drum, without pausing for breath. Chasing Schumacher to start with and then fending him off as he tore into the distance to prevent the Ferrari driver from catching him.

It was a sprint race which had not started too well. Having qualified on the second row, at first the Finn found himself blocked behind Eddie Irvine and it took him 14 laps to get past. *«It would be wrong to say I was worried. That would not be quite the right word. In a situation like that, you have to concentrate and push hard, without thinking about your state of mind. It was obvious to me that Eddie had problems as his car was all over the road. I have to admit, he did not try to stop me passing him. He was very correct.»*

At the Nurburgring, the McLaren was once again the car everyone had to beat, just as it had been back at the start of the season. *«The car worked really well, that's for sure,»* continued Hakkinen. *«On Saturday we had some set up problems, but today it was once again very easy to drive. A real pleasure.»* As he stepped out of the car, before he even took his helmet off, he stroked the nose of his car - a sign of complicity and affection.

After his mistake at Monza, Mika Hakkinen squared it all at the Nurburgring. *«He drove a fabulous race,»* said an enthusiastic Steve Hallam, a McLaren engineer. *«Mika drove better today than at any time since he joined our team.»*

In the early evening, having got over his earlier emotions, the Finn confirmed the importance of this win, not just in mathematic terms but also from a psychological point of view.

«I think that my driving today is an answer to all those who have criticised me,» he opined. *«Some said I would not stand the pressure and this proves that I certainly can,»* he added, alluding to comments from Eddie Irvine (see page 207.)

◁ *«We-have-won!» Mrs. Mika Hakkinen's joy is a joy to see after the race.*

◁ *The good lady wife was not the only one to be bubbling with joy. Mika was also in seventh heaven. The moment he stepped from the cockpit, he patted it on the Mercedes badge on the nose, a moving testament to the Finn's complicity with his car.*

The most important grand prix in McLaren's history

The McLaren team was now only one point away from winning the constructors' world championship. Thanks to David Coulthard's third place on Sunday, the Anglo- German team now had 142 points to Ferrari's 127. For the Scuderia to snatch victory in the constructors' championship - less important than the drivers' title, but more use in advertising terms - it would have to finish first and second in Suzuka, with McLaren failing to score a single point, which appeared to be verging on the impossible. After the race, Ron Dennis yet again sported a banana sized ear to ear grin and, glass of champagne in hand, he had to shout to make himself heard above the din of the music blaring out of the sound system at the team motorhome. Dennis admitted the race had been a dream. *«It is probably the most important race in the team's entire history,»* he claimed. *«It puts us back in a position of strength, in both the constructors' and drivers' championships. We will party tonight and tomorrow we get back to work.»*

◁ *The start had not gone too well for the McLarens - for once! It was Eddie Irvine who made the cleanest getaway, ahead of his team leader.*

IN THE POINTS

1.	Mika HAKKINEN	West McLaren Mercedes	1 h 32'14"789
2.	M. SCHUMACHER	Scuderia Ferrari Marlboro	at 2"212
3.	David COULTHARD	West McLaren Mercedes	at 34"164
4.	Eddie IRVINE	Scuderia Ferrari Marlboro	at 58"183
5.	Heinz-H. FRENTZEN	Winfield Williams	at 60"248
6.	Giancarlo FISICHELLA	Mild Seven Benetton Playlife	at 61"360

Fastest lap : Mika HAKKINEN, lap 25, 1'20"450, avg. 203.873 km/h

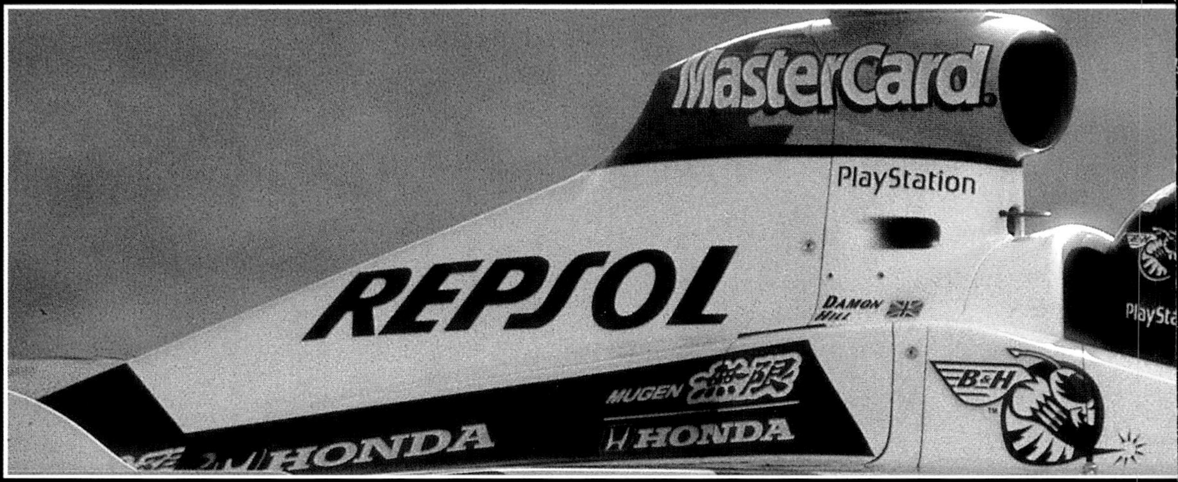

Profile of men at work
>From top to bottom: Jean Alesi, Damon Hill, Jacques Villeneuve and Mika Hakkinen.

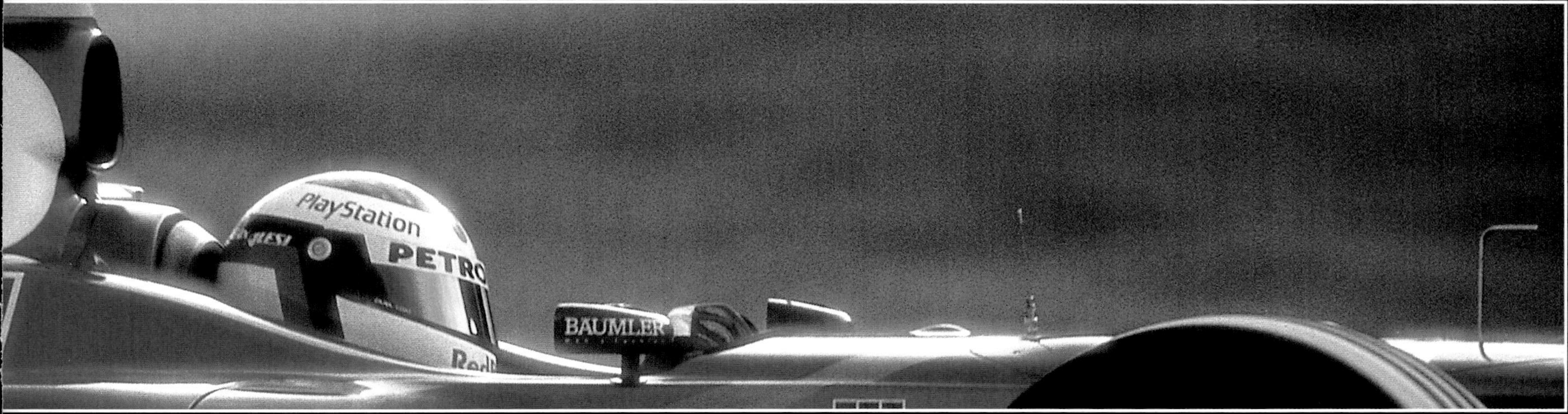

GROSSER WARSTEINER PREIS VON LUXEMBURG

Michael Schumacher was powerless and in front of his home crowd at that

Ferrari leaves 140,000 disappointed

A pursuit race at the Nurburgring. Michael Schumacher kept Mika Hakkinen under pressure throughout the whole race. The Finn did not crack. ▷▽

They also serve who stand and wait. The speed of the McLaren mechanics during the pit stops contributed in no small way to the success of the weekend. ▽

There were a few Finns who had made the trip to the Nurburgring, but only a few of them dared bring out their white flags with the blue cross on it, surrounded as they were by hordes of Michael Schumacher fans.
On Sunday, the Luxembourg Grand Prix was a sell out: 140,000 spectators had flocked there from all over Germany, wearing red T-shirts and Dekra caps to cheer on Michael Schumacher.
It was not enough. At the Nurburgring, the double world champion proved incapable of matching Mika Hakkinen's blistering pace.
The Ferrari may have lead the first lap, but its lead was soon whittled away. When the Finn took the lead during the pit stops, the German could do nothing about it.
«When Mika came out of the pits ahead of me, I was surprised to be honest,» said Michael Schumacher. *«I had a five second lead before I pitted and I do not understand how he made that up in just four laps. Especially as I was running on fresh rubber.»*
The German was actually not very happy with the handling of his Ferrari, which would explain why he did not dominate the race, in the way he had cruised to the front in qualifying. *«The balance was wrong. I realised during the formation laps and we tried to change the situation on the grid, by changing the angle of the front wing. We went in the right direction, but not far enough. I asked them to make an extra change during the pit stop, but the car was still oversteering.»*
Michael Schumacher was as disappointed as his 140,000 admirers. *«Of course I am disappointed. I sincerely thought we could here today. But all we can do is admit that we were not quick enough.»*
In the other Ferrari, Eddie Irvine complained about the handling of his F 300. *«I do not understand what happened. The understeer we managed to get rid of over the course of the weekend, came back for the race. I could not have gone any quicker without crashing.»*
In the championship, Michael Schumacher was four points down on Mika Hakkinen and needed five to win. Things were looking tough for him.» *I still think it is possible to win the championship,»* he said. *«There is still a lot of time before the Japanese Grand Prix and we will put these five weeks to good use to make a definite improvement to the car. As long as we have not lost, I will not give up.»*

A lot of effort for just one point

The Benetton team came home from the Nurburgring with just one point from Giancarlo Fisichella's sixth place. It was not a fair reward for qualifying fourth and eighth on the grid.
«A poor result? A catastrophe, that's what it was!» said Giancarlo Fisichella, not mincing his words after the race. The little Italian had missed out on his goal of beating the Williams duo, in order to hoist Benetton up the world championship order and catch up with the reigning world champion team.» *I managed to pass Frentzen for a while, but then I slid on oil from Rosset's car and he got me back. It is a real shame because fourth place was in my grasp.»*
Alexander Wurz, in the other Benetton, finished out of the points in seventh place. He could have finished fifth, but lost his chance during the pit stop, when first gear jammed and he lost several seconds while the mechanics fixed the problem and sent him on his way again.

△
Qualifying had not gone too well for Olivier Panis as he was only 15th on the grid. In the race, the Frenchman finished an unnoticed 12th.

Down to the wire

Mika Hakkinen could have been crowned at the Nurburgring. But it was not to be. For the third season in a row, the world championship for drivers would once again go down to the final round. When one considered the almost dominance of the McLaren boys in the early part of the season, the current situation seemed unbelievable. To reach that point, one had to remember the silver arrows' reliability problems, a driving error or two from Mika Hakkinen and an incredible amount of work undertaken by the Ferrari team.
Having the world championship remain undecided until the final race suits everyone. The suspense is almost unbearable and the media coverage is also unbearable! The sports sponsors had good reason to thank the unreliability of the McLarens.

▷
Alexander Wurz eats dirt during practice. At the Nurburgring there were a lot of «offs» and they came in all shapes and sizes.

PRACTICE TIMES

No	Driver	Car/Engine/Chassis	Practice Friday	Practice Saturday	Qualifying	Warm-up
1.	Jacques Villeneuve	Williams/Mecachrome/FW20/7 (G)	1'20"326	1'20"457	1'19"631	1'22"257
2.	Heinz-Harald Frentzen	Williams/Mecachrome/FW20/6 (G)	1'21"174	1'20"646	1'19"522	1'22"352
3.	Michael Schumacher	Ferrari/F300/189 (G)	1'20"461	1'19"925	1'18"561	1'21"515
4.	Eddie Irvine	Ferrari/F300/184 (G)	1'20"841	1'20"982	1'18"907	1'21"636
5.	Giancarlo Fisichella	Benetton/Playlife/198/6 (B)	1'20"325	1'20"834	1'19"048	1'21"362
6.	Alexander Wurz	Benetton/Playlife/198/4 (B)	1'21"014	1'20"819	1'19"569	1'21"870
7.	David Coulthard	McLaren/Mercedes/MP4-13/6 (B)	1'20"577	1'20"388	1'19"169	1'20"915
8.	Mika Hakkinen	McLaren/Mercedes/MP4-13/4 (B)	1'19"689	1'19"850	1'18"940	1'20"396
9.	Damon Hill	Jordan/Honda/198/3 (G)	1'21"738	1'21"050	1'19"807	1'22"582
10.	Ralf Schumacher	Jordan/Honda/198/4 (G)	1'21"351	1'20"327	1'19"455	1'22"206
11.	Olivier Panis	Prost/Peugeot/AP01/7 (B)	1'21"391	1'23"928	1'21"048	1'23"248
12.	Jarno Trulli	Prost/Peugeot/AP01/6 (B)	1'21"764	1'20"953	1'20"709	1'23"112
14.	Jean Alesi	Sauber/Petronas/C17/6 (G)	1'21"952	1'21"427	1'20"493	1'22"278
15.	Johnny Herbert	Sauber/Petronas/C17/2 (G)	1'22"603	1'21"649	1'20"650	1'22"716
16.	Pedro Diniz	Arrows/A19/7 (B)	1'22"485	1'21"781	1'21"258	1'23"398
17.	Mika Salo	Arrows/A19/6 (B)	1'24"004	1'21"704	1'21"120	1'23"997
18.	Rubens Barrichello	Stewart/Ford/SF2/5 (B)	1'21"538	1'22"276	1'20"530	1'23"104
19.	Jos Verstappen	Stewart/Ford/SF2/2 (B)	1'22"566	1'22"399	1'21"501	1'22"698
20.	Ricardo Rosset	Tyrrell/Ford/026/1 (G)	1'23"644	1'25"570	1'22"822	1'25"225
21.	Toranosuke Takagi	Tyrrell/Ford/026/5 (G)	1'22"792	1'22"968	1'21"525	1'24"333
22.	Shinji Nakano	Minardi/Ford/M198/3 (B)	1'22"967	1'23"019	1'22"078	1'23"555
23.	Esteban Tuero	Minardi/Ford/M198/5 (B)	1'23"331	1'22"893	1'22"146	1'24"178

CLASSIFICATION & RETIREMENTS

Pos	Driver	Team	Time
1.	Hakkinen	McLaren Mercedes	in 1h32'14"789
2.	M. Schum.	Ferrari	at 2"212
3.	Coulthard	McLaren Mercedes	at 34"164
4.	Irvine	Ferrari	at 58"183
5.	Frentzen	Williams Mecachrome	at 1'00"248
6.	Fisichella	Benetton Playlife	at 1'01"360
7.	Wurz	Benetton Playlife	at 1'04"790
8.	Villeneuve	Williams Mecachrome	at 1 lap
9.	Hill	Jordan Mugen Honda	at 1 lap
10.	Alesi	Sauber Petronas	at 1 lap
11.	Barrichello	Stewart Ford	at 2 laps
12.	Panis	Prost Peugeot	at 2 laps
13.	Verstappen	Stewart Ford	at 2 laps
14.	Salo	Arrows	at 2 laps
15.	Nakano	Minardi Ford	at 2 laps
16.	Takagi	Tyrrell Ford	at 2 laps
Lap	**Driver**	**Team**	**Reason**
7	Diniz	Arrows	hydraulic system
7	Trulli	Prost Peugeot	transmission
37	Rosset	Tyrrell Ford	engine
38	Herbert	Sauber Petronas	engine
54	R. Schum.	Jordan Mugen Honda	brakes
57	Tuero	Minardi Ford	not classified

FASTEST LAPS

	Driver	Time	Lap
1.	Hakkinen	1'20"450	25
2.	Coulthard	1'20"715	61
3.	M. Schum.	1'21"001	65
4.	Frentzen	1'21"394	65
5.	Fisichella	1'21"506	65
6.	Irvine	1'21"667	62
7.	Villeneuve	1'21"701	33
8.	Hill	1'21"741	66
9.	Wurz	1'21"778	61
10.	R. Schum.	1'21"881	21
11.	Alesi	1'21"979	43
12.	Herbert	1'22"712	23
13.	Panis	1'22"931	61
14.	Takagi	1'23"392	47
15.	Barrichello	1'23"412	33
16.	Salo	1'23"552	23
17.	Verstappen	1'23"944	30
18.	Tuero	1'24"024	50
19.	Rosset	1'24"161	23
20.	Nakano	1'24"210	61
21.	Diniz	1'25"285	5
22.	Trulli	1'25"328	4

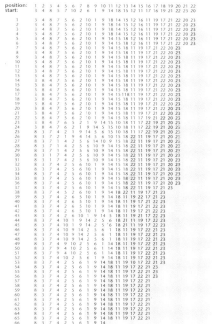

LAP CHART

position:	1	2	3	4	5	6	7	8	9	10	11	12	13	14	15	16	17	18	19	20	21	22
start:	3	4	8	5	7	10	2	6	1	9	14	18	15	12	11	17	16	19	21	22	23	20
1	3	4	8	7	5	6	2	10	1	9	18	14	15	12	16	11	19	17	21	22	20	23
2	3	4	8	7	5	6	2	10	1	9	18	14	15	12	16	11	19	17	21	22	20	23
3	3	4	8	7	5	6	2	10	1	9	18	14	15	12	16	11	19	17	21	22	20	23
4	3	4	8	7	5	6	2	10	1	9	18	14	15	12	16	11	19	17	21	22	20	23
5	3	4	8	7	5	6	2	10	1	9	14	15	18	12	16	11	19	17	21	22	20	23
6	3	4	8	7	5	6	2	10	1	9	14	15	18	12	16	11	19	17	21	22	20	23
7	3	4	8	7	5	6	2	10	1	9	14	15	18	11	19	17	21	22	20	23		
8	3	4	8	7	5	6	2	10	1	9	14	15	18	11	19	17	21	22	20	23		
9	3	4	8	7	5	6	2	10	1	9	14	15	18	11	19	17	21	22	20	23		
10	3	4	8	7	5	6	2	10	1	9	14	15	18	11	19	17	21	22	20	23		
11	3	4	8	7	5	6	2	10	1	9	14	15	18	11	19	17	21	22	20	23		
12	3	4	8	7	5	6	2	10	1	9	14	15	18	11	19	17	21	22	20	23		
13	3	4	8	7	5	6	2	10	1	9	14	15	18	11	19	17	21	22	20	23		
14	3	8	4	7	5	6	2	10	1	9	14	15	18	11	19	17	21	22	20	23		
15	3	8	4	7	5	6	2	10	1	9	14	15	18	11	19	17	21	22	20	23		
16	3	8	4	7	5	6	2	10	1	9	14	15	18	11	19	17	21	22	20	23		
17	3	8	4	7	5	6	2	10	1	9	14	15	118	11	19	17	21	22	20	23		
18	3	8	4	7	5	6	2	10	1	9	14	15	18	11	19	17	21	22	20	23		
19	3	8	4	7	5	6	2	10	1	9	14	15	18	11	19	17	21	22	20	23		
20	3	8	4	7	5	6	2	10	1	9	14	15	18	11	19	17	21	22	20	23		
21	3	8	4	7	5	6	2	10	1	9	14	15	18	11	19	17	21	22	20	23		
22	3	8	4	7	5	6	2	10	1	9	14	15	18	11	17	19	21	22	20	23		
23	3	8	4	7	6	5	2	1	9	14	15	10	18	11	17	22	19	21	20	23		
24	3	8	4	7	6	2	1	9	14	5	15	10	18	11	17	22	19	21	20	23		
25	8	3	7	4	2	1	9	14	5	6	15	10	18	11	17	22	19	21	20	23		
26	8	3	7	2	1	9	4	14	5	6	10	15	18	22	11	19	17	21	20	23		
27	8	3	7	1	4	2	5	6	14	10	9	15	18	22	11	19	17	21	20	23		
28	8	3	7	1	4	2	5	6	10	9	14	15	18	22	11	19	17	21	20	23		
29	8	3	7	1	4	2	5	6	10	9	14	15	18	22	11	19	17	21	20	23		
30	8	3	1	7	4	2	5	6	10	9	14	15	18	22	11	19	17	21	20	23		
31	8	3	1	7	4	2	5	6	10	9	14	15	18	22	11	19	17	21	20	23		
32	8	3	7	4	2	5	6	10	1	9	14	15	18	22	11	19	17	21	20	23		
33	8	3	7	4	2	5	6	10	1	9	14	15	18	22	11	19	17	21	20	23		
34	8	3	7	4	2	5	6	10	1	9	14	15	18	22	11	19	17	21	20	23		
35	8	3	7	4	2	5	6	10	1	9	14	15	18	22	11	19	17	21	20	23		
36	8	3	7	4	2	5	6	10	1	9	14	15	18	22	11	19	17	21	20	23		
37	8	3	7	4	2	5	6	10	1	9	14	15	18	22	11	19	17	21	23			
38	8	3	7	4	5	2	6	10	1	9	14	18	22	11	19	17	21	23				
39	8	3	7	4	2	6	5	10	1	9	14	18	11	19	22	17	21	23				
40	8	3	7	4	2	6	5	10	1	9	14	18	11	19	17	21	22	23				
41	8	3	7	4	2	6	5	10	1	9	14	18	11	19	17	21	22	23				
42	8	3	7	4	2	6	5	10	1	9	14	18	11	19	17	21	22	23				
43	8	3	7	4	2	6	10	1	9	14	5	18	11	19	21	17	22	23				
44	8	3	7	4	10	1	9	14	2	5	6	18	21	11	19	17	22	23				
45	8	3	7	4	10	1	9	14	2	5	6	18	21	11	19	17	22	23				
46	8	3	7	4	10	9	14	2	5	6	1	18	11	19	17	22	21	23				
47	8	3	7	4	10	9	14	2	5	6	1	18	11	19	17	22	21	23				
48	8	3	7	4	10	9	14	2	5	6	1	18	11	19	17	22	21	23				
49	8	3	7	4	9	10	2	5	6	1	14	18	11	19	17	22	21	23				
50	8	3	7	9	4	10	2	5	6	1	14	18	11	19	17	22	21	23				
51	8	3	7	9	4	10	2	5	6	1	14	18	11	19	17	22	21	23				
52	8	3	7	4	10	2	5	6	1	9	14	18	11	19	17	22	21	23				
53	8	3	7	4	2	5	6	1	9	14	18	11	19	10	17	22	21	23				
54	8	3	7	4	2	5	6	1	9	14	18	11	19	17	22	21	23					
55	8	3	7	4	2	5	6	1	9	14	18	11	19	17	22	21	23					
56	8	3	7	4	2	5	6	1	9	14	18	11	19	17	22	21	23					
57	8	3	7	4	2	5	6	1	9	14	18	11	19	17	22	21						
58	8	3	7	4	2	5	6	1	9	14	18	11	19	17	22	21						
59	8	3	7	4	2	5	6	1	9	14	18	11	19	17	22	21						
60	8	3	7	4	2	5	6	1	9	14	18	11	19	17	22	21						
61	8	3	7	4	2	5	6	1	9	14	18	11	19	17	22	21						
62	8	3	7	4	2	5	6	1	9	14	18	11	19	17	22	21						
63	8	3	7	4	2	5	6	1	9	14	18	11	19	17	22	21						
64	8	3	7	4	2	5	6	1	9	14	18	11	19	17	22	21						
65	8	3	7	4	2	5	6	1	9	14	18	11	19	17	22	21						
66	8	3	7	4	2	5	6	1	9	14												
67	8	3	7	4	2	5	6															

BRIDGESTONE

Best result for a Bridgestone shod runner:

Mika Hakkinen, McLaren-Mercedes, 1st

CHAMPIONSHIPS

(after fifteen rounds)

Drivers :

1. Mika HAKKINEN 90
2. Michael SCHUMACHER 86
3. David COULTHARD 52
4. Eddie IRVINE 41
5. Jacques VILLENEUVE 20
6. Damon HILL 17
   Alexander WURZ 17
8. Giancarlo FISICHELLA 16
9. Heinz-Harald FRENTZEN 15
10. Ralf SCHUMACHER 14
11. Jean ALESI 9
12. Rubens BARRICHELLO 4
13. Mika SALO 3
    Pedro DINIZ 3
15. Johnny HERBERT 1
    Jan MAGNUSSEN.........................1
    Jarno TRULLI 1

Constructors :

1. McLaren / Mercedes 142
2. Ferrari 127
3. Williams / Mecachrome 35
4. Benetton / Playlife 33
5. Jordan / Mugen Honda..................31
6. Sauber / Petronas 10
7. Arrows 6
8. Stewart / Ford 5
9. Prost / Peugeot 1

FIFTEENTH ROUND

GROSSER PREIS VON LUXEMBURG, NÜRBURGRING

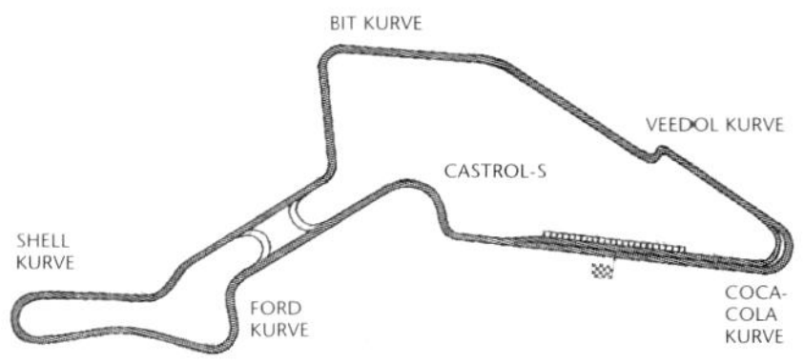

Date : September 27, 1998
Lenght : 4555 meters
Distance : 67 laps, 305.235 km
Weather : cloudy and cold, 16 degrees

WEEK-END GOSSIP

• Secret weapon at Benetton

The Benetton team was working on a new front suspension, which they considered a sort of «secret weapon» to allow the Anglo-Italian team to get back to the top in 1999. Giancarlo Fisichella refused to talk about it, except to say this new development was «interesting.»

• From Jordan to Arrows

Gary Anderson, former Jordan technical director had finally opted to work for the Arrows team, replacing John Barnard, who was due to sign a deal with the Prost team as an external consultant. However, there was some confusion over Anderson's positions as he appeared to have signed another contract to join Stewart.

• Ferrari still pushing

Despite Goodyear confirming its withdrawal from the sport at the end of the season, it seemed that Scuderia Ferrari was still pushing hard for the American company to stay in Formula 1. Luca di Montezemolo was apparently still in communication with the management of the Akron company. «*We are trying to get them to change their mind,*» was the word from Ferrari. «*Their tyres are fantastic and much of our progress this season is down to them.*»

• Sly seeks sponsors

Sylvester Stallone is still trawling the F1 paddock - he had also been in Italy - but it seemed he was having difficulties in finding the required budget for his Formula 1 film. Apparently, no Hollywood producer was keen to hand over the 25 million dollars still missing to start filming. At least Jean Alesi had already agreed to play one of the lead roles.

• Williams-BMW is building

The Williams team was setting up a second and independent test team, based in BMW premises in Munich. It would be used to develop the engine which the Bavarian constructor was preparing for the 2000 season. The other test team would work on the 1999 programme.

• Not again Jacques!

Jacques Villeneuve had been spending his money at the hairdressers yet again. After blonde, blue and mauve, this time he went black. Soon there will not be many colours left.

• Irvine attacks Hakkinen

Eddie Irvine is not known for being diplomatic. At the Nurburgring, Michael Schumacher lieutenant tried to destabilise Mika Hakkinen. «*Mika will crack under the pressure, that is obvious,*» he declared. «*Michael knows he will be able to fight for the championship again in the future, if he misses out this time, but for Mika this is likely to be his only chance. That is what creates the pressure.*»

RACE SUMMARY

- At the start, Eddie Irvine made the best start ahead of Michael Schumacher and Mika Hakkinen.
- Irvine immediately runs into handling problems. He slides at the last chicane and lets Schumacher slip through.
- Once in the lead, Schumacher pulls out a big lead while it takes Mika Hakkinen 14 laps to get past Irvine.
- Once past Eddie Irvine, Mika Hakkinen stepped up the pace and started to close on Michael Schumacher. The gap came down from 8.5 to 5.2 seconds, when the Ferrari refuels on lap 24.
- After Michael Schumacher had made his pit stop, Mika Hakkinen is out on his own in front and sets fastest lap after fastest lap. When he makes his own pit stop on lap 28, he manages to keep the lead as he rejoins the track.
- At first, Schumacher seems to be able to match Hakkinen's pace, but he gradually drops further and further back.
- The second run of pit stops do not alter the order and Mika Hakkinen takes his seventh win of the season, ahead of Michael Schumacher.

Located in the Eifel mountains, all the roads leading to the Nurburgring are minor ones. On Sunday, the 140,000 spectators trying to get it got stuck in traffic jams dozens of kilometres in length. Seeing how the traffic was being controlled near the circuit entrance (see photo,) it was easy to see how these jams came about.

World champions!

We had to wait for the very last race, but finally it was decided. Mika Hakkinen won the world championship for drivers and McLaren-Mercedes picked up the constructors' award.

The expected duel with Michael Schumacher was over before it started, as the German stalled on the grid and had to start at the back of the field. But whatever way it happened, the championship was theirs and nothing was going to spoil the McLaren-Mercedes team's celebration after the race (photo.)

FUJI TELEVISION JAPANESE GRAND PRIX
SUZUKA

During the five week gap since the Luxembourg Grand Prix, the McLaren and Ferrari teams had tested pretty much non-stop in preparation for the Japanese Grand Prix. Both claimed to have made significant improvements to their car. The result was that Michael Schumacher clinched pole after a thrilling duel with Mika Hakkinen. ▷

His third pole-position of the season

Michael Schumacher grabs the final pole

Michael Schumacher scored his tenth Ferrari pole at Suzuka as well as the twentieth of his career. It was not a simple task however, as the German had spent much of the morning session stuck in the pits with a hydraulic problem. «*One could think that I am a bit short of mileage on this circuit,*» he commented. «*But the truth is that we have tested so much recently, that we know what we want to get out of the car and how to do it. We actually owe this pole to the testing we did in Europe.*»

Ferrari had brought a special qualifying engine to Suzuka, apparently much more powerful than the standard version. Michael Schumacher was keen to scotch this rumour. «*We have a little bit more, but it is only some small details which have changed. It is not headline news and I am sure Mercedes have done something similar. Everyone has worked very hard and we have improved in all areas. We have made a lot of progress in just a few weeks.*» Despite this year's changes to the regulations, Schumacher was as quick as the previous year, which seemed amazing on such a demanding track as Suzuka. «*It's a pretty incredible result and most of this progress comes from the tyres. But it also means it is a lot more fun to drive. It is great fun to be able to throw the car into the corners on this circuit.*»

Strategy meeting for the McLaren brains after qualifying: Adrian Newey, Mika Hakkinen and Ron Dennis. ▽▷

A lot of Finns had made the trip to Suzuka. In fact, for once, there appeared to be more of them than Germans around the track. ▽

Hakkinen and Coulthard are right behind

Mika Hakkinen conceded a mere 178 thousandths of a second to Michael Schumacher. On Saturday, the two rivals were on a different planet to the rest of the field. In third place, David Coulthard was over a second behind his Finnish team- mate.

Right at the end of the session, Mika had set off on a very hot lap, as could be seen from his top speed, up 2 km/h up on his previous best. But he got his rear wheels on the grass and had to abort the lap. «*It is just one of those things that happen when you are on the limit. There is no point in talking about,*» he commented. «*It would probably have been a good lap, but we will never know. I am a bit angry with myself, because everything was going well up until then.*» Naturally the Finn was upset at being beaten by Michael Schumacher as the first part of their duel came to a close with the end of qualifying. «*Of course I am disappointed, I would have preferred to have been on pole. But it did not work and that is all there is to it. I cannot say this increases the pressure on me. Tomorrow we will see what happens.*»

The Finn refused to confirm whether or not the team had used a qualifying engine. «*You will have to ask Mario* (Ilien.) *He does not always tell me everything!*» In third place on the grid was Hakkinen's faithful lieutenant, David Coulthard. As the season wore on, the Scotsman was beaten more and more soundly by his team mate and he seemed to be wilting. In Suzuka the difference was a whole second and in the press conference he hardly had anything to say about it.

He did mention a problem with a «*lack of confidence in the car,*» to justify the gap. «*Maybe I am just a nervous person,*» he said as a joke, which fell flat with its audience. Asked what a lack of confidence meant he replied: «*I have spoken about it less this year, as the car has been less sensitive. But here, I immediately had understeer which I could not dial out. There is a big gap to the front row, but I do not think it will be so big in the race.*»

As for the tactics, the Scotsman said that he did not envisage a race against Eddie Irvine, but rather whoever was in front of him. «*Anything can happen at the start,*» he concluded. «*I might even make a very good start and lead at the first corner.*»

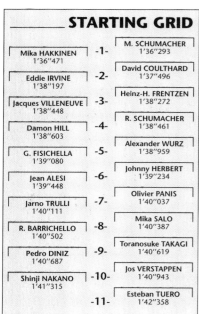

STARTING GRID

Mika HAKKINEN 1'36"471	-1-	M. SCHUMACHER 1'36"293
Eddie IRVINE 1'38"197	-2-	David COULTHARD 1'37"496
Jacques VILLENEUVE 1'38"448	-3-	Heinz-H. FRENTZEN 1'38"272
Damon HILL 1'38"603	-4-	R. SCHUMACHER 1'38"461
G. FISICHELLA 1'39"080	-5-	Alexander WURZ 1'38"959
Jean ALESI 1'39"448	-6-	Johnny HERBERT 1'39"234
Jarno TRULLI 1'40"111	-7-	Olivier PANIS 1'40"037
R. BARRICHELLO 1'40"502	-8-	Mika SALO 1'40"387
Pedro DINIZ 1'40"687	-9-	Toranosuke TAKAGI 1'40"619
Shinji NAKANO 1'41"315	-10-	Jos VERSTAPPEN 1'40"943
	-11-	Esteban TUERO 1'42"358

CHAMPION, MIKA

◁
Victory! As he drives past his team hanging off the pit wall, Mika Hakkinen allows himself a wheel locking celebration.

Mika Hakkinen did not really know what planet he was on. Once out of the car and congratulated by Michael Schumacher, he escaped from officials and ran down the pit wall to wave at a virtually no one, unable to get across to the main grandstand, before being caught and sent back for the podium ceremony.
Once this was over he tackled the traditional press conference, where he was far chattier than usual, launching into a lengthy explanation of the dream race, which had not looked so promising before the start. «*I was very nervous when the time came to get into the car,*» he admitted. «*After all, I was only second in qualifying and I was on the wrong side of the grid. It was not comfortable. I tried to tell myself: 'OK, stay calm, you can finish second.'*»
After a problem for Jarno Trulli aborted the first start, it was time for the second start and this time Michael Schumacher stalled (see page 214.) «*I tried not to think too much about what was happening to him,*» continued Hakkinen. «*But when I was told he had to start from the back, I thought, Wow! that's great.*» Leading from the start, the Finn immediately pulled out a gap on Eddie Irvine, the only Ferrari driver in a position to challenge him. «*I could not relax yet. I knew Eddie was there, ready to take the lead and then slow me down.*»
It was on lap 32, when Mika Hakkinen saw the wreck of Michael Schumacher's car that he understood it was all over and that at that moment he had become the 1998 world champion. «*I realised then it was over. I spoke to the team about it on the radio, but Ron* (Dennis, the McLaren boss) *told me to keep concentrating. He told me I still had the race to win. So I speeded up again, before lifting off towards the end of the race.*»
The champagne had been sprayed, the Finnish national anthem had been played, but Mika Hakkinen admitted he still did not understand what it meant. «*It is not real for me yet. I remember that when Damon Hill became champion here in 1996, he said he could not describe his feelings and it is the same for me. It is too big to believe. After crossing the finish line, I drove very slowly to try and understand. But I could not.*»
Mika then went back to his team for another champagne shower, while every mechanic was given a cigar. «*Now I want to celebrate,*» concluded the Finn. «*How, I don't know, but I will find a way.*»

«Well done mate.» Michael Schumacher congratulates his opponent at the end of the grand prix.
▽

A difficult wake-up call for the title candidate

Now that the title was in his pocket, Mika Hakkinen was able to admit to it without shame. Yes, he had suffered anguish and struggled through race morning. «*I got up around 6 o'clock. I tried to stay calm and focussed and not to be nervous. But really, I felt a lot of pressure. We have worked like mad all season and I knew I had to do something good this afternoon. Then I started to think about all the things that could go wrong; an engine that could explode, a puncture that could happen at any time or I might even make a driving error. So many things could happen. But it was not worth spending too much time thinking about it and I tried to concentrate on the race again. I had to be strong. Honestly, it was a bad morning for my nerves.*»
The match of the year ended up with a score of 10 - 0 in favour of Mika Hakkinen, who thus ended the year 14 points ahead of his rival.
The Finn was keen to praise his opponent. «I think Michael and I had a good fight,» he commented. «*It was very professional and always fair-play, without any comings together. I really have no negative feelings about this season. It was a very hard year but I liked it a lot. It was great. I know that some people criticised Michael a lot for his attitude this year, but personally I never had these negative thoughts.*»

IN THE POINTS

1.	Mika HAKKINEN	West McLaren Mercedes	1 h 27'22"535
2.	Eddie IRVINE	Scuderia Ferrari Marlboro	at 6"491
3.	David COULTHARD	West McLaren Mercedes	at 27"662
4.	Damon HILL	B&H Jordan Mugen Honda	at 1'13"491
5.	Heinz-H. FRENTZEN	Winfield Williams	at 1'13"857
6.	Jacques VILLENEUVE	Winfield Williams	at 1'15"867

Best lap : M. SCHUMACHER, lap 25, 1'40"190, avg. 210.703 km/h

«Did someone knock?» Toranosuke Takagi in his Tyrrell was surprised to be speared by the Minardi of Argentina's Esteban Tuero, who simply got his braking all wrong. Neither man was hurt, but it is highly likely that debris from the collision caused Michael Schumacher's puncture.

FUJI TELEVISION JAPANESE GRAND PRIX

A downcast Michael Schumacher. One has to admit, the fates had not been kind to him in Suzuka.

Lap 32. The Ferrari's right rear tyre has just exploded, causing irreparable damage to the F 300. It's all over.

Ferrari: missed again!

There are days that are tainted with bad luck and November 1st was one of those days for Michael Schumacher as the German saw his chances evaporate even before the start of the race. *«I don't know what happened,»* he explained after the race. *«When I came back to the grid, the clutch did not free, first gear selected itself and the engine stalled. We had never experienced this sort of problem.»* Having caused the start to be delayed, the German was forced to start from the back of the grid. What a start! Four corners later he was already 13th, having passed eight cars in two kilometres.

At the end of lap five, he was fifth, just twelve seconds behind Hakkinen in the lead. *«I enjoyed the start of the race,»* added Schumacher. *«It was good fun, especially as the other drivers did not make it difficult for me to get past.»* So, maybe the championship was not lost after all.

In truth it really was. Stuck behind the battling Villeneuve and Hill, the German was losing precious seconds. Once he got past these two on lap 15, he was now 33 seconds down on his Finnish rival. He got the gap down to 28 seconds, but then it stagnated for the next ten laps.

It looked as though the German was heading for a second place finish, when his right rear tyre exploded in the middle of the pit straight, possibly after running over debris from the Takagi-Tuero accident. *«I don't know if the debris caused the failure,»* added Schumacher, although Goodyear later confirmed the tyre failed because of a cut consistent with debris. *«But I had not expected problems with the rear tyres. I had flat-spotted a front, which was causing a lot of vibration and I was more worried about that tyre.»*

Surrounded by a horde of cameramen, the German did not seem too distraught. It was only an hour since the puncture, but he already appeared to got over it. *«I want to congratulate Mika. He deserves the world championship. I do not think we lost it here at Suzuka, but rather at the beginning of the season. I am not too disappointed, because we can be proud of what we have done this season. Life goes on and now we must try again next year.»*

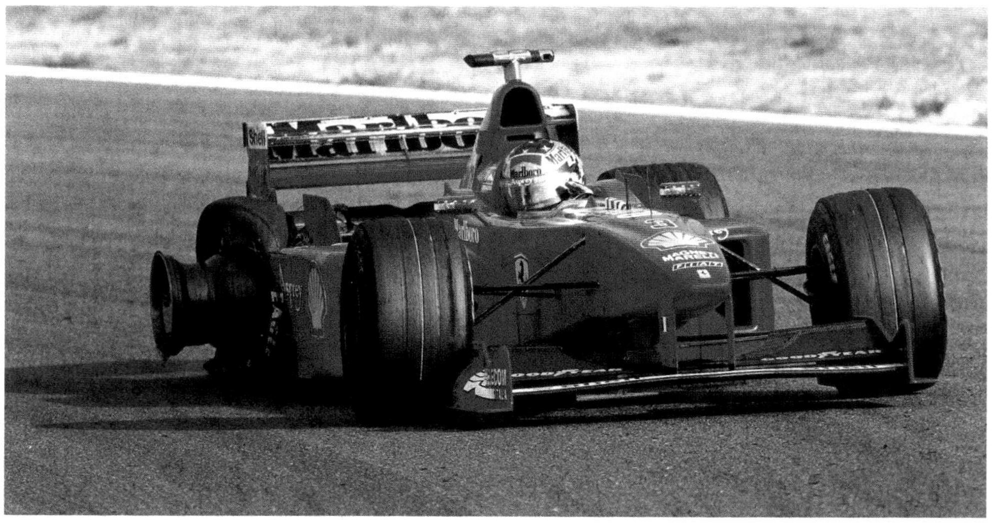

Finnish Roulette

Ferrari President Luca di Montezemolo is not a frequent visitor to the grands prix circuits, claiming he does not enjoy it. Nevertheless he was in Suzuka to boost the morale of his troops. *«I have come to show my support for all the fantastic work which the team has accomplished this year,»* he explained.

«But once again we have lost in the last round. To be honest, twice is enough! I feel a bit sad, but that is racing. When everything comes down to just one race, then it really is like playing roulette. I was hoping red would win, but it turned out to be black. But Mika could easily have stalled on the grid and had a puncture and we could now be celebrating Michael's title. In fact, what I regret is that we could not win the championship before this final round. We had a very good car, but we lost too much time at the start of the season because of the tyres. Once again that is motor sport.»

Williams wins the battle of the also-rans

The start. Mika Hakkinen leads, pulling away from Eddie Irvine. Right at the back, Michael Schumacher takes off like a rocket.

With only four points separating the Williams, Benetton and Jordan teams, it was going to be a close fight for third place in the championship at Suzuka.

There was certainly plenty at stake for the Williams mechanics, as Frank Williams had promised them a particularly good bonus if they kept third place, evidently important for attracting sponsors and for the distribution of television rights funds.

It was mission accomplished in the end, thanks to Heinz-Harald Frentzen's fifth place and Jacques Villeneuve's sixth. *«It was the toughest race I have known,»* complained «HH» at the end. *«My car lost its power steering on the first lap and it was like driving a truck.»*

Despite this, the German managed to hold off Damon Hill, until the final corner. Heinz-Harald did not close the door enough: in 1999 Damon Hill would be his new team-mate at Jordan.

The unplanned strategy

In second place, Eddie Irvine confirmed that the Scuderia was on form in Suzuka and that Michael Schumacher might have been able to win the race. If he had got away in the lead, he would no doubt have had fun slowing down Mika Hakkinen in order to let Eddie Irvine pass the Finn. All the same, the Irishman never seemed capable of menacing Mika Hakkinen. *«We had no real strategy for this race today,»* said the Ireland with a touch of humour and his characteristic phlegmatic approach. *«Over the weekend, we had looked at around fifteen possible strategies depending on what happened at the first corner. The only one we had not come up with was Michael at the back and me at the front!»*

Eddie Irvine had to settle for running his own race. *«I wanted to attack Mika, but he pulled away much too easily. My car went very well. I had copied Michael's set up just before the race. The best thing for me is that we have finally cured the back problem I have had all season, thanks to the way we have set up my seat.»*

PRACTICE TIMES

No	Driver	Make/Engine/Chassis	Practice Friday	Practice Saturday	Qualifying	Warm-up
1.	Jacques Villeneuve	Williams/Mecachrome/FW20/6 (G)	1'41"252	1'39"883	1'38"448	1'41"510
2.	Heinz-Harald Frentzen	Williams/Mecachrome/FW20/7 (G)	1'40"389	1'38"874	1'38"272	1'41"452
3.	Michael Schumacher	Ferrari/F300/189 (G)	1'39"823	1'38"429	1'36"293	1'40"431
4.	Eddie Irvine	Ferrari/F300/184 (G)	1'40"615	1'40"552	1'38"197	1'41"246
5.	Giancarlo Fisichella	Benetton/Playlife/198/6 (B)	1'42"224	1'40"265	1'39"080	1'42"611
6.	Alexander Wurz	Benetton/Playlife/198/6 (B)	1'42"628	1'41"002	1'38"959	1'42"881
7.	David Coulthard	McLaren/Mercedes/MP4-13/3 (B)	1'40"845	1'38"673	1'37"496	1'40"710
8.	Mika Hakkinen	McLaren/Mercedes/MP4-13/4 (B)	1'40"644	1'38"752	1'36"471	1'41"056
9.	Damon Hill	Jordan/Honda/198/6 (G)	1'41"098	1'40"146	1'38"603	1'41"902
10.	Ralf Schumacher	Jordan/Honda/198/4 (G)	1'40"336	1'40"003	1'38"461	1'41"119
11.	Olivier Panis	Prost/Peugeot/AP01/7 (B)	1'43"493	1'40"857	1'40"037	1'42"727
12.	Jarno Trulli	Prost/Peugeot/AP01/6 (B)	1'43"121	1'42"786	1'40"111	1'43"834
14.	Jean Alesi	Sauber/Petronas/C17/6 (G)	1'43"788	1'40"925	1'39"448	1'42"700
15.	Johnny Herbert	Sauber/Petronas/C17/2 (G)	1'43"894	1'41"543	1'39"234	1'42"837
16.	Pedro Diniz	Arrows/A19/7 (B)	1'44"468	1'41"889	1'40"687	1'44"273
17.	Mika Salo	Arrows/A19/6 (B)	1'43"634	1'41"823	1'40"387	1'42"650
18.	Rubens Barrichello	Stewart/Ford/SF2/5 (B)	1'43"854	1'41"172	1'40"502	1'44"205
19.	Jos Verstappen	Stewart/Ford/SF2/2 (B)	1'42"191	1'41"924	1'40"943	1'43"935
20.	Ricardo Rosset	Tyrrell/Ford/026/2 (G)	1'45"054	-	1'43"259	not qualif.
21.	Toranosuke Takagi	Tyrrell/Ford/026/3 (G)	1'42"833	1'41"105	1'40"619	1'43"776
22.	Shinji Nakano	Minardi/Ford/M198/3 (B)	1'44"632	1'43"013	1'41"315	1'43"593
23.	Esteban Tuero	Minardi/Ford/M198/5 (B)	1'46"396	1'43"048	1'42"358	1'45"733

LAP CHART

position:	1	2	3	4	5	6	7	8	9	10	11	12	13	14	15	16	17	18	19	20	21
start:	3	8	7	4	2	1	10	9	6	5	15	14	11	12	17	18	21	16	19	22	23
1	8	4	2	7	1	9	10	6	5	14	11	3	18	17	16	21	19	12	22	23	15
2	8	4	2	7	1	9	10	6	5	3	14	11	18	17	16	21	19	12	22	23	15
3	8	4	2	7	1	9	10	6	3	5	14	11	18	17	19	21	12	22	23	15	
4	8	4	2	7	1	9	10	3	6	5	14	11	18	17	19	21	12	22	15	23	
5	8	4	2	7	1	9	3	10	6	5	14	11	18	17	19	21	12	15	22	23	
6	8	4	2	7	1	9	3	10	6	5	14	11	18	17	19	21	12	15	22	23	
7	8	4	2	7	1	9	3	10	6	5	14	11	18	17	19	21	12	15	22	23	
8	8	4	2	7	1	9	3	10	6	5	14	11	18	17	19	21	12	15	22	23	
9	8	4	2	7	1	9	3	10	6	5	14	11	18	17	19	21	12	15	22	23	
10	8	4	2	7	1	9	3	10	6	5	14	11	17	19	21	15	12	18	22	23	
11	8	4	2	7	1	9	3	10	6	5	14	11	17	19	21	15	12	18	22	23	
12	8	4	2	7	1	9	3	10	6	5	14	11	17	19	15	21	12	18	22	23	
13	8	4	2	7	1	9	3	10	6	5	14	11	17	19	15	21	12	18	22	23	
14	8	4	2	7	1	3	9	6	5	14	11	17	15	19	21	12	18	22	23		
15	8	4	2	7	3	1	5	14	9	11	6	15	19	21	12	18	22	23			
16	8	4	2	7	3	1	14	9	11	6	5	15	21	12	19	18	22	23			
17	8	4	2	7	1	3	14	9	6	11	5	15	12	21	18	23	19	22			
18	8	4	2	7	1	3	14	9	6	5	15	11	12	18	19	21	23	22			
19	8	4	7	2	3	14	9	1	5	6	15	11	18	19	12	21	22	23			
20	8	4	7	3	2	9	1	5	6	14	15	11	18	19	12	21	22	23			
21	8	4	7	3	2	9	1	5	6	14	11	15	18	12	21	22	19	23			
22	8	4	3	7	2	9	1	5	6	14	11	15	18	12	21	22	23				
23	8	4	3	7	2	9	1	5	6	14	11	15	12	21	22	18	23				
24	8	4	3	7	2	9	1	5	6	14	11	15	12	21	22	18	23				
25	8	4	3	7	2	9	1	5	6	14	11	15	12	21	22	18	23				
26	8	4	3	7	2	9	1	5	6	14	11	15	12	22	21	23					
27	8	4	3	7	2	9	1	5	6	14	11	15	12	22	21	23					
28	8	4	3	7	2	9	1	5	6	14	11	15	12	22	21	23					
29	8	4	3	7	2	9	1	5	6	14	15	11	12	22							
30	8	4	3	7	2	9	1	14	6	5	15	11	12	22							
31	8	4	3	7	2	9	1	14	5	6	15	11	12	22							
32	8	4	7	2	9	1	14	5	6	15	11	12	22								
33	8	4	7	2	9	1	14	5	6	15	11	12	22								
34	8	4	7	2	14	9	1	5	6	15	11	12	22								
35	8	4	7	2	14	9	1	5	6	15	11	12	22								
36	8	4	7	2	9	1	5	14	6	15	11	12	22								
37	8	4	7	2	9	1	5	14	6	15	11	12	22								
38	8	4	7	2	9	1	5	14	6	15	11	12	22								
39	8	4	7	2	9	1	5	14	6	15	11	12	22								
40	8	4	7	2	9	1	5	14	6	15	11	12	22								
41	8	4	7	2	9	1	5	14	6	15	11	12									
42	8	4	7	2	9	1	5	14	6	15	11	12									
43	8	4	7	2	9	1	5	14	6	15	11	12									
44	8	4	7	2	9	1	5	14	6	15	11	12									
45	8	4	7	2	9	1	5	14	6	15	11	12									
46	8	4	7	2	9	1	5	14	6	15	11	12									
47	8	4	7	2	9	1	5	14	6	15	11	12									
48	8	4	7	2	9	1	5	14	6	15	11	12									
49	8	4	7	2	9	1	5	14	6	15	11										
50	8	4	7	2	9	1	5	14	6	15	11										
51	8	4	7	9	2	1	14	5													

BRIDGESTONE

Best result for a Bridgestone shod runner:

Mika Hakkinen, McLaren-Mercedes, *1st*

CLASSIFICATION & RETIREMENTS

Pos	Driver	Team	Time
1.	Hakkinen	McLaren Mercedes	in 1h27'22"535
2.	Irvine	Ferrari	at 6"491
3.	Coulthard	McLaren Mercedes	at 27"662
4.	Hill	Jordan Mugen Honda	at 1'13"491
5.	Frentzen	Williams Mecachrome	at 1'13"857
6.	Villeneuve	Williams Mecachrome	at 1'15"867
7.	Alesi	Sauber Petronas	at 1'36"053
8.	Fisichella	Benetton Playlife	at 2'01"301
9.	Wurz	Benetton Playlife	at 1 lap
10.	Herbert	Sauber Petronas	at 1 lap
11.	Panis	Prost Peugeot	at 1 lap
12.	Trulli	Prost Peugeot	engine

Lap	Driver	Team	Reason
3	Diniz	Arrows	spin
14	R. Schum.	Jordan Mugen Honda	engine
15	Salo	Arrows	hydraulics
22	Verstappen	Stewart Ford	transmission
26	Barrichello	Stewart Ford	hydraulics
29	Tuero	Minardi Ford	accident
29	Takagi	Tyrrell Ford	accident
32	M. Schum.	Ferrari	tyre
41	Nakano	Minardi Ford	throttle wire

FASTEST LAPS

	Driver	Time	Lap
1.	M. Schum.	1'40"190	19
2.	Hakkine	1'40"426	35
3.	Irvine	1'40"870	36
4.	Coulthard	1'40"905	42
5.	Villeneuve	1'42"273	40
6.	Hill	1'42"275	38
7.	Frentzen	1'42"331	36
8.	Fisichella	1'42"335	20
9.	Alesi	1'42"357	31
10.	Herbert	1'42"858	38
11.	R. Schum.	1'42"965	4
12.	Panis	1'43"073	49
13.	Trulli	1'43"164	42
14.	Wurz	1'43"447	18
15.	Nakano	1'44"158	37
16.	Barrichello	1'44"947	8
17.	Salo	1'45"304	14
18.	Takagi	1'45"673	23
19.	Tuero	1'45"792	21
20.	Verstappen	1'45"840	19
21.	Diniz	1'46"099	2

SIXTEENTH ROUND

FUJI TELEVISION JAPANESE GRAND PRIX, SUZUKA

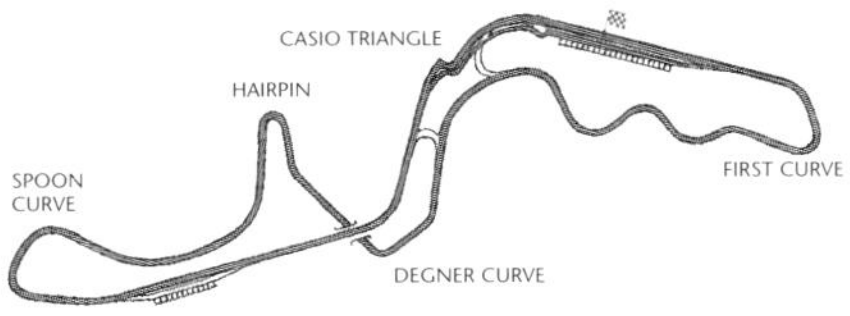

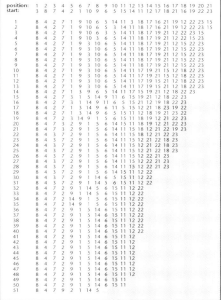

Date :	November 1, 1998
Length :	5860 meters
Distance :	51 laps, 298.868 km
Weather :	sunny, 23 degrees

CHAMPIONSHIPS

(after sixteen rounds)

Drivers :

1. Mika HAKKINEN 100
2. Michael SCHUMACHER 86
3. David COULTHARD 56
4. Eddie IRVINE................................47
5. Jacques VILLENEUVE 21
6. Damon HILL 20
7. Heinz-Harald FRENTZEN 17
   Alexander WURZ 17
9. Giancarlo FISICHELLA 16
10. Ralf SCHUMACHER 14
11. Jean ALESI.......................................9
12. Rubens BARRICHELLO....................4
13. Mika SALO.......................................3
    Pedro DINIZ 3
15. Johnny HERBERT.............................1
    Jan MAGNUSSEN............................1
    Jarno TRULLI...................................1

Constructors :

1. McLaren / Mercedes...................156
2. Ferrari...133
3. Williams / Mecachrome 38
4. Jordan / Mugen Honda.................34
5. Benetton / Playlife 33
6. Sauber / Petronas 10
7. Arrows...6
8. Stewart / Ford 5
9. Prost / Peugeot...............................1

WEEK-END GOSSIP

- **Richards dismissed because of Ford**

The surprise disappearance of David Richards from the helm of the Benetton team was put down to the Englishman's desire to sign an engine deal with Ford. The Benetton family, which controls the team, for its part wanted to continue to trust in Renault, hoping for the rapid return of the French company to F1.

It was this disagreement which led Richards to head for the door. The nomination of Rocco Benetton, the youngest of Alessandro's sons seemed a bit strange. Barely 29, he did not seem cut out for such a tough challenge.

- **Testing restricted**

It seems that the number of private test sessions next season will be severely limited, in order to reduce the running costs of the teams. The rule is taking time to put into place however, in part because it seems impossible to ban Ferrari from running at its own Fiorano circuit.

- **Bernie in the USA**

Absent from Japan, Bernie Ecclestone was rumoured to be in the United States, where he was discussing the possibility of running a Formula 1 grand prix at Indianapolis in 2000.

- **Diniz to Sauber**

The deal is done. A few days before the Japanese Grand Prix, the Swiss Sauber team announced it had signed a contract with Pedro Diniz and his 14 million dollars, for the 1999 season. Having previously had talks with Ralf Schumacher, Heinz-Harald Frentzen and Toranosuke Takagi, the team finally opted for the talent and fortune of the Brazilian.

- **Honda: still no decision**

A surprise, or rather a non-surprise at Suzuka. While the Japanese car company Honda was supposed to have taken the opportunity of the grand prix to announce its return to F1 in 2000 on the Thursday before the race, no announcement was forthcoming. It seemed the company's bosses are still divided as to whether they should make an F1 comeback, given the poor economic climate at the moment. For more information about the Japanese marque's plans see pages 52 and 53.

RACE SUMMARY

- A chaotic start. At first, Jarno Trulli stalls on the grid forcing the organisers to abort the procedure. At the end of the second formation lap, it is Michael Schumacher's turn to stall. He therefore has to start from the back of the grid. Third formation lap.
- When the race is finally underway, Mika Hakkinen heads Eddie Irvine, followed by Heinz-Harald Frentzen and David Coulthard.
- Michael Schumacher is carving through the field in spectacular fashion. Having started 21st, he is already 12th at the end of lap 1 and 7th at the end of lap 5.
- Up ahead, Irvine is unable to match Hakkinen's pace.
- Michael Schumacher is stuck behind Villeneuve and Hill for a long time. Having passed them, he is 33 seconds down on Hakkinen. He refuels and then puts in several fastest laps in succession.
- From lap 22, the German is third behind Hakkinen and Irvine who would obviously move over if the need arose.
- At the back, Esteban Tuero and Toranosuke Takagi come together on lap 29 at the chicane. It is a big crash and there is debris on the track.
- On lap 32, Michael Schumacher's right rear tyre explodes. He pulls over and retires his Ferrari.
- From that point on, Hakkinen is world champion. The Finn only has to bring his car home. In fact he does not even have to do that to take the title.

▽ *«Konichi-wa Steve-san.» At Suzuka there was no shortage of hostesses to greet the various sponsor guests. Each to their own taste.*

by Pascal Dro

High standards with four champions in 1999

Where would Formula 1 be without the glory which is bestowed on its most deserving elements? It would be a competition without a winner, like a friendly soccer match or a preliminary confrontation before the real thing. Whatever, it would not be what it is today. Formula One's strength is that it produces legends and dreams in real time. Remember the equally legendary arrogance of Ron Dennis' comment to the press: «*We make history, you are here to report it.*» Without doubt, making history constitutes an important part of the team owners' motivation. It recognises their deeds and gives it a historical perspective and flatters their egos, which are often over developed and for some of them, it is the F1 dream.
It is true that Formula 1 is for ever dishing out honours. First pole, first wins, best debuts, biggest salary, number of wins and world titles: all F1 statistics form a classification. Strangely enough, the drivers, who actually stand on the podiums, which are the source of many of these figures, seem strangely untouched by this surfeit of glory. The main motivation they admit to is money and that is linked to winning. They are all there to win and everything is done to make them seem more valuable than their competitors. They might want to win the title for themselves and for their country, but glory does not figure.
But the winner of the 1999 championship will have more glory than at any point in the recent past. The reason for this is that next season there will be four world champions on the track; Mika Hakkinen, Damon Hill, Jacques Villeneuve and Michael Schumacher. All bar Villeneuve should be in the running for not only the odd race win, but also the supreme prize itself. This is a rare enough occurrence to make it worthy of note. One has to go back fifteen years to 1985, to find four champion drivers on the track together. Then it was Lauda, Piquet, Prost and Rosberg. Even then, it was only at the last race of the year in Australia, that Prost picked up his first title. Both Senna and Mansell were in action then, but neither had yet won the big prize. The total number of champions fighting it out together actually reached seven as opposed to the four in 1999. Corneille said that «to win without danger is to triumph without glory.» In 1999 the winner's glory will be all the more intense as it will have been achieved against a first class field. One of these champions can expect to finish fourth at best. It should be a great season. Will there be a fifth world champion by the end of the season. The only real claimant to this position would have to be David Coulthard.

F1 has seen its future and it is called BAR

Like others before it, British American Racing was born out of the desire of a group of people to come together to create a team. But this time, we are looking at the creation of a team for the next millennium.
It has a colossal budget in the order of 100 million dollars per year for five years, a race car constructor of industrial scale, Adrian Reynard and Reynard Cars, a talented commercial director, Rick Gorne, a world champion driver, Jacques Villeneuve, a young hopeful, Ricardo Zonta, who comes from Brazil, one of the last stomping grounds for the tobacco companies, the best customer engine available, the Supertec V10 and a beautiful new factory to put all the elements together under a single roof. Orchestrating the whole deal is Jacques Villeneuve's former manager, Craig Pollock. It really is the team for 2000 arriving at a track near you one year early. It is the sign of a multinational looking for an audience before the sport is overrun with anti-tobacco and anti-alcohol legislation, necessitating a new breed of sponsor and signalling the end of the historic backers of the sport. Alain Prost has a good grasp of the current trend: «*At McLaren it is Mercedes which controls the team's finances. West and Mobil are there thanks to Mercedes. For a constructor, spending an additional 50% over the cost of the engines in order to become a majority shareholder in a team and eventually take it over and give it your name, is not a stupid plan. It greatly increases its visibility and it is a trend which seems perfectly normal to me.*»
At BAR, it is British American Tobacco which is paying for everything, including the purchase of the old Tyrrell team, out of whose ashes British American Racing will rise. The fight between the old and new school is almost over. Only Arrows and Minardi remain of the old order who, even if they are part of an industrial group, it is only on a very small scale. Benetton is a steel fist in a velvet glove. While the multinationals might not yet own the majority of shares in these teams, the weight of their support gives them all the voting rights. Money rules, but as long as there is plenty of it, no one complains.

Jarno Trulli at the Austrian Grand Prix. In 1999, the Italian will stick with the Prost-Peugeot team. ▽

The constructors are killing off the assemblers

In the mid-Eighties, they were known as the assemblers. It was a generic term probably invented by those scoffing foreigners and it joined together those who used the Cosworth/Hewland unit mated to a chassis of their own design. In this group could be found Arrows, ATS, Theodore, Ensign, Toleman, Tyrrell and also Brabham, Williams, Lotus and McLaren.
At the time, there was a certain amount of ill feeling between this group and the major constructors, who were beginning to make their presence felt in F1.
Some were brazen about their arrival, like Renault and Fiat through Ferrari, while others snuck in through the back door like Alfa Romeo and BMW with Brabham, Honda with Williams, Lotus and McLaren. The two camps had a different concept of what Formula 1 was all about. Eventually, Formula 1 chose to go down the constructors' path, which has led to the situation we have today, ten years on. The sport attracts a huge global audience and major car manufacturers. Its high profile image on the world stage no longer needed the little teams. Lotus and Brabham crumbled and hung on to the start of the Nineties. Today, Tyrrell has disappeared and new teams have to pay a hefty deposit simply to get in on the act. Not only does this sort out the wheat from the chaff but it also allows Bernie Ecclestone to control the number of cars on the track. Currently we have 22 machines and that number seems to suit the television cameras perfectly. It also means we no longer have to put up with half baked outfits like Andrea Moda or Life for example.
This means that the arrival of a new team is a rare occurrence and those tend to come from the major constructors. Honda is due to arrive in 2000 with its own team, chassis and all, while Toyota will for the time being, take the more conventional route of supplying engines.

◁
Michael Schumacher will be one of four world champions in action in 1999. Back in 1995, the German was the only one.

◁
Ready to go.. There will be no more than 22 cars in 1999, just like in 1998.

Waiting for Honda, Toyota, Nakano, Takagi and the rest

Japan and F1 have a long history together. Like all good stories, it has its ups and downs, linked to circumstances and the changing economic climate. In the Eighties Honda dominated the sport. We had Satoru Nakajima, Aguri Suzuki as well as fleeting appearances from the likes of Hattori in 1991 with Coloni, while Ukyo Katayama was a more serious and longer lasting competitor. Yamaha also tried to get in on the act and just as quickly as it begun, so it ended. At the end of 1992 Honda pulled out, Alain Prost retired at the end of '93 and one year later, Ayrton Senna, whose career grew with Honda, died. On the team front, March owners Leyton House disappeared, as did Footwork which pulled out of supporting Arrows and Larrousse as it crashed business wise. In Japan, Formula One's popularity declined and the country sought other foreign kicks such as cycling, football and of course its most popular sport, baseball. Formula 1 hardly ever made the papers, although Yamaha hung on with Jordan and then Arrows. It too threw in the towel, its only high point being Damon Hill's second place in the 1997 Hungarian Grand Prix. Mugen-Honda is the only organisation to have kept going with Footwork and then Ligier, who gave the Japanese engine builder its first grand prix win at Monaco with Olivier Panis in 1996. Mild Seven, the Japanese cigarette brand has remained true, recently renewing its contract with Benetton.

So the Japanese seem here to stay.

Shinji Nakano is here but nobody knows why. The same goes for Tora Takagi, who has support from Honda. He might have a role in the new team to be set up by Harvey Postlethwaite to run in 2000 and Satoru Nakajima is also linked to the project as Sporting Director. On the Toyota front, there is talk of them joining the party in 2001 and top man Hiroshi Okuda is very much aware of what its rival got out of its previous participation. Toyota is currently struggling in CART with Dan Gurney's All American Racing team. It will have completed its Le Mans programme next year and it is involved through a specialist company, in rallying, in a similar fashion to Subaru. With a total of only eleven teams allowed to play in the F1 playground, for the time being Toyota will have to settle for being an engine supplier in the style of Mercedes. But Toyota factories are springing up all over Europe and its marketing department will be pushing for some of the F1 glory to rub off.

Recap of the 1998 season

Position in championship	Driver	Make	Australian Grand Prix	Brazilian Grand Prix	Argentinian Grand Prix	San Marino Grand Prix	Spanish Grand Prix	Monaco Grand Prix	Canadian Grand Prix	French Grand Prix	British Grand Prix	Austrian Grand Prix	German Grand Prix	Hungarian Grand Prix	Belgian Grand Prix	Italian Grand Prix	Luxembourg Grand Prix	Japanese Grand Prix	Number of pole-positions	Number of victories	Number of fastest laps	Number of laps in the lead	Number of kilometers in the lead	Final classif. in Chapionship
1	Mika HAKKINEN	McLaren Mercedes	1	1	2	A	1	1	A	3	2	1	1	6	A	4	1	1	9	8	6	575	2'703	100
2	Michael SCHUMACHER	Ferrari	A	3	1	2	3	10	1	1	1	3	5	1	A	1	2	A	3	6	6	268	1'252	86
3	David COULTHARD	McLaren Mercedes	2	2	6	1	2	A	A	6	A	2	2	2	7	A	3	3	3	1	3	120	597	56
4	Eddie IRVINE	Ferrari	4	8	3	3	A	3	3	2	3	4	8	A	A	2	4	2	–	–	–	1	4	47
5	Jacques VILLENEUVE	Williams Mecachrome	5	7	A	4	6	5	10	4	7	6	3	3	A	A	8	6	–	–	–	–	–	21
6	Damon HILL	Jordan Mugen Honda	8	10	8	10	A	8	A	A	A	7	4	4	1	6	9	4	–	1	–	26	181	20
7	Heinz-H. FRENTZEN	Williams Mecachrome	3	5	9	5	8	A	A	15	A	A	9	5	4	7	5	5	–	–	–	–	–	17
8	Alexander WURZ	Benetton Playlife	7	4	4	A	4	A	4	5	4	9	11	16	A	A	7	9	–	–	1	–	–	17
9	Giancarlo FISICHELLA	Benetton Playlife	A	6	7	A	A	2	2	9	5	A	7	8	A	8	6	8	1	–	–	24	106	16
10	Ralf SCHUMACHER	Jordan Mugen Honda	A	A	A	7	11	A	A	16	6	5	6	9	2	3	A	A	–	–	–	–	–	14
11	Jean ALESI	Sauber Petronas	A	9	5	6	10	12	A	7	A	A	10	7	3	5	10	7	–	–	–	–	–	9
12	Rubens BARRICHELLO	Stewart Ford	A	A	10	A	5	A	5	10	A	A	A	A	A	10	11	A	–	–	–	–	–	4
13	Mika SALO	Arrows	A	A	A	9	A	4	A	13	A	A	14	A	A	A	14	A	–	–	–	–	–	3
14	Pedro DINIZ	Arrows	A	A	A	A	A	6	9	14	A	A	A	11	5	A	A	A	–	–	–	–	–	3
15	Johnny HERBERT	Sauber Petronas	6	12	A	A	7	7	A	8	A	8	A	10	A	A	A	10	–	–	–	–	–	1
16	Jan MAGNUSSEN	Stewart Ford	A	11	A	A	12	A	6	–	–	–	–	–	–	–	–	–	–	–	–	–	–	1
17	Jarno TRULLI	Prost Peugeot	A	A	11	A	9	A	A	A	A	10	12	A	6	13	A	12	–	–	–	–	–	1
	Then, by alphabetical order :																							
	Shinji NAKANO	Minardi Ford	A	A	13	A	14	9	7	17	8	11	A	15	8	A	15	A	–	–	–	–	–	–
	Olivier PANIS	Prost Peugeot	9	A	15	11	16	A	A	11	A	A	15	12	A	A	12	11	–	–	–	–	–	–
	Ricardo ROSSET	Tyrrell Ford	A	A	14	A	NQ	NQ	8	A	A	12	F	NQ	A	12	A	NQ	–	–	–	–	–	–
	Toranosuke TAKAGI	Tyrrell Ford	A	A	12	A	13	11	A	A	9	A	13	14	A	9	16	A	–	–	–	–	–	–
	Esteban TUERO	Minardi Ford	A	A	A	8	15	A	A	A	A	A	16	A	A	11	A	A	–	–	–	–	–	–
	Jos VERSTAPPEN	Stewart Ford	–	–	–	–	–	–	–	12	A	A	A	13	A	A	13	A	–	–	–	–	–	–

Nber of Grand Prix contested

Patrese	256
Berger	210
DeCesaris	208
Piquet	204
Prost	199
Alboreto	194
Mansell	187
G. Hill	176
Laffite	176
Lauda	171
Boutsen	163
Senna	161
Brundle	158
Watson	152
Alesi	151
Arnoux	149
Warwick	147
Reutemann	146
E. Fittipaldi	144
Jarier	135
Cheever	132
Regazzoni	132
Herbert	129
Ma. Andretti	128
Brabham	126
Peterson	123
Ickx	116
Jones	116
Rosberg	114
Tambay	114
Hulme	112
Scheckter	112
Surtees	111
Martini	119
M. Schumacher	118
Hakkinen	112
De Angelis	108
Alliot	107
Mass	105
Bonnier	102
McLaren	101
D. Hill	100
Stewart	99
Siffert	97
Barrichello	97
Amon	96
Depailler	95
Katayama	95
Capelli	94
Hunt	92
Beltoise	86
Gurney	86
Palmer	84
Surer	82
Trintignant	82
Irvine	81
Frentzen	81
Johansson	79
Nannini	77
Ghinzani	76
Panis	75
Nakajima	74
Brambilla	74
Gugelmin	74
Stuck	74
Coulthard	74
Clark	72
Pace	72
Modena	70
Pironi	70
Then :	
Morbidelli	68
Salo	68
Diniz	66
Verstappen	57
Larini	49
J. Villeneuve	49
Fisichella	41
R. Schumacher	33
Nakano	33
Rosset	32
Trulli	30
Magnussen	24
Wurz	19
Tuero	16
Takagi	16

Nber of poles

Senna	65
Prost	33
Clark	33
Mansell	32
Fangio	28
Lauda	24
Piquet	24
D. Hill	20
M. Schumacher	20
Andretti	18
Arnoux	18
Stewart	17
Moss	16
Ascari	14
Hunt	14
Peterson	14
Brabham	13
G. Hill	13
Ickx	13
J. Villeneuve	13
Berger	12
Rindt	10
Hakkinen	10
Surtees	8
Patrese	8
Coulthard	8
Laffite	7
Fittipaldi	6
P. Hill	6
Jabouille	6
Jones	6
Reutemann	6
Amon	5
Farina	5
Regazzoni	5
Rosberg	5
Tambay	5
Hawthorn	4
Pironi	4
De Angelis	3
Brooks	3
T. Fabi	3
Gonzales	3
Gurney	3
Jarier	3
Scheckter	3
Then :	
Alesi	2
Frentzen	1
Barrichello	1
Fisichella	1

Nber of victories

Prost	51
Senna	41
M. Schumacher	33
Mansell	31
Stewart	27
Clark	25
Lauda	25
Fangio	24
Piquet	23
D. Hill	22
Moss	16
Brabham	14
Fittipaldi	14
G. Hill	14
Ascari	13
Andretti	12
Jones	12
Reutemann	12
J. Villeneuve	11
Hunt	10
Peterson	10
Scheckter	10
Berger	10
Hakkinen	9
Hulme	8
Ickx	8
Arnoux	7
Brooks	6
Laffite	6
Rindt	6
Surtees	6
G. Villeneuve	6
Patrese	6
Alboreto	5
Farina	5
Regazzoni	5
Rosberg	5
Watson	5
Gurney	4
McLaren	4
Coulthard	4
Boutsen	3
P. Hill	3
Hawthorn	3
Pironi	3
Then :	
Herbert	2
Panis	1
Panis	1
Alesi	1
Frentzen	1

Number of fastest laps

Prost	41
M. Schumacher	34
Mansell	30
Clark	28
Lauda	25
Fangio	23
Piquet	23
Berger	21
Moss	20
D. Hill	19
Senna	19
Regazzoni	15
Stewart	15
Ickx	14
Jones	13
Patrese	13
Arnoux	12
Ascari	11
Surtees	11
Andretti	10
Brabham	10
G. Hill	10
Hulme	9
Peterson	9
J. Villeneuve	9
Hunt	8
Coulthard	8
Laffite	7
G. Villeneuve	7
Hakkinen	7
Farina	6
Fittipaldi	6
Gonzalez	6
Gurney	6
Hawthorn	6
P. Hill	6
Pironi	6
Scheckter	6
Frentzen	6
Pace	5
Watson	5
Alesi	4
Alboreto	4
Beltoise	4
Depailler	4
Reutemann	4
Siffert	4
Then:	
Fisichella	1
Wurz	1

Total number of points scored

Prost	798.5
Senna	614
M. Schumacher	526
Piquet	485.5
Mansell	482
Lauda	420.5
Berger	385
Stewart	360
D. Hill	353
Reutemann	310
G. Hill	289
E. Fittipaldi	281
Patrese	281
Fangio	277.5
Clark	274
Brabham	261
Scheckter	255
Alesi	234
Laffite	228
Hakkinen	218
Regazzoni	212
Jones	206
Peterson	206
McLaren	196.5
Alboreto	186.5
Moss	186.5
Arnoux	181
Ickx	181
Ma. Andretti	180
Surtees	180
J. Villeneuve	180
Hunt	179
Coulthard	173
Watson	169
Rosberg	159.5
Depailler	141
Ascari	139
Then :	
Irvine	99
Frentzen	88
Herbert	83
Barrichello	55
Panis	54
Fisichella	36
R. Schumacher	27
Wurz	21
Salo	15
Verstappen	11
Katayama	5
Diniz	5
Trulli	4
Nakano	2
Larini	1
Magnussen	1

Number of laps in the lead

Senna	2'999
Prost	2'705
Mansell	2'099
Clark	2'039
Stewart	1'893
M. Schumacher	1'836
Lauda	1'620
Piquet	1'572
D. Hill	1'351
G. Hill	1'073
Brabham	827
Andretti	799
Peterson	706
Berger	695
Scheckter	671
Reutemann	648
Hakkinen	641
Hunt	634
J. Villeneuve	634
Jones	594
Patrese	568
G. Villeneuve	533
Ickx	529
Arnoux	506
Rosberg	506
Fittipaldi	459
Hulme	436
Coulthard	430
Rindt	387
Regazzoni	361
Surtees	310
Pironi	295
Watson	287
Laffite	279
Alesi	271
Alboreto	218
Tambay	197
Gurney	191
P. Hill	189
Jabouille	184
Amon	183
Brooks	173
Depailler	165
Boutsen	164
Von Trips	156
Bonnier	139
Then :	
Frentzen	76
Trulli	37
Herbert	27
Fisichella	31
Irvine	24
Panis	16
Barrichello	4

Nber of km in the lead

Senna	13'613
Prost	12'575
Clark	10'189
Mansell	9'642
Stewart	9'077
M. Schumacher	8'463
Piquet	7'465
Lauda	7'188
D. Hill	6'243
G. Hill	4'618
Brabham	4'541
Andretti	3'577
Berger	3'456
Reutemann	3'309
Peterson	3'304
Hunt	3'229
Ickx	3'067
Hakkinen	3'022
J. Villeneuve	2'972
Jones	2'877
Scheckter	2'837
Patrese	2'571
Arnoux	2'561
G. Villeneuve	2'244
Rosberg	2'137
Surtees	2'131
Fittipaldi	2'122
Coulthard	2'052
Rindt	1'905
Hulme	1'900
Regazzoni	1'855
P. Hill	1'715
Brooks	1'525
Gurney	1'518
Laffite	1'476
Alesi	1'297
Watson	1'245
Pironi	1'238
Jabouille	978
Tambay	975
Alboreto	927
Von Trips	787
Amon	784
Boutsen	662
Siffert	636
Bandini	615
Then :	
Frentzen	379
Trulli	160
Fisichella	154
Herbert	149
Irvine	129
Panis	53
Barrichello	18

Abbreviations : A = retired; NQ = not qualified; NPQ = not prequalified; F = forfeit; D = disqualified, NC = finished but not classified (insufficient distance covered). ARG = Argentina; AUS = Australia; AUT = Austria; BEL = Belgium; BRE = Brazil; CAN = Canada; DAL = Dallas; ESP = Spain; EUR = Europe; FIN = Finland; FRA = France; GB = England; GER =Germany; HOL = The Netherlands; ITA = Italy; JAP = Japan; MEX = Mexico; MON = Monaco; NZ = New-Zealand; PAC = Pacific; POR = Portugal; RSM = San Marino; SA = South Africa; SUE = Sweden; SUI = Switzerland; USA = Etats-Unis; USAE = East USA; USAW = West USA; VEG = Las Vegas. NB : Laps in the lead only since 1957.

The 49 World Champions

Year	Driver	Nationality	Make	Nber of races	Nber of poles	Nber of victories	Nber of fastest laps
1950	Giuseppe Farina	ITA	Alfa Roméo	7	2	3	3
1951	Juan Manuel Fangio	ARG	Alfa Roméo	8	4	3	5
1952	Alberto Ascari	ITA	Ferrari	8	5	6	5
1953	Alberto Ascari	ITA	Ferrari	9	6	5	4
1954	Juan Manuel Fangio	ARG	Mercedes/Maserati	9	5	6	3
1955	Juan Manuel Fangio	ARG	Mercedes	7	3	4	3
1956	Juan Manuel Fangio	ARG	Lancia/Ferrari	8	5	3	3
1957	Juan Manuel Fangio	ARG	Maserati	8	4	4	2
1958	Mike Hawthorn	GB	Ferrari	11	4	1	5
1959	Jack Brabham	AUS	Cooper Climax	9	1	2	1
1960	Jack Brabham	AUS	Cooper Climax	10	3	5	3
1961	Phil Hill	USA	Ferrari	8	5	2	2
1962	Graham Hill	GB	BRM	9	1	4	3
1963	Jim Clark	GB	Lotus Climax	10	7	7	6
1964	John Surtees	GB	Ferrari	10	2	2	2
1965	Jim Clark	GB	Lotus Climax	10	6	6	6
1966	Jack Brabham	AUS	Brabham Repco	9	3	4	1
1967	Dennis Hulme	NZ	Brabham Repco	11	0	2	2
1968	Graham Hill	GB	Lotus Ford	12	2	3	0
1969	Jackie Stewart	GB	Matra Ford	11	2	6	5
1970	Jochen Rindt	AUT	Lotus Ford	13	3	5	1
1971	Jackie Stewart	GB	Matra Ford	11	6	6	3
1972	Emerson Fittipaldi	BRE	Lotus Ford	12	3	5	0
1973	Jackie Stewart	GB	Tyrrell Ford	15	3	5	1
1974	Emerson Fittipaldi	BRE	McLaren Ford	15	2	3	0
1975	Niki Lauda	AUT	Ferrari	14	9	5	2
1976	James Hunt	GB	McLaren Ford	16	8	6	2
1977	Niki Lauda	AUT	Ferrari	17	2	3	3
1978	Mario Andretti	USA	Lotus Ford	16	8	6	3
1979	Jody Scheckter	SA	Ferrari	15	1	3	1
1980	Alan Jones	AUS	Williams Ford	14	3	5	5
1981	Nelson Piquet	BRE	Brabham Ford	15	4	3	1
1982	Keke Rosberg	FIN	Williams Ford	16	1	1	0
1983	Nelson Piquet	BRE	Brabham BMW Turbo	15	1	3	4
1984	Niki Lauda	AUT	McLaren TAG Porsche Turbo	16	0	5	5
1985	Alain Prost	FRA	McLaren TAG Porsche Turbo	16	2	5	5
1986	Alain Prost	FRA	McLaren TAG Porsche Turbo	16	1	4	2
1987	Nelson Piquet	BRE	Williams Honda Turbo	16	4	3	4
1988	Ayrton Senna	BRE	McLaren Honda Turbo	16	13	8	3
1989	Alain Prost	FRA	McLaren Honda	16	2	4	5
1990	Ayrton Senna	BRE	McLaren Honda	16	10	6	2
1991	Ayrton Senna	BRE	McLaren Honda	16	8	7	2
1992	Nigel Mansell	GB	Williams Renault	16	14	9	8
1993	Alain Prost	FRA	Williams Renault	16	13	7	6
1994	Michael Schumacher	GER	Benetton Ford	14	6	8	9
1995	Michael Schumacher	GER	Benetton Renault	17	4	9	7
1996	Damon Hill	GB	Williams Renault	16	9	8	5
1997	Jacques Villeneuve	CAN	Williams Renault	17	10	7	3
1998	Mika Hakkinen	FIN	McLaren Mercedes	16	9	8	6

Constructor's championship 1998

Position	Team	Nber of points	Nber of poles	Nber of victories	Nberot fastest laps	Nber of laps in the lead	Nber ot kil. in the lead
1.	McLaren Mercedes	156	12	9	9	695	3'300
2.	Ferrari	133	3	6	6	269	1'256
3.	Williams Mecachrome	38	0	0	0	0	0
4.	Jordan Mugen Honda	34	0	1	0	26	181
5.	Benetton Playlife	33	1	0	1	24	106
6.	Sauber Petronas	10	0	0	0	0	0
7.	Arrows	6	0	0	0	0	0
8.	Stewart Ford	5	0	0	0	0	
9.	Prost Peugeot	1	0	0	0	0	0

Nb. of constructor's championship titles

(exists since 1958)

9 : Williams 1980 - 81 - 86 - 87-92 - 93-94-96-97

8 : Ferrari 1961 - 64 - 75 - 76 77 - 79 - 82 - 83

McLaren 1974 - 84 - 85 - 88-89 - 90 - 91 98

7: Lotus 1963 - 65 - 68 - 70-72 - 73 - 78

2 : Cooper 1959 - 60
Brabham 1966 - 67

1 : Vanwall 1958
BRM 1962
Matra 1969
Tyrrell 1971
Benetton 1995

Number of poles per make

Ferrari	124
Lotus	107
Williams	107
McLaren	92
Brabham	39
Renault	31
Benetton	16
Tyrrell	14
Alfa Roméo	12
BRM	11
Cooper	11
Maserati	10
Ligier	9
Mercedes	8
Vanwall	7
March	5
Matra	4
Shadow	3
Lancia	2
Arrows	1
Honda	1
Jordan	1
Lola	1
Porsche	1
Wolf	1

Number of victories per make

Ferrari	119
McLaren	116
Williams	103
Lotus	79
Brabham	35
Benetton	26
Tyrrell	23
BRM	17
Cooper	16
Renault	1
Alfa Roméo	10
Maserati	9
Matra	9
Mercedes	9
Vanwall	9
Ligier	9
March	3
Wolf	3
Honda	2
Hesketh	1
Penske	1
Porsche	1
Shadow	1
Jordan	1

Nber of fastest laps per make

Ferrari	132
Williams	109
McLaren	80
Lotus	70
Brabham	41
Benetton	37
Tyrrell	20
Renault	18
BRM	15
Maserati	15
Alfa Roméo	14
Cooper	13
Matra	12
Ligier	11
Mercedes	9
March	7
Vanwall	6
Surtees	4
Eagle	2
Honda	2
Shadow	2
Wolf	2
Ensign	1
Gordini	1
Hesketh	1
Lancia	1
Parnelli	1
Jordan	1

Family picture of the 1998 championship, a few hours before the finale in Suzuka. Standing, from left to right: Jos Verstappen, Rubens Barrichello, Jean Alesi, Johnny Herbert, Jarno Trulli and Olivier Panis. Middle: Mika Salo, Pedro Diniz, Giancarlo Fisichella, Alexander Wurz, Esteban Tuero, Shinji Nakano, Toranosuke Takagi and Ricardo Rosset. Sitting: Heinz-Harald Frentzen, Jacques Villeneuve, David Coulthard, Mika Hakkinen, Michael Schumacher, Eddie Irvine, Damon Hill and Ralf Schumacher.

Sporting regulations

The FIA will organise the FIA Formula One World Championship (the Championship) which is the property of the FIA and comprises two titles of World Champion, one for drivers and for for constructors. It consists of the Formula One Grand Prix races which are included in the Formula One calendar and in respect of which the ASNs and organisers have signed the organisation agreement provided for in the 1997 Concorde Agreement (Events). All the participating parties (FIA, ASNs, organisers, competitors and circuits) undertake to apply as well as observe the rules governing the Championship and must hold FIA Super Licences which are issued to drivers, competitors, officials, organisers and circuits.

LICENCES

10. All drivers, competitors and officials participating in the Championship must hold a FIA Super licence. Applications for Super Licences must be made to the FIA through the applicant's ASN. The driver's name will remain on the super license for one year.

CHAMPIONSHIP EVENTS

12. Events are reserved for Formula One cars as defined in the Technical Regulations.

13. Each Event will have the status of an international restricted competition.

14. The distance of all races, from start signal referred to in Article 144 to the chequered flag, shall be equal to the least number of complete laps which exceed a distance of 305 km. However, should two hours elapse before the scheduled race distance is completed, the leader will be shown the chequered flag when he crosses the start/finish line (the Line) at the end of the lap during which the to hour period ended. The Line is a single line which crosses both the track and the pit lane.

15. The maximum number of events in the Championship is 17, the minimum is 8.

17. An Event which is cancelled with less than three months written notice to the FIA will not be considered for inclusion in the following year's Championship unless the FIA judges the cancellation to have been due to force majeure.

18. An Event may be cancelled if fewer than 12 cars are available for it.

WORLD CHAMPIONSHIP

19. The Formula One World Champion Driver's Title will be awarded to the driver who has scored the highest number of points, taking into consideration all the results obtained during the events which have actually taken place.

20. Points will not be awarded for the Championship unless the driver has driven the same car throughout the race in the Event in question.

21. The title of Formula One World Champion for Constructors will be awarded to the make which has scored the highest number of points, taking into account all the results obtained by a maximum of 2 cars per make.

22. The constructor of an engine or rolling chassis is the person (including any corporate or unincorporated body) which owns the intellectual property rights to such engine or chassis. The make of an engine or chassis is the name attributed to it by its constructor. If the make of the chassis is not of the same as that of the engine, the title will be awarded to the former which shall always precede the latter in the name of the car.

23. Points for both titles will be awarded at each Event according to the following scale :

1st : 10 points; 2nd : 6 points; 3rd : 4 points; 4th : 3 points; 5th : 2 points; 6th : 1 point.

24. If a race is stopped under Arts. 158 and 159, and cannot be restarted, no points will be awarded in case A, half points will be awarded in case B and full points will be awarded in case C.

25. Drivers finishing first, second and third in the Championship must be present at the annual FIA Prize Giving ceremony. Any such driver who is absent will be liable to a maximum fine of US $ 50,000.00. All competitors shall use their best endeavours to ensure that their drivers attend as aforesaid.

DEAD HEAT

26. Prizes and points awarded for all the positions of competitors who tie, will be added together and shared equally.

27. If two or more constructors or drivers finish the season with the same number of points, the higher place in the Championship (in either case) shall be awarded to :

a) the holder of the greatest number of 1st places,

b) if the number of first places is the same, the holder of the greatest number of second places,

c) if the number of second places is the same, the holder of the greatest number of third places and so on until a winner emerges,

d) if this procedure fails to produce a result, the FISA will nominate the winner according to such criteria as it thinks fit.

COMPETITORS APPLICATIONS

43. Applications to compete in the Championship may be submitted to the FIA at any time between 1 November and 15 November each year (...). Successful applicants are automatically entered in all events of the Championship and will be the only competitors at Events.

45. A competitor may change the make and type of engine at any time during the Championship. All points scored with an engine different (in make and type) to that which was first entered in the Championship will count (and will be aggregated) for the assessment of Benefits and for determining team positions for pre-qualifying purposes, however such points will not count towards (nor be aggregated for) the FIA Formula One Constructors Championship.

46. (...) All applicants who did not take part in the entire Championship for the previous year must also deposit US$500,000.00 with the FIA when submitting their application. (...)

47. All applications will be studied by the FIA which will publish the list of cars and drivers accepted together with their race numbers on 1 December (or the following Monday if 1 December falls on a week-end), having first notified unsuccessful applicants as set out in article 43.

48. No more than two entries will be accepted from any one competitor.

INCIDENTS

54. Incident means any occurrence or series of occurrences involving one or more drivers, or any action by any driver, which is reported to the stewards by the race director (or noted by the stewards and referred to the race director for investigation) which :

- necessitated the stopping of a race under Article 158;

- constituted a breach of these Sporting Regulations or the Code;

- caused a false start by one or more cars;

- caused an avoidable collision;

- forced a diver off the track;

- illegitimately prevented a legitimate overtaking manoeuvre by a driver;

- illegitimately impeded another driver during overtaking.

55. It shall be at the discretion of the stewards to decide, upon a report or a request by the race director, if a driver or drivers involved in an incident shall be penalised. If a driver is involved in a collision or incident (see Art. 54) he must not leave the circuit without the consent of the stewards.

56. The stewards may impose a time penalty on any driver involved in an incident.

57. Should the Stewards decide to impose a time penalty, the following procedure will be followed :

a) The stewards shall, no later than twenty-five minutes after the moment at which the Incident occurred, give written notification of the time penalty which has been imposed to an official of the team concerned. Notification of the penalty, which will include the time at which the steward's decision was made, will also be displayed on the timing monitors.

b) Subject to e) below, from the time the steward's decision is notified on the timing monitors, the relevant driver may cover no more than three complete laps before entering the pits and proceeding to his pit where he shall remain for the period of time penalty. During the time the car is stationary it may not be worked on unless the engine stops, in which case it may be started after the time penalty period has elapsed.

c) When the time penalty period has elapsed the driver may rejoin the race.

d) Any breach or failure to comply with Articles 57 b) or 57 c) may result in the car being excluded.

e) If an incident for which a time penalty is imposed occurs with 12 or less complete laps remaining to the finish of the race, the stewards shall have the right to add the time penalty to the elapsed time of the driver concerned.

58. Any determination made or any penalty imposed pursuant to Article 56 shall be without prejudice to the operation of Articles 160 or 161 of the Code.

CHANGES OF DRIVER

61. During a season, each team will be permitted one driver change for their first car and will be permitted to have three drivers for their second car who may be changed at any time provided that any driver change is made in accordance with the Code and before the start of qualifying practice. After 18:00 on the day of scrutineering, a driver change may only take place with the consent of the stewards. In all other circumstances, competitors will be obliged to use the drivers they nominated at the time of entering the Championship except in case of force majeure which will be considered seperately. Any new driver may score points in the Championship.

NUMBER OF CARS PARTICIPATING

63. The number of cars allowed to start the race is limited to 26. For practice the number is limited to 30, except for the free practice on race day which is open only to those cars which have qualified for the race.

64. Should the number of cars entered in the Championship exceed 30 the following procedure will be used :

- 26 places in qualifying practice will be reserved for constructors' cars according to the classification in the World Championship for Constructors of the two previous half seasons (...)

- 4 places will be made available to other cars according to pre-qualifying practice.

- Those cars not included in the 26 automatically admitted to qualifying practice will take part in a timed practice session two days before the race (see Art. 118) and the 4 fastest of them will then be allowed to take part in free and qualifying practice sessions (see Arts. 119 and 120) together with the aforementioned 26.

RACE NUMBERS AND NAME OF CAR

65. Each car will carry the race number of its driver (or his replacement) as published by the FIA at the beginning of the season. When a car is shown on a 25 cm television monitor in such a way as to substantially fill the screen in at least one dimension, its race number must be clearly visible from the front and from either side of the car respectively.

66. The name or the emblem of the make of the car must appear on the front of the nose of the car and in either case be at least 25 mm in its largest dimension. The name of the driver will also appear on the bodywork, on the outside of the cockpit, or on the driver's helmet and be clearly legible.

PIT LANE

69. a) For the avoidance of doubt and for description purposes, the pit lane shall be divided into two lanes. The lane closest to the pit wall is designated the «fast lane» and the lane closest to the garages is designated the «inner lane», and is the only area where any work can be carried out on a car.

b) Competitors must not paint lines on any part of the pit lane.

c) No equipment may be left in the fast lane. A car may enter the fast lane only with the driver sitting in the car behind the steering wheel in his normal position even when the car is being pushed.

d) Team personnel are only allowed in the pit lane immediately before they are required to work on a car and must withdraw as soon as the work is complete.

SPORTING CHECKS

71. At the first Event of each Championship, the FIA will check all licences.

SCRUTINEERING

73. Initial scrutineering of the car will take place three days (Monaco : four days) before the race between 10h00 and 18h00 in the garage assigned to each team.

74. Unless a waiver is granted by the stewards , competitors who do not keep to these time limits will not be allowed to take part in the Event.

75. No car may take part in the Event until it has been passed by the scrutineers.

76. The scrutineers may :

a) check the eligibility of a car or of a competitor at any time during an Event.

b) require a car to be dismantled by the competitor to make sure that the conditions of eligibility or conformity are fully satisfied.

c) require a competitor to pay the reasonable expenses which exercise of the powers mentioned in this Article may entail.

d) require a competitor to supply them with such parts or samples as they may deem necessary.

78. The race director or the clerk of the course may require that any car involved in an accident be stopped and checked.

80. The stewards will publish the findings of the scrutineers each time cars are checked during the Event. These results will not include any specific figure except in respect of fuel analysis or where a car is found to be in breach of the Technical Regulations.

SUPPLY OF TYRES IN THE CHAMPIONSHIP AND TYRE LIMITATION DURING THE EVENT

81. Supply of tyres : No tyre may be used in the Championship unless the company supplying such tyre accepts and adheres to the following conditions :

- one tyre supplier present in the Championship: this company must equip 100% of the entered teams on ordinary commercial terms.

- two tyre suppliers present : each of them must, if called upon to do so, be prepared to equip up to 60% of the entered teams on ordinary commercial terms.

- three or more tyre suppliers present : each of them must, if called upon to do so, be prepared to equip up to 40% of the entered teams on ordinary commercial terms.

- each tyre supplier must undertake to provide only two specifications of dry-weather tyre and three specifications of wet-weather tyre at each Event, each of which must be of one homogenous compound only;

- if, in the interests of maintaining current levels of circuit safety, the FIA deems it necessary to reduce tyre grip, it shall introduce such rules as the tyre suppliers may advise or, in the absence of advice which achieves the FIA's objectives, specify the maximum permissible contact areas for front and rear tyres.

82. Quantity and type of tyres :

a) The same driver may not use more than a total of forty dry-weather tyres and twenty-eight wet-weather tyres throughout the entire duration of the Event.

Prior to the qualifying practice each driver may use two specifications of dry-weather tyres but must, before qualifying practice begins, nominate which specification of tyre he will use for the remainder of the Event.

For qualifying practice, warm up and the race each driver may use no more than twenty-eight tyres (fourteen front and fourteen rear).

b) All dry-weather tyres must incorporate circumferential grooves square to the wheel axis and around the entire circumference of the contact surface of each tyre.

c) Each front dry-weather tyre, when new, must incorporate 3 grooves which are : - arranged symmetrically about the centre of the tyre tread;

- at least 14 mm wide at the contact surface and which taper uniformly to a minimum of 10 mm at the lower surface;

- at least 2.5 mm deep across the whole lower surface;

- 50 mm (+/- 1.0 mm) between centres.

d) Each rear dry-weather tyre, when new, must incorporate 4 grooves which are : - arranged symmetrically about the centre of the tyre tread;

- at least 14 mm wide at the contact surface and which taper uniformly to a minimum of 10 mm at the lower surface;

- at least 2.5 mm deep across the whole lower surface;

- 50 mm (+/- 1.0 mm) between centres.

The measurements referred to in c) and d) above will be taken when the tyre is fitted to a wheel and inflated to 20 psi.

e) A wet-weather tyre is one which has been designed for use on a wet or damp track. All wet-weather tyres must, when new, have a contact area which does not exceed 300 cm2 when fitted to the front of the car and 475 cm2 when fitted to the rear. Contact areas will be measured over any square section of the tyre which is normal to and symmetrical about the tyre centre line and which measures 200 mm x 200 mm when fitted to the front of the car and 250 mm x 250 mm when fitted to the rear. For the purposes of establishing conformity, only void areas which are greater than 2.5 mm in depth will be considered. Prior to use at an Event, each tyre manufacturer must provide the technical delegate with a full scale drawing of each type of wet-weather tyre intended for use. With the exception of race day, wet-weather tyres may only be used after the track has been declared wet by the race director and, during the remainder of the relevant session, the choice of tyres is free.

83. Control of tyres :

a) All tyres which are to be used at an Event will be marked with a unique identification.

b) At any time during an Event, and at his absolute discretion, the FIA technical delegate may select the dry-weather tyres to be used by any Team from among the total stock of tyres which such Team's designated supplier has present at the Event.

c) During initial scrutineering, each competitor may have up to forty-four dry-weather tyres and thirty-six wet-weather tyres for each of his drivers ready for marking in his garage. Tyres not marked during initial scrutineering can be marked at other times by arrangement with the FIA technical delegate.

d) From among the twenty-eight dry-weather tyres chosen for each car for qualifying practice, warm up and the race, the FIA technical delegate will choose at random sixteen tyres (eight front and eight rear) which are the only dry-weather tyres which such car may use in qualifying practice.

e) A competitor wishing to replace an already marked unused tyre by another unused one must present both tyres to the FIA technical delegate.

f) The use of tyres without appropriate identification is strictly forbidden.

84. Wear of tyres : The Championship will be contested on grooved tyres. The FIA reserve the right to introduce at any time a method of measuring remaining groove depth if performance appears to be enhanced by high wear or by the use of tyres which are worn so that the grooves are no longer visible.

WEIGHING

85. The weight of any car may be checked during the Event as follows :

a) All drivers entered in the Championship will be weighed, wearing their complete racing apparel, at the first Event of the season. If a driver is entered later in the season he will be weighed at his first Event.

b) During qualifying practice

1) the FIA will install weighing equipment in an area as close to the first pit as possible, this area will be used for the weighing procedure;

2) cars will be selected at random to undergo the weighing procedure. The FIA technical delegate will inform the driver by means of a red light at the pit entrance that his car has been selected for weighing;

3) having been signalled (by means of a red light), that his car has been selected for weighing, the driver will proceed directly to the weighing area and stop his engine;

4) the car will then be weighed and the result given to the driver in writing;

5) if the car is unable to reach the weighing area under its own power it will be placed under the exclusive control of the marshals who will take the car to be weighed;

6) a car or driver may not leave the weighing area without the consent of the FIA technical delegate.

c) After the race : Each car crossing the line will be weighed. If a car is weighed without the driver the weight determined under 2 above will be added to give the total weight required under Article 4. of the Technical Regulations.

d) Should the weight of the car be less than that specified in Article 4.1 of the Technical Regulations when weighed under b) or c) above, the car and the driver will be excluded from the Event save where the deficiency in weight results from the accidental loss of a component of the car due to force majeure.

e) No solid, liquid, gas or other substance or matter of whatsoever nature may be added to, placed on, or removed from a car after it has been selected for weighing or has finished the race or during the weighing procedure. (...)

f) Only scrutineers and officials may enter the weighing area. No intervention of any kind is allowed there unless authorised by such officials.

86. Any breach of these provisions for the weighing of cars may result in the exclusion of the relevant car.

SPARE CAR

89. A competitor may use several cars for practice and the race provided that :

a) he uses no more than two cars (one car for a one car Team) for free practice on each of the two practice days;

b) he uses no more than three cars (two cars for a one car Team) during qualifying practice;

c) they are all of the same make and were entered in the Championship by the same competitor;

d) they have been scrutineered in accordance with these Sporting Regulations;

e) each car carries its driver's race number.

90. Changes of car may only take place in the pits under supervision of the marshals.

91. No change of car will be allowed after the green light (see Article 142) provided always that if a race has to be restarted under Article 160 Case A, the moment after which no car change will be allowed shall be when the green light for the subsequent start is shown.

GENERAL SAFETY

93. Drivers are strictly forbidden to drive their car in the opposite direction to the race unless this is absolutely necessary in order to move the car from a dangerous position. A car may be pushed to remove it from a dangerous position as directed by the marshals.

94. Any driver intending to leave the track or to go to his pits or the paddock area must signal his intention to do so in good time making sure that he can do this without danger.

96. A driver who abandons a car must leave it in neutral or with the clutch disengaged and with the steering wheel in place.

97. Repairs to a car may be carried out only in the paddock, pits and on the grid.

99. Save as provided in Articl 141, refuelling is allowed only in the pits.

102. Save as specifically authorised by the Code or these Sporting Regulations, no one except the driver may touch a stopped car unless it is in the pits or on the starting grid.

104. During the periods commencing 15 minutes prior to and ending 5 minutes after every practice session and the period between the green lights being illuminated (Article 142) and the time when the last car enters the parc fermé, no one is allowed on the track with the exception of :

a) marshals or other authorised personnel in the execution of their duty;

b) drivers when driving or under the direction of the marshals;

c) and mechanics under Article 143 only.

105. During a race, the engine may only be started with the starter, except :

a) in the pit lane where the use of an external starting device is allowed (...).

107. A speed limit of 80 km/h in practice and 120 km/h during the warm up and the race, or such other speed limits as the Permanent Bureau of the Formula One Commission may decide, will be enforced in the pit lane. Except in the race, any driver who exceeds the limit will be fined US$250 for each km/h above the limit (this may be increased in the case of a second offence in the same Championship season). During the race, the stewards may impose a time penalty on any driver who exceeds the limit.

108. If a driver has serious mechanical difficulties during practice or the race, he must leave the track as soon as it is safe to do so.

109. The car's rear light must be illuminated at all times when it is running on wet-weather tyres. The technical delegate may check the light at any time until 15 minutes before the green light. No penalty will be imposed if the light fails during a race, nor need the car be stopped.

110. Only six team members per participating car (all of whom shall have been issued with and wearing special identification) are allowed in the signalling area during practice and the race. (...)

112. The race director, the clerk of the course or the FIA medical delegate can require a driver to have a medical examination at any time during an Event.

113. Failure to comply with the general safety requirements of the Code or these Sporting Regulations may result in the exclusion of the car and driver concerned from the Event.

PRE-QUALIFYING PRACTICE, FREE PRACTICE, QUALIFYING PRACTICE AND WARM UP

115. No driver may start in the race without taking part in qualifying practice.

116. During practice there will be a green/red light at the pit exit. Cars may only leave the pit lane when the green light is on.

117. During the Event, the circuit shall not be used for any purpose other than the Event except after all practice has finished on each day and during the period beginning after the free practice on race day and ending 60 minutes before the pit lane is opened or at other times with the written consent of the FIA.

118. Should it be necessary for certain cars to pre-qualify in accordance with Article 64, the practice session will take place two days (Monaco, three days) before the race from 08h00 to 09h00.

119. Free practice sessions will take place :

a) two days (Monaco : three days) before the race from 11.00 to 12.00 and from 13.00 to 14.00.

b) the day before the race from 09.00 to 9.45 and from 10.15 to 11.00.

120. Qualifying practice will take place :

a) The day before the race from 13.00 - 14.00.

b) Each driver is allowed a maximum of 12 laps qualifying practice. Should a driver complete more than 12 laps, all times recorded by the driver will be cancelled.

121. Warm up : a free practice session will take place

on race day; it will last 30 minutes and start 4 hours and 30 minutes before the starting time of the race.

122. The interval between the free and qualifying practice session may never be less than 1 hour and 30 minutes.

Only in the most exceptional circumstances can a delay in free practice or other difficulty on race morning result in a delay to the starting time of the race.

123. If a car stops during practice it must be removed from the track as quickly as possible so that its presence does not constitute a danger or hinder other competitors. If the driver is unable to drive the car from a dangerous position, it shall be the duty of the marshals to assist him. If any such assistance results in the car being driven or pushed back to the pits, the car may not be used again in that session. Additionally, if the assistance is given during a pre-qualifying practice or qualifying practice session, the driver's fastest lap time from the relevant session will be deleted. In the event of a driving infringement during practice, the Stewards may delete any number of qualifying times from the driver concerned. In this case, a team will not be able to appeal against the Stewards' decision.

124. The clerk of the course may interrupt practice as often and for as long as he thinks necessary to clear the track or to allow the recovery of a car. In the case of free practice only, the clerk of the course with the agreement of the stewards of the meeting may decline to prolong the practice period after an interruption of this kind.

Furthermore if, in the opinions of the stewards, a stoppage is caused deliberately, the driver concerned may have his times from that session cancelled and may not be permitted to take part in any other practice session that day.

126. Should one or more sessions be thus interrupted, no protest can be accepted as to the possible effects of the interruption on the qualification of drivers admitted to start.

127. All laps covered during qualifying practice will be timed to determine the driver's position at the start in accordance with the prescriptions of Article 132. With the exception of a lap on which a red flag is shown (see Article 158) each time a car crosses the Line it will be deemed to have completed one lap. On a circuit where the Line is situated before the first pit, any car which stops on the circuit having already completed its total allocation of laps, will be deemed to have covered an extra lap.

STOPPING THE PRACTICE

128. Should it become necessary to stop the practice because the circuit is blocked by an accident or because weather or other conditions make it impossible to continue, the Clerk of the Course shall order a red flag and the abort lights to be shown at the start Line. Simultaneously, red flags will be shown at all marshal posts. When the signal is given to stop all cars shall immediately reduce speed and proceed slowly back to their respective pits and all cars abandoned on the track will be removed to a safe place. Any lap during which the red flag is shown will not be counted towards a car's total lap allocation for that session. At the end of each practice session all drivers may cross the Line only once.

PRESS CONFERENCES

129. The FIA press delegate will choose a maximum of five drivers who must attend a press conference in the media centre for a period of one hour at 15:00 on the Thursday of the Event (on Wednesday in Monaco). These driver's Teams will be notified no less than 48 hours before the conference. In addition, a maximum of two Team personalities may be chosen by the FIA press delegate to attend this press conference.

On the Friday of the Event (on Thursday in Monaco), a minimum of three and a maximum of six drivers and/or team personalities, (other than those who attended the press conference on the previous day and subject to the consent of the team principal), will be chosen by ballot or rota by the FIA press delegate during the Event and must make themselves available to the media for a press conference in the media centre for a period of one hour at 15:30.

130. Immediately after qualifying practice the first three drivers in qualifying will be required to make themselves available for television interviews in the unilateral room and then attend a press conference in the media centre for a maximum period of 30 minutes.

THE GRID

131. At the end of qualifying practice, the fastest time achieved by each driver will be officially published (see Article 63).

132. The grid will be drawn up in the order of the fastest time achieved by each driver. Should two or more drivers have set identical times, priority will be given to the one who set it first.

133. The fastest driver will start the race from the position on the grid which was the pole position in the previous year or, on a new circuit, has been designated as such by the FIA safety delegate.

134. Any driver whose best qualifying lap exceeds 107% of the pole position time will not be allowed to take part in the race. Under exceptional circumstances however, which may include setting a suitable lap time in a previous free practice session, the stewards may permit the car to start the race. Should there be more than one driver accepted in this manner, their order will be determined by the stewards.

135. The final starting grid will be publihed after the warm up on race day. Any competitor whose car(s) is (are) unable to start for any reason whatsoever (or who has good reason to believe that their car(s) will not be ready to start) must inform the clerk of the course accordingly at the earliest opportunity and, in any event, not later than 45 minutes before the start of the race. If one or more cars are withdrawn the grid will be closed up accordingly.

137. Any car which has not taken up its position on the grid by the time the ten minute signal is shown will not be permitted to do so and must start from the pits in accordance with Article 140.

BRIEFING

138. A briefing by the race director will take place one hour after the end of warm up on race day. All drivers eligible to take part in the race, and their Team Managers, must be present throughout the briefing; absence may result in exclusion from the race.

STARTING PROCEDURE

139. 30 minutes before the time for the start of the race, the cars will leave the pits to cover one reconnaissance lap. At the end of this lap they will stop on the grid in starting order with their engines stopped. Should they wish to cover more than one reconnaissance lap, this must be done by driving down the pit lane at a greatly reduced speed between each of the laps.

140. 17 minutes before the starting time, a warning signal announcing the closing of the pit exit in 2 minutes will be given.

15 minutes before the starting time, the pit exit will be closed and a second warning singal will be given. Any car which is still in the pits can start from the pits, but only under the direction of the marshals. It may be moved to the pit exit only with the driver in position. Where the pit exit is immediately after the Line, cars will join the race when the whole field has passed the pit exit on its first racing lap. Where the pit exit is immediately before the Line, cars will join the race as soon as the whole field has crossed the Line after the start.

141. Refuelling on the starting grid may only be carried out prior to the 5 minute signal and by using one unpressurised container with a maximum capacity of 12 litres. Any such container may not be refilled during the starting procedure and must be fitted with one or more dry break couplings connecting it to the car.

142. The approach of the start will be announced by signals shown ten minutes, five minutes, three minutes, one minute and thirty seconds before the start of the formation lap, each of which will be accompanied by an audible warning.

When the ten minute signal is shown, everybody except drivers, officials and team technical staff must leave the grid.

When the five-minute signal is shown all cars must have their wheels fitted. After this signal wheels may only be removed in the pits. Any car which does not have all its wheels fitted at the five-minute signal must start the race from the back of the grid or the pit lane.

When the one minute signal is shown, engines will be started and all team technical staff must leave the grid.

When the green lights are illuminated, the cars will begin the formation lap with the pole position driver leading. When leaving the grid, all drivers must proceed at a greatly reduced speed until clear of any Team personnel standing beside the track. During the formation lap practice starts are forbidden and the formation must be kept as tight as possible.

Overtaking during the formation lap is only permitted if a car is delayed when leaving its grid position and cars behind cannot avoid passing it without unduly delaying the remainder of the field. In this case, drivers may only overtake to re-establish the original starting order.

Any driver who is delayed leaving the grid may not overtake another moving car if he was stationary after the remainder of the cars had crossed the Line, and must start the race from the back of the grid. If more than one driver is affected, they must form up at the back of the grid in the order they left to complete the formation lap. If the Line is not situated in front of pole position, for the purposes of this Article only, it will be deemed to be a white line one metre in front of pole position.

A time penalty will be imposed on any driver who, in the opinion of the Stewards, unnecessarily overtook another car during the formation lap.

143. Any driver who is unable to start the formation lap must raise his arm and, after the remainder of the cars have crossed the Line, his mechanics may attempt to rectify the problem under the supervision of the marshals. If the car is still unable to start the formation lap it will be pushed into the pit lane by the shortest route and the mechanics may work on the car again.

144. When the cars come back to the grid at the end of the formation lap, they will stop on their respective grid positions, keeping their engines running. Once all the cars have come to a halt the five-second signal will appear followed by the four, three, two and one second signals. At any time after the one second signal appears, the race will be started by extinguishing all red lights.

146. Any car which is unable to maintain starting order during the entire formation lap or is moving when the one second light comes on must enter the pit lane and start from the pits as specified in Article 140.

147. If, after returning to the starting grid at the end of the formation lap, a driver's engine stops and he is unable to restart the car, he must immediately raise his hands above his head and the marshal responsible for that row must immediately wave a yellow flag.

If the start is delayed, (see Article 148) a marshal with a yellow flag will stand in front of the car concerned to prevent it from moving until the whole field has left the grid. The driver may then follow the procedure set out in Articles 143 and 146. As in Article 144, other cars will maintain their grid positions and the vacant position(s) will not be filled. Should there be more than one driver in this situation, their new positions at the back of the grid will be determined in accordance with their relative positions on the grid at the start of the formation lap.

148. If a problem arises when the cars reach the starting grid at the end of the formation lap the following procedure shall apply :

a) If the race has not been started, the abort lights will be switched on, all engines will be stopped and the new formation lap will start 5 minutes later with the race distance reduced by one lap. The next signal will be the three minute signal.

b) If the race has been started, the marshals alongside the grid will wave their yellow flags to inform the drivers that a car is stationary on the grid.

c) If, after the start, a car is immobilised on the starting grid, it shall be the duty of the marshals to push it into the pit lane by the fastest route. If the driver is able to re-start the car whilst it is being pushed he may rejoin the race.

d) If the driver is unable to start the car whilst it is being pushed his mechanics may attempt to start it in the pit lane. If the car then starts it may rejoin the race. The driver and mechanics must follow the instructions of the track marshals at all times during such a procedure.

149. Should Article 148 apply, the race will neverthelesss count for the Championship no matter how often the procedure is repeated, or how much the race is shortened as a result.

150. No refuelling will be allowed on the grid if more than one start procedure proves necessary under Article 148.

151. A time penalty will be imposed for a false start judged using an FIA supplied transponder which must be fitted to the car as specified.

152. Only in the following cases will any variation in the start procedure be allowed :

a) If the track is dry throughout all practice sessions but becomes wet (or vice-versa) after the end of the warm up and at least 60 minutes before the starting time, a 15 minute free practice may be allowed.

b) If it starts to rain after the five-minute signal but before the race is started and, in the opinion of the race director teams should be given the opportunity to change tyres, the abort lights will be shown on the Line and the starting procedure will begin again at the 15 minute point. If necessary the procedure set out in Article 148 will be followed.

c) If the start of the race is imminent and in the opinion of the race director, the volume of water on the track is such that it cannot be negotiated safely even on wet-weather tyres, the avort lights will be shown on the Line simultaneously with a «10» board with a red background.

This «10» board with a red background will mean that there is to be a delay of ten minutes before the starting procedure can be resumed. If weather conditions have improved at the end of that ten minute period, a «10» board with a green background will be shown. The «10» board with a green background will mean that the green light will be shown in ten minutes.

Five minutes after the «10» board with the green background is shown, the starting procedure will begin and the normal starting procedure signals (i.e. 5, 3, 1 min., 30 second) will be shown.

If however, the weather conditions have not improved within ten minutes after the «10» board with the red background was shown, the abort lights will be shown on the Line and the «10» board with the red background will be shown again which will mean a further delay of ten minutes before the starting procedure can be resumed.

This procedure may be repeated several times.

At any time when a «10» board (with either a red or green background) is shown, it will be accompanied by an audible warning.

d) If the race is started behind the safety car, Article 157 n) will apply.

THE RACE

154. A race will not be stopped in the event of rain unless the circuit is blocked or it is dangerous to continue (see Article 158).

155. If a car during the race (except under Article 148 c and d), it must be removed from the track as quickly as possible so that its presence does not constitute a danger or hinder other competitors. If the driver is unable to drive the car from a dangerous position, it shall be the duty of the marshals to assist him. If any such assistance results in the engine starting and the driver rejoining the race, the car will be excluded from the results of the race.

156. During the race, drivers leaving the pit lane will do so on their own responsibility. However, a flashing yellow light will be shown at the pit exit and a marshal with a blue flag will warn of cars approaching.

SAFETY CAR

157. (...) b) 30 minutes before the race start time the safety car will take up position at the front of the grid and remain there until the five-minute signal is given. At this point (except under n) below) it will cover a whole lap of the circuit and enter the pit lane. If Article 152 a) applies, the safety car will take up its position at the front of the grid as soon as the 15 minute practice session has finished.

c) The safety car may be brought into operation to neutralise a race upon the decision of the clerk of the course. It will be used only if competitors or officials are in immediate physical danger but the circumstances are not such as to necessitate stopping the race.

d) When the order is given to deploy the safety car, all observer's posts will display immobile yellow flags and a board «SC» which shall be maintained until the intervention is over.

e) During the race, the safety car with its revolving lights on, will start from the pit lane and will join the track regardless of where the race leader is.

f) All the competing cars will form up in line behind the safety car no more than 5 car lengths apart. All overtaking is forbidden (except under n) below), unless a car is signalled to do so from the safety car.

g) When ordered to do so by the clerk of the course the observer in the car will use a green light to signal to any cars between it and the race leader that they should pass. These cars will continue at reduced speed and without overtaking until they reach the line of cars behind the safety car.

h) The safety car shall be used at least until the leader is behind it and all remaining cars are lined up behind him.

Once behind the safety car, the race leader must keep within 5 car lengths of it and all remaining cars must keep the formation as tight as possible.

i) While the safety car is in operation, competing cars may stop at their pit, but may only rejoin the track when the green light at the pit exit is on. It will be on at all times except when the safety car and the line of cars following it are about to pass or are passing the pit exit. A car rejoining the track will proceed at reduced speed until it reaches the end of the line of cars behind the safety car.

j) When the clerk of the course calls in the safety car, it must extinguish all the revolving lights, this will be the signal to the drivers that it will be entering the pit lane at the end of that lap. At this point the first car in line behind the safety car may dictate the pace and, if necessary, fall more than five car lengths behind it. As the safety car is approaching the pit entrance the yellow flags and SC boards at the observer's posts will be withdrawn and green flags will be displayed for one lap.

k) When the safety car has pulled off the circuit and the cars are approaching the Line, green lights will be shown. All observer's posts will then show a green flag. Overtaking remains strictly forbidden until the cars pass the green light at the Line. The green flags will be withdrawn after one lap.

l) Each lap completed while the safety car is in service will be counted as a race lap.

m) If the race is stopped under Case C, the safety car will take the chequered flag and all cars able to do so must follow it into the pit lane and into the parc fermé.

n) In exceptional circumstances, the race may be started behind the safety car. In this case, at the five-minute signal its revolving yellow lights will be turned on. This is the signal to the drivers that the race will be started behind the safety car. When the green lights are shown, the safety car will leave the grid with all cars following in grid order no more than 5 car lengths apart. There will be no formation lap and race will start when the leading car crosses the line for the first time.

Overtaking, during the first lap only, is permitted if a car is delayed when leaving its grid position and cars behind cannot avoid passing it without unduly delaying the remainder of the field. In this case, drivers may only overtake to re-establish the original starting order.

Any driver who is delayed leaving the grid may not overtake another moving car if he was stationary after the remainder of the cars had crossed the Line, and must form up at the back of the line of cars behind the safety car. If more than one driver is affected, they must form up at the back of the field in the order they left the grid.

A time penalty will be imposed on any driver who, in the opinion of the Stewards, unnecessarily overtook another car during the first lap.

STOPPING A RACE

158. Should it become necessary to stop the race because the circuit is blocked by an accident or because weather or other conditions make it dangerous to continue, the clerk of the course shall order a red flag and the abort lights to be shown at the Line.

Simultaneously, red flags will be shown at all marshal posts.

When the signal is given to stop all cars shall immediately reduce speed in the knowledge that :

- the race classification will be that at the end of the penultimate lap before the lap in which the signal to stop the race was given,

- race and service vehicles may be on the track,

- the circuit may be totally blocked because of an accident,

- weather conditions may have made the circuit undriveable at racing speed,

- the pit lane will be open.

159. The procedure to be followed varies according to the number of laps completed by the race leader before the signal to stop the race was given :

Case A. Less than two full laps. If the race can't be restarted, Article 160 will apply.

Case B. Two or more full laps but less than 75% of the race distance (rounded up to the nearest whole number of laps). If the race can be restarted, Article 161 will apply.

Case C. 75 % or more of the race distance (rounded up to the nearest whole number of laps). The cars will be sent directly to the Parc Fermé and the race will be deemed to have finished when the leading car crossed the line for the penultimate time before the race was stopped.

RESTARTING A RACE

160. Case A.

a) The original start shall be deemed null and void.

b) The length of the restarted race will be the full original race distance.

c) The drivers who are eligible to take part in the race shall be eligible for the restart either in their original car or in a spare car.

d) After the signal to stop the race has been given, all cars able to do so will proceed directly but slowly to either :

- the pit lane or,

- if the grid is clear, to their original grid position or,

- if the grid is not clear, to a position behind the last grid position as directed by the marshals.

e) All cars may be worked on.

f) Refuelling will be allowed until the five minute signal is shown.

161. Case B.

a) The race shall be deemed to be in two parts, the first of which finished when the leading car crossed the Line for the penultimate time before the race was stopped.

b) The length of the second part will be three laps less than the length of the original race less the first part.

c) The grid for the second part will be a standard grid with the cars arranged in the order in which they finished the first part.

d) Only cars which took part in the original start will be eligible and then only if they returned under their own power by an authorized route to either the pit lane or to a position behind the last grid position as directed by the marshals.

e) No spare car will be eligible.

f) Cars may be worked on in the pits or on the grid. If work is carried out on the grid, this must be done in the car's correct grid position and must in no way impede the re-start.

g) If a car returns to the pits if may be refuelled. If a car is refuelled it must take the re-start from the back of the grid and, if more than one car is involved, their positions will be determined by their order on the penultimate lap before the race was stopped. In this case their original grid positions will be left vacant.

162. In both Case A and Case B :

a) 10 minutes after the stop signal, the pit exit will close.

b) 15 minutes after the stop signal, the five minute signal will be shown, the grid will close and the normal start procedure will recommence.

c) Any car which is unable to take up its position on the grid before the five minute signal will be directed to the pits. It may then start from the pits as specified in Article 140. The organiser must have sufficient personnel and equipment available to enable the foregoing timetable to be adhered to even in the most difficult circumstances.

FINISH

163. The end-of-race signal will be given at the Line as soon as the leading car has covered the full race distance in accordance with Article 14. Should two hours elapse before the full distance has been covered, the end-of-race signal will be given to the leading car the first time it crosses the Line after such time has elapsed.

164. Should for any reason (other than under Article 158) the end-of-race signal be given before the leading car completes the scheduled number of laps, or the prescribed time has been completed, the race will be deemed to have finished when the leading car last crossed the Line before the signal was given. Should the end-of-race signal be delayed for any reason, the race will be deemed to have finished when it should have finished.

165. After receiving the end-of-race signal all cars must proceed on the circuit directly to the parc fermé without stopping and without receiving any object whatsoever and without any assistance (except that of the marshals if necessary).

Any classified car which cannot reach the parc fermé under its own power will be placed under the exclusive control of the marshals who will take the car to the parc fermé.

PARC FERME

166. Only those officials charged with supervision may enter the parc fermé. No intervention of any kind is allowed there unless authorised by such officials.

167. When the parc fermé is in use, parc fermé regulations will apply in the area between the Line and the parc fermé entrance.

168. The parc fermé shall be sufficiently large and secure that no unauthorised persons can gain access to it

CLASSIFICATION

169. The car placed first will be the one having covered the scheduled distance in the shortest time, or, where appropriate, passed the Line in the lead at the end of two hours, All cars will be classified taking into account the number of complete laps they have covered, and for those which have completed the same number of laps, the order in which they crossed the Line.

170. If a car takes more than twice the time of the winner's fastest lap to cover its last lap this last lap will not be taken into account when calculating the total distance covered by such car.

171. Cars having covered less than 90 % of the number of laps covered by the winner (rounded down to the nearest whole number of laps), will not be classified.

172. The official classification will be published after the race. It will be the only valid result subject to any amendments which may be made under the Code and these Sporting Regulations.

PODIUM CEREMONY

173. The drivers finishing the race in 1st, 2nd and 3rd positions and a representative of the winning constructor must attend the prize-giving ceremony on the podium and abide by the podium procedure (...), and immediately thereafter make themselves available for a period of 90 minutes for the purpose of television unilateral interviews and the press conference in the media centre.

COMPETITORS' REIMBURSEMENT

174. The reimbursement is a percentage of the gross receipts (as certified by the FIA's auditors) from all moving picture rights associated with the Championship plus a fixed sum (...), plus, for those competitors who competed in every event of the previous season and finished among the top ten in the Championship, assistance with transport to events outside Europe in the traditional manner. Any team which contracts with the FIA to enter the Championship for more than one year will be paid according to the terms of its agreement with the FIA, which will incorporate the above reimbursement.

Meaning of the flags

White flag	service vehicle on track
Blue flag :	(immobile) : a car is close behind you (waving) : a car is about to overtake you
Yellow flag :	(immobile) : overtaking is prohibited, danger (waving) immediate danger, slow down
Red flag :	(by marshals and the Clerk of the race) : stopping of the race on the Line
Green flag :	end of danger, free track
Yellow with red stripes flag :	danger, slippery surface
Black flag :	(with car number) : stop on the next lap
Black with yellow circle flag :	your car is in danger
Black and white flag :	non-sporting behaviour, warning
Chequered flag :	end of the race or of the practice

BRIDG
West
Schweppes
KENW
ON TOP OF
THE WORL
Congratulations to Mika Hakkinen for winning the
1998 Formula One Drivers' World Championship
and to the West McLaren Mercedes team for winning the
1998 Formula One Constructors' World Championship.
Tyres By
F1 DRIVERS' AND CONSTRUC